Social Learning and Cognition

Social Learning and Cognition

TED L. ROSENTHAL

Department of Psychology
Memphis State University
and Department of Psychiatry
University of Tennessee Center for the
Health Sciences, Memphis, Tennessee

BARRY J. ZIMMERMAN

Ph.D. Program in Education
The Graduate School and University Center
The City University of New York
New York, New York

ACADEMIC PRESS
New York San Francisco London 1978
A Subsidiary of Harcourt Brace Jovanovich, Publishers

ACADEMIC PRESS, INC.
111 Fifth Avenue, New York, New York 10003

United Kingdom Edition published by
ACADEMIC PRESS, INC. (LONDON) LTD.
24/28 Oval Road, London NW1 7DX

Library of Congress Cataloging in Publication Data

Rosenthal, Ted L.
Social learning and cognition.

Bibliography: p.
1. Learning, Psychology of. 2. Cognition in children. 3. Socialization. I. Zimmerman, Barry J., joint author. II. Title.
BF318.R67 155.4'13 78-4549
ISBN 0-12-596750-0

PRINTED IN THE UNITED STATES OF AMERICA

To Renate and Diana
for patient understanding,
and to Al Bandura
who modeled the way

Every sort of skill perfects its work
in this way, by observing the mean and
bringing its work up to this standard.

—*ARISTOTLE, The Nichomachean Ethics*

Contents

Foreword

The recent years have witnessed substantial developments in theorizing and experimentation in the field of social learning. One of the major subjects of interest concerns the cognitive mechanisms of social learning and the social learning determinants of cognitive competencies. In the present volume, Rosenthal and Zimmerman systematically examine the burgeoning literature in this field, to which they themselves have contributed heavily.

The authors apply the explanatory principles of social learning to the highest manifestations of human intellect—judgment, language, and thought. Through incisive analysis of theory and a wealth of research, they show how the study of cognition can be enriched by considering the influential role of social learning determinants. This publication should help to break down the still prevalent isolation of scholars working in the areas of social and cognitive development.

The practitioner also has much to gain from this book. It provides a conceptual framework for analyzing cognitive functioning and suggests means for developing conceptual and linguistic skills. Unlike the traditional stage doctrines, which underestimate human capabilities and dwell on limitations, the authors' approach directs our attention to the potentialities for cognitive development.

The mark of a promising conceptual approach is its ability to produce the phenomena it purports to explain and to specify the processes by which the effects are achieved. The theory proposed in this volume fares well on both counts. But there is still much to be explained. By identifying important issues to be resolved, Rosenthal and Zimmerman offer new directions of inquiry that hold promise of deepening further our understanding of human thought and behavior.

ALBERT BANDURA

Preface

The 1960s witnessed the milestone publication of Albert Bandura's research, work which demonstrated the potency of adult modeling on children's behavior. These studies returned scientific legitimacy to the topic of vicarious learning. Previously, observational learning had either been ignored, dismissed as artifactual, or its status denigrated, merely as a special case of instrumental conditioning. In view of its significance, a comprehensive historical survey of the research and theorizing on vicarious learning, showing how the *Zeitgeist* of previous eras led psychologists to neglect the observational realm, is included in the present book.

Bandura's research showed the pervasiveness of social modeling, that it could teach without overt practice or direct incentives, and that learning gains persist over time, although they may not emerge until long afterward. The conceptual implications of such commonly witnessed, but scientifically little appreciated, phenomena led Bandura to devise a new theory of social learning, cognitive in emphasis. Unlike many viewpoints, the social learning approach does not advance a complete set of formal propositions to be confirmed or refuted. Rather, its scope and precision have evolved with close ties to empirical research—often prompted by shortcomings in alternative conceptual frameworks: first, by the mental disease and psychic energy constructs of psychodynamic views; later, by nonmediated behaviorist assumptions that overt practice and reinforcement are the key determinants of learning; and by the logical circularity and pessimistic view of humanity typically found in trait-factor approaches to human functioning. These concerns inform this book. Its thrust, from a social learning standpoint, is a critical scrutiny of structural stage theories of children's development.

Prominent among the structural positions considered are Piaget's theory of intelligence, psycholinguistic accounts of innately governed language development, and Piaget's and Kohlberg's theories of moral development. In this book, we have sought to illuminate some of the theoretical and empirical shortcomings of certain aspects of structuralist positions. We have attempted to explicate a social learning perspective on the social origins of complex abilities, and how these progressively evolve as children grow older. The possibility of synthesizing the major strengths of both social learning and structural contributions is considered.

This book differs from earlier discussions of social learning processes in its emphasis on rule-governed conceptual behavior. Most previous efforts have given priority to clinical issues and personal adjustment skills such as antisocial behavior, altruism, self-control processes, and aggression (e.g., Bandura, 1969, 1977). To date, there has been no book-length treatment of recent social learning contributions in such cognitive spheres as concept formation, language learning, relational and categorical decision making, moral judgments, creativity, problem solving, and conceptual reasoning strategies. The only previous comprehensive discussion of these topics was a journal-length review of then current research which we published in the *Psychological Bulletin* (Zimmerman & Rosenthal, 1974). This book represents our attempt to treat the issues and literature central to that article in much greater depth, and in light of the subsequent research that has burgeoned in the area of children's cognition and information processing.

The format of this book is unusual, as it comprises just four chapters. Chapter 1 is composed of three minichapters, all of which have a common theme: that human cognitive processes and observational learning are intimately and inseparably linked. The first minichapter deals with the distinguishing characteristics of cognitive explanations for human behavior, and the kinds of evidence that cognitive theorists cite in support of their position. Then, the major psychological theories that address abstract, rule-governed activities are described. The second section of Chapter 1 is devoted to a full historical review of research on imitative and vicarious learning—probably the most thorough coverage available anywhere—as it stood before Bandura's work revivified the topic in the 1960s. In the final section of the chapter, we illustrate recent evidence on observational rule acquisition, describe the major competing theories to explain it, and analyze the adequacy of each stance as illustrated by its capacity to handle these new results.

Chapter 2 concerns children's acquisition and refinement of language. Here we discuss the objections and misunderstandings raised by psycholinguists to counter modeling explanations of language learning. We then summarize the current research, which clearly shows that children can learn language rules through modeling influences. Finally, effort is made to integrate the evidence and concerns of both behavioral and psycholinguistic writers, as their ideas relate to social guidance and covert cognitive processes.

In Chapter 3, the research and theorizing on moral and cognitive development associated with Piaget, Kohlberg, and their colleagues is contrasted and compared with social learning alternatives. The structuralist viewpoint, and supporting data, are examined carefully and critically. A social learning explanation is proposed to account for the typical developmental patterns that have been observed. Research that has challenged certain key assumptions of the structuralist formulations is surveyed and discussed, placing emphasis on how it concurs with social learning interpretations. The theoretical and practical advantages, and further potentialities, made possible by a social learning reanalysis of the issues are presented.

In the final chapter, we summarize and integrate research bearing upon the effect of modeling influences on a wide diversity of conceptual activities, ranging from the formation of simple concepts to elaborate intellectual demands that involve complex styles of reasoning and strategies for seeking and organizing information. Current literature from other areas of research on symbolic performance and information processing are integrated with the data based on exemplary guidance methods, and common theoretical conclusions are drawn. The pervasive evidence of executive mediation when observers acquire, retrieve, and utilize these sorts of highly complex, abstract solutions is reviewed. Finally, the challenge that such results pose for nonmediational explanations of vicariously derived conceptual feats is examined.

This book is designed for an audience of advanced undergraduates, graduate students, and professionals from such diverse fields as child development, social psychology, psychiatry, social work, clinical psychology, education, and rehabilitation. The social learning perspective appeals to readers from many varied disciplines because its scope is broad and its implications relevant to diverse behavioral specialities. As a case in point, author Ted Rosenthal is a clinical psychologist and author Barry Zimmerman is an educational psychologist. Our disciplines and careers are both directly concerned with the application of psychological principles to real-life human problems. We undertook the writing of this book in the belief that its research conclusions and conceptual guidelines would have positive impact on people trained to educate and counsel children. As a result, we often mention practical applications and implications of research evidence and theoretical interpretations. However, this book was not written as a guide to the use of modeling techniques. Rather, it is an attempt to provide a broad, integrated framework through which people from various backgrounds can understand children's thought and language, as achievements or problems, in relation to the sociocultural environment and its influences. The advantage of a social orientation such as ours is to allow educators, counselors, and other professionals to appreciate that things can be *done* about children's cognitive and language skills and their development. For we believe that human advancement is the ultimate criterion by which a psychological theory can be judged.

We are thankful to Albert Bandura who took time from his crowded schedule to comment on preliminary versions of the manuscript. Other colleagues whose thinking particularly influenced ours are Geary Alford, John Bergan, David Bearison, Gene H. Brody, Barry Gholson, John E. Kelley, Glenn M. White, and Grover Whitehurst. Special thanks are due Kathleen Snow-White who first alerted us to the role of modeling in classic rhetoric. Our thanks also to Max Weiner and Margaret Lilly whose administrative support was instrumental in getting the manuscript typed and reproduced. Lynda Clemons, Rebecca Hayes, Jan Lockett, and Carolyn Weber merit special thanks for their assistance in typing and proofreading the manuscript.

1

Cognition, Behavior Change, and Social Learning

COGNITIVE PHENOMENA AND THEORIES TO EXPLAIN THEM

What Is Cognition?

Cognition is "a generic term for any process whereby an organism becomes aware of or obtains knowledge of an object. . . . It includes perceiving, recognizing, conceiving, judging, reasoning [English & English, 1958, p.92]." Perhaps the key word in this definition is *knowledge;* cognitive psychologists have devoted much effort to studying how knowledge influences more overt forms of behavior.

For many years, it was fashionable to treat the acts of thought as givens, speaking only in terms of their observable outcomes, rather than trying to examine their characteristics. Recently, analyses of human thinking have again become bold and detailed. Instead of simply accepting that previous knowledge is an array of cues that influences performance, investigators have attempted to determine what functional mental events transpire while a person actually behaves. To these psychologists, cognition is a *method of processing information.* It refers to all of the processes that enable an individual to represent and deal with the external environment symbolically or imaginally. The individual does not react to stimulation from the distal environment in raw physical form, but first interprets and represents these stimuli. These representations then instigate and guide most subsequent behavior. By representation of stimuli, we mean the way in which stimuli are fitted into a person's cognitive organization, which is both a repository of past experiences and a complex information processing device.

It is apparent from these two definitions that the term *cognition* refers to a variety of mental phenomena. There are certain classes of human behavior that are more likely to be described as cognitive, namely, those involving *abstraction* and *transfer,* where symbolic or logical activities during learning and responding seem particularly evident. In the case of abstraction, an individual acts selectively, reacting to certain abstract dimensions of objects before him and not to others. In the case of transfer, he is obviously adding some personal component to his original learning experience. Thus, more than the literal, external properties of stimuli guide the individual's behavior.

Abstraction and transfer are particularly prominent during rule learning. Much of what psychologists refer to as knowledge can be described in terms of *rules.* By a rule, we mean that two or more objects or events are related to one another in a systematic way. For example, we learn that a flashing red traffic light signifies stopping before crossing an intersection. Later, we exhibit transfer of this rule by stopping when we unexpectedly see a flashing red light beside a stalled car on a highway.

Not only do we learn individual rules, but we also adopt superordinate rules. Thus a fisherman acquires certain rules for catching bass and a different set of rules for catching trout. But he must learn a superordinate set of rules for deciding whether the trout or bass strategy will be more likely to pay off in a remote pond or stream. A hierarchy of embedded rules can be described as a *structure* of knowledge. Like its constituent rules, structures involve abstraction and transfer.

The term cognition also refers to the way people *perceive* and *interpret* events. Here again, the term is more likely to be invoked when people react in a manner that is in some way discrepant with the concrete details of the external stimulus situation. Gestalt psychologists (see Hilgard & Bower, 1966) have reported evidence suggesting that an ambiguous stimulus such as

will be interpreted as a familiar object such as a triangle. Evidence also indicates that individuals perceive and interpret ambiguous or novel stimuli on the basis of a mental set. For example, Neisser (1967) has concluded that the reason adults tend to display extremely slow recognition of curse words flashed briefly by tachistoscope, was that they did not expect an experimenter to present such stimuli. Further evidence indicates that once beliefs are formed, considerable contrary evidence is required before they are altered (Mahoney, 1974a; Rosenthal & Siegel, 1959).

The term cognition is also used to describe *covert processing of information*. The accomplishments of storage and retrieval are commonly cited as important cognitive processes. As will soon be described in detail, research on storage and retrieval activities during learning and recall indicates that information is selectively coded (reduced to essential elements) and then elaborated (missing parts are filled in). It thus appears that a learner makes a personal cognitive contribution during learning and recall. Most information processing formulations include a logical component as well as a storage component to explain coding and elaboration activities. Often, this logical component has been spoken of in terms of "executive processes [Kintsch, 1970]." The decision to code a stimulus one way versus another is attributed to executive processes.

Historically, the notion of *awareness* has played a central role in most cognitive formulations. By awareness, cognitive psychologists refer to a person's ability to report experience, or his skill in selectively exposing himself to particular experiences. Mental sets whether inductively formed or created by instructions are assumed to directly affect one's awareness. Later, we will describe research indicating that attempts to manipulate a person's awareness will affect his reaction to experience.

An important question to pose at this point is: How do cognitive phenomena differ from the acquisition and production of purely terminal responses? Why should psychologists make assumptions about cognitive processes that are not readily verifiable through direct observation? Would it not be more scientific to deal only with overt responses? Not necessarily. Cognitive processes are postulated when changes in a person's behavior cannot be explained on the basis of the external stimulus environment. That is, attempts to relate each one of an individual's responses to a particular stimulus in his environment have failed in a variety of situations. Numerous studies, which will be summarized below, now indicate that learning outcomes will not be accurately predicted if one assumes that responses are additively combined in a gradual fashion. While the learning of simple motor responses can to some degree be explained by an incremental learning view, complex learning involving abstraction cannot. Early Gestalt psychologists used the word *insight* to describe the suddenness of this type of learning, as well as its discontinuity from prior responding.

Molecular analyses of behavior on learning and transfer tasks often reveal little point-to-point response similarity; however, regularity on an abstract level can be found. For example, if in an art lesson, a young child is taught to draw a person such as a policeman, the youth may learn that a head, a torso, two arms and legs must be included. The subsequent pictures drawn by the child, such as a ballerina, often bear little resemblance to the model originally used for instruction: The ballerina is not dressed in a blue uniform, does not wear a hat, and is of a different sex. However, the ballerina does possess the same major body parts. Thus, the transfer of learning to new stimuli cannot be explained simply on the basis of discrete stimulus or response elements. Rather, it seems necessary to assume that selectivity or abstraction has occurred. The child in our example has added quite dissimilar response elements that were not directly related to his original learning. It is this constructive activity, so pervasive during complex learning, that defies explanation by simple notions in which antecedent cues are merely linked to terminal responses.

Why Is It Necessary to Assume Cognitive Mediation of Behavior?

A substantial amount of research indicates that *abstraction is something more than combining discrete stimulus–response associations.* Among notable research in this sphere is the work of the Kendlers (e.g., Kendler & Kendler, 1959, 1962). They devised an ingenious experiment in which subjects were taught to discriminate a particular stimulus attribute such as large size (see Figure 1-1). The nature of concept formation was then examined by presenting the subjects with a new concept to learn, involving either the same stimulus dimension (a reversal shift) or a new dimension (a nonreversal shift). In the example, a switch from large to small would be a reversal shift since the same conceptual dimension of size was involved. A switch from large size to black color is a nonreversal shift since the conceptual dimension had to be altered (from size to color), as did the target stimulus attribute (from large to black). The Kendlers shifted concepts during training without informing the subjects, and the speed of learning nonreversal and reversal shifts from feedback was compared.

This experimental paradigm was important because it permitted comparison of two different explanations for concept learning. According to a nonmediational additive model, which focuses only on overt responses, subjects should be able to make nonreversal shifts easier than reversal shifts. From this viewpoint, learners making nonreversal shifts have already been rewarded for *black* responses on half of the original training trials. The opposite response, *small,* was never reinforced. However, according to a mediational, nonadditive formulation, the reversal shifts should be easier since a conceptual discrimination of *size,* as well as the *large* responses, was learned during initial training.

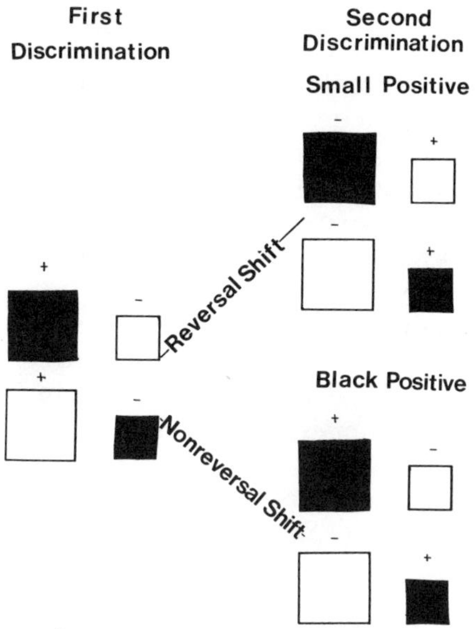

Figure 1-1 A schematic outline of the reversal shift paradigm. [After H. H. Kendler & T. S. Kendler. *Psychological Review,* 1962, *69,* 1–16. Copyright 1962 by the American Psychological Association. Reprinted by permission.]

The size concept did not have to change after reversal shifts. On the other hand, nonreversal shifts required altering both the specific response and the conceptual discrimination. The Kendlers found that individuals made reversal shifts more easily than nonreversal shifts. This series of studies dramatically demonstrated that mental abstraction was a real phenomenon. The set or preference for one organizing dimension over another was not predictable by nonmediational, incremental learning theory.

Paired associate (PA) research also indicates that cognitive processes are critical factors in learning and recall. The PA paradigm involves learning to associate a list of pairs of words, such as *record* and *scissors.* After seeing the first word, the subject must, for learning to be demonstrated, recall the second word of each pair. Experiments (e.g., Jensen & Rohwer, 1965) indicate that if a subject is told to make up a sentence involving the PA words, recall is greatly improved. The subject might create the sentence *You don't use* **scissors** *to cut a* **record.** By embedding words in a meaningful sentence, a person cognitively links his previous experiences with each of the paired associates. Evidence also (Yuille & Paivio, 1968) suggests that instructions to create a vivid image of the interaction of two associates also enhances recall. The subject might imagine a giant scissors cutting a record in two. Notice that in both types of studies, the learner was not given any additional details to link the PAs but was given an abstract strategy to generate his own cognitive codes. The fact that these *instructions to code* greatly promoted recall indicates the important role of cognitive processes.

There are a number of studies which indicate that *extraneous stimulation can interfere* with cognitive processes. Bourne and Bunderson (1963) conducted a clever study to examine the importance of cognitive activity in concept formation. Cognitive psychologists believe that feedback received during concept learning is mentally examined and that old hypotheses concerning the concept are changed to fit the feedback. Nonmediational explanations for learning ignore an individual's covert activity and tend to emphasize the immediacy of feedback after a response is made. With animals, delays in presenting reinforcement retards learning (Skinner, 1953).

Bourne and Bunderson's concept task required college students to decide whether or not each picture of a geometric form exemplified a given concept. The pictures varied along several dimensions such as size, color, shape, etc., and the conceptual rule was conjunctive, such as the selecting of all red squares. It was reasoned that if covert cognitive activity were important, then the amount of time following the reception of feedback (the postfeedback interval) should be critical. If not enough time was allowed before presenting the next card, learning would be disrupted. From a nonmediational stance, the amount of time between the presentation of the picture and the reception of feedback would be the most critical (the feedback interval). The results strongly confirmed that it was the postfeedback interval that most influenced concept formation and not the feedback interval. Thus, it appears that stimulus events, such as the presentation of new items, that intrude upon cognitive processing hamper learning.

Other evidence shows that overt responding can interfere with cognitive processes and impede learning. Hillix and Marx (1960) studied the role of overt activity during problem solving. The task involved throwing switches to determine an underlying pattern for correctly lighting a display board. One group directly pulled switches and watched the light display for feedback. Another group learned by watching the experimenter pull switches in the same order as done by the overt performers in the first group. Thus, both groups received the same information, but one was spared having to actively respond. The researchers expected that overt performance would improve learning since it involved practicing the terminal acts to be learned. Instead, they found that the "passive" observers achieved better concept acquisition. Vicarious exposure could surpass direct performance training!

Research on *mental sets* and *awareness* indicates that these cognitive processes also play prominent roles in mediating human behavior. Self-reports about an individual's awareness during motoric responding are of great assistance in predicting behavior. In an aversive conditioning study, Fuhrer and Baer (1965) found that only those subjects who recognized the relationship between the pitch of a stimulus tone and the onset of a painful shock displayed conditioned emotional reactions. Other subjects, who remained unaware of the contingency, failed to condition. Some psychologists (e.g., Skinner, 1953) have argued that it is conditioning that creates awareness rather than the reverse. However, there is evidence to the contrary. Very early, Cook and Harris (1937) showed that an individual's expectations were at least as important in creating conditioned emotionality as the actual aversive pairings. Chatterjee and Ericson (1962) found that subjects who were led to believe that shock would be administered contingent upon certain stimulus words conditioned rather rapidly. Others who were told that the shock was unrelated to any class of words displayed no conditioned reactions. Thus, it was the anticipation of a contingent relationship rather than the actual contingency itself that influenced learning. In addition, further evidence shows that during conditioning, instructions informing the learner that aversive consequences would no longer be applied promptly eliminate conditioned emotional responses (Grings & Lockhart, 1963; Notterman, Schoenfeld, & Bersh, 1952; Wickers, Allen, & Hill, 1963), while uninstructed persons display very gradual extinction curves. Thus, rather well-established response histories can be abruptly altered simply by making a person aware of a change in contingencies.

Information processing psychologists have devised an imaginative dichotic listening task to examine the role of awareness in learning (Broadbent, 1958). In these studies, the learner simultaneously received two different auditory messages, one through each ear via earphones. Although receiving both signals at the same auditory levels, the learner was able to attend to one signal more than the other. Furthermore, directions to the listener to concentrate on one message and ignore the other greatly affected what was learned. Very little information from the nonattended signal was acquired. These studies demonstrated signal monitoring on a purely cognitive level, monitoring that was independent of the reaction of sense receptors to overt stimuli of equal physical intensity.

It is clear from the preceding research that cognitive processes such as awareness and mental sets play a central role in learning. This does not mean that cognition fluctuates independently of the external environment; rather, it is affected by important setting events such as instructions, the nature and consistency of feedback, and the importance of the task to the learner.

Research on *memory* and recall also reveals the pervasiveness of cognitive influences. Most psychologists distinguish between short- and long-term memory. Short-term memory refers to recall within a few seconds after information is presented. Some significant evidence of cognitive functioning during short-term memory has been derived from error patterns displayed during recall. Conrad (1964) examined immediate recall of six letter sequences. Sequences having a single letter error were analyzed in a matrix to determine which letters were confused. Since the task was visual, one would expect from a nonmediational viewpoint that similar-looking letters would be confused. However, he found that the errors involved letters that *sounded* alike. Thus, it appears that the visually presented information was covertly recoded into auditory form.

The role of cognitive processes is even more evident in long-term memory. Bousfield (1953) found that people tended to cluster words into conceptually similar groups, spontaneously and covertly organizing information during learning and recall. Tulving (1962) found that the amount of recall was directly correlated with the degree of the subjects' mental organization. Simply rehearsing the words covertly did not significantly improve recall unless some cognitive reorganization occurred (Tulving, 1966). In much of this research on subjective organization, different individuals used different types of categories to group words for recall. Thus, it was not the specific category label that affected recall, but rather the fact that the person organized the information in some way that was meaningful to him.

Some psychologists have suggested that the categories used to organize words for recall need not be thought of as mental abstractions but simply as networks of associations. Cofer (1965) designed an experiment to test this claim. He set up a number of PA word lists. The stimulus and response word on each list varied along two dimensions: associative strength (as derived from word associate norms) or conceptual relatedness. For example, the words *bed* and *chair* were conceptually related but were not verbally associated, whereas the words *bed* and *dream* were conceptually unrelated but were strongly associated verbally. He found that conceptual organization made a clear, separate contribution to recall. It played a particularly key role for word pairs having no associative strength.

We have already cited PA research showing that meaningful coding improves recall. Likewise, the research on subjective organization also revealed that cognitive categorization assisted free recall. Considerable additional research suggests that most aspects of behavior involve mental abstraction, transformation, and reconstruction. For example, rather than the incidence, the typicality of *structure* determined how easily items were learned, classified, and generated (Rosch, Simpson, & Miller, 1976). This evidence opposes the "response" learning accounts, that assume behavior to be holistically learned, stored, and retrieved without mental representation and transformation. Perhaps the most convincing evidence that action is cognitively directed centers on the *constructive* qualities of behavior.

Bruner (1957) has argued that even the simple act of *perceiving* involves active constructions. This process is most evident in difficult perceptual tasks, as demonstrated by Bruner's attempt to recognize an obscure object across his partially darkened study. Because the visual information was impoverished, Bruner was forced to hypothesize as to which object he was observing, until he was able to identify it. He suggested that we often remain unaware that we form hypotheses or categorize during perception because identification can usually be made instantaneously. He also summarized a range of studies showing that "perceptions" can be manipulated on complex tasks if a person expects to see something else. For example, the stimulus

would be perceived as a "4" rather than an "H" if the viewer expected (or was "set" to encounter) a number. Neisser (1967) used the term *figural synthesis* to describe this perceptual construction process.

Some of the first evidence for the constructive nature of human thought emerged from research on *recall.* Bartlett (1932) studied how subjects remembered short stories, retesting his experimental subjects several times on the same story to detect systematic changes in recall. He noticed that an individual's memory for even the simplest stories was highly inaccurate. Usually only a rough outline of the story was remembered, and the details tended to be filled in on a rational basis during retelling. The stories became more coherent and stereotyped with each retelling. Not only does mental activity during learning affect what is stored, but one's activity during recall affects how the stored partial trace is elaborated. This cognitive activity is selective. An individual's general hypotheses determine what aspects of the story are emphasized.

Recent prose learning research indicates that the comprehension of grammatical statements involves extensive mental transformation of input. When a sentence is understood, it is cognitively transformed into its covert meaning, and the original word elements are largely lost during storage (e.g., Begg & Paivio, 1969; Moeser, 1974; Sachs, 1967). Consequently, subjects experience great difficulty identifying initially heard sentences from lexically equivalent passages. However, subjects can easily detect sentences that are semantically altered. The discovery that meanings, rather than individual words, are units of storage is incompatible with theories that treat abstract learning in terms of discrete stimulus–response units.

Underlying the notion of reconstructive mental operations is the assumption that what is stored for recall is incomplete. In an ingenious study, Brown and McNeill (1966) found evidence for the selective nature of stored representations by examining the "tip-of-the-tongue" phenomenon. This experience is familiar to nearly everyone. We know a particular word, cannot recall it at the moment, but can recognize it if someone else says it. Brown and McNeill investigated this phenomenon by selecting word definitions from the dictionary and asking subjects to supply the word. They found that individuals had a general idea of the words, remembering such elements as the first letter, the shape of the word, and the number of syllables. Thus, there was unambiguous evidence of partial recall. This research sheds light on the storage and retrieval process. Even single words are not recalled as units, having been selectively coded for storage. When a sufficient number of storage cues are retrieved, the word can be reconstructed.

The importance of cognitive processes in human behavior is also evident from the way in which meaning controls overt action. Suppes (1974) has argued that conceptual meaning (as well as social contingencies) guides behavior, wondering why people say *biggest red barn* instead of *red biggest barn*. He analyzed patterns of adjective modification of nouns in several languages and found a constant order. He found that adjectives of intensity *(biggest)* preceded adjectives of classification *(red)*. Suppes believed this ordering to be logically restricted and describable in terms of set theory notions. The sequence of adjectives is based on the partitioning of sets. For illustration, let us assume there is a set of barns varying in color and size. All barns vary along the size dimension, but only some barns fit the category of redness. Therefore if a person says, *Find the red biggest barn,* he may well be referring to an empty set, in which none of the biggest barns happen to be red. This will never occur with properly sequenced adjectives. *Find the biggest red barn* will prove informative since only the set of red barns will be ordered according to size for this decision. Suppes' analysis is rather complicated, but it does indicate that meaning is not an arbitrary phenomenon based on haphazard association. It is constrained by the reference environment. Meaning restricts and directs human action in systematic ways, such as word order patterns. Because the abstract consequences of cognitive patterning affect overt human behavior, we contend that mediation cannot be excluded from a comprehensive explanation of human functioning.

Theoretical Explanations of Cognitive Phenomena

ASSOCIATIONIST AND REINFORCEMENT POSITIONS

Main Features of the Position

John B. Watson (1919) had a profound effect on the theoretical direction of psychology in America. His impassioned arguments urging psychologists to break with the "mentalism" of the past and focus on observable behavior struck a responsive chord during the first quarter of the twentieth century. His plea for minimal inference beyond observed behavior fitted well with scientific parsimony. Beginning with Watson, and continuing until the present, explanations for psychological functioning that dealt with observables (stimuli or responses) have been preferred. Watson and his contemporaries attempted to explain all psychological phenomena in terms of stimuli and responses. This tradition affected several generations of psychologists and is alive and well today. The most prominent contemporary spokesman for nonmediational theory is B. F. Skinner. Among other psychologists who have made substantial contributions to the position are Baer, Bijou, and Gewirtz.

How do nonmediational behaviorists explain cognitive phenomena? In general, they distrust any attempts to deal with covert mental processes. Skinner (1953), although talking about mental phenomena at length, concludes that these processes are not distinct from bodily events. Gewirtz (e.g., 1971a) questions the existence of imagery. As a result, most nonmediational behaviorists avoid any reference to covert processes in their study and discussion of human functioning. In addition, their position also assumes that thought and language are learned through reinforcement of overt responses. Behavioral functioning is described in terms of external stimuli. *Reinforcement* of overt responses is necessary for learning to take place. Nonmediational behaviorists disavow any notions that basic learning can occur without direct reinforcement. *Practice* is also stressed in this account. During practice, responses can be shaped or refined through systematic reinforcement. It is assumed that learning can be more effectively controlled if covert responses can be made overt.

Concept formation is explained in terms of *stimulus control.* The processes of discrimination and generalization are the main elements in a stimulus control formulation. Discrimination is the accentuation of a particular aspect of a stimulus by means of selective reinforcement. Abstraction is a form of discrimination in which a behavior is "brought under the control of a single property or special combination of properties of stimuli while being freed from the control of all other properties [Skinner, 1953, p. 134]." Abstraction, it must be noted, involves only a subset, rather than all of the properties of the stimulus configuration. If, for example, the red color of an object were reinforced, and other stimulus properties such as shape and size were varied, a subject would discriminate the color attribute. Thus, concept formation is not treated as the acquisition of a new response in the usual sense, but rather is considered to be the selective attachment of a response to a particular stimulus configuration. Transfer or generalization to other settings where the critical stimulus properties are present will occur. Skinner believes that transfer is not an activity performed by a subject; rather, he explains the phenomenon simply as the control acquired by one stimulus being shared by other stimuli with common properties.

Nonmediational behaviorists explain forgetting in terms of operant extinction (Skinner, 1957). In their view, a response is weakened if not reinforced. Forgetting also occurs when new responses become attached to an old stimulus. In fact, the term forgetting is not generally used by these psychologists since it alludes to covert processes deemed unnecessary in explaining the coupling and uncoupling of stimuli and responses.

Nonmediational associationists put less emphasis on reinforcement. They treat concept formation as a process whereby new linkages are formed between two events, such as between the words *cat* and *knife* in a PA paradigm. In this view, *contiguity* is considered to be the major explanation for learning. The assumption is made that two stimuli or a stimulus and response become associated if they co-occur in time or space. For example, some associationists would define the presented word *cat* as the stimulus, and the answer word *knife* as the response. Presentation of the written word list after each PA trial is often thought of as reinforcement. Other psychologists such as Staats (1968) discuss this associative process in terms of classical conditioning, treating the stimulus word as the unconditioned stimulus and considering the response word to be the conditioned stimulus. In any event, whatever their theoretical preference, these associationistic psychologists agree that learning can be explained without making inferences about mediational acts such as the formation of hypotheses or reasoning. Thus, the strength of an association can be directly related to the recency and frequency of pairings of the stimulus elements. The more often the words *cat* and *knife* are presented together, the stronger the learning.

Associationists generally explain forgetting in terms of interference. Two types of interference have been identified. *Retroactive* interference occurs when later experiences interfere with prior learning. For example, if a subject has more trouble remembering the first verse of a poem after learning the second, retroactive interference has occurred. A second type of interference, *proactive,* occurs when prior learning acts to inhibit subsequent learning. Accordingly, if learning the first verse of a poem makes the acquisition of a second verse more difficult, proactive interference has occurred.

Thought is treated as a fractional anticipatory associative response by some associationists (Staats, 1968). Thus a child associates the word *dog* with his attention to a dog and stroking of the animal's smooth fur. The word may later elicit an attentional response from the child. This alerting response precedes the sight of the dog and represents a fraction of the child's total response to dogs. Associationists (Staats, 1961) suggest that human knowledge can be represented by networks of associations termed *habit families* (see Figure 1-2). For example, a dog is associated

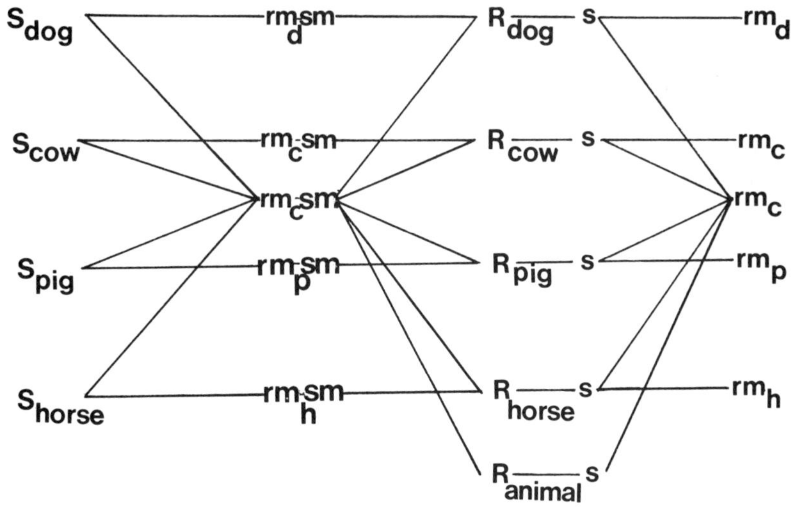

Figure 1-2 A schematic outline of a verbal habit family for the concept of animal. [After A. Staats, *Psychological Review,* 1961, *68,* 190–204. Copyright 1961 by the American Psychological Association. Reprinted by permission.]

with a network of other animals such as cows or pigs. Pigs and dogs are associated because both are animals. Transfer is thus explained on the basis of a common connection. This formulation is avowedly mechanistic: stimuli and responses must be directly associated. Thought is elicited by and responds to overt stimulation. Individuals cannot personally affect these linkages.

Strengths and Limitations of Associationist and Reinforcement Positions

Perhaps the most notable advantage of these orientations is the element of parsimony that both contain. These psychologists have resisted the temptation to postulate any unobservable events. Behavior must be explained in terms of the overt stimuli that precede or follow every response. No redefinition of overt behavior in terms of covert responses is permitted. If this strategy is proved to fit the myriad examples of human conceptual behavior, its simplicity and elegance would make it a very attractive explanatory framework.

Because of the philosophical emphasis on overt behavior, learning events have always been equated with overt performance, a restriction not found in other approaches we will soon examine. Many opposing theories deal primarily with mental processes and have largely neglected performance factors. Since associationists make no distinction between mental activities and observable behavior, no separate set of principles is needed to explain such performance parameters as motivation, storage, and retrieval.

Nonmediational behaviorists have done much to stimulate research on such difficult human problems as retardation and autism. They have been most successful in improving children's performance by creating favorable contingencies. At the same time, because they have relied so heavily on the use of shaping procedures to teach new responses (e.g., Skinner, 1953), the application of more effective cognitive techniques (e.g., modeling or instructions) has been delayed.

The narrow focus on overt behavior has limited the effectiveness of nonmediational accounts and applications in explaining certain aspects of psychological functioning, in particular, complex cognitive phenomena. Associationist positions cannot adequately explain the evidence of constructive activity in perception, learning, and recall. As we noted earlier, there is extensive evidence (e.g., Neisser, 1976) to confirm that stimuli are not simply perceived and associated with a particular response. Treating all learning in terms of overt responses to direct stimulation fails to allow for the important symbolic intervening activities whose overt consequences are pronounced.

Research on learning and memory also suggests that one does not acquire topographically whole responses, but rather images and verbal meanings. Neither words nor images are complete or fixed; they instead, are composed of selected elements sufficiently informative to permit one to cognitively reconstruct a reasonably close representation of what had previously been seen or heard (Neisser, 1967). Evidence for this constructive activity has been particularly clear in the error patterns displayed during overt responding. Performance errors are not random. They are directional and consistent with the assumptions and hypotheses guiding the problem solver at the moment.

From a nonmediated, associationist standpoint, however, why should directions either to form images of two paired-associate words, or to embed these words in a meaningful sentence, enhance a subject's learning and recall? No new practice or response information has been given. These cognitive "actions" are in no way observable. Why should directions to organize objects into conceptually related categories help a subject's recall? Because this formulation does not deal with the informative characteristics of experience per se, the existence and effects of mental operations are not predictable, nor can they even be easily explained.

Likewise, why should stimulus intrusions during active covert mental processing interfere with performance? Overt pairings and consequences are not altered. Nonmediational positions only consider the timing and dosage of reinforcement (Bourne & Bunderson, 1963), giving no formal attention to what occurs covertly after reinforcement, such as hypothesis reformulation. Further, why should attempts to elicit overt task performance (rehearsal) during problem solving interfere with acquisition (Hillix & Marx, 1960) or prove to be less effective than a more cognitive procedure? From a nonmediational standpoint, such procedures should have the *opposite* effect. Here, overt behavior was executed directly in regard to the relevant stimuli, presumably optimal learning conditions according to a nonmediational explanation. Direct practice interfered, but symbolic exposure improved learning. This shows that the two forms of practice are *not* identical in their effects, and that covert mental activity cannot be ignored without hazard.

Another problem of many nonmediational positions is their insistence that reinforcement must be present for learning to occur; this assumption has been challenged for years. Perhaps the first research to seriously question the need for reward was conducted by Tolman and his associates (e.g., Tolman & Honzik, 1930), studying animal maze learning. A group of rats was first permitted to explore a maze without receiving any rewards, and was later trained to earn rewards for running the same maze. These animals, with their initially nonreinforced experience, learned the maze in significantly less time than did another group, who were given no opportunity to explore prior to training. Tolman's interpretation was that while learning can occur cognitively without reinforcement, reinforcement does affect performance. The same essential implications arose from research with children (Bandura, 1965).

In conclusion, the nonmediational associationist position has challenged other theories by offering parsimonious and concrete explanations for complex psychological phenomena. This narrow focus has been of great consequence in dealing with certain aspects of behavior, and has stimulated other theorists to rebut associationist assertions with research evidence. At the same time, this position is of limited assistance in helping us understand how symbolic guidance may be applied in behavioral change procedures.

STRUCTURALIST POSITIONS

A second group of theories that we will call *structural* stress understanding the organization of general knowledge as the best way to explain how people think. In this approach, behavior is of secondary importance because it is assumed to imperfectly reflect the manner in which knowledge is organized. No single all-encompassing structural theory has yet emerged. All of the prominent competitors have thus far limited their focus to some subset of human behavior such as language, intellectual development, or moral growth. Three prominent theories attracting attention today are psycholinguistic theory (Chomsky, 1957), Piaget's (1952b) theory of intellectual development, and Kohlberg's (1968) theory of moral development. We will briefly describe some main features of each.

Piaget's Theory

Piaget (1952b) has described changes in a child's intellectual functioning in terms of four major periods. The first, which extends from birth to approximately 2 years of age, is termed *sensorimotor*. During this period, the child forms primitive concepts that center on motoric actions and on the resulting sensory experience. According to Piaget, motor control evolves from an infant's tendency to repeat behavior that brings unanticipated changes in the environment. This tendency is termed a *circular reaction*. From these sensorimotor experiences, the child learns perceptual accuracy. That is, he learns to treat certain environmental stimuli as constants despite the fact that the retinal images of each stimulus vary in different viewing positions and according to the surrounding context. These perceptual "schemata" or protoconcepts which eventually form the framework for the logical thought that occurs later in development, embody only direct sensory qualities during the sensorimotor period. The infant learns *object permanence*, meaning that he is aware of the existence of an object even when he can not see it. He also learns the *causality* between sensory motor events.

The second stage, termed the *preoperational period*, extends from approximately 2 to 7 years of age. During this period, the child learns to form symbols such as language, numbers, and letters. The child's concepts are based on sensory experience, and include the visual dimensions of height, width, or length. Piaget believed that the child possessed only limited logical skills, and was capable of treating only one stimulus dimension at a time. It was also concluded that the child could not mentally manipulate symbols. The child's thought was described as *transductive*, meaning that he was not capable of reasoning from the particular to the general (or the reverse), since this involved manipulating more than one thought. Instead, the child reasoned from particular to particular in an "intuitive" fashion.

At approximately 7 years of age, a child enters the third stage of cognitive development, the *concrete operations* period. He can now logically manipulate symbols; he can reason inductively and deductively; he can reason backward as well as forward (reversibility); and he can mentally deal with more than one stimulus dimension at a time. He can conserve, seriate, classify, and reason transitively. According to Piaget, his thought is limited in only one respect: He cannot reason logically about phenomena he has not directly experienced; he cannot test hypotheses about potential explanations for an event in a systematic way. These latter accomplishments designate the final period of mental development termed the *formal operations* period. Children generally enter this period at around 11 years of age. Thus, in Piaget's theory, the evolution of thought is characterized by four qualitatively distinct periods.

Psycholinguistic Theory

Most structural psychologists approach language in terms of Chomsky's (1957) theory of transformational grammar, which we will briefly characterize; more detailed summaries are available (e.g., Deese, 1971). Chomsky suggested that linguistic functioning might be described on two levels: It embodies a *surface structure*, which is generally depicted using diagrams of the usual parts of speech, and a covert, unobservable *deep structure*. Deep structure is the meaning level of language; it can be depicted as a simple declarative sentence expressing a particular thought such as *John hit the ball.* This meaning can be expressed in many different ways, such as the intransitive form *The ball was hit by John* or as the question *What did John hit?* Chomsky devised a series of *transformation* rules for explaining all of the ways in which a single core meaning can be syntactically manipulated into grammatically correct surface structure sentences. He assumes that meaning exists apart from and prior to each spoken or written sentence. Thus, linguistic functioning is explained on the basis of a deep structure and a system of rules for permuting that structure into grammatically correct sentences.

Psycholinguists have attempted to explain systematic changes in a child's language skill by means of transformations and implied deep structure. The child maps meaning onto language more accurately as he acquires language competence; a number of phases in language development have now been identified. The earliest phase, babbling, is not given much attention by psycholinguists because little meaning is evident. The first meaningful words are spoken around 1 year of age (McNeill, 1970). Children at this age use one-word utterances such as *dada,* speech which is termed *holophrasic.* Psycholinguists feel that such single-word utterances imply more meaning than is evident in the surface structure. The next major phase in speech development occurs around 18 months of age, when the child begins to use two-word utterances; these utterances reflect a crude level of syntactic regularity, and one word often acts as a "pivot" such as *doggie* ***go*** or *kitty* ***go.*** At roughly 28 months of age, children begin to speak in three- and four-word utterances, but transformation rules are not yet evident in their speech. By the time a child is 36 months old, he is using two dozen transformation rules. When the children reach 4 years of age, their syntactic development is practically complete (McNeill, 1971), and they can use all transformation rules. Thus psycholinguistic theory à la Chomsky has emphasized progressive, age-related changes in children's syntactic development, in changes which are described with respect to an underlying linguistic structure and transformation rules.

Moral Development Theories

Another prominent structural theory, originally proposed by Piaget (1948), deals with moral development; the approach was later greatly refined by Kohlberg (1968). Both versions share the assumption that moral development proceeds via a series of qualitatively distinct stages related to intellectual development. Piaget studied how children evaluated a protagonist for various misdeeds such as lying, stealing, or causing accidents. He found that a very young child makes judgments of moral propriety on the basis of the amount of damage that results.

TABLE 1-1
Kohlberg's Stages of Moral Development[a]

Classification of moral judgment into levels and stages of development		
Levels	Basis of moral judgment	Stages of development
I	Moral value resides in external, quasi-physical happenings, in bad acts, or in quasi-physical needs rather than in persons and standards.	Stage 1: Obedience and punishment orientation. Egocentric deference to superior power or prestige, or a trouble-avoiding set. Objective responsibility.
		Stage 2: Naively egoistic orientation. Right action is that instrumentally satisfying the self's needs and occasionally others'. Awareness of relativism of value to each actor's needs and perspective. Naive egalitarianism and orientation to exchange and reciprocity.
II	Moral value resides in performing good or right roles, in maintaining the conventional order and the expectancies of others.	Stage 3: Good-boy orientation. Orientation to approval and to pleasing and helping others. Conformity to stereotypical images of majority or natural role behavior, and judgment by intentions.
		Stage 4: Authority and social-order maintaining orientation. Orientation to "doing duty" and to showing respect for authority and maintaining the given social order for its own sake. Regard for earned expectations of others.
III	Moral value resides in conformity by the self to shared or sharable standards, rights, or duties.	Stage 5: Contractual legalistic orientation. Recognition of an arbitary element or starting point in rules or expectations for the sake of agreement. Duty defined in terms of contract, general avoidance of violation of the will or rights of others, and majority will and welfare.
		Stage 6: Conscience or principle orientation. Orientation not only to actually ordained social rules but to principles of choice involving appeal to logical universality and consistency. Orientation to conscience as a directing agent and to mutual respect and trust.

[a] Adapted from Theodore R. Sizer, *Religion and Public Education,* "Moral and Religious Education and the Public Schools" by Lawrence Kohlberg. Copyright © 1967 by Houghton Mifflin Company. Used by permission.

The child thus concludes that a boy who accidentally breaks many of his mother's glasses is more culpable than his brother who intentionally smashes only one glass. At around 8 years of age, the child passes from this initial stage of *objective* morality to a stage of *subjective* morality, wherein intentions are given prime consideration. Now, the child will consider a protagonist to be most blameworthy if he intends to commit a misdeed. In the example cited above, the latter brother would be judged as the more blameworthy.

In Kohlberg's (1968) elaboration of the theory (see Table 1-1), the child passes through three major stages, each composed of two substages. In the first, *preconventional,* stage, moral justifications are based on whether the act escapes punishment or whether rewards are obtained for the protagonist. Morality is decidedly self-centered and geared toward the immediate consequences of deeds. In the second, i.e., *conventional* morality stage, moral justifications are based on social convention. Acts which adhere to social norms are judged as the most moral, and social mores or laws are treated as absolute standards for judging behavior. In the third or *postconventional* stage, moral justifications become abstract and separate from group influences. Man-made laws are seen as relative, and subordinate to higher laws such as Kant's categorical imperative or the Golden Rule. In sum, Kohlberg's approach studies the child's justification for his moral judgment, and not the actual judgment itself.

Common Features of Structural Theories

As part of our brief overview of structuralist theories of language, thought, and moral judgment, let us consider some of their common features. Structural theories are *basically nativistic.* Many structural psychologists would be vexed by this characterization and would counter that their formulations are essentially interactional. Experience, as well as maturation, must be given a role. This claim is true to a degree. However, it is important to point out that in all of these views, the role of experience is delimited by the structure the child possesses. Experience can provide symbolic content for the structures, or can even provoke a structure to emerge, but it cannot create the structure. As Hans Furth, an eminent interpreter of Piaget's position (1969), puts it: "Note also that the internal structure is not something that at any time was external and gradually became interiorized, rather it is developmentally and phylogenetically related to the living organization itself which at no level can be considered as being outside the organism [pp. 75–76]." Psycholinguists closely adhering to a Chomskian view react similarly; language is considered as a biological phenomenon, a product of "evolutionary specialization [McNeill, 1971, p. 19]." They too believe that the structures (of grammar) cannot be inferred from direct experience. "The deep structures are never displayed in the form of examples, stimuli, responses, or anything else [McNeill, 1971, p. 18]." Thus, while structuralists give experience a role in their theories, structures are assumed to exist before experience can be apprehended. However, the reverse is not assumed to be true; experience cannot create structures.

A second aspect common to all structural theories is their concern with *qualitatively different stages* of development. This feature also reflects their preference for a biological conception of development. Each stage is characterized by the emergence of a particular structural component. Maturation is given primary importance in accounting for the emergence of each structure, and for this reason, the stages are generally age related. According to such views, the sequence of structural development is assumed to be invariant. No stage can be skipped, nor is it possible to reverse development.

Structuralist positions tend to emphasize *logical* and *rule-governed* aspects of thought and language and to deemphasize such content factors as the associative strengths or reinforcement histories of words and stimuli. Thus, Piagetians would devote little attention to the fact that when highly discriminable stimuli are presented, a child is able to display mental evidence of advanced logical operations, but when cues are subtle, the same is not possible (Borke, 1975). Similarly, psycholinguists have given little attention to the semantic content of speech and have instead placed their theoretical stress on syntax; it seems likely that experience would play a more obvious role in mental functioning if greater significance were assigned to content dimensions.

A final shared assumption is that the structure reacts *holistically*, and is equal to more than the sum of its component rules. Kohlberg (1968) states this tenet as follows, "Basic development involves basic transformation of cognitive structure which cannot be defined or explained by the parameters of associative learning (contiguity, repetition, reinforcement, etc.) and which must be explained by parameters of organizational wholes or systems of internal relation [p. 348]."

Strengths and Limitations of Structuralist Theories

What are the strengths of this approach? First, it attempts to provide an explanation for typical developmental patterns in the emergence of language and thought—at a global level of analysis, involving, for example, changes in behavior patterns over periods of several years. Second, structuralist approaches attempt to deal with the full spectrum of thought and language and not just small segments of the intellectual process. Chomsky's theory can account for all of syntactic development; Piaget's attempts to explain all of the logical or operational aspects of intelligence. Third, structuralist approaches provide an analysis of complex thought and language in terms of more elementary accomplishments. For example, Piaget's notion of conservation and seriation further refined his analyses of the child's concept of number.

There are several notable limitations to the structuralist orientation. The assumption that fixed homogeneous stages underlie the child's behavior does not fit the empirical evidence. There is far more variability in children's behavior than would be expected. For example, while Kohlberg's theory assumes the sequential emergence of six types of moral thought, there is little evidence of adherence to any single type of thought. Various mixtures of judgmental criteria are used during every presumed stage. Thus, adopting a structural viewpoint requires considerable selectivity in interpreting obtained data. Above all, these approaches cannot handle very well the systematic impact of experience on behavior. As already noted, the role of experience in explaining behavioral change is subservient to the importance given to the inner structures. A cognitive balance or equilibrium notion is usually advanced to account for the response changes attributable to direct stimulation. These explanations are not totally satisfactory, since the question of which real-world event intensities, sequences, or optimal arrangements create key imbalances is never specified. A structuralist position tends to ignore social and functional factors, and as a result, the determinants of behavior change are relatively neglected. Piaget uses the terms *functional* and *operational* to distinguish behavioral changes from structural changes. Psycholinguists use the terms *performance* and *competence* to describe the same distinctions in regard to language. The relationship between alterations in action and in structure remains poorly specified.

Because of these assumptions, the structuralist position does not address molecular changes in behavior very well. For example, structuralist theories cannot offer *a priori* predictions concerning the particular type of training that will promote a child's acquisition of rules of conservation or syntax.

The structuralist model can handle typical patterns of development at a rather gross level. All children are assumed to traverse the same road of development; hence, this formulation cannot explain atypical developmental patterns. For example, why should potters' children conserve substance before manifesting other types of conservation (Price-Williams, Gordon, & Ramirez, 1969)? The accuracy of structural explanations for typical developmental patterns is often questionable (Zimmerman, 1978) particularly in cases of moral judgments. A structuralist stance also has trouble explaining response variability among tasks differing in stimulus characteristics but which share the same underlying rule (e.g., Borke, 1975). Nor can structuralist notions explain reverses in developmental sequences as the result of particular experiences (e.g., Miller, 1973; Rosenthal & Zimmerman, 1972b).

Another limitation of structuralist models is their inability to account for behavioral change once it is assumed that the structure has fully emerged. This means that Piagetians have difficulty explaining differences in conceptual performance after approximately 13 years of age, and psycholinguistic models are not useful much beyond the age of 4.

Finally, structural models are of limited assistance in guiding instruction. Their focus is on explanation rather than on prediction, and a predictive model is necessary to offer useful guidance in choosing among teaching procedures and in other applied situations.

INFORMATION PROCESSING THEORY

Main Features of the Position

These approaches to human cognitive behavior coevolved with the growth of cybernetics and developments in modern electronic computer technology. The application of machine analogues to human cognition cannot be attributed to one individual, nor is it the focus of a coherent and integrated program of research. Instead, a systems approach became appropriate when parallels between human efforts and machine attempts to handle information became obvious, and because this approach proved flexible for describing complex logical functioning.

Information processing psychologists have generally rejected the *reflex arc* notion of learning, whereby information flows from sensory receptors along afferent nerves to the central nervous system and back through efferent nerves to the muscles, which then respond overtly. This linear and rather automatic model of information processing was both inflexible and cumbersome to use when programming a computer. Correspondingly, many psychologists concluded that this model was unfit to describe human thought for the same reasons.

Thus, information processing psychologists abandoned the reflex arc and developed a more suitable model, capable of handling complex monitoring and testing during information storage, processing, and retrieval. Miller, Galanter, and Pribram (1960) proposed a new paradigm for explaining cognitive functioning in terms of testing input against some of a subject's already-established criteria. If the result of the test is negative or incongruous, responding continues until the incongruity is resolved. A *recursive loop* is thus posited, in which feedback from a particular action is monitored during a testing phase. Miller *et al.* termed their model of human functioning a *TOTE unit,* an acronym for Test, Operate, Test, Exit. It is presented in Figure 1-3.

Concept learning can be described in terms of TOTE units. The initial test phase consists of checking selected hypotheses against known information. If the hypothesis is consistent with accepted knowledge (i.e., if it passes the initial test), it is applied to current conceptual learning. If the hypothesis proves inconsistent with known information, it is discarded, and a new hypothesis is selected. According to this formulation, information is selectively processed on the basis of a complex monitoring system. This emphasis on monitoring is evident in other aspects of information processing theory.

Information is thought of as potentially passing through three systems of representation or memory. These phases are depicted in Figure 1-4. Information is first registered in *sensory storage.* All incoming stimulation regardless of whether it is visual, auditory, or of another modality, is registered in sensory storage for a brief instant. Sperling (1960) has provided much evidence concerning this type of memory. Whereas all information is registered, most is retained only very briefly, for about 200 msec. Unless *attention* is directed to some portion of the stimulus field, the information is not processed further. If attention is

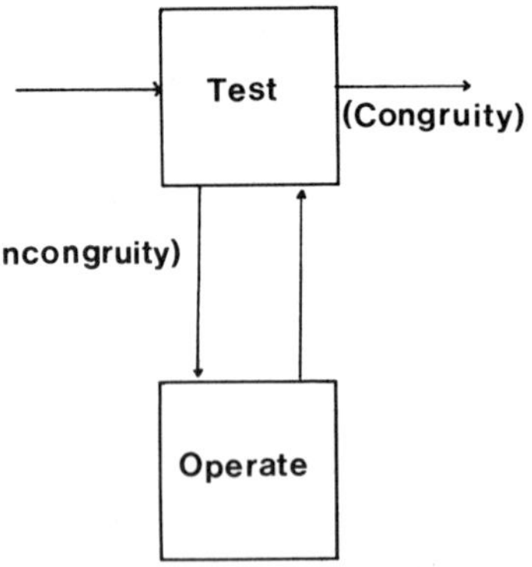

Figure 1-3 A TOTE unit. [From *Plans and the Structure of Behavior* by George A. Miller, Eugene Galanter, and Karl H. Pribram. Copyright © 1960 by Holt, Rinehart, and Winston. Adapted by permission of Holt, Rinehart, and Winston.]

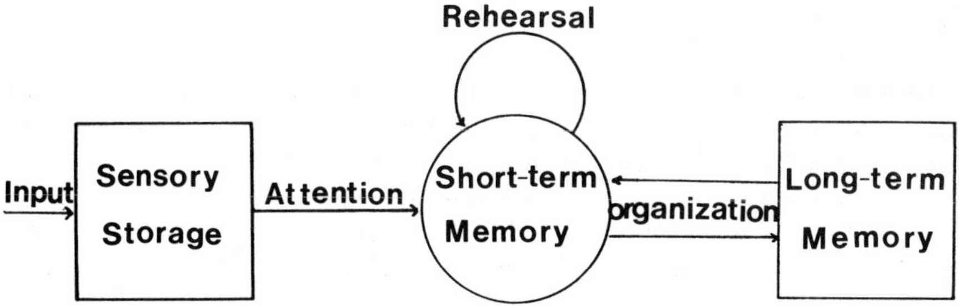

Figure 1-4 A schematic outline of the memory system.

directed, the second stage of processing, termed *short-term memory*, ensues. Much less information can be processed during this stage; however, information is analyzed more completely. Neisser (1967) described short-term memory as a sequential mode of processing, in contrast to the parallel mode evident during sensory storage. Short-term memory is of limited capacity to store information. Typically, it can handle 7 ± 2 units of information (Miller, 1956), an amount which will be retained for less than 17 seconds. Forgetting can be prevented if a subject *rehearses* the information. A digit span test is one common measure of this type of mental storage.

The third stage of information processing is *long-term memory*. Information must be coded or organized before it can enter long-term memory. Once represented there, it is assumed to persist indefinitely, although it may not be easily retrieved. Research concerning the importance of coding and organization on long-term memory has already been discussed.

Information processing psychologists thus depict cognitive functioning in terms of successive circuits monitored by check points. In order to enter short-term memory, information must be attended, and before entering long-term memory, it must be organized. This monitoring formulation assumes that individuals play a rather active role in directing much of their thought. We have already discussed the role of attention in dichotic listening research (Broadbent, 1958), and there is recent evidence (Neisser & Becklen, 1975) that visual information is cognitively controlled in similar fashion. It is believed that the criteria used for monitoring the information signal are derived to a significant degree from previous experience. For example, a person at a cocktail party will shift his attention to the conversation behind him if he hears his name mentioned.

Strengths and Limitations of Information Processing Theory

The information processing formulation views cognition as an active and constructive process. The criteria set up to govern processing are constructed by an individual depending upon his beliefs or expectations about the situation. The way in which a person codes or organizes information is similarly affected by his beliefs about what will be needed during recall and by his knowledge of different coding strategies. Thus, information processing theory is able to well explain the evidence of selection and construction in human thought.

This position can also explain the role of awareness in cognition. Research on dichotic listening (Broadbent, 1958) had indicated that attention could influence what was heard by subjects. Information processing theory was well able to account for this phenomenon: It had the advantage of being specifically designed to explain the evidence suggesting separate subsystems of representation or memory, and evidence that information is advanced for successive levels of analysis based on repeated monitoring of the information signal.

There are, however, several limitations to this viewpoint that deserve mention. An information processing position does not, by itself, explain how information is extracted from the social and physical environment. In his recent book, Neisser (1976) rejects a linear information processing approach because it minimizes the reciprocal relationship between congnitive events and information derived from the environment. He also questions some conclusions drawn by information processing psychologists regarding the human capacity to process information. Neisser now believes that poor perceptual and conceptual performances are better attributed to deficient cognitive skills than to mechanical incapacities. Information processing theories do not explain how knowledge becomes translated into action, and they ignore the motivational determinants of the acquisition and utilization of information. Questions such as how social contexts affect particular styles and emphases of processing are not addressed.

Thus, issues such as an individual's motivation are left largely untreated by this position. Little attention is directed at the way in which knowledge is translated into overt motoric responses. Finally, this position has not attempted to *predict* patterns of cognitive development in children. Efforts have been made to *explain* known developmental differences in cognitive functioning using an information processing model (Farnham-Diggory, 1972); however, to date, these attempts have not produced any comprehensive theories.

SOCIAL LEARNING THEORY

Recently, another formulation, social learning theory, has been advanced to explain cognitive phonomena as well as more overt behavioral functioning (Bandura & Walters, 1963; Bandura, 1969a, 1977b). This apparoach represents a marriage of information processing concerns and behavioral emphases. In this synthesis, particular attention is given to the impact of social variables, such as the behavior of models, on human cognitive processes. Thus, symbolic and behavioral events are studied in natural situations that closely approximate transactions in everyday life. The social learning approach emphasizes a *reciprocal* relationship between the processes of cognition and the information derived from the environment, whereas information processing theorists emphasize a *linear* flow of information. Social learning theory seeks to recast the old but ever-developing hypotheses about the nature of learning into a framework which best fits the existing data. Let us consider some of these recurrent issues and a social learning explanation.

Recurrent Questions

One such question is: "Is behavior controlled by cognitive factors or external stimuli?" Bandura (1969a, 1977b) concluded that both factors are involved, and operate in a reciprocal relationship. Cognitive processes, determined by stimulus influences from the environment, in turn act to transform the environment. The context of the stimulus that elicits an action is itself modified by the actions that are evoked. Every individual lives in a control/countercontrol relationship with his environment. A particular joke deserves mention: i.e., how the new rat in the Skinner box is told by the resident rat how to influence the behavior of graduate students by pressing the bar in the corner. The point of this anecdote is to illustrate that the relationship between behavior and the environment is reciprocal. Bandura (in press) treats psychological functioning as a continuous interaction among behavioral, cognitive, and environmental influences. As indicated in Figure 1-5, a change in any one element of this tripartite system simultaneously affects both other elements. In a social learning approach, reciprocal determinism becomes a generic principle for analyzing psychological phenomena ranging in complexity from the individual's organization of knowledge and action to interpersonal functioning, and finally, to the level of social systems effects.

Viewed from a social learning stance, environment is never considered as a fixed entity, not even for the lowliest rodent. Admittedly

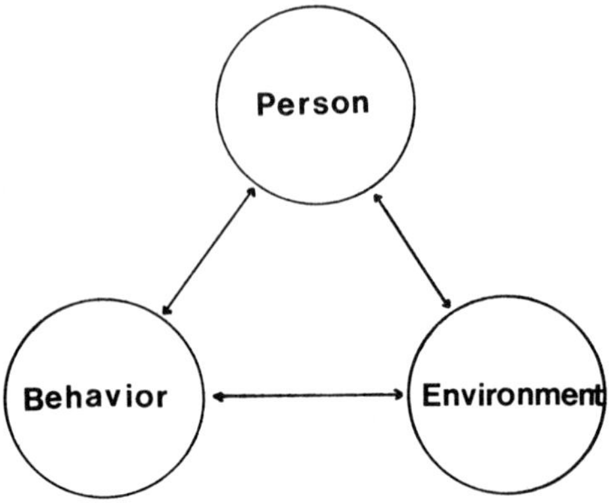

Figure 1-5 A schematic representation of a social learning reciprocal conception of interaction.

more rigid at certain points than at others, the environment remains a set of potentialities that must be activated by certain patterns of behavior. An aggressive child will face a far more hostile peer group than an obliging youngster. Few of us find the environment to be a homogeneous realm where probabilities of antecedent and consequent stimulus events are equal in all quarters. The actions displayed and sanctioned at a gay liberation gathering are likely to differ from those exhibited at a Veterans of Foreign Wars convention. Beliefs about the environment, even if largely inaccurate, can often compel people to expose themselves selectively to that small set of circumstances in which the belief will be modeled and reinforced. Indeed, the actions of others may be the triggering mechanism which creates the environment, as occurs in the "self-fulfilling prophecy" instance of the aggressive boy. The discrepancy between the actual and the potential world is probably greatest when the controlling stimuli depend on other people, as in social learning situations. During human interaction, the contingencies influencing each participant's response are constantly changing, as a result of the actions of all those involved. This reciprocity thus reverses the familiar formulation that behavior (B) is a function (f) of the environment (e) such that if one solves the equation for the environment $e = f(B)$, it emerges in turn as a function of behavior. Bandura (1977b) conceptualizes this interactive relationship between an individual and his environment in terms of three components: stimulus controls, reinforcement controls, and cognitive controls. The import of this tripartite formulation will be elaborated later in this chapter.

A second recurring question concerns *whether complex behavior can be adequately explained without reference to covert processes, as nonmediation-*

lists maintain, or whether cognitive subprocesses must be taken into account. Social learning theory assumes that neither thought nor environmental context can be studied or even profitably discussed in mutual isolation. Cognitive processes cannot be ignored because stimulus and reinforcement controls exert little impact on behavior unless they are first represented mentally (e.g., Chatterjee & Ericson, 1962; Fuhrer & Baer, 1965). Thus, evidence of how well information is received, comprehended, and recognized is helpful in predicting behavioral outcomes. Knowledge of people's preexisting beliefs is also necessary in order to predict how a particular experience will be interpreted. Real-life experiences seldom are so totally informative that they can be represented in only one way. There is evidence (Cook & Harris, 1937) that expectations are at least as important as actual experiences in determining learning.

In addition to knowing the general cognitive set used to construe experience, it is also important to know how information is internally processed during learning in order to predict behavior. Answers to such questions as: "Can the subject discriminate the relevant information?" and "How is this information being converted into symbols?" are essential for predicting learning and recall (Bandura & Barab, 1971; Bandura & Jeffery, 1973). Thus, social learning theory systematically considers cognitive factors during learning. Several specific cognitive subprocesses have been emphasized, including *attention, coding* or representation, and *retention.*

Bandura (1965) has concluded that it is empirically and theoretically useful to distinguish between cognitive acquisition and behavioral performance. Acquisition and performance are affected by different variables. In a reciprocal interactive analysis, *acquired concepts* influence attention to stimuli and in turn are themselves modified by what is perceived. Similarly, individuals' *performances* are affected by their conceptions about the contingency, schedule, and meaning of consequences, which in turn act to alter their conceptions. Unlike most cognitive formulations, however, social learning theory does not relegate overt responses to trivial status. Observable activities and cognitive determinants are involved in a complex interactive process. In order to account fully for performance, *incentive* and *motoric* variables must be given weight. These terms refer to an individual's willingness and capacity to perform. Thus, during learning, a number of subprocesses are involved, each to some degree. Consideration of each subprocess is necessary to understand psychological functioning and to optimally predict behavior. Later in this chapter, the interrelationships among several subprocesses will be illustrated in detail.

A third recurring question that has been debated involves the *role of reinforcement in learning*. Cognitive psychologists feel that reinforcement is unnecessary to explain acquisition, whereas many nonmediational theorists believe it is essential. Reality rarely involves a simple dichotomy; it seems evident from research that both positions are partially correct. As indicated above, Bandura (1965, 1971a,b) believes that without reinforcement, *acquisition* can occur simply on the basis of observation and inference, as suggested by cognitive psychologists. People need not display or implement the information they have learned unless incentive conditions for performing are favorable. Reinforcement affects cognitive processes as well. Incentives can direct attention, planning, and can also prompt rehearsal. Although reinforcement does not create new learning, it does affect how various sub-processes involved in acquisition are executed.

A fourth controversial issue concerns *the nature of the learning process*. Is learning merely passive reception, in which stimuli and responses are rather mechanically linked? Or is learning an active, constructive process that proceeds somewhat independently of environmental constraint? Research (Bandura & Jeffery, 1973) has provided evidence to indicate that learning does involve active constructions of symbols by the subject, and that the properties of coding frameworks greatly affect later retention (Bandura, Jeffery, & Bachicha, 1974). However, rather than considering it to be a process that is *in toto* personally directed or unpredictable, cognitive coding is treated as a learned skill or rule that can be cued by environmental stimuli. Thus, although there is hypothesis-formation during learning, the rules permitting hypotheses to be generated and tested can be traced to previous environmental experiences and usage norms.

A final question involves the nature of *developmental changes*. Should children's cognitive functioning be described in terms of a single, genetically endowed monolithic structure that primarily emerges through maturation? Or can development be better described in terms of the successive acquisition of cognitive skills or rules, without making firm structural and maturational assumptions? Although recognizing that typical structural frameworks might be useful in describing the modal changes in thought and language, a social learning view suggests that the organizing structures can usefully be examined in terms of component rules and operating assumptions. Since these rules can be learned through experience, no assumptions of fixed maturation or innate sequences of development need be made. This formulation enables both short- and long-term changes in behavior to be explained by the same principles.

From a social learning viewpoint, a theory's value is ultimately judged by the power of the procedures it generates to *create* psychological changes rather than to merely *describe* them. Social learning theory has been a source of very effective methods to promote personal and social change.

A Sociocultural View of Concept Formation

The preceding discussion described how social learning theory is able to integrate seemingly discrepant findings into a single encompassing viewpoint that is both cognitive and behavioral. Why do *social* variables receive so much emphasis in this account? The sociocultural fabric of an individual's environment sets limits on, and prompts, the particular behavior he will display. Thus, it is crucial for an adequate theory to account for the most obvious human characteristic: the social nature of mankind. Later, we will present evidence showing the pervasive influence of social forces on a wide variety of responses including those involving abstractions such as concepts, language, and reasoning.

How are cognitive rules and structures acquired from a sociocultural perspective? Children's thoughts are molded from birth by the social milieu in which they are raised. Their awareness of certain abstract dimensions of their environment, as well as the strategies they use to collect, process, and interpret information are primarily drawn from countless exposures to the behavior patterns of the people around them. It is probable that even the organized aspects of the physical environment, such as mathematical relationships, usually are not gleaned directly or intuitively, but instead are mediated by others' manipulations and symbolizations of that environment. It is unlikely that direct learning occurs solely from first-hand physical contracts, because this process is inefficient. The inefficiency arises from an individual's ability to sample only small aspects of his environment—a result of limited resources, time, and mobility. Socially mediated experiences greatly expand an individual's fund of knowledge. Most theories of cognitive development, whether favoring behavioristic, information processing, or Piagetian orientations, focus almost exclusively on cognitive change by means of feedback from direct experimentation. In a social learning analysis of cognitive development, conceptions about oneself and the nature of the environment are developed and verified through four different modes for gaining information: enactive, vicarious, social, and logical (Bandura, 1977b).

How can a sociocultural approach explain "universal" structural characteristics in thought, language, and morality? *Interperson similarities* in knowledge and behavior can be explained in several ways.

First, social norms and cultural practices constrain the behavior of adult models in a systematic manner. Commonly held concepts, skills, and cultural beliefs are displayed by most people. Because modeled behavior displays consistencies with certain phenomena, an observer is able to abstract the common theme or rule underlying the responses; he will then use this framework to organize his knowledge and guide his overt activity. A second factor, one which creates similar sequences of conceptual development among different children, involves the interrelationships among rules and normative standards. Most rules are interdependent to some degree; thus, the learning of one rule will affect acquisition of others. Commonalities in mental structure between individuals of disparate cultures can be explained on the basis of functional importance as constrained by shared biological capacities. Possessing certain concepts permits obvious control over the physical environment, such as the ability to use the sun as a directional guide. Such common objects and events as heavenly bodies, plants, animals, geographical formations, and the biological regularities of human life will create similar concepts and social demands in societies that are otherwise culturally different.

An equally important psychological question is often overlooked: Namely, how are *inter-* and *intraperson differences* in knowledge and behavior to be explained? A sociocultural formulation suggests that differences arise from variations in social experience. For example, the son of a physicist will probably have a different explanation for natural phenomena like lightning, thunder, and cloud movement than will the offspring of a baker. Because the social environment is not homogeneous, sociocultural influences can also explain variations in behavior across settings. Different responses are modeled and reinforced in different quarters. There is considerable evidence (Mischel, 1968) that behavior, even conceptual behavior, varies greatly according to the physical and social setting. Evidence of situational variability in responding indicates that the *use* of a conceptual rule as well as its formal *meaning* is affected by social experience. Thus, sociocultural regularities not only color the acquisition of knowledge but also affect the ultimate use of knowledge in the natural environment.

In conclusion, a sociocultural framework is well suited to explain the uniquely human dimensions of learning and behavior: Namely, the ability to learn vicariously, the capacity to form abstractions of structural regularities among events, and the ability to flexibly adapt to particular situations. In large part, cognition is a socially determined process.

THE ORIGINS OF OBSERVATIONAL LEARNING

The history of people watching as a means of learning obviously precedes formal scholarship. Yet, early in antiquity, the importance of imitative techniques in education was clearly recognized. Much thought and effort were devoted to analyzing and refining the pedagogical uses of modeling. The ancient Greeks used the word imitation *(mimesis)* to mean observational learning from a wide variety of sources: from the overt actions and orations of others, or from the visual form of events, to abstract models exemplifying prose style and moral propriety. Greco–Roman literary criticism not only addressed esthetics but also sought to select the best models for imitation in teaching the younger generation (Clark, 1957).

Perhaps the first enduring account of imitation as a planned educational device was written by Isocrates, circa 390 B.C. (see Norlin, 1929). He urged teachers not just to expound upon the principles of oratory, but to model appealing speech so that students could emulate graceful examples. The Roman writer Lucian (see Fowler & Fowler, 1905) likewise endorsed the discerning use of imitation for the instruction of young historians. As a concept, *mimesis* is probably derived from dramatic poetry and first meant the copying of a person or creature in dance, speech, or gesture; it was later extended to include various imitative representations (Clark, 1957; Preminger, 1965). In *The Republic,* Plato (1920 ed., Books 3 & 10) discussed the relationship between drama and *mimesis,* using the idea of imitation to explain how ideal objects become particularized and represented in experience, which then serves as the basis for poetry. In contrast, Aristotle was far more concerned with *mimesis* as drama, and in his *Poetics* the concept of imitation served to integrate his analysis of all art forms. Of interest in this connection was his definition of tragedy as a representation of action, or "an imitation through action rather than narration [1942 ed., p. 11]," in which he primarily emphasized the empathic experiences of the audience observing the players. In essence, he stressed *mimesis* as generic vicarious experience, and not the mimicry of specific, molecular details.

This broader conception of imitation was passed in large part to the Romans. Quintillian noted that the "whole conduct of life" involves emulating positive examples displayed by others, whether it is music, painting, or farming that is modeled. From imitating the carefully selected qualities of models, a boy could acquire purity, manliness, and a wide vocabulary. Cicero told how a master can improve the oratory of his pupils, and made the guidance of students to appropriate models his first teaching precept. Seneca the elder advised his sons to choose their models wisely, and whether imitating living men or earlier writers, his sons were instructed to emulate a range of people lest they become too similar to any one model. Clark (1957) gives a fuller discussion of imitation in Greco–Roman pedagogy and mentions that St. Augustine favored modeling as a method of teaching student preachers (p. 148). From the Middle Ages through the eighteenth century, many writers and teachers urged the use of modeling to train rhetoric and elocution (see Bahn & Bahn, 1970). Even popular authors, including Lewis Carroll (1964 ed., p. 121) and Agatha Christie (1970, p. 83) have, in their writing, taken vicarious phenomena for granted as part of the human situation.

The Instinctual Thrust

In recent times, the French sociologist Tarde (1903) was probably the first to successfully draw serious scientific attention to imitative processes. He was mainly concerned with social phenomena and made imitation the keystone of his system, accounting for the formation, maintenance, and change of social regularities in not only legal and political institutions, but fashions and customs, and shared desires and beliefs as well. Invention was seen as a new combination of prior imitations; however, observing others could, and often did, instigate new behavior. Tarde discussed many aspects of societal and large-group phenomena in terms of imitative practices and their effects, noting that persons of lower social status typically emulate high prestige figures like kings, courtiers, and celebrities.

Tarde said much less about vicarious factors in individual behavior. He discerned that the products of modeling are conveyed in relatively complete form, and hence "spared the fumblings of the first workman." For vicarious experience to be adopted, it must overcome conflicting tendencies to execute previously established, antagonistic responses. He felt that imitation may be either vague or precise, and that visual or auditory sense impressions were more likely to be emulated than were inputs of smell or taste. However, these psychological issues earned little analysis. He assumed that social man possessed innate, instinctual tendencies to imitate, a view which Lloyd Morgan (1896) and Ross (1908) among others came to share. Apart from noting that the developing child might acquire language, accent, manners, and gestures observationally, especially from the dominant parent, Tarde was largely concerned with adult behavior, scarcely mentioning children or the educational potentials of modeling. During that era, Faculty Psychology espoused imagery (e.g., Galton, 1883) and photography was newly invented. It is hard now to assess which of these strands tugged harder when Tarde proposed, as a psychological explanation, that imitation was the "quasi-photographic reproduction of a cerebral event" by the observer, whether done willfully or not—a statement that smacks of current interests in imaginal and covert processes.

William James (1890) also accorded imitation an instinctual basis, often drawing on this conception in his *Principles.* James accounted for human socialization largely in terms of the maturing child's instincts to emulate sounds and gestures, instincts that were followed by an interest in imitative games. James explicated neither the phenomenon nor its means of operation, leaving imitation as a pervasive but unexplained fact. He asserted that overt movement is immediately followed by its mental representation (1890, Vol. 2, p. 552). But especially for Thorndike (1911, 1913), all of this was speculative foolishness. Because they shared a common source in James, Thorndike lumped imitation, together with ideomotor (suggestion) effects, and inferential processes generally, hurling eloquent refutations against such offensive, mentalistic notions.

William McDougall treated imitation as an important, innate tendency; yet, in stricter usage, he restricted the term, applying it to one person copying the actions or bodily movements of another (1926, p. 106). Refusing to consider it a separate instinct, McDougall listed five types of imitation: *(a)* sympathetic expressive acts, e.g., responding to a smile by smiling; *(b)* simple ideomotor action based on suggestion, as in hypnosis; *(c)* deliberate emulation of a skilled or admired model's movements; *(d)* imitating the effects created by a model's deeds but not his literal motor patterns; and *(e)* infants' reproducing observed movements that do not express affective states, e.g., sticking out the tongue when another does so. McDougall felt that moral judgments were imitative if they were based on normative social influences rather than on strongly aroused emotions, and he followed Tarde's view that imitation was the main source of sociopsychological regularities. The child develops his sense of self and interaction standards by imitative role taking, based on adult precedents, as practiced in solitary play and during contacts with peers. In any event, McDougall had no better luck than James in making vicarious explanations palatable to environmentalists. For example, G. H. Mead (1909, pp. 404–405) protested that more caution was needed before any behavior could be considered instinctive or specific actions could be thought imitative.

The Behavioristic Parry: Reflex Circles

E. L. Thorndike soon took the lead in opposing the view that anything could be learned from observation. Thorndike did not closely examine the possible mechanisms since he doubted the existence of imitation, in part because he believed the concept required that an *idea* intervene between stimulus and response. He also disputed the Tarde–James–McDougall premise that observation of an action could elicit a drive to emulate the action. After Thorndike (1911) utterly failed to confirm imitative learning in animals, he repeatedly criticized the view that an association could be formed between an object and an action involving it "through an idea gained from watching [p. 213]," or that perceiving a response to a situation by another "tends in and of itself to connect that response to that situation [p. 250]". Considering all to be discredited concepts, Thorndike grouped suggestion or idea-motor action with inference and imitation, and concluded then:

> Various forms of statement, most of them vague, have been and would be used in describing the potency of a perceived response, a thought-of-response, or a train of inference, to produce a response and bind it to the given total situation. Any forms will do for the present argument. . . . I shall try to show that they cannot; that, on the contrary, the laws of exercise and effect account for all learning [p. 251].

Half-heartedly, he granted that perception of a familiar, already learned response may activate the old habit, but concluded that symbolic exposure to a new behavior cannot instate the response as new learning (p. 257).

If anything, Thorndike was even more vehement in his *Educational Psychology*, where he took sharp issue with James and McDougall, denying that "imitation exists as a force whereby the preception of R, in connection with S, in another man's behavior creates a bond between R and S in the perceiving individual [1913, p. 174]." Yet, as before, he allowed an exception: The behavior of others as models might influence one's own speech or manners (1913, p. 175). Was Thorndike straining toward the realization that an observed stimulus was a stimulus like any other functional cue? One cannot tell. He never performed nor encouraged further empirical research on vicarious effects, and even in his final writings, Thorndike (1940, p. 151; 1943, p. 12) took pains to deny that observational learning had any relevance to the action repertoires of men or animals. He left the impression that imitative processes were a quagmire of mentalistic pseudoscience, and that, in any case, whatever might be real could be explained by the usual laws of habit formation. These laws, as construed by Thorndike, required that an overt action must be performed in order for learning to occur. Elevated to dogma, this assumption greatly influenced later behaviorists interested in modeling, among them Miller and Dollard (1941, pp. 307–308) who credited Thorndike with a major role in correcting the theory of imitation.

Like Thorndike, J. B. Watson (1914) denied that imitation could establish new learned coordinations in people or animals. He stressed the lack of consensus about the meaning of the term, arguing that it should refer to the rapid regrouping of prior habits (p. 277); he also attacked Lloyd Morgan's classification of imitation as misconceived and anthropomorphic (pp. 278–279). Watson reported some experiments with monkeys and reviewed the research of others; as a result, he allowed that there was some slight evidence for vicarious learning (p. 288). He later dismissed imitation along with all of man's other "so-called social instincts," concluding that although it plays little role in the acquisition of manual habits, imitation deserved special status in the development of language repertoires, a capacity which Watson felt was shaped by parental modeling and differential rewarding of the baby's vocal responses (1919). The topic became peripheral in later books (Watson, 1924, 1928), where it was mentioned mainly as part of his attack on instinctual explanations, viewed as false extrapolations from Darwinian theory. Also reflecting a Behavioristic *Weltanschauung* was his stance toward imagery: "What then becomes of images: Why do they remain unproven—mythological, the figment of the psychologist's terminology . . . [1928, p. 76]." The next year, Watson and McDougall (1929) published their debate *The Battle of Behaviorism*. Their vigorous diatribes centered on their opposing philosophies of science, and as a result, such substantive issues as the properties of imitation, became coopted, used as slogans and epithets, and were lost in the combat between warring camps. Although an amusing donnybrook, the debate did not mention imitative behavior.

Smith and Guthrie (1921) were not content just to disparage. Instead, they proposed an associationistic account of emulative phenomena. Refreshingly open to the flavors of life, they attempted to address consciousness, images, perception and imagination in operational terms. They granted that imitation was real and frequently occurring, and attributed it to chains of conditioned responses. Their theory was elegant and ingenious. Stimuli are contiguously attached to movement responses that may be either gross or minimal; these movements, acting in Watsonian fashion, i.e., as the "subvocal expression of word response tendencies [p. 163]," affect cognition. As examples, they cited the fractional lip movements that occur during reading, and the incipient attack or defense gestures of spectators at a boxing match responding in tune with the actions in the ring. These minimal movements comprise part of the perception of situations; "since they themselves offer proprioceptive stimulation, such movements may be the cues for further responses [p. 164]." Movement-produced cues perpetuate such chained, serial acts as talking, so that many overt utterances were seen as linked habits which recur repeatedly without change, and which often were first established by imitating others' speech. Sentence novelty was thus produced, by the multiple responses attached to each word, with momentary response thresholds dictating the exact verbal sequence. This device allowed some variability in language production, but not enough to account for the diversity of natural language combinations. Smith and Guthrie failed to consider the option of hierarchically organized habit families, namely, Miller and Dollard's (1941) "higher order habits," and by failing to do so, made subsequent theory-building problematic. But they did attempt to tie overt stimuli to phenomenology, to deal with images (through the lag between cessation of external inputs and the central representations thereof), and to relate memory to an event's recency, duration, and the amount of attention it evokes. Using language acquisition as their example, Smith and Guthrie analyzed imitation as learned behavior in the following way: Various stimuli provoke the baby to utter a huge variety of vowel and consonant sounds, which accompany the movements that continue or reiterate them. The sounds become conditioned stimuli for their own production, which, when uttered by others, are then imitated by the baby. Before imitation is possible, the baby must practice playing with the sounds: This activity prepares him to imitate the phonemes of his language. "Imitation is seldom an exact replica of the act that is imitated. The imitator's response is that habitual act of his that most nearly resembles the act he observes [p. 132]."

While it was hardly a complete theory, and an approach that ruled out "nonresponse" observational learning, Smith and Guthrie's view was a step toward a systematic contiguity explanation of the process of imitative learning. Shortly thereafter, Allport (1924) proposed a very similar account of the mechanism, and, although he devised it independently, he cited their priority (p. 185). Dashiell (e.g., 1949, pp. 531–533) also adopted this type of analysis, crediting it to Allport. Later on, Guthrie (1935) held to the same basic position, admitting the facts of imitative behavior and ascribing them to a circular reaction based on contiguous association between stimuli and acts. Such reasoning invites protests (e.g., Miller & Dollard, 1941) regarding how a response ceases. If a cue evokes action that contains component stimuli, which, in turn, effectively elicit performance of the action, why does the cycle not go on forever? From their later writings, one can assume that Smith and Guthrie would probably invoke two types of plausible answers: because other stronger stimuli, more able to incite competing acts, may enter the situation to overpower the cues maintaining the ongoing sequence; because repeating the response-chain adds new fatigue or satiation cues that reduce the net threshold strength of the ongoing response; or the effects of both of these ploys in concert (see Hilgard, 1956). But the limitations of the circular reaction position should be viewed in the context of Smith and Guthrie's main goal: to offer a plausible, behavioristic explanation for the genesis of imitation. They did not really explore, or extend, the range of vicarious phenomena, and as a result, made no sustained efforts to fit many facts with theory, nor to conceptualize the problem in refined detail.

In the same associationistic vein, George Humphrey (1921) contributed a fascinating paper on social learning that never earned the attention it deserved. He noted the importance of imitation for education, placing special emphasis on the use of modeling demonstrations in pedagogy. Denying that imitation was instinctive, he explained it as arising from learned circular reactions whose conditional stimuli are similar in form to the reaction, as occur, for example, in the case of a crying baby:

> Although the original stimulus to which the child responds was perhaps a pain, as he cries, the child hears himself crying. Thus, S is producing R, and with it the auditory stimulus S_2, the sound of the baby's cry in the baby's own ears. Hence, by the law of substitution of stimuli, S_2, the auditory stimulus, produced R, the reaction [p. 4].

Once the cycle is established, it makes no difference to the infant whether he or another child produces the cues. Upon hearing the sound of crying he will cry. Humphrey tried to analyze response integration in Pavlovian terms (citing Pavlov's papers in the *Journal de Psychologie, 1913*), using the concepts of *inhibition* to explain cessation of response, and *inhibition of inhibition* to join response tendencies. The following is a schematic outline of Humphrey's account: Imitation arises when a primary stimulus, e.g., a bright object, leads to a reaction such as reaching, and the sight of the arm moving becomes a conditioned S to evoke repetition of the act. This soon inhibits because the primary S is absent, but when a fresh stimulus such as a comb in one's hand, is added, this new S substitutes for the prior "moving arm" input and inhibits the inhibition of the former reaction. The baby now moves his arm in response to the visual cues of comb-held-in-hand, but the movements made are not novel. They are responses learned earlier. Thus, a new stimulus "captures" and disinhibits an older dormant action pattern whose effective cues overlap with the actions (transfer stimuli) newly modeled by others.

Humphrey extended this view of response integration to more complex cases involving sets of nested component systems. By conditioning, these smaller reflex units can join into progressively larger wholes that retain an imitative character. Whether imitative or not, responses and small action chains can be hierarchically organized and subordinated to the functional control of larger situational demands (see Humphrey, 1921, p. 12). Humphrey discussed the motivations for imitation in terms of psychological drives, prophetically noting that a boy will imitate the man holding the power to bestow upon him what the boy enjoys (cf., Bandura, Ross, & Ross, 1963). Like most associationists, Humphrey felt that overt practice must first teach a response before observation can affect it: "The organism cannot acquire a new activity by imitation [p. 15]." He failed to see that shaping an already-available response (so that it is only elicited by progressively more distinctive stimuli, and is extinguished to prior cues not meeting the added requisites) entails the acquisition of many new discriminations. But he did concern himself with practical pedagogy, raising the question: Who is the better training model, another child or the teacher? He urged empirical research on this issue for all the tasks in which imitation enters the learning process.

Floyd Allport (1924) strongly opposed all views maintaining that imitation was the least bit instinctual or was a valuable aid to learning. He rebutted McDougall's theory of sympathetic induction of emotions, i.e., that a state of emotion perceived in another's behavior created vicarious arousal. According to Allport, it was not perception, but knowledge of the conditions affecting another person that rouses our understanding and sympathy. He sought to expel all notions of automatism, whereby the exposure to emotion necessarily evokes either arousal or affect of the same type as was observed. His counterexplanation was based on the transfer of past emotional conditioning, a process mediated by cues common to a spectator's past experience and a model's present plight. Taken literally, would vicarious affective response be precluded in conditions truly novel for observers? Not so. Under these new conditions, the observer "carried out thought reactions tinged with emotion similar," even though the events were never encountered (p. 236). This was a cognitive gambit that gave some ground to McDougall, in particular because observers typically perceive situations, and the feelings of those acting in them, simultaneously. Obviously, it cannot be denied that either clear situational *or* affect (e.g., pain) cues can elicit vicarious emotionality; however, in this game, the importance of controversy was never subordinated to the discussion of such mundane details. Except for reflex circles, which were mentioned in his account of the conditioning of infants' repetitive vocalization, Allport treated all imitative behavior as instrumental, to gain the desired outcomes, and also denied that useful acts could be learned by observation. He proposed as common drives in childhood, the wish to be grown up (in order to explain imitative family games and the copying of parental models), and the "compensatory striving for power" (which spurs the emulation of policemen, robbers, and train engineers). These tactics allowed him to reject the notion that valued goals, and the skills necessary to attain them, originate in the behavior of others. Modeling might simply inform observers that a given act, already learned by practice, might earn certain consequences (cf., Miller & Dollard, 1941). Allport was content to conclude that, other than using it to merely describe behavioral regularities, "we may dispense with the conception of imitation [pp. 241–242]."

Very different was Holt's (1931) comprehensive discussion of conditioned circular reflexes mediated by proprioception. He tied his reasoning to Sherrington's (1909) physiological research, Bok's (1917) account of Pavlovian reflex circles, and Humphrey's (1921) extension of this paradigm to infants' reiteration of sounds, maintaining the concept of inhibition as an explanatory device. While opting for the Humphrey–Smith–Guthrie–Allport reflex circle view of imitation, Holt added to this the notion of environmental response selection through differential reinforcement, offering some tentative drive-reduction interpretations. Those affinities may have led Miller and Dollard (1941) to assign Holt the lion's share of credit for the circular reflex conception of imitation. But Holt's actual contribution was a detailed expansion of the notion plus recognizing how the same mechanism might create new behavior. Namely, during activity, an adult may introduce some new motion, which the child may copy without any prior circular reaction. Proprioceptive afferent impulses, returning to the central nervous system after the child moves his eyes, gain motor outlet by passing into the muscles that move the hand or leg in the same direction. Thereafter, the child may imitate movements "in this plane which he sees another person execute. . . . It is empathy or empathic imitation through the mediation . . . of proprioceptive impulses set up by adient or exploratory eye movements [pp. 118–119]." This, for Holt, was "genuine imitation," because it accounted for the physical stimuli arising from a model's behavior that affected an observer via his own nervous system. Thus, Holt was among the first writers of this century to extend reflex circle premises to "nonresponse" learning based on visual observation. He did not further develop the idea, since it was only tangential to his main concerns. Instead, he constructed an exhaustive account of response integration in conditional reactions, accentuating neural facilitation and inhibition processes.

The First Refractory Phase and Baldwin's Unclaimed Legacy

Shortly thereafter, interest in modeling began to wane. Consider Woodworth's (1918) initial approach to social learning. He took issue with all instinct notions except for simple reflexes, arguing that once aroused, any mechanism can provide its own drive or lend drive impetus to other mechanisms. Although he accepted Thorndike's conclusion, i.e., that modeling did not exist in animals, Woodworth thought it was possible in children *if* one includes trial and error learning in the process. The child can imitate models only after learning to mimic, but cannot reflexively sustain this ability to imitate, beyond following some tendency to imitate, i.e., having "the ability to perceive the act imitated with sufficient precision to serve as a check on the correctness of his attempt [pp. 184–185]." Later, Woodworth (1921) decided that anthropoid apes, unlike lower animals, might profit from modeling—a process which he preferred to call "learning by observation." At best, he had little more to say on the subject; as a concern, imitation was gutted by the instinct controversy, and Woodworth ignored it as dead in his later books (1940, 1958). A similar policy of discarding modeling as a defunct topic was evident among the newer works of some writers (e.g., Morgan, 1929, 1933) who formerly had been staunch advocates of the imitation doctrine.

Images became an outdated concern of the structuralists. Imitation had been mated to discredited instinct theories and shared their purgatory; at best, it was reduced to explaining a circular mechanism. Science boycotted teleology. Weathered by such tides of intellectual history, the work of J. M. Baldwin went unrecognized, a misfortune in the light of contemporary thought. As early as 1894, he addressed imitative factors in human cognitive development, dealing cogently with topics last in fashion during Greco–Roman times. Much of his thought was predicated on now-discarded assumptions and on intuitive speculations. Yet, much rests on careful observation, inviting empirical tests and further refinement. Drawing on biology and the theories of Darwin and Spencer, Baldwin traced neurological determinants for imitation, seeking to formulate an overall synthesis, as Tarde had done. Baldwin (1906) tried to show that life necessitated the spontaneous natural selection of stimulus-motor response units, including imitative activity of two main types: *organic imitation,* such as circular reactions leading to positive hedonic outcomes, and *conscious imitation,* the basis for the emulation and practice of most habits. He was apparently the first to apply James' (1890) reflex circle notion to vicarious phenomena, which, in evolutionary terms, were serially cast in order of complexity, moving from the experience of lower animals and culminating in human memory. He pondered the relationship between imitation and *ideomotor suggestion,* whereby a meaningful stimulus imagined or revived from memory was centrally depicted or cognized (James, 1906, p. 123).

From his systematic observations, Baldwin felt that his own children began social imitation around the age of 9 months, after which it quickly spread to new activities. Intermixed with now dubious views on genetic and racial development are his interesting behavioral commentaries concerning, e.g., the roles of exposure and novelty in producing social poise, and the effect of fearless modeling by an older child to reduce the shyness of a younger one. Baldwin dealt with imitation in language learning, with the events that provoked his daughter's incipient dog phobia, and with the use of aversive consequences (bending fingers backward), to break his baby's habit of scratching people's faces. Studying his daughter's attempts to imitatively draw objects or sketched replicas, Baldwin observed developmental gains (between months 10 and 27) in her reproductions. Over time, she grew able to produce recognizable sketches just from memory. He thus concluded: "*Here, therefore, is the rise of tracery imitation of the child's own mental picture*—a fact of great theoretical interest [1906, p. 84]." His analysis was extended to the origins of handwriting as a two-step process, i.e., first as the "tracery imitation of an external copy," and then as "the similar imitation of a memory picture or form." Baldwin explained this learning series in terms of progressively evolving associations between visual stimuli (or their memorial representations), and the child's motor and optical responses that guide drawing; this account bears resemblance to some current nonverbal, imitative training methods (e.g., Lovaas, Frietas, Nelson, & Whalen, 1967).

Of the greatest relevance for contemporary psychology, Baldwin conceptualized response refinement and skill acquisition as relying heavily on modeling. Thus, a musician first imitates the movements and sounds of his instructor; later, he plays from printed rules, and eventually the name of a selection can elicit "subconscious" sound and muscle movements, copies whose vicarious heritage is forgotten (pp. 289–291; cf. Skinner, 1953, pp. 118–121). In this way, reactions first drawn from imitations of external stimuli may later become governed by internal memory cues that supersede their emulative origins: A child may begin by copying a word as it is sounded by others, but he later reserves its correct use for the object it designates. Visual images of the object now elicit the word in speech, replacing the original auditory model.

Baldwin ascribed stimulus selection to attention, noting that an act of imitation unites contiguous stimuli; the functional union of these stimuli creates a synthesis of meaning among the several elements that are joined. To Baldwin, abstraction and inference developed via the organizing effects of attention upon mediated stimuli—stimuli which become structured into "great nets" or "mental categories" as the result of differential attention. Consider his example of the perception and classification of a peach (pp. 297–299). Attention to the peach evokes some feedback by means of cues common to a wide range of stimuli (e.g., sensations of gross muscle contraction), triggers off the action of other components shared by a narrower set of objects (e.g., special sense cues like the muscular adjustments made by the eye as it accommodates to objects of comparable size), and initiates feedback limited to objects sharing specific visual details. These separable targets of attention all transmit inputs that alter the mental correlate of the stimulus, joining it with other correlates linked to earlier peaches, ultimately becoming subsumed within the category of Peach. In addition to motoric memories, images from prior peach experiences are evoked in this act of recognition and grouping. Thus, one's sense of familiarity with an object derives from the cognitive reinstatement of earlier examples, and images support one another so as to arouse the feeling of recognition. Baldwin assumed that abstract paradigms as well as class commonalities can be imitatively established by generalizing from the framework of elements linked in this manner: "Imitation is the method by which our *milieu* of thought and feeling . . . [gets] reproduced within us in a system of relationships . . . [p. 308]." He then relates the story of a friend's daughter who, after bumping her head, began calling all bodily pain "bump-bump," whereupon her younger brother further generalized the term to indicate all mental distress, like unpleasant emotions and fears. Since the child's performance repertoire is more limited than the range of stimulus events he encounters, a cluster of related stimuli will elicit the same essential response, initially overgeneralized, but later more discriminative until a "rectification of the concept [p. 309]" is achieved.

Overly inclusive concepts, such as the belief that red squares designate *all* colors, are honed by further perceptions and practice into more veridical classes. Red becomes a grouping within the larger set of colors, and squareness is no longer required to designate the color red. Thus, *boat* is first conceived of as having the elements of spread sails, three masts, and sailors in the rigging. "Then sailors are dropped, sails and masts go, etc. What is left is said to be abstracted, as for instance, the concept color, a quality abstracted from particular instances. But true abstraction is not a singling out, it is rather a paring down, a wearing off, an erosion . . . It represents that which is essential in an experience, not only as tested by its uninterrupted recurrence and shifting and drifting details, but more especially by its regular calling-out force upon me in some great fixed way of acting [pp. 311–312]." Baldwin then empirically defined the general or abstract as an attitude, expectancy, or motor tendency that fits numerous specific experiences. As in the peach example, common feedback patterns are triggered by elements of the same class, and distinctions among categories are mediated by differential attention to nonoverlapping features (pp. 313–315). Overt input stirs self-produced echoes; thus, category recognition is jointly governed by distal and stored cues. He applied similar reasoning to vicarious emotional responding. A child weeps at a picture of another's tearful grief because it evokes memory copies of personal suffering that prompt habitual emotional reactions.

Baldwin took pains to deny that new behavior requires graduated overt practice or reinforcement (cf. Bandura, 1962, 1965). Citing his daughter's attempt to imitate a complex response first demonstrated for her, he asked: "How long would it [take] if she had waited for experiences actually pleasurable to build up this motor combination? In cases of persistent imitation there is more than association as such. The movements initiated are new, as combinations. . . . [Cognition is not confined] to past experiences held in memory, but issues a new and more adaptive co-ordination of them [pp. 362–363]." From his developmental observations, he proposed that the child first practices auditory and then visual images before addressing many sensorimotor feedback cues. Thus, auditory and visual memories get a head start over motor cues in steering attention which, in turn, governs the probability that a stimulus will elicit an imitative response. "Attention is the go-between between the copy imitated and the imitation which copies it. It is, therefore, *the central and essential fact in all voluntary motor control* [p. 450].'' From this, he proposed a theory of inhibition. If movements lead to a painful outcome, they are suppressed by *positive* inhibition. However, what about diffuse or random acts that serve no purpose and earn no visible consequences? These fail to attract attention and hence suffer *negative* inhibition. Since attention is required to select movements, and to make them persistent, orderly, and habitual, unattended actions give way to competing responses having more compelling functional significance. It is interesting to ponder what might have occurred had Baldwin attracted students who operationalized his ideas and subjected them to experimental testing. As it was, the time was not ripe. With the rise of peripheralistic behaviorism in the United States, his work suffered from the negative inhibition of scholarly attention, although it was sometimes mentioned with scorn by the victors.

Although Kimball Young (1930) may have drawn upon Baldwin's work, he criticized Baldwin for using imitation to explain too much. Young provided a synthesizing viewpoint rather than introducing new concepts. He adopted the reflex circle to explain repeated vocalizations in infants, and treated all imitation in terms of response integration by association. Young was original because he was willing to readmit covert central processes into analyses of human behavior, i.e., that cerebral events intervene between overt stimuli and responses, and are manifested as attitudes, images, and ideas. Attitudes are incipient habits; images arise from the retentive capacities of the cortex; concepts derive from imagery and are related to language growth. One can manipulate imaginal representations of external objects and symbolic concepts to better control one's environment. Perhaps of most interest, he linked imagination and thought to social conditioning and communication, citing this as a means for sociocultural control of conduct. Thus, overt events are construed in light of the ideas and values established by socialization, which creates a frame of reference that directs and gives meaning to behavior. Young was striving to meld the concerns of individual and social psychology, using symbolic mediating activity as an integrating device, but such an approach was atypical of the era. For example, when Murphy, Murphy, and Newcomb (1937) tried to organize the main achievements of social psychology, imitation received scant notice most of which, both pro and con, concerned Tarde. Of the few research studies that were cited, interest centered mainly on those of Gurnsey, summarized by Bühler (1931), and on the work of Valentine (1930), who pursued some of Baldwin's interests, as well as his method of genetic observation, contributions introduced more than a generation earlier. No mention of Baldwin's own work was made.

Divergent Continental Interpretations

Baldwin's approach was more congenial to European perspectives, but his influence there was qualified by a dissimilar intellectual orientation. Thus, Paul Guillaume (1925, trans. 1971) used Baldwin's genetic observation strategy to study his son's and daughter's two first years of life. Although owing much to their views, he criticized Tarde's and Baldwin's theories as "philosophies [p. 1]." Guillaume assumed that all acts have instinctual roots that interact with past and present learning to regulate current actions. Perception plays an executive role (like attention did in Baldwin's theory), and imagery helps one to conceptualize or think about an action. All of these strands of the total mental state must be given weight, for behavior to be explained. Images can assist in analyzing modeled examples and in assuring a better overt match before action is performed, akin to what Muenziner (1938) would later call *vicarious trial and error.*

For Guillaume, the term "imitation" spanned multiple meanings and a broad range of response examples. Namely, the act that one person copies from another might represent an educative step the observer could not have attained on his own; alternatively, it might be vicarious instigation of behavior already in the child's repertoire. Guillaume recognized that the concept of imitation was not unitary or absolute, but instead involved properties that can be abstracted and studied in regard to such diverse criteria as function, purpose, effects, or physical topography viewed as an assembly of movements. His most illuminating remarks stem from his sensitivity to the social conditions of early development. Accordingly, Guillaume felt that cognition derives from the social realities that surround the infant. Human displays are particularly compelling as stimuli, and modeling by adults has special impact on the baby. Thus, behavior comes to be regulated more by the attitudes and precedents of other people than by the objective properties of events (cf. Festinger, 1950); reality is socially defined. Long before example can initiate new acts, parents are actively prompting, praising, and manually steering the baby to perform. Such parental activities train and select behavior that is valued by the social environment. For example, a babble that approximates *ma ma* or *da da* earns caresses, sweets, and other forms of social approval. Over time, imitation becomes more accurate because previous experience becomes organized and exerts a corrective influence on what the child extracts from new modeling episodes.

How, then, does imitation come about? The question is easier asked than answered. First, considerable trial and error learning is involved.

Using sound production as an example, he accepted that some role may be played by a circular reaction; however, vocal responses must become subordinated to auditory perception if performance is to be reliable. An appropriate affective state must also play a part. Guillaume believed that interesting or unusual, rather than necessarily pleasant, sensations may instigate a circular reaction. Recognition of his progressive improvement in matching his own responses to the stimulus is a sensation that will strengthen the child's desire to imitate. In choosing words to imitate, the child is influenced by verbal significance; eventually, a direct, contemporaneous model is no longer needed and the child will imitate from memory.

Guillaume's writing is evocative rather than systematic. He draws attention to many important issues, makes some interesting inferences, and orchestrates the interplay of many constructs and themes symphonically. But the functions of and relationships among these constructs are not well developed. Sometimes inconsistent, sometimes lacking logical continuity, his thoughts are often poorly juxtaposed, and the logic from one level of discourse often conflicts with that from another. It seems clear that no consistently integrated set of explanatory principles is being advanced. Explicit variables are not isolated and further probed. The notion of multiple causation, which, under given conditions, typically involves the shifting contributions made by a variety of determinants gets Guillaume's major attention. A similar strategy of explanation is found in Piaget's (1962) views of imitation, which are discussed later in this chapter, and which were greatly influenced by Guillaume. One sharp difference between their approaches, however, requires mention. Guillaume assumed that imitation could result from association between sense perceptions and movement responses; the more closely his response follows or matches the sensory signals that are modeled, the better the imitation from the child's standpoint.

Piaget (1962, p. 81) strongly rejected this reasoning. In his account, imitation progresses as an intrinsic part of cognitive development in general. Any response that is to be emulated must already be endowed with meaning; the child is not concerned with matching his own behavior to modeled stimuli, but instead seeks to reproduce a meaningful event. Like Guillaume, Piaget is interested in imitation as part of an evolving equilibrium among cognitive states and structures that arise with development. He discusses such issues as selecting, grouping, and concept–formation, but gives scant emphasis to the environmental variables governing social imitation. Experimental manipulations are not his goal. Like Guillaume, Piaget offers nothing to suggest possibilities for research on the acquisition of new concepts from training models, nor does he advocate the use of observational learning techniques as a means of teaching abstract strategies or styles. Although Piaget's work has been a great impetus to the developmental study of cognition, it has done little to prompt research on social learning phenomena. His methodology and style of explanation seem very alien to the conventions of American experimental psychology. In tenor and emphasis, the Piagetian approach is somewhat reminiscent of psychoanalytic thinking—a theory long concerned with certain facets of imitative phenomena which, at this point, are appropriate to summarize.

In the psychoanalytic literature, social learning influences are usually discussed in terms of *identification,* which is of two main types: *primary* or *anaclitic;* and *defensive* or *identification with the aggressor.* Anaclitic identification is basic in the primitive perceptual and libido development of the infant, who is ambivalent toward the persons who care for and protect him. In the first, oral, phase of libido development, the child's emotions run parallel to his dominant frame of reference, namely, the experience of feeding. At this developmental stage, any craved-for goal object is eaten and, while annihilated in its own right, the object becomes part of (is incorporated by) the child. Perception, like feeding, involves a taking in or rejection of stimuli, and the early reactions of imitating what is perceived are conceptually akin to oral incorporation of perceived stimuli. The structural properties and effects of anaclitic identification retain their continuity throughout the child's life. Because identification derives from such a close association with perception (Fenichel, 1945, p. 37), the ontogenetic linkage continues throughout development. Ideation and other key mental processes (Freud, 1955a,e) are similar to identification, i.e., are structured such that significant external stimuli are assimilated; the covert representations of these stimuli then operate to steer behavior. As the child's cognitive capacity increases, the defensive form of identification becomes dominant and the focus of cognition shifts to the handling and resolution of the Oedipal situation (see Freud, 1955a,b,c,d, 1959a).

At first, the little boy takes a special interest in his father, whom the child also wishes to emulate. But at the same time, the male child is erotically attached to his first love object, his mother. Both emulative and erotic goals would be fulfilled if the boy could supplant his father and take his place as mother's lover; this creates a rivalry between father and son, and tinges their relationship with hostility. By the Oedipal stage, identification with father (wanting to *be* like him) has become differentiated from making the object–choice of father (wanting to *have* his prerogatives). Accordingly, by the process of defensive identification, "a person's own ego [is molded] after the fashion of the one that has been taken as a model [Freud, 1955d, p. 106].'' Both the boy's erotic desire for mother, as well as his fear of retaliation by father, lead the child to renounce mother in fearful deference to the dominant father who, if the boy behaves otherwise, might castrate him—or so the boy thinks. In resolving his Oedipal strivings, the boy gives up mother and adopts the attitudes and moral stance of the aggressor, i.e., the presumably jealous father. The boy also incorporates aspects of the lost love object, his mother, so that the child identifies with *both* parents to varying degrees (Freud, 1959c). Identification is a major and general psychological process, not something simply confined to childhood or the Oedipal situation. Two qualifications deserve mention, however: Freud's earlier thinking (e.g., 1955d, pp. 106–107, 1959b, p. 159) underwent elaboration, revision, and change over time (e.g., 1955f, p. 129–130); our summary of identification has navigated around numerous technical subtleties, for example, the extent of imitation following identification with various social figures (see A. Freud, 1946).

Fine points aside, identification with the aggressor has had wide currency as the psychoanalytic version of social learning phenomena. Thus, Freud considered emotional identification with the *leader* as the basis of group membership and cohesion (1955d, pp. 108–109). Freud was familiar with the then current views of imitation (e.g., Tarde's), but discarded them because he felt the concept was too snarled with issues of suggestion (1955d, pp. 88–89). Defensive identification, his alternative construct, has been used to account for the effective management of delinquent youngsters (Aichorn, 1935), for value changes among concentration camp prisoners (Bettelheim, 1943; Frankl, 1954, 1959), and as a main explanatory principle in psychoanalytic accounts of social psychology (Sargent & Williamson, 1958). Psychoanalytic logic has been critically discussed by experimentally oriented writers (e.g., Bandura, 1969a; Rachman, 1963; Ullmann & Krasner, 1975), and a competing, social learning analysis of aggression is available (Bandura, 1973).

The heuristic contributions of Freud, Piaget, and their colleagues must be acknowledged. During a long drought when most behavioral psychologists showed little real concern for imitative phenomena, organismic and psychodynamic scholars helped maintain interest in modeling processes. Certainly, Lewin (1935) and Tolman were spurred by psychoanalytic notions. Originally, Tolman (1932) had little to say about social learning, and merely listed imitativeness along with curiosity and gregariousness in the group of acquired drives. Doubtless among his main contributions was stressing the importance of cognitive factors, even in learning by lower animals; he also stimulated research (e.g., on latent learning) not readily explained by simple conditioning premises. Although a self-avowed behaviorist, Tolman and his students kept cognitive explanations alive within the psychology of learning. By showing that rats could acquire "maps" of "means–end field relations" rather than sheer movement habits, Tolman confirmed a type of observational learning. To this day, Tolman's distinction between performance and learning has remained relevant. He later accepted the Freudian idea of identification and, in this guise, social learning was given prominence—as occurs, for example, when a child identifies with an adult whose interests and career pattern he adopts (Tolman, 1942, p. 67; cf. Freud, 1955d, p. 105). Tolman (1942) also assigned a high priority to utopian modeling applications as practical devices for improving the social order. In his later work, Tolman (1948) continued to insist that symbolic mediating events intervene between overt stimuli and responses. During an era dominated by Hull's (e.g., 1943, 1952) peripheralistic behavior theory, a dissenting, cognitive viewpoint was exemplified by Tolman and Lewin. Contemporary social learning interpretations owe a debt to this influence.

A Reminiscence Effect: Modeling Briefly Revisited

Miller and Dollard's *Social Learning and Imitation* (1941) was the next milestone in the history of modeling. The book has three main emphases: to establish the importance of imitative learning in acquired (not instinctual!) social, behavior; to replace the associative contiguity accounts minimizing the effects of reinforcement (e.g., Humphrey, 1921; Smith & Guthrie, 1921) with a Hullian drive-reduction analysis of imitation; and to support their stance with *experimental* evidence, going beyond the naturalistic observations offered by previous writers. They sketched an outline map of important issues that needed further exploration, calling attention to many problems of subsequent research interest, and sifted and synthesized ideas scattered throughout the literature. For example, Miller and Dollard postulated the concept of imitative "savings," allowable because observers need not repeat all the units of a model's actions, as long as the final (goal) responses are similar. They explained the phenomenon of learning to pay attention as an acquired cue discrimination process. They implicated teachers' pessimism, leading to restricted delivery of attention and reward, as social determinants of poor schoolwork by lower-class children. Neither present concern with the matters they either ignored or glossed over, nor our specific disagreements with their theorizing, are intended to denigrate the significant contributions of Miller and Dollard, such as their pioneering efforts to study human modeling through controlled laboratory experiments.

Miller and Dollard's dominant thesis asserted and reiterated that imitation was learned instrumental behavior. They separated *imitativeness*, an acquired social drive (cf. Crown & Marlowe, 1964), from the reinforced habits of *imitation*, which was further separated into three classes: *Same* behavior occurs when similar responses are instigated, among people who react to common cues; some external eliciting stimulus is responsible for evoking simultaneous performance and not the social situation or relationship among observers. This occurs when all drivers stop because a traffic light turns red. *Matched-dependent* behavior means using a model as a discriminative cue to discern when and where to respond in order to earn a reward; the model does not elicit new actions or alter the form of available responses, but steers the observer to the locus of reinforment. In *copying*, one must learn to guide one's own acts from observing a model's cues and responses. An example is learning to sing on key by a process of sharpening both stimulus and response discriminations through guided demonstrations and feedback. Miller and Dollard defined copying as matched-dependent behavior *augmented by* the use of sameness and difference cues. These latter cues are derived from the closeness of match between the model's and observer's responses. The copying and matched-independent categories were treated as polar opposites, the end points of the narrow potential range assigned to all observational learning.

Miller and Dollard's experiments with animals and children were very similar in design and intent. For example, they showed that when a child model finds candy in one of two otherwise identical boxes, child observers rapidly adopted a similar strategy, choosing the model's box for candy. Another group of children was given the reverse contingencies; these observers promptly learned to earn reward by picking the box avoided by the model. Imitation (and reverse imitation) was then generalized to a new choice-box task, to new models, and to a different (but simple) two-choice response. In another study, either following or reversing a model's choice of boxes activated a relevant light signal, and this cue assisted correct performance. None of the experiments were directed at their more complex form of imitation, i.e., copying; the possibility of learning or refining skills or concepts from watching a model's efforts was not tested. The topography of the emulative response, and its potential utility for daily living were ignored. The model's main function was to disclose the locus of payoff. As Bandura (e.g., 1969a) has noted, data derived from such narrow operations fail to depict *social* learning adequately: If the model were eliminated and cues indicating place (e.g., symbols or colors) were instead exposed on the boxes, it is likely that the discrimination would have been learned just as quickly, if not faster than before. The experiments of Miller and Dollard did confirm that systematic matching or reversal of a model's choices was subject to reinforcement control. But the studies tell little about vicarious processes, and less about the range or complexity of behavior that modeling can teach and elaborate. Indeed, had the model chosen a correct five-step path among many identical boxes or buttons, some particular advantages of demonstration would have been disclosed. Whereas dichotomous choices yield as much information from false as from proper responses, multiple-step discriminations do not. Much more information is conveyed when a model selects the correct combination from numerous possibilities; in contrast, much trial and error practice is required when only external cues of color or position are available without vicarious guidance. These extensions were not attempted, nor were they made salient, in the context of Miller and Dollard's effort to validate reinforcement control; instead, the constraining frame of reference implied by their drive-cue-response-reward analysis hampered Miller and Dollard's penetration of observational learning.

For instance, in Miller and Dollard's first illustrative case (1941, pp. 133–137), one need not accept their assumption of a "long-established imitative pattern" to explain why a hungry child craves a familiar food she sees another child eating. Arousal of the child's appetite would be better described as vicarious instigation (closer to their *same* behavior) than as imitation. Their second illustration, a "peek-a-boo" case example (pp. 137–143), highlights the problem vividly. They imposed a labored reward analysis on a child's playing peek-a-boo games with mother. But the least plausible element of their explanation is how the word "peek" comes to be imitated: "On some one occasion, he happens to say 'peek' or something like it, to himself; he finds that hearing himself say this is rewarding; thereupon he repeats it and begins to stabilize the response [p. 141]." Notice that the roles of social example and interaction are subordinated to the child's directly producing some approximation to the target response. Although the game is often initiated by mother, (presumably rewarding the baby's utterances that are similar to 'peek'), some independent, overt source of original, reinforced learning is the explanation resorted to by these investigators. Like some of the other writers discussed earlier, Miller and Dollard apparently felt that a modeled act cannot itself instate new behavior. Oddly, the child in this view is allowed to discern mother's "increased interest" when he makes the sound, but is not allowed to acquire the sound from her repeated vocalizations. Their history of psychological views about vicarious behavior was similarly anchored in preconceptions. For example, they criticized Hobhouse (1915) for concluding that his pet had benefited from observing a model's performance: "He did not grasp the fact . . . that the watching animal must be *performing* the act while the leader animal is performing it and must then be rewarded for its total watching-performing behavior [1941, p. 309]." Throughout their historical survey, their rigid theory appeared to color their perceptions. The reader is invited to test this directly by comparing, for example, their account of Baldwin, Holt, Humphrey, or Smith and Guthrie with the original sources.

If a crucial role of social models is to establish and refine complex response ensembles and not just spatial discriminations (see Bandura, 1977b), it is instructive to trace Miller and Dollard's thinking about the scope of vicarious learning. They assigned a purely supplementary role to imitation; it served only as a means to prime correct overt response (which could then be rewarded and acquire some true strength) faster than would otherwise occur. Thus, they noted that *copying* plays an important part in language acquisition, but treated it as a springboard to "independent" learning, rather than as a method in its own right. In order for modeling to influence acquisition of a particular response, the response must first be present in the learner's repertoire: "Imitation cannot be used to produce either a sound or a novel combination of sounds in a new situation, unless the component cue-response matchings have been already learned [p. 206]." This stance rules out demonstrations as means of teaching novel stimulus and response combinations when, in fact, modeling serves very well for this purpose. Miller and Dollard did feel that imitation could expedite the learning of manual, mechanical, and athletic skills. Their clearest suggestion of a new activity that could be learned through imitation involved athletic skills: They described how a boy who knew how to watch and match, might more easily "learn how to throw a curve with a baseball by seeing how another boy puts his hand on the ball than by puzzling out the solution for himself [pp. 151–152]." Yet when stating the conditions under which imitation would assist learning, they ignored this illustration (pp. 210–211); they denied that a model's actions can themselves provide the cues needed to acquire a new response.

In Miller and Dollard's two-choice imitation studies, children showed a strong tendency on the first trial to pick the box the model had *not* selected. Also, the reverse-modeling group made fewer errors than the group rewarded for duplicating the model's choice of boxes. Later writers (e.g., Scheerer, 1954) have noted that those data suggest the children did not learn imitative *habits* through reward. Instead, the children generalized inferentially from past experience with related games in which a law of probability has become evident: Typically, if one of two options has just paid off for somebody else, the remaining choice becomes more promising. Likewise, aficionados of Las Vegas do not rush to patronize the slot-machine that has just dispensed a jackpot. Instead, they try to remember which machine has *not* paid off for a long time and hence is a better bet to play. However, once children perceived they would get candy where the model did, they kept "imitating" not from increased habit strength, but from a changed expectancy about the probable locus of reward. Miller and Dollard did not directly address this competing ("cognitive") interpretation of their data, but adhered instead to a reinforcement analysis of incremental response changes across trials. Yet they were fully aware of this alternative explanation. Early in the book they alluded to a little girl who, as the result of past experience with hiding games, might tell herself "He'll probably change the place now that I know it [p. 16]." Such willingness to ignore implications incompatible with their preferred drive-reduction account of imitation may help to clarify their failure to experimentally investigate abstract, conceptual modeling, despite their obvious interests in broader symbolic behavior.

Miller and Dollard treated thought as implicit speech, and gave cue-producing, mediating acts a central role in the reasoning processes. They granted that learning to attach the proper responses to word labels (or to observing another person) that are serving as cues prompts, in the case of language (or imitation), a marked reduction in random trial and error; hence, correct responses are elicited faster (p. 26). They pointed out that abstraction entails responding to similar cue classes in diverse contexts and plays a major role in the higher mental processes (p. 72). But excluded from their discussion was the human capacity to respond *selectively* to subtle cues. This exclusion is perplexing in light of their earlier allusion to a child's inferential thought, i.e., telling herself that the other participant will probably switch to a new hiding place after the first one was discovered. Yet, Miller and Dollard would not entertain the notion of a child telling himself that "an apple is like an orange because they're both round, fruit, and good to eat."

They even cited one of Miller's (1934) own studies showing how, if trained to find candy under a yellow box placed among three red boxes, a young child will promptly generalize, and seek reward beneath a purple box placed among three green boxes. They acknowledged that the cue of color difference was independent of the specific colors presented, but they never adapted this research design to study observational learning. Had they compared the performance of child observers with that of children who had chosen and been rewarded overtly, research on vicarious concept attainment would have been well underway! Surely, given Miller's brilliant experiments in other spheres, one might assume a simple next step of varying the numbers of boxes, the types of containers, and the dimensions of disjunction (e.g., one cup versus several bags, one large versus several small receptacles, or one metal versus several wooden boxes). In that way, rapid transfer by observers across familiar grouping dimensions could have been manifested. As it was, when Miller and Dollard tried to extrapolate from their imitation paradigm to naturalistic abstract learning, their most ambitious attempt was a very cautious one, with their effort remaining confined to overt, reinforced response-matching. They concluded that while the model is responding, the observer must be performing the act directly, and must then earn reinforcement for the net sequence of observing–emulating activity. However, this conclusion was not derived from their data, it was merely assumed—a legacy from the past that they chose to accept.

A final irony was Miller and Dollard's neglect of Hull's doctoral research studies that were among the first experiments on concept formation established by observation. To anticipate our later discussion, a *model* is merely a stimulus array, and whether human or not, it is organized such that it conveys information efficiently. The arrangement, that is, patterning, or accentuation of key stimulus components can itself transmit guidance about the concept to be learned. Demonstrating the desired target response, or emphasizing its crucial attributes, can create abstract learning inferentially. In common sense terms, if an observer can see live examples reflecting the type of concept he must adopt, he can use the examples to guide his behavior.

Hull (1920) studied whether the learner must himself act to develop concepts from concrete experiences, or whether he can instead profit from having the common elements displayed before him—a device that spares the learner from the need to identify and abstract the constant attribute on his own. To his surprise, Hull found that observing the common elements was functionally equivalent to the learner developing the concepts independently. Hull next showed that presenting abstract (common) elements *plus* concrete examples was superior to either method alone. Hull then devised a study even more pertinent to observational learning. He questioned whether demonstration, by drawing the learner's attention to the essential concept attribute, could improve concept mastery. His stimuli were Chinese characters (ideographs), and when presented to the demonstration group, the constant attribute was drawn in red; this was not done for the controls, who only received black ideographs. The results distinctly favored the demonstration format. In essence, this was abstraction, based on the modeling of the essential core attribute of his stimuli. Improved conceptual performance required neither overt practice nor drive reduction; it was the result of a more informative restructuring of the stimulus arrays, in order to guide observational discrimination. Miller and Dollard's conception of imitation as a set of response habits, and their bias requiring reinforced overt performance, did not dispose them to make the connection between Hull's results and observational learning.

The Second Refractory Phase: Darkness before Dawn

Not much happened in social learning for almost 20 years after the appearance of Miller and Dollard's (1941) book. L. L. Bernard (1942) deserves mention for reiterating the role of models in transmitting sociocultural mores. While he gave no real analysis of mediating mechanisms, Bernard, like Tarde, underscored the continuity between vicarious learning and social influence phenomena. Melton (1950) took a fresh look at the possibilities for expanding the range of learning techniques by inviting research on the method of tuition or guidance, as used in formal pedagogy, and on imitation as another type of guidance that reduces wasteful trial and error. He concluded that the virtues of modeling result "because the learner acquires a better orientation toward the significant relationships or objects in the problem situation rather than because the learner imitates the specific adequate response and excludes all inadequate response [pp. 675–676]." This view marked a step toward interpreting modeling as a source of information, rather than as a habit-training device. Melton cited the work of Carr (1930) and his students, studies showing that various forms of guidance—manual prompting, visual cues, graphic mnemonic maps, and verbal directions—improved performance on stylus mazes. In the realm of concept formation, however, Carr's student Waters (1928) found that demonstrating the correct response on a complex bead-removal puzzle had clearly detrimental effects as compared to other techniques. Although more recent work (Kirby, 1973) suggests that Waters' results may involve procedural artifacts (the induction of a confusing solution set), Waters' early negative findings very likely discouraged any further study of vicarious concept learning by Carr's group.

Skinner (1953) offered an interesting analysis of imitative repertoires based on discrimination processes. He took the example of *drawing from copy*, very similar to Baldwin's tracery imitation. The skilled copyist has developed an elaborate repertoire that undergoes sustained use and refinement because the approximations matching the sample stimulus earn selective reinforcement. Similar contingencies affect the ability to sing or play music by ear, and imitation in general. Although not allowing for novel learning through unreinforced observation per se, Skinner offered a sophisticated account of the linkages that can integrate imitative sequences. His notions concerning the matching of a stimulus that controls a learner's response, and generalizing from a prior history of reinforced social emulation, have exerted subsequent influence. For example, Gewirtz (1971a,b) has adopted a similar position in an effort to explain the genesis of all imitative behavior.

Overall, though, it was an era of famine for modeling. How far had the psychological study of social learning progressed by the mid-1950s? On the learning end, little was in the air. In his classic compendium, Osgood (1953) listed imitation as a possible method for producing the correct response, but theorists preferred to analyze this sequence in terms of trial and error or conditioning paradigms. He also dealt with imitation in language development, merely noting: *(a)* that imitation has been offered as one explanation for the origin of speech in primitive man; *(b)* that infants' speech production has been credited to imitation in Allport's (1924) and Holt's (1931) reflex circle accounts; and *(c)* that verbal object labels are rapidly acquired once an infant has verbal skill and a "readiness" to imitate. Hilgard's (1956) second edition of *Theories of Learning* confined discussion to Melton's (1950) ideas, which we summarized earlier.

On the social end, another yardstick was Lindzey's (1954) *Handbook of Social Psychology*. It treated Freudian identification in both individual and collective behavior. Gordon Allport gave imitation some space in his historical chapter, especially crediting Tarde and Baldwin, and recounting the bygone instinct controversy. Allport (1954) further noted that "imitation" alludes to, but fails to clarify, the role of models in societal influence processes. Experimental research was very sparse, and consisted primarily of Miller and Dollard's matched-dependent studies, spurring Scheerer's (1954) rejoinder. Modeling was alloted broad scope in reference to sociocultural implications, but was vastly more restricted in regard to learning and pedagogy than it had been during Greco–Roman times. Research such as had been attempted on observational concept learning was either forgotten or out of vogue. In short, the field was something of a sleeping giant. Not long afterward, Albert Bandura roused it with new research and theory which, as central concerns of this book, will be discussed presently.

VICARIOUS LEARNING AND COGNITIVE PROCESSES

Contemporary Theoretical Accounts to Explain Imitative Performance

Contemporary views of vicarious learning differ in many respects, but particularly important are the following considerations: *(a)* whether modeling phenomena are best treated in terms of the copying or reproduction of overt responses (an *imitation* stance), or whether modeled events are instead used as cognitive guides for future conduct (a symbolic *informational* stance); *(b)* the role in learning and performance to be assigned to reinforcement and affective arousal; and *(c)* the provisions to be made for modeling in establishing novel behavior.

RESPONSE REINFORCEMENT VIEWS OF IMITATION

Main Features

In the tradition of Thorndike (1913) and Watson (1924), a number of contemporary theorists (e.g., Baer & Sherman, 1964; Gewirtz, 1971 a,b; Parton, 1974; Skinner, 1953) have attempted to describe vicarious learning as a form of instrumental conditioning. Imitative behavior is considered as a generalized response class that is acquired relatively early during development, at a time when a child's approximations to a model's behavior are selectively reinforced on the basis of response similarity. This formulation is depicted according to the standard three-component instrumental conditioning paradigm $S^d \rightarrow R \rightarrow S^r$ in which the S^d represents the modeled behavior, R denotes the overt matching response, and S^r indicates the reinforcing stimulus.

According to this response-reinforcement formulation, imitative learning is theoretically equivalent to the match-to-sample paradigm. The model's behavior functions as the "sample," and the matching response chosen from the array of alternatives is the "imitation" response. Recall that Miller and Dollard (1941) first proposed this interpretation under the rubric "matched-dependent" behavior.

Reinforced matching is stressed in this analysis, i.e., behavior will not be imitated unless reinforcement follows. "Negative imitation" is theoretically possible if contrary responses are reinforced instead of the modeled responses. Once *the* imitation response class is formed, it is assumed to be maintained on an intermittent reinforcement schedule in the natural environment. Children are often praised inconsistently, e.g., for emulating their parents' etiquette at the dinner table one evening and not the next. Intermittent reinforcement will maintain high levels of imitative responding even during periods of nonreinforcement. This explanation is proposed in order to account for imitation in the absence of direct rewards. Thus, learning that appears to occur via observation alone is believed to be under reinforcement control. The person who imitates will discontinue unless some minimal amount of reinforcement is forthcoming.

The response reinforcement formulation puts great emphasis on overt performance as well as reinforcement to explain imitation. How, then, can we explain vicarious acquisition without performance? For example, a young child watches his parent use a chair as a platform to remove elevated objects, such as a cookie jar, from the cupboard. Several days later, in the absence of either parent, the child uses the chair to reach the cookie jar himself. According to the response reinforcement position, the imitation response (as a generalized class) had already been learned. It is assumed that the chair-using response was already known, or the child could not have imitated without practice and reinforcement. The response had merely to be shifted from the model to the cookie jar. This can occur via the pairing of the conditioned stimulus (the model) and the neutral stimulus (the cookie jar). Neither reinforcement nor performance is theoretically required to explain such shifts.

The response reinforcement position explains transfer of imitation responses to unfamiliar models and to new physical and social settings on the basis of identical elements. That is, unfamiliar models are assumed to share body elements and behavioral characteristics with familiar models whose behavior, when imitated, was reinforced. Therefore, an observer will imitate new models because cues from social exemplars were reliably related to past reinforcement. Similarly, responses can be generalized to a new context because of common environmental elements. For example, the child might transfer his chair-use skill to get a ball from the shelf in his closet. In this case, the ball and shelf shared with the cookie jar and cupboard the stimulus properties of shape and perhaps elevation; these common elements enabled the imitative response to be transferred.

In essence, the response reinforcement account assumes a discrimination learning model. It preserves the historical premise whereby no new behavior can be acquired solely from vicarious experience. New responses can only be learned through shaping, or prompting, or by physical guidance (Gewirtz, 1968). There is, however, evidence that responses with a zero-order probability of being displayed can be learned vicariously (Rosenthal, Alford, & Rasp, 1972). The response reinforcement interpretation of such findings is that no new responses are being learned. The depiction of novel responses simply involves the reorganization of known behavioral elements. This shifting of known responses to a new organization of familiar stimuli can occur without reinforcement or performance.

Limitations of the Response Reinforcement View of Imitation

First, while the theory is reasonably well able to explain performance of known responses on the basis of the stimulus discrimination hypothesis, it does not account for evidence that vicarious acquisition of novel responses can occur without being accumulated in a piecemeal fashion (e.g., Zimmerman & Rosenthal, 1972a,b). It has been argued that acquisition of such novel responses is just the reorganization of known behavioral elements (e.g., Gewirtz, 1968, 1971a,b). To merit serious consideration, this analysis must provide an operational definition of "new" response. In the strictest sense, very little human accomplishment—from quantum mechanics to Dali paintings—is based on fundamentally original response components. It is the rearrangement of familiar elements into unfamiliar configurations that marks progress for the person and the species. However phrased, if exposure to modeling leads observers to grasp and perform molar acts and sequences not previously available to them, important learning has occurred whether or not all of the *components* of the output were familiar.

A second limitation of the response reinforcement analysis involves the assumption that vicarious learning can be treated as a single response. Treating imitation as a unitary response class does not explain how an abstract feature of a model's performance will be imitated when there is no matching of constituent responses. This phenomenon has been widely reported in research on vicarious rule learning (Zimmerman & Rosenthal, 1974c). For example, Rosenthal, Zimmerman, and Durning (1970) found substantial learning of a model's conceptual style of questioning with very little acquisition of his specific responses. It appeared that what was learned was an abstract rule which, in turn, was used by the observer to select responses already available to him. Thus, it was the *organization* of the observer's behavior that was primarily affected by vicarious experience, not his individual responses.

There are other problems with the operant formulation. It casts all model-created learning into a single *imitative* response class despite the heterogeneity of behavior that can be vicariously instigated. The failure to examine the particular properties of modeled behavior leads to a conceptual impasse. Why can a child imitate certain responses, like a simple scale on a piano, but not other modeled performances, like a

Mozart sonata? However one views vicarious effects, it is obvious that the complexity of the modeled acts and the observer's level of skill or competence will codetermine the results of exposure to modeling displays.

Another difficulty for a strict S–R position centers on whether transfer can be explained on the basis of identical elements. The stimulus discrimination explanation for transfer does not account for the generalization observed in complex modeling studies. For example, Rosenthal *et al.* (1972a) vicariously trained children to select stimuli from an array in which objects (e.g., small autos, etc.) and colors were varied according to a rule. The youngsters were able to generalize this rule to *new* objects and *new* colors without additional training. In a very stringent test of transfer, Rosenthal and Zimmerman (1976) found significant generalization when all four stimulus dimensions of a modeling task were varied during assessment of transfer. Thus, an S–R formulation appears only able to specify the range of stimuli (i.e., the class boundaries of rule-governed responses) after the fact. This is because the stimuli and responses are defined in literal, external terms and not in reference to their significance or meaning. Such results indicate that the abstract features of modeling demonstrations, as well as the literal stimulus elements, must be considered when predicting transfer. Thus, with highly novel response configurations, bright college students, who have received much reinforcement in the past for matching and have fully acquired an "imitative response class," showed little or no observational learning unless they transformed the modeled patterns into symbolic codes (e.g., Bandura & Jeffery, 1973). The three-element paradigm ($S^d \rightarrow R \rightarrow S^r$) and the "imitative response class" notions cannot explain these results. All of the conditions required by an operant viewpoint were met, and yet imitation failed to occur.

A final problem attendant to a response reinforcement formulation concerns the heavy emphasis placed on the role of reinforcement. The assumption that reinforcement pervasively determines learning seems questionable since there is ample evidence that vicarious learning can occur without direct rewards (Bandura, 1965). In several studies, incentives have failed to discernably affect acquisition (Rosenthal & Kellogg, 1973; Rosenthal, Moore, Dorfman, & Nelson, 1971; Zimmerman, 1974). Response-reinforcement psychologists claim that the pervasive phenomenon of vicarious learning without rewards is in fact under the control of an intermittent schedule. This explanation makes assumptions about an observer's learning histories that cannot usually be substantiated in natural environmental situations. Further, even theoretical research on generalized imitation has failed to explain observational learning on the basis of reinforcement alone, as Gewirtz (1968) acknowledges. As a practical matter, there is little experimental basis for believing that vicarious learning will be enhanced if direct rewards are used unless the behavior is boring or unpleasant, or the population of observers is highly atypical, e.g., retarded or autistic (Zimmerman & Rosenthal, 1974c). Under these circumstances, rewards seem to affect primarily motivation rather than learning per se.

STRUCTURALIST EXPLANATIONS FOR IMITATION

Another explanation for vicarious learning has been proposed by developmental psychologists adhering to a mental structure position. We described the general tenets of this formulation earlier and will now consider the views of prominent structural psychologists on imitation. Of this group, only Piaget (1962) has studied imitation as a separate phenomenon. However, psycholinguists have studied the role of imitation in general language development. Both of these accounts will be summarized below, after which some of the basic tenets and limitations of a structuralist approach to imitation will be discussed.

Piaget's View of Imitation

Piaget (1962) describes imitation in terms of a series of developmental stages, corresponding to a child's acquisition of sensorimotor concepts or schemata. Schemata initially arise when a child engages in action, and they become increasingly differentiated with maturation and experience. Piaget did not consider imitation to be a reflexive, innate class of responses; rather, in his view, it requires maturation and some degree of experience in order to emerge. He has identified six stages in the genesis of imitation that correspond to six stages in children's sensorimotor development.

Imitation does not occur during the *first stage* (lasting until a month after birth), although at this time certain reflexive acts that are triggered by similar responses from another person are seen. For example, the sounds of one child's weeping can elicit sustained crying in an observing child. Piaget believes that the observer fails to distinguish between his own crying and the other child's, and this lack of discrimination will sustain the crying by the observer even after the first child has stopped.

Imitation first emerges during the *second stage,* a period that extends from 1 to 4 months of age. During this stage, a child will imitate only if he is contingently mimicked by another person. For example, a child may pick up a rattle, shake it, and then put it down. If an adult does likewise, the child will generally give a startled look and then repeat the sequence. According to Piaget, a child is stimulated to engage in repetitive imitative actions because he is attempting to form primitive sensorimotor concepts. Once these schemata are formed, the mere sight or sound of the constituent responses will trigger performance of the action.

The latter accomplishment marks the onset of the *third stage,* which typically begins at 4 or 5 months of age. Contingent mimicking is no longer necessary to instigate imitation. Notice Piaget's assumption that a sensorimotor concept must be formed before children can imitate without being mimicked. He also reported that imitation was not selective during this stage; the entire sensorimotor action sequence seemed to operate as a unit, consistent with his conclusion that imitation is determined by and reflects general intellectual functioning.

During the *fourth stage* (starting at months 8 or 9), the child begins to imitate actions (such as facial gestures) that he cannot see himself make. For example, Piaget noticed his daughter imitate his mouth movements, actions which included smacking the lips or contorting the mouth. He interpreted these feats as indications that his daughter was reacting to a model symbolically for the first time. In order to imitate, she now had to integrate information from the visual mode with feedback from auditory or haptic modes.

At about 1 year of age, a child begins to imitate *new* responses, marking the onset of Piaget's *fifth stage* of imitative development. The model can now function as an information source for the child. The impact of the model's behavior on the physical and social environment can be appreciated, and these vicarious experiences can be abstracted and utilized during imitation. However, a considerable amount of trial and error is necessary before the child can imitate unfamiliar responses. At about month 16, the child begins to imitate new responses without groping; this is the hallmark of *stage six.* To Piaget, imitation has become fully covert and symbolic. He calls this process "interiorization." Overt imitation is now redundant; short-circuited by the child's ability to imagine the effects of his own emulative acts. Accordingly, images are viewed simply as covert imitative responses. Such symbolic representation permits the child to imitate new responses after long delays in time outside the presence of the model.

In conclusion, Piaget believed that imitation is related to and limited by a child's general level of intellectual development. He assumed that mental structures must precede a child's ability to imitate and not the reverse. During the six stages of development, imitation becomes increasingly covert and finally forms the basis of imaginal representation. Little is said about the role of modeled guidance after infancy.

The Psycholinguistic View of Imitation

Psycholinguistic scholars tend to assign heavy emphasis to maturation in explaining language development (e.g., McNeill, 1970, 1971), while environmental variables occupy a rather limited role. Reinforcement as a cause of language development was largely ruled out based on research by Brown, Cazden, and Bellugi (1969), who analyzed parent–child verbal interaction. They found little contingent reaction to the grammatical form of a child's utterances even though the adult did respond to the informative content of the child's statements. That is, when a child says *Bus stop*, an adult might correct him, telling the child that the vehicle was not a bus, but a truck, while failing to correct the improper verb form.

Perhaps the most intuitively compelling evidence for the influence of the social environment on a child's linguistic functioning involves imitation. When one considers the influence a parent's accent has on the speech of a child, the importance of the social environment seems demonstrated. However, for reasons we will soon discuss, psycholinguists have concluded that language content is influenced by experience, whereas grammatical structure is not.

Psycholinguists believe that grammatical structure precedes a child's capability to imitate an utterance containing that structure. Thus, a child cannot imitate an adult's use of a particular verb tense until he understands abstractly what the verb tense indicates. Psycholinguists therefore believe that imitation cannot promote grammatical development. They also invoke research suggesting the *competence,* that is, nonverbal acknowledgement of language meaning, typically precedes verbal use (or *production*) of the structure in speech.

There is, however, evidence that children can imitate a linguistically advanced structure if they are instructed to do so (Fraser, Bellugi, & Brown, 1963; Slobin & Welch, 1973). As a result, many psycholinguists (e.g., Lovell & Dixon, 1967; McNeill, 1970) consider imitation as one of the earliest measures of linguistic competence. But this conclusion seems contrary to common sense: Why conclude that comprehension creates imitation, and not the reverse? Psycholinguists have studied children's imitation of linguistically advanced statements and have found evidence (e.g., Clay, 1971) indicating that youngsters will systematically distort or change a model's utterances in a manner believed to be linguistically concurrent with the child's competence. Thus, while they assume that imitation faithfully reproduces an observed linguistic response, they view it as a constructed approximation dictated by a child's present level of linguistic competence.

Another reason why psycholinguists deny that imitation can sponsor structural development is based on language "universals [McNeill, 1970]." There is evidence suggesting that certain aspects of language, such as verb tense changes, are common to all languages. Since individuals differ greatly in culture, environmental context, child rearing practices etc., psycholinguists think it unlikely that the commonality of linguistic structure can be ascribed to social experience. As a result, they have concluded that structures are genetically determined for all human beings.

Psycholinguists have advanced a third argument, based on the so-called "generative" property of language (Slobin, 1968), which goes as follows: Language cannot be learned through imitation because of its heterogeneity of form. Children often make statements that adults rarely model, such as a child's use of the plural *mans* instead of *men*. By defining "imitation" to mean the mimicking of observed response elements, psycholinguists have concluded that modeling processes cannot account for the infinite variety of speech that is typically displayed.

Finally, most psycholinguists favor *expansion* as the social learning experience that is most likely to enhance language development of a nonstructural sort (McNeill, 1970). In this procedure, in contrast to imitation, an adult's utterances are actively related to a child's own speech and hence to his meaning structure. The adult thus reformulates the child's sentences in a more grammatically correct manner. For example, if the child says *Me go,* the adult responds *You want to go.* This is assumed to be an optimal procedure because it keeps instruction geared to the child's level of linguistic structural development.

Limitations of the Structural View of Imitation

The conclusion that structures cannot be derived from imitative experiences is far from universally accepted. There is evidence (Slobin & Welch, 1973) suggesting that if children are instructed to imitate linguistically advanced statements, they can do so accurately even if they cannot speak on such a level spontaneously. Also, there is a growing body of data (Whitehurst & Vasta, 1975) indicating that novel language structures can be learned via modeling and reinforcement. There is also considerable evidence (e.g., Rosenthal & Zimmerman, 1972b; Zimmerman & Rosenthal, 1974b) that children can acquire Piagetian operational (mental structure) skills by observing a model. In these studies, youngsters displayed conservation even though there was no evidence that they had yet reached Piaget's period of concrete operations. Further, some of these children were 4 years old, displaying these skills about 3 years sooner than the expected onset of concrete operations. Other research indicates that moral judgment rules can also be learned via modeling (Bandura & McDonald, 1963). Thus, the language and conceptual skills described as structural by psycholinguists and Piagetians can be taught through vicarious experience. Such findings clash with structuralist assumptions that mental structures totally determine an observer's reactions to a model's performance.

The criticism that modeling cannot account for the *generative* aspect of language (or any conceptual behavior for that matter), is predicated upon a mimicry definition of imitation. But there is considerable evidence (Zimmerman & Rosenthal, 1974c) suggesting that mimicry (or exact response reproduction) constitutes only a small part of what can be legitimately defined as the modeling process. Vicarious rule learning, for example, falls outside this definition. During rule learning, observers abstract certain regularities from a modeling sequence. The rules are then used to selectively combine the vicariously acquired information with past personal experience. This synthesis is then manifested in the resulting overt imitative behavior. The generative aspect of responding can be viewed as transfer of a conceptual rule from a modeling experience to tasks having similar abstract properties. Thus, when a child hears a model add an *s* to words describing multiple objects, the observer can abstract this suffix from the noun stems. Abstraction occurs because the observer learns that noun stems vary across instances of objects, whereas the suffix *s* is demonstrated each time the model encounters multiple objects. One consequence of treating generative language in terms of *transfer* is that a certain degree of *overgeneralization* can be expected. If a child observes a model produce plurals with only regular nouns, he would be expected to apply the same rule to irregular nouns such as adding an *s* to the word *man*. There is evidence to indicate that this phenomenon actually does occur during imitative rule learning (Guess, Sailor, Rutherford, & Baer, 1968). Notice that this is the same phenomenon thought by psycholinguists to be incompatible with an imitative basis for language development. Thus, no inherent conflict exists between imitative learning and rule-governed phenomena.

Another major deficiency of structural theories is their inability to predict *performance*. They can explain *competence* or knowledge but offer relatively little a priori guidance about how the knowledge will be behaviorally manifested, a limitation that becomes particularly important once the structure is assumed to have fully emerged. McNeill (1971) believes that language development is largely complete by the age of 4 years; for Piaget, conceptual development is fully attained only early in adolescence. Yet there is extensive evidence that older children and adults will alter their language and conceptual responses in accordance with vicarious experience (Zimmerman & Rosenthal, 1974c). For example, Rosenthal and Carroll (1972) showed that junior high school children changed the grammatical structure of their verbs and sentences to agree with those of a model. Structural theories offer little assistance in predicting these types of imitative performance outcomes.

It is important to note that no single encompassing *structural theory* to explain vicarious learning for all aspects of human behavior has yet emerged. Every position thus far has been devised to handle a selected content area such as intelligence, language, or morality. Efforts to cross-relate and integrate structural theories have not been very successful (Nelson, 1974). In explaining human behavior in a natural context, few sharp distinctions can be made between thought and language. The two are intimately linked, and a single theoretical framework is thus not only desirable but is also crucial for comprehensive explanations of human behavior.

Finally, while structural theories emphasize *rule-governed* aspects of behavior, they tend to ignore *content* dimensions. A careful examination of the psycholinguistic model reveals that it deals almost exclusively with syntactic rules, while paying very little attention to semantics or to the content of speech. Similarly, in Piaget's theory, the operational qualities of intelligence are stressed, while the phenomena that are operated upon are treated cursorily. However, as Haygood and Bourne (1965) have persuasively argued, abstraction involves both attributes (content) and rule elements. It is clear that the content of tasks will affect vicarious acquisition and transfer. Conservation of number, for example, is typically attained several years before conservation of weight. Zimmerman and Lanaro (1974) have suggested that the failure of Piagetians to predict or find transfer in their training studies, while other approaches have been successful, might be attributed to the latter's systematic approach to content factors. Thus, content factors, as well as rule elements, should be included in comprehensive descriptions of cognitive functioning.

AN AFFECTIVE FEEDBACK VIEW OF IMITATION

This formulation assumes that vicarious learning can only be explained in terms of covert changes in an observer's affective states. Mowrer and Aronfreed are two major proponents of this viewpoint, and we will consider their respective positions in detail.

Mowrer (1960) formulated a two-factor theory of imitation, placing heavy emphasis on affective arousal. One type of learning, which he termed *imitation*, occurs when, after watching a model perform a response, an observer receives rewards for duplication of this performance. Since they are repeatedly associated with direct rewards, the model's actions become secondarily reinforcing to the observer; hence, they are copied. Basically, this is an instrumental conditioning explanation, much like Miller and Dollard's (1941). Mowrer recognized another type of vicarious learning, *empathy,* which occurs when the model not only illustrates responses but when he receives rewards for them as well. This phenomenon has been termed vicarious reward by other writers (Bandura, 1971b). Mowrer suggested that the observer must "intuit" the model's satisfactions (or dissatisfactions) in order to learn empathically. The observers experience some of the sensory consequences of the model's behavior in a form parallel to the model's sensations and must also "intuit" the model's reactions to incentive operations. Under these conditions, the element of empathy is added to the determinants of simple imitation. Mowrer's account does not mention how the observer learns to "intuit" the model's satisfactions—whether, for example, "imitative" learning precedes "empathic" learning. The key requirement in Mowrer's position is that imitation occurs because of affective cues created by the association of a model's behavior with rewards.

Affective feedback reasoning was further elaborated by Aronfreed (1968). He assumed that, for a young child, the behavior of models occurs in a highly valenced social context. This association endows the behavior and its cognitive results with a positive affective value that is maintained to some degree in other social contexts. Not only the behavior (including proprioceptive feedback) is conditioned—the cognitive representation of the response is handled similarly. If the behavior acquires positive affect, then wherever the behavior is enacted, the observer will experience positive affect. His intentions to imitate will also elicit positive affect because of the association of the affect and the cognitive representation of the behavior. This account does not specify why, once elicited, imitative responses do not continue indefinitely. However, Aronfreed (1968) has acknowledged that "imitative performance is jointly controlled by its intrinsic value and by the external reinforcement structure of specific situations [p. 286]." The term *vicarious* describes the observer's affect, elicited here by the stimulus conditions confronting another person. Thus, with empathy, it is the model's *subjective reaction* which valences the modeled behavior, but in vicarious learning, *environmental consequences* valence the modeled responses. Since especially for training purposes, one would expect congruence between the model's covert and overt experiences, it is doubtful that this distinction would apply to many empirical events. Notice that with both empathy and vicarious learning, behavior is explained by changes in affect. *Imitation* is seen as a special subclass of observational learning, in which the properties of a model's behavior influence an observer's subsequent response. Thus, imitation can be created through direct reward as well as through vicarious or empathic experience.

Aronfreed (1968) discusses the association of an observer's responses with another person's expressive cues based on a social conditioning paradigm. Initially, a child learns to discriminate the subjective cues of others through repeated association of these cues with direct consequences to himself. This would happen, for example, when a child, after seeing the delight of a peer who gets a new bike, then gets to ride on it himself. As the cues become conditioned, they begin to elicit the child's affective responses even when he does not expect to be directly reinforced. Aronfreed suggested that the rather sudden and precise alterations made by an observer after watching a model perform appear to require some assumption of cognitive processing. He termed this capacity a "cognitive template," but did not fully elaborate its properties. He did suggest that affective cues aroused by modeled events can become attached to a cognitive representation, and the reward value of emulation "would be a function of the match between the template and the flow of imitative behavior [1968, p. 282]." Thus, although it needs further clarification, Aronfreed's description of how the template actually functions during responding implies a belief that cognitive events do not directly determine behavior. Instead, an intervening affective process is assumed. Cognitive events must first trigger some degree of emotional arousal before being manifest in overt response.

Limitations of the Affective Feedback View of Imitation

The major problem with this theory is its lack of scope. According to this position, an observer can only learn if events are emotionally arousing. Another drawback to the affective feedback theory is its lack of completeness and specificity. Indeed, what is meant by arousal? Are Mowrer and Aronfreed referring to somatic arousal as indicated by the usual physiological measures such as heart rate, blood pressure, Galvanic skin response (GSR), or are they referring to arousal at a cognitive level? If the latter type of arousal is also implied, how is it to be measured? If one considers arousal only at a cognitive level, then it is impossible to disprove the assertion that arousal does not occur.

If one defines arousal according to somatic indicators, there is considerable evidence that learning occurs without affect or afferent feedback. The results of curare experiments in which animals are skeletally immobilized during training indicate that learning can occur mentally without the proprioceptive feedback associated with movement (Black, 1958; Black, Carlson, & Soloman, 1962; Soloman & Turner, 1962). Similar findings were reported when nerves were surgically severed (Taub, Bacon, & Berman, 1965; Taub, Theodoru, Ellman, Bloom, & Berman, 1966).

A somatic arousal assumption is hard to reconcile with the rapid behavioral changes that are typically observed during imitation in the natural environment. Researchers studying human affect by such measures as GSR, heart rate, etc., find that environmental stimuli activate or inhibit affect responses rather slowly because of the involvement of involuntary muscle groups in emotion. These reactions are rather organismic in nature and seem an unlikely basis for governing the precise action sequences involved in most imitative behavior. Clinical accounts of the therapeutic use of techniques such as desensitization on phobic patients generally suggest that reconditioning of affect proceeds rather deliberately (e.g., Wolpe, 1969). Further, the synchronization between affective cues or states and observable behavior is imperfect at best (Rachman & Hodgson, 1974).

Thus, the arousal notion needs further clarification. Also unclear is the role of the cognitive template in the arousal formulation. Precisely what is meant by a template? A template suggests an isomorphic representation of modeled events. Many modeled activities are learned and retained in symbolic codes that bear little resemblance to observed stimuli. Symbolic coding is a constructive process whose coded representations are not necessarily structurally isomorphic with their overt referents. A symbolic coding process (e.g., reductive or elaborative codes in verbal or imaginal form) has greater applicability than a template matching process. Still another problem involves how a template notion interfaces with affective arousal. While arousal undoubtedly occurs during much vicarious learning, there seems insufficient reason for placing on affective conditioning the burden of explaining all vicarious phenomena.

A SOCIAL LEARNING VIEW OF IMITATION

How Does Learning Occur?

It will be recalled that social learning theory (Bandura, 1969a, 1977b) considers learning from a combination cognitive–behavioral perspective. In the case of imitation, a distinction is made between vicarious *acquisition*, that is, observational learning, and imitative *performance*. The importance of this distinction is illustrated in a clever study by Bandura (1965). He exposed three groups of children to a modeling sequence. One group saw the model being punished for his actions; for a second group, the model was ignored; for the third group, the model was rewarded. The children were then placed again in the same setting, this time alone, and their imitative behavior was recorded. The group that viewed the rewarded model showed the most imitative behavior, the ignored-model group was intermediate, and the punished-model group displayed the least imitation. Then, without further training, all of the children were promised rewards if they would demonstrate what they had learned. All three groups displayed comparable levels of acquisition.

This study demonstrated that vicarious acquisition was not necessarily reflected in imitative performance unless certain incentive conditions were present. Acquisition occurs through observation and by the cognitive processing of modeling stimuli; these stimuli can be meaningfully grasped or interpreted by observers. Imitative performance, on the other hand, is influenced by direct, observed, and self-generated outcomes. Both acquisition and performance must be explained in an adequate theory of imitation.

To accomplish this goal, Bandura (1969a, 1977b), in his formulation of social learning theory, has synthesized elements of information processing theory with elements of reinforcement reasoning. A marriage of these two viewpoints is necessary to explain imitation; reinforcement theories cannot handle the covert cognitive activity that occurs during acquisition and transfer, whereas information processing theory neglects performance factors.

As mentioned earlier, Bandura (1971a, 1977b) treats acquisition in terms of the component cognitive (attention, retention) and behavioral reproduction (motoric responding and motivation) subprocesses that are depicted in Figure 1-6. *Attention* refers to observers' orienting and perceptual activities when they register overt events. In the case of imitation, observers must attend to and perceive a modeling episode before they can profit from its guidance. In support of this distinction, a very close relationship between an observer's attention to a model and subsequent learning has been found (Yussen, 1974). By *retention*, Bandura is referring to evidence that modeled behavior must be adequately discriminated and symbolically represented by the observer if he is to subsequently act successfully (Bandura & Barab, 1971; Rosenthal *et al.*, 1972a). Both availability and effectiveness of mediating codes in organizing information have been found to be directly related to recognition and recall (Bandura & Jeffery, 1973; Bandura *et al.*, 1974; Ellis, Parente, & Shumate, 1974). Even when input is well comprehended, it must be organized in a form or a mnemonic framework that permits

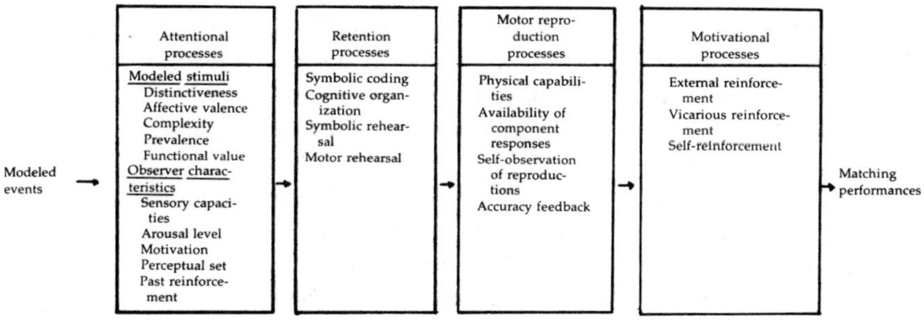

Figure 1-6 Subprocesses in the social learning view of observational learning. [After A. Bandura, *Psychological Modeling: Conflicting Theories*. Reprinted by permission of the publishers, Lieber-Atherton, Inc. Copyright © 1971. All rights reserved.]

future retrieval, in order for there to be effective retention after delay (Bandura *et al.*, 1974). Even when an observer scrutinizes, registers, and then correctly recalls modeled events, it must still be asked whether he has the *motoric skills* to translate this knowledge into action. An aspiring artist may vicariously grasp a particular drawing technique long before he has attained the technical mastery to use it imitatively. Some analysis of the motoric requirements for such behavior is necessary in order to account for the quality of responding. Finally, *motivation* is treated as a subprocess to explain and highlight the fact that what people are able to perform imitatively often departs from what they choose to perform. Incentive conditions often dictate the extent to which correct acquisition will be expressed in overt performance (Bandura, 1965).

Thus, selective attention, encoding, the organization or retention framework applied, and functional relevance all determine the fate of modeled information. Consider the example of a novice tennis player attempting to learn to serve. How well he learns to serve by watching an instructor's demonstration will depend on how well he attends to such critical aspects of the stroke as body positioning, ball throw, taking the racquet back and following through the swing. If he can verbally encode this complex sequence into a series of self-instructions, or generate clear mental images of the assembly of motions, recall will be enhanced. Finally, the expectancy that learning an effective serve may give him desired access to certain tennis social groups will help to motivate him to practice the stroke until the motoric elements are mastered. Thus, even when a skill such as a tennis serve is available, its implementation will depend on incentive consequences like the expected social rewards it brings.

Obviously, an adequate account of vicarious phenomena must address the several subprocesses that govern the extraction, storage, and utilization of modeled information.

What Influences Learning?

Social learning theory views human functioning in terms of three interdependent sources of influence, namely, antecedent determinants, consequent outcomes, and cognitive determinants of behavior. Antecedent determinants refer to the impact of objects or events that precede a subject's behavioral change. These include meaningful signs and predictive properties of the environment. Social learning psychologists believe that the most important antecedent stimuli are social. In this view, a model can influence an observer's behavior in two ways. A model can instigate the display of a particular response, as occurs when a neighbor's mowing reminds an observer that his own lawn needs tending. A model can also teach new responses. An observer might learn yoga from watching a demonstration on television.

Social learning can occur either from exposure to physical stimuli or via instructions, in the absence of viewing a live performance (Alford & Rosenthal, 1973). When a model performs, he will often leave tangible traces of his behavior imprinted on the physical environment. For example, an artist's painting techniques might be inferred from his brush strokes. Learning from a book is social in the sense that the written word is a physical record of a person's verbal dialogue or solitary thoughts. Bandura has termed this learning process *symbolic* modeling, which, in addition to occurring under the above conditions, can also occur via verbal instructions. From a social learning perspective, it makes little difference whether the modeling stimuli are cast in the form of enacted episodes or as symbolic instructions. The important point is whether the alternative modes convey the same amount of information so that the observer can discriminate the information.

A second source of control over behavior is *cognitive*. During vicarious learning, observers usually respond to models in a selective fashion (Zimmerman, 1974). Some aspects of a model's behavior will be emulated, while other aspects will be ignored. For example, an aspiring composer might imitate stylistic elements of an established master but would certainly not exactly imitate the latter's compositions. The central role of cognitive processes is particularly evident during transfer after modeling. The fact that the observer shifts the vicariously learned response to an altered stimulus context and perhaps adds personal response components to the performance indicates the importance of covert cognitive activity.

In order to understand learning by observation, an analysis of covert processes is necessary. There is considerable evidence that cognitive representations guide an observer's performance. These representations include verbal or imaginal restatements of modeled sequences (e.g., Gerst, 1971), various structured codes or mnemonic devices to preserve the witnessed events in durable form, and self–instructions about how to implement the stored data (Bandura & Jeffery, 1973; Bandura *et al.*, 1974). It is these cognitive events, and not the literal stimuli or past reinforcement, that steer the observer's integration of performance demands. The clarity with which observers grasp a modeled routine will affect how well they can register, store, and later utilize the information.

An observer's awareness or expectancy affects his cognitive interpretations of modeled events. For example, consider the observer who views a brief film depicting a man accidentally bumping into a woman and then helping her to her feet. The observer's interpretation of the action sequence would be entirely different if the protagonist had been portrayed as a pickpocket instead of as a conscientious citizen. Rosenthal and Zimmerman (1972a) found that instructions that made observers differentially aware of the nature of a rule underlying a model's performance affected imitation.

An observer's expectation of incentives will qualify how much attention he pays and how much covert effort he may devote to grasping modeled content. If he expects a vicarious display to have little personal relevance, he may turn his attention to other things and largely negate the potential guidance of the model. For example, if a modeling episode depicts guidance that is no longer useful, monitoring is diminished (Kanfer *et al.*, 1971); or, if highly stressful and aversive events are portrayed, individuals may actively seek to eliminate the distressing content either by diverting their attention or by self-producing competing thoughts (Bandura & Rosenthal, 1966).

Social learning psychologists believe that reinforcement must be cognitively represented before it affects behavior to any significant degree. Thus, the expectancy of reinforcement—as well as the delivery of the reinforcing events—will greatly influence behavior. While it is true that a person's beliefs or expectancies concerning the receipt of rewards can be created and eventually changed by the actual experience of receiving or failing to receive them, it is interesting to ascertain how much additional experience is necessary to alter an expectancy once it is formed. Kaufman, Baron, and Kopp (1966) compared a person's beliefs concerning the type of reinforcement contingencies that were operative during his performance on a motor task with the actual contingency being used. Beliefs about the reinforcement contingency were far more significant in determining response than the actual contingency that was involved. In a similar vein, performance directions to child observers controlled their responses more strongly than did the reinforcement schedules given to the training model (Feist, 1974; Ziesat, 1973). In a postexperimental interview, Bandura and Barab (1971) found that children who displayed generalized imitation of a model's highly discriminable but unreinforced responses justified their actions with the erroneous belief that their continued imitation might alter the experimenter's reinforcing practices.

Thus, it appears that, unless the subject is aware of the contingency in effect, behavior is only weakly controlled by reinforcing consequences. Inaccurate assumptions concerning the conditions of reinforcement will direct behavior until objective reinforcing events compel an alteration of the expectancy. Failure to recognize the mediating role of cognition in relating behavior to incentives is especially hazardous when analyzing reinforcement effects in the natural environment. In a natural setting, the consequences of a particular action often are temporally delayed and occur in unexpected forms. Unlike what occurs in a controlled laboratory setting, various peers and social agents may bestow rewards according to highly discrepant or opposing standards. In the face of such variability, individuals may develop imperfect hypotheses that nevertheless regulate their behavior. It is not unusual for subjects to infer and adhere to causal assumptions that are remote from actual contingencies (Rosenthal, White, & Rosenthal, 1975). Because of all of these factors, it can be difficult to detect response-guiding rationales just from studying response-incentive correlations, and the role of cognitive guidance in regulating instrumental behavior may unwisely be overlooked. Later in this chapter we will introduce some research conclusions showing that cognitive processes are necessarily involved in mediating observational learning.

Finally, social learning theory views reinforcement as having two separable functions, i.e., *incentive* and *informative* roles. Both functions are confounded in the usual operant design, wherein a child receives candy for imitative approximations of a new behavior that is displayed by a model. The candy is both an incentive to respond, as well as a cue to indicate a successful performance. Social learning psychologists have demonstrated that if these functions are separated by giving informative feedback in a form that is not an incentive, incentives do little to enhance learning (Rosenthal & Carroll, 1972; Rosenthal *et al.*, 1971; Zimmerman, 1974). These findings were obtained with normal children under nontedious task conditions. For atypical populations, e.g., the retarded, or under demanding working conditions, incentives may be necessary to motivate performance. This conclusion harkens back to the previous distinction between acquisition and performance. However, even with severe retardates, tangible incentives do not necessarily improve vicarious learning (Rosenthal & Kellogg, 1973).

Thus, these three types of control—stimulus, reinforcement, and cognitive—reciprocally influence one another. Reinforcement practices can invest or divest antecedent stimuli with their controlling function. Conversely, stimulus control procedures can remove an individual from a setting in which a particular contingency is operative. Stimulus control procedures, such as a model's behavior, can influence a person's cognitive formulations. On the other hand, an individual can cognitively alter the stimulus conditions to which he exposes himself. Reinforcement variables can also shift one's beliefs by providing affirming or disconfirming feedback. And, the reciprocal relationship also holds—cognitive attributions can negate the effects of external consequences.

Which Behavioral Phenomena Can Be Explained by Social Learning Theory?

Three major effects of vicarious experience have been identified: inhibition–disinhibition, facilitation, and novel learning. *Inhibition* refers to suppression of a known response because vicarious experiences indicate that it will be punished. In Puritan communities, social transgressors were publicly punished by flogging or by being put in the stocks, in order to vicariously deter potential violators. *Disinhibition* refers to the manifestation by an observer of a formerly punished response because of a model's fearless behavior. A child whose first attempt at swimming brought him a mouthful of water might be induced to try again if he observes a friend manage to execute a few successful strokes. *Facilitation* refers to vicarious instigation of a known but not punished response. For example, a person going on an all-day summer outing might be reminded to bring his sunglasses if he noticed a friend wearing his pair. Finally, *novel behavior* can be vicariously acquired; this occurs when a homeowner learns to fix his automobile by watching his high-priced mechanic. Social learning theory is well suited to explain these phenomena, since learning is assumed to result from cognitive activities, without requiring either reinforcement or overt performance. Yet, the impact of rewards or punishment, as in the case of disinhibition or inhibition, can easily be explained in terms of the subprocess of motivation.

Social learning theory can also explain how *enculturation* occurs: It highlights the role of social stimuli in influencing human behavior, an emphasis that fits well with anthropological reports on how children are socialized (Bandura & Walters, 1963). These accounts suggest that important societal skills during childhood (such as toilet training, feeding, and danger avoidance) as well as instrumental adult competencies (such as sex role responses, tool making and use, and aggression or defense) are primarily learned through observation.

Thus, the *normal* behavior patterns that children display can be attributed to the children's observation of common responses modeled by adults. *Deviant* patterns can be learned from atypical models. For example, there is extensive evidence (Bandura, 1973) that aggressive children are often raised in homes where severe punishment is used to control them. This modeled use of violence as a means of control, and the parental approval of aggressive styles of conduct, lead to emulation by the youngsters. This focus, emphasizing the characteristics of the human exemplars that each individual encounters allows social learning theory to explain the development and display of both typical and atypical behavior.

Because of its emphasis on social processes, social learning theory is particularly suited to deal with group performance as well as individual responding. Social phenomena, such as group norms and mores, can be readily addressed both in terms of the exemplary acts of others, and with respect to the social consequences that accrue when a person matches or defies group standards. Social learning theory is well suited to explain the influential role of human models (or symbolic descriptions of them) in the diffusion of behavior patterns from one society to another. This theory, as previously described, can handle the induction and use of a common rule or belief from diverse social examples. The role of social sanctions in maintaining compliance to group beliefs can also be dealt with in terms of cognitive self-guidance to maintain favorable incentive outcomes.

By viewing behavioral functioning in terms of a reciprocal interaction between individuals and their surroundings, social learning theory can explain how a person alters his environment, as well as the reverse process. This feature is of tremendous social importance. It has triggered a wave of innovative research on self-control (e.g., Thoreson & Mahoney, 1974). Subjects have been taught to be more effective in directing their own behavior by efforts at monitoring, setting goals, arranging incentives, and by restructuring the influences of their environment. In many cases (e.g., Bandura & Perloff, 1967; Mahoney, 1974b) self-imposed contingencies were as effective as those which were externally controlled. These procedures are being therapeutically applied to difficult human problems such as weight control, gambling, and drinking (Mahoney, 1974a; Thoreson & Mahoney, 1974).

Because of the emphasis on social observation and feedback as the primary means by which individuals learn and alter behavior, the continuity of cultural groups can be easily explained. Tradition and knowledge can be transmitted to the youth who observes the rituals as well as the less formal behavioral practices of adults. From these modeling sequences, concepts or rules can be abstracted and refined by social consequences; these cognitions in turn guide the observer when he reaches adulthood. Witnessed by the next generation, his actions aid in perpetuating this socially mediated cycle for passing on important information. In technologically sophisticated societies, symbolic models such as books, records, photographs, or films can augment or replace live modeling performances.

Finally, social learning theory is able to explain how new developments occur within a society through social experience. We will describe this research in detail in Chapter 4. Let us briefly mention several ways in which creative behavior can arise from modeling. One widely accepted definition of a creative act is a novel recombination of known elements. There is evidence (Harris & Evans, 1973; Zimmerman & Dialessi, 1973) that observers can learn strategies for innovatively recombining behavior (of his own and of the model) via observation of a model's creative performance. Such acquisition is similar to the way in which problem solving strategies are learned, as we will see in subsequent chapters. The only difference is in the nature of the rule that is learned. A creativity rule tends to be divergent and expansive in nature, whereas a problem solving strategy tends to be convergent or focusing. Thus, the introduction of technological developments, new musical compositions, or innovative works of art can be analyzed as the joint product of social experience and an observer's personal symbolic contribution.

Empirical Data in Search of a Theory of Vicarious Learning

Since 1960, much research has been devoted to learning by observation. The present section will enumerate some of the key results (which are dealt with in later chapters), which competing theories must address. The scope of a more satisfactory conceptual scheme will then be illustrated.

RESEARCH EVIDENCE TO BE EXPLAINED

In capsule form, here is an overview of some empirical conclusions that must be accounted for by an adequate theory of observational learning. Each point serves to test competing positions.

New Learning Can Occur by Observation and without Performance

This has been demonstrated for tasks as diverse as maze learning (Rosenbaum & Hewitt, 1966), dimensional judgment preferences (e.g., Ryan & Kobasigawa, 1971), language patterns (e.g., Carroll, Rosenthal, & Brysh, 1972), conceptual problems (e.g., Zimmerman & Rosenthal, 1972a), and styles of responding (e.g., Debus, 1970; Ridberg, Parke, & Hetherington, 1971). Indeed, task-relevant overt performance can interfere with vicarious learning (Zimmerman & Bell, 1972). Recall of previous learning after long delays can occur without practice of terminal responses (Flanders, 1968). There is also evidence (Bandura & Jeffery, 1973) that when a task involves extensive cognitive coding, practice of overt terminal responses may not assist recall. Therefore, views that require direct experience or firsthand effort are called into question. But explanations based on the symbolic processing of modeled information are not strained by these results.

Acquisition Can Occur without Direct Rewards to Either Observers or Models

This has been demonstrated in numerous studies, where specific action sequences (Bandura, 1965) and more abstract rules (e.g., Zimmerman & Rosenthal, 1972a) were the tangible goals of training. In fact, the provision of tangible rewards (e.g., Rosenthal & Kellogg, 1973; Rosenthal & Whitebook, 1970), the promise of future rewards (e.g., Rosenthal & Carroll, 1972), and the attempts to create subjective expectations of personal success (Rosenthal, Feist, & Durning, 1972; Rosenthal & Zimmerman, 1972a) all have had rather trivial impact on normally cooperative learners. Thus, theories assuming that acquisition *requires* reinforcement are called into question. However, when target performance violates social norms (Bandura, 1965) or with recalcitrant populations such as autistic children (Lovaas, Berberich, Perloff, & Schaeffer, 1966), there can be value in transmitting information within a context of reward operations. Thus, rewards and punishments administered to a model or to oneself can affect learner response (Bandura, 1965, 1976). These results challenge structuralist views that discount external motivators. In contrast, these results are no problem for a stance that assumes incentives to primarily affect the monitoring of input and the willingness to perform, but not the acquisition of knowledge.

Vicarious Learning Is Not Well Predicted by Associative Strengthening

Associative theories emphasize prior response strength as an indication of previous learning, and treat the gradual increase in response strength in terms of successive pairings with the stimulus. There is evidence (Rosenthal & White, 1972a) that vicarious changes in response are often abrupt and unrelated to prior response strength. During rule learning, acquisition is generally sudden, occurring as if a conceptual "insight" had been achieved. From an associationist standpoint, repeated pairings of a stimulus and response are the optimal conditions for learning. However, research shows (Bandura & Jeffery, 1973) that without cognitive transformation into meaningful symbols, rehearsal of an overt response often does little to improve the recall of vicariously learned information. Finally, there is extensive evidence (e.g., Rosenthal *et al.*, 1970; Zimmerman & Brody, 1975) that individuals who are entirely unfamiliar, and thus of no associative value as models, are imitated nonetheless. Vicarious learning will occur regardless of whether the observer was instructed to do so (Carroll *et al.*, 1972; Rosenthal *et al.*, 1970), whether or not the model has been rewarding (Bergen & Johanson, 1968), and whether the model has been protrayed as highly competent (Zimmerman & Dialessi, 1973) or not (Harris, 1973). This is not to imply that such associative variables and other situational factors do not influence the amount and precision of imitative response. Rather, it is simply to illustrate that observers will emulate unfamiliar models even when lacking any obvious environmental cues to do so. These data pose problems for theories viewing observational learning strictly in terms of stimulus–response habits, but not for positions emphasizing cognitive interpretation and transformation of information.

Transfer after Vicarious Learning Fails to Adhere to Associationist Assumptions

It will be recalled that associationistic theories treat transfer in terms of identical stimulus elements within learning tasks. This formulation does not account for the range of stimuli that have been found to govern observationally acquired responses. Several studies (Rosenthal *et al.*, 1972a; Rosenthal & Zimmerman, 1976) have reported generalization on transfer tasks that shared no literal stimulus elements with the training task. During performance after vicarious rule learning, subjects select many response elements from their own behavioral repertoires. Analyses of mimicry or exact copying after vicarious rule learning reveal that observers rarely duplicate the model's exact responses, e.g., less than 11% for children (Rosenthal *et al.*, 1970),less than 13% for adults (Robert, White, & Rosenthal, 1975) on various conceptual tasks. Most imitation occurs on a more abstract level. Response selection during generalization is often unrelated to the prior associative strength of the behavior (Rosenthal & White, 1972a). This generative aspect of transfer is, as psycholinguists have reminded us, a very pervasive aspect of language and thought.

Another Important Aspect of Vicarious Learning Is the Presence of Covert Cognitive Activity

The coding of modeled phenomena into symbols affects both acquisition and recall (Bandura & Jeffery, 1973; Bandura *et al.*, 1974; Gerst, 1971). In the preceding studies, the coding was done personally by the observer; however, other evidence suggests that if a verbal code is offered by a model (Alford & Rosenthal, 1973; Rosenthal *et al.*, 1972a) or by another person, e.g., an experimenter (Zimmerman & Rosenthal, 1972a), acquisition is enhanced. In addition, there is further evidence supporting the role of cognitive factors in vicarious learning. Both the quality and the quantity of the organization of information in modeling sequences have also been shown to affect conceptual behavior (Rosenthal & Zimmerman, 1973, 1976). In these studies, the same discrete units of information were presented in varying degrees of sequential organization, in concurrence with the structure of the conceptual rule. Conceptual organization substantially affected imitation, transfer, and recall. Finally, as mentioned earlier, we have found that an observer's awareness or cognitive set affects both acquisition (Rosenthal & Zimmerman, 1972a) and imitative performance (Rosenthal *et al.*, 1970). The evidence described above, namely, that symbolic transformations of observed phenomena influence vicarious learning, creates explanatory problems for nonmediational theories or accounts that emphasize passive associationism. However, these results are consistent with analyses that view observational learning in terms of symbolic processing of information.

Vicarious Social Experience Affects Both the Structural Form and Content of Children's Thought and Language

The cognitive skills that are assumed to reflect qualitative differences in mental structure can be taught precociously to children via modeling.

Children as young as four years old who showed no evidence of attaining Piaget's concrete operations stage were able to learn to conserve (e.g., Rosenthal & Zimmerman, 1972b; Zimmerman & Lanaro, 1974). Similarly, preadolescents who gave no indication of having reached the formal operations stage learned through demonstration and practice to reason in a hypothetical deductive manner (Siegler, Liebert, & Liebert, 1973). Language rules of a syntactical nature have also been taught by means of modeling (Brown, 1976). In addition, typical patterns of cognitive development can be reversed, with evidence of less mature levels of cognition being manifest as a result of vicarious experience (Bandura & McDonald, 1963; Rosenthal & Zimmerman, 1972b). While age and general experience affect vicarious learning (Zimmerman, 1974; Zimmerman & Lanaro, 1974; Zimmerman & Rosenthal, 1974a), age considerations per se offer little guidance in making predictions about a particular child's ability to learn vicariously, and have rather weak explanatory value unless relatively gross differences in age are compared (Gholson & Danziger, 1975). Theories which assume that reactions to vicarious experience are limited by the emergence of innate structures in discontinuous stages have difficulty explaining these results. However, formulations which treat a structure as a tentative organization of information created from, and sensitive to, experience, appear to concur with the evidence.

In summary, then, a satisfactory theory of observational learning should account for mediating activities, such as the representation and transformation of information. The position must be able to allow for both learning and performance, as well as for differences between acquisition and overt responding. Finally, the position should be able to integrate sociocultural influences, such as group standards and developmental usage norms, with the evolution and maintenance of cognitive skills.

A SOCIAL LEARNING APPROACH TO VICARIOUS PHENOMENA

A number of the conceptual and empirical issues that have been raised thus far will receive further consideration in the chapters that follow. At this point, then, it may be timely to review these major issues, showing how they gain coherence when interpreted from the standpoint of social learning theory.

How do cognitive phenomena differ from the acquisition of purely terminal responses? With cognitive events, there appears to be no direct linear relationship between stimulus and response. Molecular analyses of responding often reveal no point-to-point similarity between learning and performance although changes on an abstract level can be noted. Stimuli are responded to selectively, according to certain meaningful cue features and abstract properties; previous knowledge is combined with direct experience in a unique and constructive fashion. The categorically organized and influential covert activity is particularly evident during transfer to new stimuli. From a social learning standpoint, these distinctive characteristics of cognitive phenomena require covert activity to be considered in a comprehensive psychological analysis.

Why is it necessary to assume that behavior is cognitively mediated? Research indicates that abstraction is something more than the summation of discrete associations. Most skills are acquired when a learner symbolically codes task stimuli in a systematic fashion. There is also evidence that the external events accompanying cognitive activity can interfere with learning even when they contain task-relevant information. Mental sets, whether experimentally or idiosyncratically created, strongly affect learning. It has been widely reported in research on recall that organizing schemes directly affect memory. Finally, there is considerable evidence from research on perception, learning, transfer, and recall that human thought is selective and constructive in nature. Social learning theory recognizes the importance of cognitive processes and treats them as a major contributor to behavioral control.

Are reinforcement and overt performance necessary for learning? Research in laboratory settings has shown that learning can occur without discernable rewards or overt practice. Also, careful observation of children's learning in naturalistic situations has failed to confirm any pervasive occurrence of systematic reward practices, such as would be anticipated by reinforcement theories. Social learning theory suggests that acquisition can occur observationally without reinforcement and performance, although anticipated reinforcement can facilitate learning by encouraging symbolic coding and rehearsal. Anticipated reinforcement also aids in explaining more overt types of performance.

Can concept formation be explained solely on the basis of associative principles? The evidence tends not to support this conclusion. An associationist explanation cannot eaily handle the evidence for constructiveness in learning, perception, and recall. Associationistic principles do not explain why stored images or words are incomplete, why subjective organization should enhance recall, or why external events that occur after the pairing of stimuli and responses can interfere with learning. Nor can associationistic principles explain why instructions that direct a subject to code stimuli meaningfully should enhance learning. All of the above can be easily handled within a social learning framework, since the important mediating roles of cognitive processes are recognized.

Are cognitive structures innately endowed and do they emerge largely as a result of maturation? Evidence does suggest that mental and linguistic structures can be systematically taught. These patterns vary in form among people having different types of prior experience. Such evidence conflicts with assumptions that innate structures determine an individual's ability to profit from experience. While recognizing that structural regularities may be useful for describing gross changes in thought and language for the majority, a social learning position emphasizes vicarious and direct experience, rather than maturation, in determining cognitive development. This stance has the advantages of explaining the atypical as well as the typical patterns of development and behavior, and can predict more detailed short-term changes in performance. Training interventions that can be tailored to particular groups of learners are also highlighted.

Can modeling phenomena be adequately explained in terms of response copying? There is extensive evidence to the contrary, data gathered from careful comparisons of a model's performance and observers' subsequent imitation. Instead, vicarious learning seems to typically involve the abstraction of rules and meaningful implications from a model's performance; these inferences are then used to integrate previously stored information and to create the appropriate terminal imitative responses. As a result, an observer's imitation often satisfies the abstract principles guiding a model's performance, while remaining topographically dissimilar in terms of responses. Social learning theory can readily accommodate abstraction during vicarious acquisition since cognition is treated as an important subprocess determining behavior.

Is affective arousal necessary for vicarious learning to occur? Although some affective arousal of physiological systems often accompanies vicarious learning, there is little evidence to suggest that it is a necessary precondition for learning. Learning can occur when response-produced feedback is surgically or chemically blocked. In addition, the covariation between somatic indicators and behavior change is poor. Social learning theory assumes that affective conditioning can occur via observation but is not necessary for vicarious acquisition to occur. In fact, high arousal can actually disrupt vicarious learning (Bandura & Rosenthal, 1966). Rather, the crucial determinants of behavior are assumed to be the extraction and symbolic representation of meaningful information, and its implementation through cognitive processes.

How is the vicarious acquisition of novel behavior to be explained? Theories that emphasize response-reinforcement deny that new acts can be learned without overt practice. There is, however, evidence suggesting that novel behavior can be acquired through observation alone. Social learning psychologists accept this evidence at face value. The efforts to dismiss such learning (based on the argument that certain response components were previously known) are questionable, since much of what is conventionally termed "learning" would then be excluded by this definition. Instead, learning is viewed as central, representational phenomena rather than the gradual accretion of response-elements through reinforcement. Reinforcement, however, is important in explaining performance, and in altering the attention-value of cues and events; it is thus treated as a separate subprocess governing behavior.

Can a stimulus discrimination interpretation account for the type of transfer typically witnessed in modeling studies? Attempts to treat transfer in terms of discrete stimulus and response elements do not adequately specify the stimulus or response class boundaries. Unlike discrimination learning, observational learning typically occurs in a relatively holistical fashion, rather than as a molecular, piecemeal accumulation. Abstract structures and meaningful inferences, rather than literal stimulus–response elements, appear to guide generalization. These findings are coherent with the social learning emphasis on a symbolic rather than an associative determination of behavior.

How can an "imitation" learning theory explain the infinite variety of unique linguistic and conceptual responses that are typically displayed? Evidence indicates that most phenomena legitimately considered to be imitative do not involve mimicry. They are imitative only on an abstract or molar level. Considerable evidence confirms that abstract rules can be learned vicariously, and these rules can promptly be transferred to a wide variety of situations, objects, and events. By using the modeled principles to organize one's individual responses on the transfer task, a grammatically or logically correct—but statistically infrequent—terminal response is produced, novel by an objective definition. The *generative* aspect of thought and language involves the conceptual transfer of guiding rules that can either be acquired purely vicariously, solely through direct practice, or from infinite combinations of informative influences, both literal and symbolic.

Finally, structural similarities in the language and thought of different people can be explained on the basis of common modeling experiences and social continuities. Parallels in cognitive structures of individuals in the same cultural groups derive in part from common social experiences and in part from functional relationships between cognitive rules. Usually, such rules and social norms are interdependent to some degree. The rules and mores acquired early on will steer and qualify subsequent learning, enhancing some conceptualizations and actions at the expense of alternative solutions. Finally, similar concepts are formulated by different cultural groups because of similar human needs and capacities and common features of each group's physical environment.

Thus, a social learning position suggests that most learning occurs via the symbolic interventions of other human beings, primarily by means of observation, explanation, and social feedback. Few psychologists question the impact of social factors on obvious classes of behavior such as self-care skills, interpersonal etiquette, or motor accomplishments like dancing. However, the influences of modeling on such abstract classes of behavior as concepts, problem solving strategies, and language have not been widely recognized, perhaps because they are less obvious. In our opinion, the frequent neglect of social forces as determinants of conceptual processes can be attributed to theories about cognition and learning that ignore either (and sometimes both) covert symbolic activity, or social factors. In the ensuing chapters, we will discuss both of these variables from a social learning standpoint, illustrating how this position represents a tangible advance toward a comprehensive explanation of how people acquire knowledge, and develop paradigms or strategies for abstract reasoning.

2

Language and Verbal Behavior

Children grow up in a world mediated by the actions, beliefs, and value systems of others. At birth, the baby girl is swaddled in pink, the boy in blue, and both are stamped with relatively sex-specific names. The social agents who minister to the infant are themselves constrained by the extant cultural norms and usages. Parental expectations about the potential careers and life patterns of their newborns may differ sharply among families, based on societal role distinctions. While parents may hope for wee Dick to become a senator, a sports hero, or aviator, they instead assume that tiny Jane will become a nurse, fashion designer, or wife and mother. Attached to such sex-typed role expectations are other norms involving dress, manner, assertiveness, activity level, and proper conduct. In mother's daydreams, boylike (Dick with bat and ball) and girllike (Jane with dolls and toy furniture) interests are presumed long before the baby comprehends anything about these particular diversions.

The pervasive role of social influences upon the course of human development has been discussed at length by other writers, including such theorists as Baldwin (1906) and Young (1930), met in Chapter 1. In this connection, we have already suggested that abstract behavior is shaped in part by social forces. The canons of logic and appropriateness have no reality unless man gives them form and importance. These are normative conventions, instated and maintained by communities sharing common assumptions and discriminations about proper symbolic usage. Societies, for example, create language systems and also determine which utterances are acceptable, ungrammatical, or particularly in vogue.

It is hardly surprising, then, that Chinese children learn Chinese and

Finnish children Finnish. One readily assumes that from observing others verbalize in French, by attempting to emulate parts of what is witnessed, and by being rewarded with attention and cooperation for his acceptable efforts, or corrected and prompted for those insufficient, the French baby eventually learns to express himself in French. In this connection, it is of interest that Hanlon (1971) was able to influence the spoken accent of fourth grade children by exposing them to audiotaped models of British speakers. Without receiving any instructions to emulate the model, the children's articulation changed after hearing the tapes, becoming more like the British pronunciations. Status characteristics attributed to the speaker also affected imitative performance. Changes in children's accents were more pronounced when the model was described as nurturant and powerful than when depicted as helpless.

Nonetheless, some prominent scholars have argued that social learning processes cannot account for children's acquisition of the essentials of language (e.g., Braine, 1963; Chomsky, 1965; Ervin, 1964; Menyuk, 1964; Miller, 1965; Slobin, 1968). They have primarily disputed learning theories which assume that, in order to be learned, responses must be performed imitatively and reinforced. Instead, these writers believe language to be governed by systems of rules enabling the competent user to create novel combinations of linguistic elements that still conform to the grammatical rule constraints of the symbol system. However, these criticisms do not conflict with approaches such as social learning theory, which treat language acquisition in terms of abstract rules that can be acquired without performance or reinforcement.

PSYCHOLINGUISTIC VIEWS OF MODELING: SOME CONTROVERSIES AND REBUTTALS

Psycholinguists have devoted considerable attention to the role of *imitation* in children's acquisition of language. Many of the behavioral studies soon to be discussed were prompted by the theoretical controversy concerning whether language progress depends on innately determined or on experimental mechanisms. This brief overview will attempt to acquaint the reader with some typical strategies of psycholinguistic research, and to highlight a number of theoretical disputes. Such a background will hopefully foreshadow the emphasis on the mainly behavioral investigations that will comprise much of this chapter. No attempt will be made to provide any comprehensive summary of psycholinguistic thinking, nor will we address technical matters like "deep" versus "surface" structure or the properties of recursion. Those topics lie beyond the province of this book, which deals with language only as one type of symbolic behavior. Detailed elaborations of language are best left to professional psycholinguists. The reader is referred to the original sources, plentifully cited, and available from the references. One may well ask if it is necessary or sensible to impose a dichotomous choice between the contributions of logical relationships internal to the structure of a symbol system such as language, and the contributions of external events like the tutelary and rewarding actions of social agents. One may anticipate that no either/or disjunction will prove tenable. However, it is easy to forget that scientists are fallible beings, disposed to conceptual allegiances and enthusiasms. When individuals seek to obtain evidence that will cheer their cohorts and tax the opposition, science often advances in the process.

Psycholinguists make an important distinction between overt speech *performance* and linguistic *competence* (Chomsky, 1957). Listening to a child talk will not necessarily offer an accurate index of his linguistic power or competence in controlling and flexibly modifying the elements of language. His overt performance is not the same as his grasp, that is, his covert repertoire, of language. From a social learning standpoint, Bandura (1965) has made a parallel distinction, differentiating between response acquisition and performance. Individuals may not publicly display behavior they are perfectly capable of executing. Both approaches acknowledge that overt activity is influenced by situational, social, and internal regulatory events. Because contextual variables may restrict linguistic output, descriptive analyses of children's spontaneous speech must be interpreted with caution. There does seem to be empirical consistency to the order in which different language skills are mastered.

Frazer *et al.* (1963) studied children's facility on three dependent language measures: *imitation,* by repeating modeled sentences; *comprehension,* by selecting appropriate pictures to fit the meaning of sentences; and *production,* by formulating a particular sentence when prompted. The imitation scores tended to surpass the comprehension responses which, in turn, were more easily accomplished than production. Lovell and Dixon (1967) replicated these results with British children, both normal and retarded. Since imitation skill regularly precedes production skill, Osser, Wang, and Zaid (1969) suggested that ability to imitate marked the beginning of language competence, and adduced data to support their conclusion. Operationally, there remains the task of separating measures of performance and competence.

Psycholinguists have attempted to deal with this problem by conducting longitudinal studies on the spontaneous speech of individual children. Their hope is that a broad-based description extending across particular occasions and contexts would yield an accurate sample of changes in children's language competence (e.g., Brown, 1968; Klima & Bellugi, 1966; McNeill, 1966). However, since a child's environment itself is continuous over time, location, and social composition, one wonders how representative are such findings, and to what extent environmental events have instigated or inhibited particular classes of verbal response.

Clay (1971) attacked the same problem with a comparative analysis, using children aged 5 to 7 years, from various ethnic and language backgrounds in New Zealand. She presented English sentences that both varied in linguistic complexity and contained more words than children could store discretely in short-term memory. The child was asked to repeat each stimulus sentence, and his utterances were analyzed for both accuracy and types of errors. Thus, language competence was measured by the child's ability to reproduce an explicit set of verbal sequences. Accuracy in copying improved with age, and the linguistic complexity of the sentences determined the difficulty encountered by the children in their attempts to emulate. However, cultural and social class origins influenced the adequacy of imitation: English-speaking children from professional homes copied best; English-speaking children of working-class parents were the second most able; English-speaking Maori children were next; and Samoan children, who were generally bilingual, showed the poorest imitations. If one accepts that sentence copying is a fair measure of language mastery, then Clay's (1971) data revealed that social background did qualify children's linguistic competence and not just their performance. Of course, a child of this age has not yet attained his full competence. His language repertoire will continue to expand and permit greater flexibility for clothing ideas in a diversity of outward garbs, or particular forms of utterance. However, even with these young children, imitation was not simply a rote reiteration of observed sequences. Copying depended on prior social experience and involved active interpretation and transformation, consistent with the child's previous language learning.

One controversy associated with psycholinguistic thinking concerns nativist assumptions. Many, and probably most, psycholinguists have emphasized that young children's language seems unresponsive to either direct teaching or other forms of environmental stimulation. Yet, psycholinguists differ considerably among themselves on this issue. Scholars such as Chomsky and McNeill adhere to the more nativistic end of the continuum. In Chomsky's (1965) view, children are endowed with an innate capacity which determines the patterning that language must take: "As a precondition for language learning, [the child] must possess a linguistic theory that specifies the form of a grammar of a possible human language [1965, p. 25]." Not only are the structure and mechanisms of language considered innate, but so are the child's concepts about language (p. 48).

To justify this position, Chomsky argues that the universal properties of human languages must reflect the nature of the human capacities involved in language learning. There seems little argument that human language must conform to human capabilities. A language demanding strings of units much longer than what users could readily process would not only be inconvenient, but would be most unlikely to have resulted from spontaneous efforts to communicate by members of a tribe or culture. However, universality does not require innate causation. Incest taboos are essentially universal, but are certainly not assumed to be innate. If they were, a large fraction of Greek tragedy would be rendered pointless. Conventions are established when there is some need or rationale for them (e.g., Rosenthal & Siegel, 1959). The need to communicate for the most diverse of purposes is universal across cultures. The use of tools is also found in all human societies, but this does not imply an innate predisposition to manufacture adzes and spears. One need only assume that cultures can recognize the usefulness of implements, and therefore appreciate that a sharp chip of flint can cut better than a blunt one, or that longer sticks can more easily reach fruit-bearing boughs than can shorter sticks. Since there is considerable overlap in social and physical experience among individuals from different cultures and nations, common experience could account for many shared semantic categories, and influence the order in which the elements of language are acquired.

Chomsky (1965) further argues that language learning would be impossible without some *innate* restriction on the range of possible structures the child is able to acquire. This reasoning would seem to imply that, if cultures do not develop weapons too heavy for convenient use, then it can be assumed that the actual weights of weapon artifacts must be governed by the innate determinants of their manufacturers. It does not seem credulous or cynical to suppose that, if any easy way could be found to drop mountains or icebergs on one's enemies, man long ago would have taken up these practices with gusto. But if such means of combat have not been developed, this reflects the limitation of human capacities; it does not imply any innate determinants of proper weapon size. Much the same reasoning could be applied to flying, before the advent of airplanes and dirigibles.

Without necessarily accepting Chomsky's assumptions about innate linguistic structures, many psycholinguists appear to treat "maturation" as the most significant factor in a child's acquisition of language. They argue that associationist explanations of language learning do not fit the available data. For example, there is little basis for concluding that directed overt practice or reinforcement play major roles in language acquisition. There is even evidence that language learning can occur without speech practice (Lenneberg, 1967). Some psycholinguistic scholars (Brown *et al.*, 1969) have postulated that mothers seldom spontaneously correct the form of children's utterances, although they usually do redress errors in the content or truth value of statements. But this widely cited conclusion seems questionable in light of recent research. Moerk (1976) examined verbal interchanges between parents and their young children and found that parents are active language teachers. They frequently provided phonetic, semantic, and grammatical corrections after incomplete or incorrect statements by their youngsters. Their corrective feedback included both linguistic modeling as well as social reactions to the children's utterances. Earlier psycholinguistic analyses of parent reinforcement practices had focused on verbal approval. However, the child accrues as benefits other, more powerful rewards when his language influences other people and events. Hart and Risley (1968) found that young children more readily acquired advanced language features that were modeled if they earned appropriate stimulus materials contingently than if they received only verbal approval. This type of reinforcement is present in every conversation or social interchange. Thus, conclusions about the role of maturation in the child's development of language seem more to require positive evidence linking language acquisition to specific neurological processes rather than to rely on the supposed weakness of incentive operations. Clearly, contingent social reactions can and do operate in linguistic contexts.

Furthermore, new descriptive research on mother–child verbal interactions raises the possibility that, to some extent, the "babyish" characteristics of young children's speech may derive from parental modeling. This naturalistic evidence questions assumptions that language acquisition is relatively independent of environmental input.

Snow (1972) investigated the speech displayed by middle-class mothers when talking to their 2- or 10-year-old children. Their speech to the babies was much simpler and more redundant than when they conversed with their older children. Shorter sentences, as well as many more verbfree sentence fragments, were directed to the babies. These results suggest that the language exposure of young children contains simpler examples, including incorrect usage, of language than are available to the older, maturing child. Snow's conclusions were supported by a related but independent study. Phillips (1973) worked with younger groups of infants, aged 8, 18, and 28 months. Phillips discovered that mothers modeled simpler words and grammatical forms when speaking to their offspring than they did in conversation with a fellow adult. Maternal verbalizations did not differ between the 8- and 18-month age groups, but more adult utterances were directed at the 28-month-olds. This evidence, that mothers do not demonstrate competent, adultlike, language usage with young children, underlines the necessity of compiling much more careful naturalistic, longitudinal data if the typical environmental influences on children's speech development are to be better understood.

Children also reduce the complexity of their speech when talking to younger siblings and friends. Shatz and Gelman (1973) found that when 4-year-olds spoke to 2-year-olds, their utterances were shorter, grammatically simpler, and more designed to sustain attention than when they spoke either to other 4-year-olds or to adults. Thus, even the peer group differentially models language on the basis of a child's age.

The child's sex is another characteristic that elicits differential language modeling. Lewis and Freedle (1973) found that mothers verbally responded more to girls than to boys at just 3 months of age. Moss (1967) reported that mothers of girls imitated their daughters' utterances more than mothers of boys. It will be recalled from Chapter 1 that there is extensive evidence that contingent imitation of a child's vocalizations will elicit greater imitation of adult speech (see also Parton & Priefert, 1975).

In a recent study, Cherry and Lewis (1976) studied the interactions of mothers and their 2-year-old children on the basis of the child's sex. These researchers found that mothers of girls spoke to them more often, asked more questions, repeated more of their child's utterances, and used longer statements, as compared to mothers of male children. Interestingly, there were no sex-related differences in the children's verbal behavior at this young age. Cherry and Lewis concluded, "This suggests that it is the mothers who are responding differentially to their children as a function of sex rather than children differing as a function of sex [p. 281]." Thus, the often-cited evidence that school-age girls and women are more verbally facile than boys or men might be traced to their exposure to a richer language environment almost from the moment of birth.

The studies showing differences in language models based on children's age or sex support a core premise of a social learning explanation for development advanced in Chapter 1. That is, the social environment for children is not homogeneous or identical, but varies on the basis of the child's age, sex, home milieu, and undoubtedly, on the basis of many other factors. This fact permits explanations for age- and sex-related differences without forcing assumptions about maturation or biological factors.

Two other descriptive studies of mother–child verbal interaction support a social learning explanation for language development. Reichle, Longhurst, and Stepanich (1976) studied the verbal interaction of mothers with their 2- or 3-year-old children. Maternal modeling (also termed expatiation) occurred more frequently than expansion, which accounted for less than 4% of the mother's verbal behavior. It will be recalled that many psycholinguists believe expansion to be the primary mechanism by which children acquire language. The complexity of modeled utterances was significantly greater for the 3-year-olds than for the 2-year-olds. Also, maternal modeling often occurred in conjunction with question asking. Both types of maternal language stimulation occurred more frequently with the older children. These findings suggest that modeling is a major process by which children acquire language, and that a mother's language modeling, like her speech in general, varies according to her child's age.

One would expect that if a child acquires language by hearing and observing the speech of his or her mother, there should be some correlation between a child's language facility and the degree of the mother's linguistic stimulation. Clarke-Stewart (1973) found that the language ability of 9- to 18-month-old children was closely related to the amount of verbal stimulation received from their mothers ($r = .68$). Further, the mothers' nonresponsive verbal behavior (a subset of total stimulation) correlated more with language development than did maternal responsiveness to vocalizations. Maternal responsiveness refers to the mother's *contingent* reactions to the child, whereas nonresponsive speech means the input *independent* of the child's actions. Nonresponsive speech appears to be identical to what Reichle *et al.* (1976) described as modeling or expatiation. From her study, Clarke-Stewart concluded that children need "a language model more than a language reinforcer [pp. 68, 70]," to promote a verbal response repertoire and to understand others' communications during the early stages of language development. Her conclusion may be a bit strong given the correlational nature of the study, but it offers evidence that children can profit from simply hearing the speech and observing the behavior of their mother.

Psycholinguists tend to dismiss "imitation" as a mechanism to account for language acquisition. This viewpoint is illustrated by the rather extreme conclusions drawn from quasi-naturalistic research, which Slobin (1968) has summarized as follows: "Such findings certainly cast strong doubt on the supposition that imitation can be considered a useful explanatory device in accounting for the child's syntactic development [p. 438]." The accounts reviewed by Slobin may be less representative than Chomsky's (1964) position: "In general, it is a mistake to assume that—past the very earliest stages—much of what the child acquires is acquired by imitation. This could not be true on the level of sentence formation, since most of what the child hears is new and most of what he produces, past the very earliest stages, is new [p. 37]."

It can be seen that psycholinguists assign much weight to the novelty of output. But children frequently display rule-consistent constructions which markedly depart from the norms of English usage and which, therefore, were probably never directly modeled for them by adults. Examples of this usage would include idiosyncratic utterances like *a this truck* or *allgone pacifier*. Minimizing the contribution of modeling appears to rest on the assumption that, as a theoretical construct, "imitation" is the same as absolute mimicry, that is, one-to-one response matching, and therefore could not explain the generative aspects of children's language. If we address our analysis to the details of words, or to particular utterances, one may grant the novelty of such productions. Clearly, adults are not very likely to model responses like *eated* for children. However, this type of example does approximate regularity on a syntactic level of analysis, a conclusion extensively documented in psycholinguistic research. It is entirely possible that such utterances as *hitted*, *mouses*, or *candy wants the baby* are incomplete or inappropriate *generalizations* of vicariously acquired syntactic rules. Hence, the degree of regularity that is evident in children's early language responses might well be a product of the social environment. However, these overgeneralizations from regular to irregular nouns indicate that the children are actually imitating the model's language too well! The situation is further complicated by an individual child's mistransfer of pluralization rules; for example, when the child says *womans* for *women*, he models an error for his peers, some of whom may adopt it.

As we shall see, a rather large number of recent experiments suggest that mimicry constitutes only a small portion of the phenomena that legitimately comprise imitative learning. Mimicry itself can be influenced by the type of demonstration exhibited by the model, the properties of the tasks performed by the model and observer, and by a number of other variables (Zimmerman & Rosenthal, 1974c). An explanation of language acquisition based solely on absolute mimicry or copying presumes single-unit S–R connections, links through which individual words or phonemes are each learned discretely. We shall provide considerable evidence to the contrary, confirming beyond any shred of doubt, that vicarious learning affects complex, rule-governed abstractions, as well as discrete elements. By observation, children can acquire organized symbolic rules that govern linguistic patterning in overt verbal productions (e.g., Brown, 1976; Carroll *et al.*, 1972; Guess *et al.*, 1968) and in covert labeling (Mann & Baer, 1971), as well as the rules for forming abstract but extralinguistic concepts (Rosenthal *et al.*, 1972a; Alford & Rosenthal, 1973).

Ervin (1964) and McNeill (1970) have argued against the utility of imitative learning on empirical grounds. Ervin (1964) drew her inferences from the spontaneous speech patterns of five children, all 2 years of age. She found that their unprompted imitations of an adult's speech were grammatically no more complex than their normal speech. As a result, she ruled out imitation as a vehicle for language development. But there are several reasons to question Ervin's conclusions. First, her analysis was predicated on the restricted definition of imitation as mimicry, thereby precluding imitation of the structural properties of language. Second, delayed imitation was excluded from consideration, since Ervin only considered duplicate utterances occurring immediately after they were modeled by the adult. Third, Sherman (1971) has pointed out that Ervin's conclusion was based on the questionable sensitivity of her method in analyzing grammatical complexity. Fourth, it has been found that if children are *instructed* to imitate, the child's responses will be more linguistically advanced than his ordinary speech (Fraser *et al.*, 1963; Slobin & Welsch, 1973). More recently, Menyuk (1969) analyzed young children's prompted imitations as well as their natural productions of grammatical and nongrammatical sequences. The youngsters' imitations contained more advanced phrase structure, transformations, and morphology than were displayed in their unprompted speech. The older children could reproduce contrived and erroneous utterances, even though these conflicted with their own grammatical style. The younger children tended to alter both grammatically correct and erroneous sentences to conform with their own grammatical rules. It thus appears that the limitations on a child's information-processing facility may to some extent circumscribe his ability to reiterate accurately (see also, Liebert, Odom, Hill, & Huff, 1969; Vasta & Liebert, 1973).

It is also important to realize that examining the naturally occurring utterances of a child that are identical to those just performed by a model will only partially reveal vicarious factors that enter language learning. This is one of the major weaknesses of the descriptive–correlational research methodology used by most of the psycholinguists studying imitation. Ignored are structural changes in language that are not immediately performed. Later, we will present evidence showing that if a model's performance, as well as incentives and instructions to perform, are experimentally manipulated structural changes in children's speech can be unambiguously related to social factors. In the psycholinguistic research described above, evidence of structural change emerged only when the youngsters were asked to imitate.

Bandura (1969a, 1977b) has repeatedly emphasized that vicarious changes can take place covertly, by means of cognitive elaborations of observed events. Other than the witnessing and discrimination of action sequences, no overt, "direct" response is mandatory. Consequently, a social learning interpretation permits language rules to be acquired via tacit observation of the regularities in the speech of others, and by the recurrent pairings of these regularities with extralinguistic events. For example, parental modeling of interrogative and imperative constructions will often be tied to compelling events that affect the baby's immediate well-being. Questions such as *Does Clare want milk or juice? Does that hurt?* are asked with regard to the child's desire for food, play, and comfort-producing changes. Demands, cast in the imperative mood (*Stop crying! Don't pull that!*), are imposed, in order to redirect the child's ongoing activity. In this regard, a social learning stance emphasizes some of the same variables deemed important by several psycholinguists. Macnamara (cited by Ervin-Tripp, 1971), for example, suggested that meaning must be obvious in order for language to be acquired: "Optimal conditions at first must require that nonlinguistic events be redundant and matched quite simply with what is said . . ., Children's learning from other children, which is the usual condition in many societies, might be efficient because of its tie to activities [Ervin-Tripp, 1971, p. 195]." There is recent evidence to support Macnamara's suggestion. Brown (1976) found that children learned language rules far better when linguistic modeling was supported by concrete perceptual referents.

Like Macnamara, several other prominent psycholinguists (e.g., Bloom, 1970; Brown, 1970; Schlesinger, 1971) have rejected purely syntactic explanations for language development. They believe that because this theoretical model is incomplete, a syntactic approach requires language structures to be "wired in." They feel that biological determination of structures is unnecessary (and inaccurate) if a theory also emphasizes the role of semantics in language development.

Much recent attention has been devoted to semantic development. Nelson (1973) studied the first 50 words learned by children. Her research was unique in that she studied the social and physical environmental context in which words were acquired and used. She found that a child's first words described the moving or changing properties of people, animals, and things. The phenomena to which a child's words referred changed in some way either as a result of a child's actions or perhaps the actions of others. Thus, to a young child, the most salient properties of stimuli are *dynamic* and functional, rather than static. For example, the conceptual properties that a child initially attaches to the word *ball* are its bouncing and rolling qualities, rather than its roundness or color. These functional and dynamic meanings that a child gives to his first words are highly dependent on context. The meaning of *ball* is related to the persons who play with it and the settings in which it is bounced and rolled. The static properties that adults use to define words are not learned until much later. However, the static properties of stimuli transcend situations, and therefore enter into most lexical definitions of words. Static facets also permit the most error-free generalization of the concept to new instances.

Nelson (1974) believes that these early concepts are not first induced from a series of instances but are attached to a single instance. The concept is generalized to other stimuli which share characteristics with that first instance. Thus, seen for the first time, a wheel will be mislabeled as a *ball*, since it, like a ball, also rolls. This reasoning is consonant with evidence indicating that very young children can perform conceptually, but cannot reason well inductively until much later. This explains some common speech errors among young children, such as calling an unfamiliar man *daddy*.

Nelson's data are consistent with many of the studies cited previously, and her overall account fits well with the social learning interpretation advanced here. Evidence that a child's concepts arise from the dynamic and functional properties of stimuli is consistent with our emphasis on the role of adult behavior in directing abstractions by younger children, and on the contingent reactions of the environment to these conceptually directed performances. Certainly much of the movement and change in a child's environment is centered on or caused by the behavior of others. Nelson's observation that a child's concepts are initially and fundamentally dependent on the surrounding context coheres nicely with the emphasis of social learning psychologists on situational factors in thought and behavior (e.g., Mischel, 1968, 1973).

Some recent research also supports Macnamara's suggestion. Leonard (1975) found that nonlinguistic events affected how very young children learned a semantic structural rule. The subjects in this study were children varying in age between 28 and 40 months who had not yet begun to speak with subjects and verbs. Using modeling and reinforcement, the children were taught several types of subject–verb relationships. Those children who saw pictures or live demonstrations of the modeled statements learned the semantic rule more efficiently than those who did not see the sentences portrayed, a result indicating that nonlinguistic, as well as social and environmental, stimuli play an important role in the acquisition of word meaning.

Macnamara's suggestion has also been supported by recent research on the communication of children, i.e., a child's skill in using language to express meaning to another person. According to Krauss and Glucksberg (1969), this involves adapting one's speech to both the phenomena being described and to the listener. Whitehurst (1976) devised a clever task using stimuli that varied along several conceptual dimensions (e.g., color, size, patterns) to study how children communicate. This task permitted a detailed examination of the adequacy of 6- to 9-year-olds' descriptions to an adult. The meaning of the child's statements, as well as his skill at expression, could be determined objectively. The children's descriptions became more complete and redundant as they grew older. Older children tended to supply more than the minimal amount of information when they described something to another person.

These developmental changes could be explained in either of two ways: The child might learn to avoid making uninformative descriptions to another person because of experiencing firsthand the frustration of receiving incomplete messages. Or, the child might become a better speaker as he grows older because he is more able to imitate the communicative style of adults. It was found that children imitated the communicative style of an adult model with little regard for its suitability to the listener. This result was surprising, since the child received both direct rewards (when he responded correctly as a listener) as well as vicarious rewards (when the adult to whom the child spoke received rewards based on the child's explanations) for accuracy of communication. Such data indicate that children's communicative skills are greatly influenced by the behavior of adult models, and support Macnamara's emphasis on the redundancy of nonlinguistic events in a listener's extraction of meaning from explanations. Children clearly become more effective speakers with age, because they describe nonlinguistic events more accurately and redundantly.

Thus, many psycholinguists are moving away from Chomsky's nativistic posture, because of recent data relating semantic development to the social and nonsocial environment. Leonard's study found that word meanings could be extracted more efficiently if language was socially exemplified in the appropriate environmental context.

A social learning approach acknowledges that physiological maturation can surely limit a child's motor accomplishments, such as the articulation of sounds. It is also plausible that certain information-processing skills are prerequisite to others. If, for example, the child cannot discriminate among colors, shapes, or morphemes, he would not be readily able to grasp rules for organizing or recombining such elements. If "maturation" means some analogous and dependent "layering" of skills, then there would seem to be little grounds for dispute. There has been some social learning research on sequential dependencies in language skill attainment. For example, Lovaas (1966) developed a rather detailed analysis of autistic children's language skills in terms of phoneme matching, word matching, memory training, linguistic rule learning, and generative speech. More of this type of empirical task analysis is needed. Thus, productive speech may emerge rather suddenly, without lengthy environmental shaping of overt responses. As we shall see, operant researchers have made contributions bearing on such questions. It may be that the mobility of normal children brings them to so many situations requiring speech for communication and into the presence of so many models, that most will exhibit speech as soon as their motoric and covert symbolic skill repertoires permit. Other children, however, such as retardates, will not acquire full control of language spontaneously, and might benefit from more structured programming of environmental inputs. For example, Guess *et al.* (1968) found that vicarious techniques could instate both words and language forms in retardates; among the children who profited from systematic modeling and reinforcement programs were a number who could not, at the outset, imitate spontaneously. Their failure to emulate may, in part, have accounted for their original inability to acquire speech until specially trained.

In a number of aspects, then, social learning theory is consistent with psycholinguistic biases: Both views reject simple, single-unit association as the explanation for language or symbol acquisition. Both views also reject response modulation via shaping as the typical means by which language is developed. Both positions accept that complex learning can be covert, able to take place in the absence of external performance and explicit reinforcement. Both recognize that language acquistion demands the assimilation of intricate grammatical rules as well as discrete phonemes and morphemes. It seems necessary for psycholinguists to appreciate that rule learning and concept-attainment research have great relevance to language phenomena. Similarly, covert acquisition of linguistic features can result from tacit observations of social behavior; the overt matching of speech samples is only a fraction of the role that vicarious processes can play in language development. On the other hand, social learning theory must take greater account of sequential skill dependencies in the elaboration of language and other symbolic repertoires.

Very possibly, the nativistic assumptions of psycholinguists will largely prove to be red herrings, especially if adopted as a means of resisting simplistic accounts of language learning based on molecular associationism. Postulating "innate" propensities or structures provokes behavioral psychologists, who hear echoes of the instinct doctrine (Chapter 1) long laid to rest by experimental psychology. Unless a psycholinguist adheres to nativistic biases, he may be able to forego innate assumptions if offered alternative explanatory paradigms that acknowledge the complexities of language phenomena. Social learning theory provides this type of framework.

Certainly, spheres of interest are understandably and legitimately different. Psycholinguists are mainly concerned with the properties of language in its own right. For most psychologists, especially those interested in the processes of psychological change, language is merely one important category of symbolic activity. Psycholinguists and psychologists concur that man has a unique, species-specific capacity for complex speech and abstraction (but see, Mellgren, Fouts, & Lemmon, 1973; Fouts, Mellgren, & Lemmon, 1973; Premack, 1970). But this genetic endowment will *not* make a facile speaker of a child exclusively raised by complete mutes, however nurturant they may be. Unless the environment provides experience with the cultural conventions of language, whether through live, filmed, or recorded social agents, the child will not blossom forth with communicative discourse.

Perhaps the fundamental difference between psycholinguistic and social learning approaches lies in their respective emphases on sequence-dependent structural repertoires versus social determinants in language acquisition. In this light, disputes would bow, as they should, to the empirical data bearing on the relative contributions of each source of causation. Structural analyses of language are useful techniques for describing the typical interrelationships of syntactic rules, but a complete theory of language also requires that the relationship between the elements of the structure and the external social and physical environment be specified. Once such linkages are indicated, strategies for accelerating language development can be devised. Behavioral approaches have concentrated on establishing these linkages, even though their consideration of structural variables has been relatively unsophisticated. However, even at present levels of linguistic sophistication, social learning approaches have proven very useful in assisting individuals with language problems. This research will be described in detail in the rest of this chapter. It is now appropriate to turn to the experimental evidence that stimulated much of the preceding discussion. Bearing in mind the assumptions and reservations about modeling advanced by many psycholinguistic writers, the reader should now be prepared to draw his own conclusions from the data.

SOCIAL LEARNING OF SYNTACTIC CONSTRUCTIONS

A direct attack on the social modification of language usage was made in a pioneering study by Bandura and Harris (1966). They reasoned that children cannot acquire words or grammatical structures without exposure to the illustrative verbalizations of socializing agents. Hence, modeling factors must play an important role in language acquisition and in mediating verbal changes. Bandura and Harris sought to show that the observation of a model could rapidly influence a child's subsequent production of two syntactic constructions, the prepositional phrase and the passive voice.

They presented common nouns, which were printed on index cards, to second-grade boys and girls. For baseline purposes, the children were directed to make up a sentence using the words on the individual cards. Other cards were introduced for training and testing, but the child's task was always to make up a sentence for each card. The *reinforcement plus set* condition involved no model; the child was rewarded with paper stars (exchangeable for gifts) and verbal praise for producing the desired constructions; the problem-solving set directed children to pay careful attention to the sentences and to try and determine what aspect of a sentence would earn them a star. In all of the modeling variations, the model alone first demonstrated the selected construction (passive verbs) and then took turns with the child in making sentences. Only 75% of the model's sentences contained the passive form; other verb forms were displayed in the remaining sentences. This arrangement was used to increase the plausibility of the episode, since the experimenter cast the model, like the child, in the role of a learner, rather than presenting the model as an expert. For the *basic modeling* condition, the adult read his sentences as if inventing them spontaneously, but neither stars nor praise rewards were supplied. For the *modeling plus reinforcement* condition, stars and praise were dispensed whenever the model or the child created an instance of the desired construction, but no directions to focus attention were given. The attention-focusing problem solving instructions were added for the *modeling plus reinforcement plus set* condition.

Even after modeling, passive voice constructions remained quite rare. There was a significant increase in passives as the result of training, but most of this change was based on the superiority of the modeling plus reinforcement plus set condition, which generated the best performances. The no set, modeling plus reinforcement children did show a borderline increase over their baseline production of passives. Among the children who watched the model display passives before the prepositions were made salient, there was further evidence of learning; passive responses persisted at the onset of the switch to prepositions. The nonmodeling, reinforcement plus set group, the basic modeling only group, and the control children all failed to generate more passives than under baseline conditions.

With the much more familiar prepositional phrases, the results were somewhat more pronounced. For the combined experimental groups, there was a strong increase in prepositional constructions from baseline to later testing. The training variations differed sharply. Only the modeling plus reinforcement plus set, and the nonmodeling reinforcement plus set groups exceeded their baseline means. The no set, modeling plus reinforcement group showed a borderline increase, but neither the basic modeling nor the control subjects gave evidence of improvement. It is noteworthy that children rarely imitated the model's complete utterances. Although usage changed under the more informative conditions, this seemed to reflect recognition of the appropriate constructions rather than indiscriminate mimicry of the model's verbalizations. The desired syntactic forms were often embedded in quite novel, grammatically deviant sentence responses, e.g., *Ice are put in boxes sometimes.* Generalization of syntactical changes was not directly studied, and, except when augmented by set and reinforcement operations, modeling proved ineffective in stimulating prepositions and passives. Nonetheless, the Bandura and Harris (1966) experiment did reveal, under laboratory conditions, that social influences could modify the syntactical productions of young children, even in a brief procedure that allowed only very little direct practice. Note that learning occurred even though the model demonstrated only *partial* fidelity to the governing rule. This suggests that, as is the case in most naturalistic situations, social learning effects may accrue, even though social agents manifest some inconsistency in their behavior.

Odom, Liebert, and Hill (1968) set out to replicate the prior results with prepositional phrases, and to see if children would adopt minor alterations in phrase form if permuted phrases were modeled. In a study with second graders, they also used simple nouns, each typed on a separate index card. Children assigned to a *control* condition invented 30 sentences when neither training nor reinforcement was given. In the *grammatical rule* condition, the model demonstrated sentences, 75% of which ended in correct English phrases (e.g., *at the door*), while the remaining 25% contained no phrases of any kind. In the *nongrammatical rule* condition, the model's performance was similar, except that his phrases were in the order article–noun–preposition (e.g., *the door at*). In both modeling treatments, the model first performed 15 sentences and then alternated with the child in blocks of five trials. As in the Bandura and Harris (1966) procedure, modeling conditions were given an attention-focusing instructional set, and praise and rewards (poker chips to be traded for a prize afterward) were dispensed to child and to model for producing the desired phrases. Both modeling groups surpassed the controls in producing grammatical, *correct* phrases after training, confirming the Bandura and Harris results. The grammatical and nongrammatical rule groups did not differ in producing normal phrases, even though the former group was reinforced for such responses and the latter group was not. No evidence suggested that children adopted the model's altered, deviant phrases. Instead, the nongrammatical rule children appeared to readjust the order of the modeled phrase to agree with the familiar, correct syntactical pattern. In an attempt to determine if children had misperceived the inverted phrase form when it was modeled, or instead had actively corrected the skewed phrases, Odom, Liebert, and Hill conducted a second study.

They reasoned that if children were required to repeat verbatim the model's deviant phrases, but still produced their own correct phrases, the misperception hypothesis could be ruled out, on the grounds that an active correction to match normal phrase form had taken place. Thus, a new group of second grade children was required to either repeat the ungrammatical sentences modeled, or, in another variant, to repeat correct phrases. Aside from the repetition of normal versus inverted phrases, the previous procedures were again followed.

Both groups of children showed comparable and significant increases in their production of syntactically correct phrases. Only one ungrammatical phrase was ever given by any child, supporting the prior failure to instate the deviant phrase order. Indeed, although children could repeat the correct model with virtually no errors, the "ungrammatical" test children had significantly more difficulty in merely reproducing the model's deviant phrases.

Next, Liebert, Odom, Hill, and Huff (1969) studied the effect of age, as an index of linguistic facility, on the adoption of grammatical and ungrammatical modeled phrase forms. They reasoned that successful emulation of inverted phrases should decrease with age if phrase ordering is primarily determined by the amount of experience with the English language. On the other hand, if the ability to abstract the new rule depends on increased cognitive flexibility in solving problems, then deviant phrases should be more easily generated by older children. Their task and procedures were very similar to those of the prior experiments, with youngsters aged 5, 8, and 14 uttering either natural prepositional phrases or a deviant phrase sequence.

General increases in the modeled constructions were found, and these changes were strongly influenced by age, with the eldest group outperforming both of the younger groups. There was no overall difference between the changes wrought by the grammatical and inverted phrase models, but age again played an important role in the nongrammatical conditions. The youngest children, as before, showed increased production of normal—but situationally undemanded—phrases. In contrast, both older age levels showed decreased grammatical and increased inverted phrase production, following the form of the model's examples. Similarly, nearly all of the children exposed to the grammatical model were able to repeat his sentences accurately; significantly more errors were made by the group repeating deviant phrases. The oldest children more consistently spoke the ungrammatical construction verbatim than either younger group. The results thus confirmed that children could better emulate a model who adhered to established symbolic conventions. Greater experience with English did not hamper manipulation of the inverted constructions. Instead, the older groups were better able to adopt both grammatical and distorted phrase paradigms, suggesting that as cognitive repertoires become more supple and elaborate with experience, the child can more readily integrate rule-governed symbol patterns, whether relatively novel or banal.

We have seen from the Odom *et al.* (1968) results that although 7- and 8-year-olds failed to learn the inverted phrase order, their production of regular prepositional forms did increase. In the Liebert *et al.* (1969b) study, although the teenagers adopted the deviant phrases, 8-year-olds could not. What specific mechanisms or causal processes might explain such outcomes?

Vasta and Liebert (1973) hypothesized that these age-related effects stemmed from the poorer verbal discrimination skills of younger children. Using an auditory *recognition* task, they compared first-graders with third-graders according to their ability to discriminate inverted phrases within spoken sentences. During training, an audiotaped child model created sentences in response to stimulus words presented by the experimenter. For each sentence containing an inverted phrase, the experimenter praised the model, but supplied negative feedback to sentences devoid of phrase inversions. The child observers overheard the model receive a prize at the end of his participation. The model always spoke 20 inverted phrase sentences and either 10 regular prepositional sentences (demanding a fine-grained discrimination between phrase formats) or 10 sentences without any prepositional phrases (entailing only a grosser discrimination). After the modeling tape, all of the children received a mixed set of new sentences, and were required to identify the type of sentences (inverted phrases) the experimenter liked. No feedback was given, but a prize was promised for performing well.

As expected, the older group discriminated with significantly greater accuracy. In separate comparisons, they were more often able to judge correctly inverted phrases, regular phrases, and nonphrase sentences as falling within the "preferred" type than were the first graders. The variety of normal sentences heard during modeling did not affect the results. However, in recognition testing, fewer correct judgments were made with nonprepositional sentences than with either the regular or inverted phrase forms. Further, age interacted with type of test sentence. Third-graders could identify all three sentence forms equally well. In contrast, younger children made more errors with nonprepositional sentences than any other type, but distinguished the inverted phrases as well as the regular phrases.

From these results, it seemed that, at least in part, a child's previous inability to *produce* inverted phrases after modeling may result from age-linked skill differences in facility with syntactical forms. As we shall see, research by Mann and Baer (1971) suggests that increased familiarity with objects improves verbal labeling. Generalizing from extensive psycholinguistic evidence, Vasta and Liebert (1973) pointed out that comprehension of speech precedes the ability to construct verbal utterances. Thus, their first graders showed some capacity to distinguish inverted from regular phrases, when this discrimination required only a recognition response. In the previous studies (Odom *et al.*, 1968; Liebert *et al.*, 1969b), young children had failed when asked to produce, or even repeat, the deviant phrases. Perhaps some covert—and tenuously achieved—discrimination between regular and inverted phrases had broken down through interference when overt verbalization was demanded. Also, the previous studies used adult models. Conceivably, younger children may have interpreted the situation differently, asking themselves questions like: Why did the grown-up man make those mistakes? Are both adults trying to trick me? Is it a test to see if I give the right answer even when the man makes mistakes? To the extent that such questions were concerns of the younger children, less resigned to the arbitrary wiles of adults, they might *(a)* have inhibited the production of inverted phrases or *(b)* distracted the children from more careful attention to the ongoing experimental procedures.

In a related study, Odom, Liebert, and Fernandez (1969) explored the effects of audiomodeling tapes on the immediate and delayed production of phrases by educable mental retardates. During baseline, the child was shown simple nouns and asked to construct a sentence for each. Modeling groups then heard a tape which contained sentences all ending with normal prepositional phrases. Depending on the test condition, the experimenter either did or did not supply verbal praise for the modeled sentences. Then, after learning that the experimenter would award tokens (exchangeable for a prize) to sentences she liked, each child was given a new series of nouns for sentence production. The results showed that each experimental group surpassed the untrained controls. Adding verbal praise for the model's constructions did *not* influence performance. Essentially the same results were obtained in the retention phase 3 weeks later.

Shantz and Wilson (1972) used a modeling procedure to improve young children's oral communication skills. Second graders were given the task of describing geometric stimuli to a listener. Children in the experimental condition were trained for several sessions in triads, in which the roles of speaker, observing listener, and responding listener alternated among the three youngsters. As rated by adult judges, the trained children improved the quality of their spoken communications significantly more than did the untrained controls. Some transfer of training to a different communication task was also found.

A model's personal characteristics and the nature of his interactions with observers should plausibly affect the strength of social learning. It has been found, for example, that nurturant models will in *general* sponsor better acquisition (Bandura & Huston, 1961; Mischel & Grusec, 1966), that children more often spontaneously solicit attention from positively reinforcing teachers (Rosenthal, Underwood, & Martin, 1969), and verbalize more frequently with such encouraging instructors (Friedman, 1973a). Similarly, Friedman (1973b) found that under naturalistic classroom conditions, first graders more often emulated several aspects of highly rewarding teachers' verbal styles than the speech modes of less rewarding teachers. The theoretical conditions under which a model's nurturance may and may not foster defined types of imitative performance has been discussed in some detail by Bandura (1969b). When, for example, a nurturant model adopts stringent criteria for self-reward, children may be *more* likely to depart from the demanding standards than if the adult enacts a less supportive role.

Carroll, Kossuth, and Rogers (1971) used observation to teach second-graders a simple tense discrimination. Ten common—but semantically unrelated—verb stems were displayed in columns on a blackboard. The children were directed to pay careful attention while the adult model responded. The model then placed a minus (−) sign above half of the stems, while vocalizing each and adding a suffix (*-ing*) aloud. She introduced a plus (+) sign for the remaining stems, and instead spoke the past tense (*-ed*) suffix. The suffixes were not added visually to the written stems. No symbols were given to control children to differentiate *-ing* from *-ed* verbs. After training, the model orally presented a new list of present progressives and simple past tense verbs, and the children responded by designating plus or minus signs on response sheets. Both modeling groups surpassed the controls in correctly designating the alternative tenses.

Kossuth (1972) then compared modeling along with modeling plus translation in the acquisition and transfer of a novel language rule. The *modeling only* group observed a demonstration of the criterion rule behavior. The *modeling plus translation* involved exposure to the process of transforming an English sentence into its equivalent version according to a new symbolic convention. Oral presentation was contrasted with the use of pictorial stimuli for training, and the performance of second versus sixth grade children was also compared. The children were told that they would be taught a funny new language which they would use for creating sentences to describe pictures. The modeled sentences always consisted of three key words, i.e., a subject (S), a verb (V), and an object (O), whose order (e.g., SVO, OSV, etc.) was not important. The rule involved attaching arbitrary inflectional endings as follows: *-ub* to the subject (actor) stem; *-um* to the verb (action) stem; and *-ul* to the object (acted upon) stem. Thus, the English sentence *The lamb talks to the pig* became, in the new language, *Lamb**__ub__** talk**__um__** pig**__ul__***, in any ordering of the three new words. Previous pilot testing had shown that the novel constructions never occurred spontaneously in children's speech and that, by themselves, instructions to use the invented inflectional endings brought very little suffix utilization. After modeling training, the first set of pictures was again presented in an imitation phase, and the child was required to construct a new-language sentence for each. In the generalization phase, new pictures were introduced and the children were asked to formulate a sentence for each one.

The performances in both modeling conditions surpassed those of the untrained controls for proper use of the arbitrary language, during both imitation and generalization phases. Overall, performance was better for imitation than for generalization. Sixth-graders outperformed the younger children, and girls surpassed boys. Adding the translation step to the modeling procedure significantly improved rule use, as did displaying the pictures during training. (It was found that modeling-only children showed evidence of both learning and transfer with and without the translation sentence prop.)

Malouf and Dodd (1972) also confirmed that quite young children could learn an arbitrary grammatical rule, one that was artificial, but neither violated nor contravened their more usual language experiences. Malouf and Dodd compared *exposure* (observation without practice) with *expansion* (presenting only visual cues first, with subsequent practice, and then auditory cues), using first-grade children and an ingenious cartoon animal, the *wug*. The youngsters had to learn to associate English adjectives with various features of the wug's appearance. The visual stimuli contained combinations of attributes relating to the wug's body surface (furry, spotted, or striped), limbs (booted, finned, or whiskery), and antennae (curly, horned, or rounded). These visual cues were coordinated with recordings of spoken sentences describing the particular composite of visual characteristics, e.g., a spotted whiskery wug. The sentences always fit the rule that adjectives about body covering should be placed first, about limbs next, and about antennae last. Two of the three serial positions were included in each training sentence, and then the child was tested to see if he maintained the correct order when all three attributes had to be arranged in sequence.

Training was conducted either by exposure (pictures and sentences jointly presented without the child responding overtly), imitation (stimuli presented as above while the child also described the wug aloud), or expansion (the child saw the picture, gave an oral description of it, and then heard the corresponding sentence). An untrained control group was shown all of the pictorial stimuli, but neither received sentence descriptions nor was asked to characterize the pictures.

The untrained controls made significantly more errors than the children in any of the experimental groups. The exposure ("pure" modeling) group showed definite rule learning, but did not perform as well as the observation plus practice children. There were no significant differences between the "imitation" and "expansion" techniques, although expansion tended to create weaker performance. Of greater concern is Malouf and Dodd's (1972) evidence that all three modeling variants successfully taught quite young children a novel and arbitrary grammatical rule. The possibility was thus raised that, in the research discussed earlier (Odom *et al.*, 1968; Liebert *et al.*, 1969b) younger children's difficulties may have been less due to the arbitrary form of the inverted prepositions, than to the fact that inversion violated a rather familiar usage norm. Natural prepositional phrases would normally be encountered by the children, and exemplified by many adults. Ordinarily, adults might be expected to censure and correct departures from normative usage by school-age children. In contrast, older subjects would be better able to flexibly adhere to or depart from the usual phrase form to meet situational social demands, like those in an experiment or game. As was previously proposed, younger children, who were presumably less cynical about adults' inconsistencies, may have been thrown off course when the adult model created inverted phrases. Also recall that in the Vasta and Liebert (1973) study, first-graders discriminated inverted and normal phrases equally well, when tested with a recognition task.

In most of the preceding research, the children were measured on imitative syntactic productions. Transfer of natural linguistic constructions to entirely new stimuli was not directly assessed. Thus, Carroll *et al.* (1972) studied adoption of a model's sentence pattern, verb tense, and word content in a design that enabled the generalization effects for the sentence and verb forms to be separately measured. They used third and fourth graders who were economically disadvantaged, primarily Mexican-Americans.

During the baseline test, each child was shown pictures mounted on cards and, in the guise of a game, was asked to make up a sentence for each. After baseline was established, the experimental groups observed an adult model orally create a sentence for each card. Children were told to watch and listen carefully to the model's sentences, and to try and figure out in what way they were the same. The youngsters, however, were not directed to emulate the model's utterances. After modeling, the stimuli were presented again, and the children's sentences were recorded; this comprised the imitation phase. Finally, with no further training, new pictures were introduced and the child's sentence productions served to measure generalization.

In each experimental variant, the model's sentences followed a structural pattern of noun subject, auxiliary plus transitive main verb, plus noun object. Three tense constructions were studied. In the present condition, the present progressive tense was always modeled, e.g., *The hunter* ***is aiming*** *the bow*. In the past condition, the imperfect tense was modeled, e.g., ***was aiming.*** In the future condition, the simple future tense was used, e.g., ***will aim.*** Except for these changes in tense, the modeled sentences were identical, and only contained instances of the desired ("correct") structure and tense forms. In each tense variation, half of the children received a verbal prompting before the imitation phase test. In the present tense condition, the children were asked to tell *what* ***is happening*** *in each picture;* in the past condition, *what* ***was happening;*** and in the future condition, *what* ***will happen.***

In the present tense variation, relative to untrained controls, modeling established significant increases over baseline for all three (sentence structure, tense, and word content) response measures. There were no differences between prompted and unprompted modeling groups. In the past variation, the results, while basically similar, were generally more pronounced. On all response measures, modeling children surpassed their own baselines and the performance changes of the control group, but prompted and unprompted children did not differ. In the future variation, there were again significant across-phase changes, with the modeling children superior to control children on all dependent measures. Here, where the future construction was relatively rare, prompting improved tense performance, but aided the modeling subjects more than the controls.

These results illustrate the responsiveness of rather elaborate syntactical features, presented simultaneously within sentences, to brief modeling displays. Systematic changes were made despite a complete absence of explicit rewards to either child or model. In several categories, there was clear generalization of the grammatical rules to new stimuli without any additional training. The data suggest that a social learning approach can contribute to an understanding of how language behavior is modified. As well, modeling variables may help to explicate such extralinguistic determinants of language performance as the affective relationship between children and tutelary social agents, the discriminability of selected language features, the strengthening or alteration of the personal language rules that the child may already possess, and the encoding variables concerning the formats and media properties of diverse methods for transmitting language.

Rosenthal and Whitebook (1970) replicated some main features of the foregoing experiment. They were concerned with the effectiveness of weaker directions plus a promised money reward relative to stronger directions with no offer of incentive. They also wanted to show that when the experimenter served as her own model the results would be similar to those obtained when the roles of experimenter and model were occupied by different persons. They used the same stimuli and basic procedures as before, but confined tense modeling to past ("was aiming") constructions. The subjects were third- and fourth-graders. After the baseline was established, the *weak instructions plus money* modeling group was directed as follows:

> I want you to watch and listen carefully to my sentences and learn as much as you can. Later, you will have another turn and, if you do a good job when it is your turn, I will give you a dime at the end of the game.

In the *specific instructions no money* treatment, incentives were not mentioned, and the child was told:

> I want you to watch and listen carefully to my sentences and learn my sentences as well as you can. Later, you will have another turn, and I will want to see just how close to my sentences you can come when it is your turn. If you can, copy my sentences perfectly.

Notice that the specific instructions group was openly urged to reproduce the modeled sentences if possible. The experimenter-model then proceeded identically for both groups, supplying the same sentences as in the earlier study, but casting all verbs in the past progressive tense, e.g., *The tiger was watching the deer.* After this training exposure, all modeling children again responded to the first set of pictures and then, without further guidance, to the new generalization stimuli.

During the imitation phase, in both modeling treatments, the children significantly surpassed their baseline scores on each dependent grammatical class: sentence structure, verb tense, and word content. The alternative modeling subjects performed comparably on both the tense and structure measures, but the specific instructions children more closely reproduced the model's word content. During generalization, each experimental group again surpassed its baseline means for structure and tense, with negligible differences among the modeling variations. In contrast, the control children showed no evidence of changing grammatical usage between the baseline and generalization phases. These results, with the experimenter serving as her own model, were in striking numerical agreement with the data obtained from the corresponding conditions of the Carroll *et al.* (1972) study. Of greater importance was the fact that instructions urging reiteration of the model's *sentences* affected only word choices, and not the more generic structure or tense features. The promise of a money incentive had no discernible effects on either reproduction or transfer of the modeled language parameters, as compared with the earlier experiment, in which no incentives were offered.

Rosenthal and Carroll (1972) set out to further investigate the roles of instructional and incentive information, as well as their placement in a time sequence. They selected a much more difficult sentence pattern and verb tense and used older, economically disadvantaged, seventh graders. Since in all of the prior research on natural syntactical constructions, children were studied individually, and the results were based on spoken responses, it was decided to conduct this experiment under background circumstances more similar to typical classrooms. For a baseline, groups of children were given mimeographed word lists that were arranged in alphabetical order for word classes of articles, connectives, nouns, pronouns, and verbs. The children were directed to "make up 12 sentences using the words on the list" and to neatly print them on response sheets. The experimenter gave instructions and introduced the model, who displayed complicated sentences using the same word list the children had used for baseline. Afterward, the word lists and new response sheets were supplied and the children wrote their imitation phase sentences as before. The model's sentences were complex in structure and contained the past perfect verb form. For example, *When the rocket had reached the moon, the crew explored the surface* and *Since the sun had melted the snow, the gardener planted the flowers*. The experiment compared boys and girls on the effects of stronger or weaker instructions, the offer or nonoffer of a large reward for the best performance, and the sequence of positioning this information either before or after the model's demonstrations.

The *strong* instructions drew attention to the model's sentences, and, noting that all had two parts and involved past action, requested the children to try and emulate his sentences. In the *weak* instructions condition, the children were only told to watch the model and play the game. As a concession to economic inflation, quite a tempting reward was invoked. Children in the *incentive* condition were promised a party during school time with $20 provided for treats if they did well as a group. The *no incentive* group was told nothing. The *before-modeling* information sequence presented the relevant combination of incentive and instructional data immediately prior to the model's sentence demonstrations, while the *after-modeling* sequence was given directly after the sentence demonstrations. At this point, before moving on to the results, the reader is invited to ponder what he or she thinks will be the effect of the before- versus after-modeling information variations, and to jot on a piece of paper his hunches and predictions about how the alternative sequences might affect the children's grammatical output.

The combined modeling children far surpassed a control group in producing the complex sentence and pluperfect tense constructions. It was evident that observing the model was very effective in altering the children's use of the two grammatical forms studied. On both dependent measures, the strong instructions children scored higher than the weak, and boys outperformed girls. Promising or omitting the very substantial incentive had no effect, for either response measure, on the children's syntactical output, which was consistent with prior results using smaller, dime rewards (Rosenthal & Whitebook, 1970).

The sequence of introducing information, before or after the model performed, also had no discernable effects. Since 180 children were studied, this seems important. First, consider what is intuitively plausible (consulting your jotted prediction slip if appropriate). Does it not seem that with the stronger orienting instructions, when a large reward was also offered for good performance, and especially because both were given conjointly, that the sequence presenting the information before the model performed should be better than giving the same information afterward? One might look to primacy effects, or to the dominance of a prior set that qualifies the interpretation and integration of subsequent material (e.g., Hovland & Pritzker, 1957). Or one might advance the intuitive premise that, for example, if I know that I should notice how the model's sentences are organized, that is, if we do the best job, we get a party. I will strive harder to attend to, and utilize, whatever the model shows me. In contrast, if I do not learn about the incentive contingencies, and what to look for in modeled sentences until after the model performs, I'm stuck with whatever happens to have lodged in my memory. Indeed, at the end of the experiment, numbers of children in the after-modeling group spontaneously complained, protesting that they should have been told about the party before the man showed them his sentences. Nevertheless, the after sequence performed as well as the before condition, and there were no interactions among any of the variables studied.

What makes this result so intriguing is Bandura's (1969a, 1977b) theory of vicarious acquisition processes. He assumes that observational exposure to short-run perceptual inputs creates relatively enduring, retrievable images of the modeled activities. Later, the symbolic mediators so developed serve as guides for overtly reproducing matching responses. In the present case, stronger and weaker instructional sets did affect performance. The children's capacity to store and retrieve the model's complicated sentence rubrics had to be very robust to overcome the positioning differences between the before and after sequences. From these results, from the nonsignificant results in the Malouf and Dodd (1972) experiment, i.e., between standard and interference intertrial formats, and from other data yet to be discussed, it would seem that human symbolic storage capacities are quite stable over time. This stability would support a theoretical basis for human information-processing that does not require precise temporal positioning, or simplistic linear stimulus–response units, in the apprehension, coding, and maintenance of abstract information.

The practical implications of the complex sentences study must also be mentioned: Modeling procedures effectively stimulated the production of quite sophisticated language constructions under classroomlike conditions. The results were obtained from children whose economic backgrounds were disadvantaged. For many of them, Spanish was the language first learned and was typically spoken at home (as was the case with the Carroll *et al.* [1972] sample). Yet, the offer of a quite tantalizing incentive for good performance added no measurable gain to the attention-compelling information that was present in both the schoollike learning setting and the modeling display. In contrast, orienting the students about how to proceed, and providing cues about what to discriminate in the model's sentences, had a clearly facilitating effect on imitative language performance.

There is research indicating that social incentives such as praise play a rather minor part in language learning. Clinton and Boyce (1975) compared the effects of *informative* feedback, in which the experimenter cued the child to the accuracy of his response, with *incentive* feedback, in which the experimenter gave positive comments for correct responses. The task was to teach 7- to 10-year-old normal and retarded children to use plurals generatively. It was hypothesized that retardates would be more influenced by praise. Feedback improved language learning, but praise did not augment knowledge of results, even for the retarded group. These results are consistent with Bandura's (1969a, 1977b) view that the incentive dimension of reinforcement does little to assist learning, but instead affects performance.

Harris and Hassemer (1972) investigated the effects of modeling on the length and complexity of a child's sentences in a situation that minimized any implication that the model's sentences were desirable or should be emulated. They also studied the effects of language background by comparing English-speaking children who heard English sentences with children bilingual in English and Spanish who heard the sentences cast in either of the two languages.

During the baseline, the child constructed sentences for a series of picture cards. The child then produced sentences to the cards, taking turns with an adult model. The adult modeled either simple one-clause sentences or complex two-clause sentences, using Spanish with bilingual children in one condition, and English for both others (bilingual or English backgrounds). Within each condition, the model began with complex sentences for half of the children. Then some conversation with the child was interposed, after which sentence alternation continued but the model switched to demonstrating simpler sentences. For the remaining subjects, simpler sentences were modeled first and more complex constructions afterward.

The modeled verbal expressions influenced the children's utterances. Sentences produced during the complex phase contained more words than either in baseline or during simple sentence modeling. Complex modeling led to more sentences containing prepositional phrases and complex clauses, as well as fewer simple sentences and sentence fragments, than were produced during baseline or simple sentence modeling. The complex-first modeling sequence sponsored somewhat longer sentences than did the reverse order. Fourth-graders created longer sentences than second-graders; this grade difference was the sharpest for the bilingual children who were addressed in Spanish, with smaller grade differences elsewhere.

Thus, receiving neither external reinforcement nor instructional cues to invite emulation of the model, the children produced sentences that reflected the length and complexity of the modeled exemplars. The first sentences modeled seemed to create a kind of primacy effect, affecting children more than the second set of sentences. Although older children produced wordier sentences, there were no differences between grade levels or sexes in the structural complexity of sentences. And, perhaps of greatest pedagogical interest, the bilingual children's response to modeling was comparable to that shown by the monolingual children, regardless of whether the bilinguals observed a modeled use of Spanish or English.

In a recent study of vicarious influences on language patterns, Harris and Siebel (1976) presented to fifth- and sixth-graders an audiotape of a model's reactions to a series of pictures. All of the modeled sentences contained conditional clauses, animal names, and three adjectives. The children were subsequently asked to compose sentences to the same (imitation) and to new pictures (generalization). As before, no directions were given to emulate the model's performance. Compared to the responses of no-model controls, youngsters who heard the model produced significantly more conditional clauses in both imitation and generalization. They used more animal names and wrote longer sentences during imitation. Girls tended to be more affected by the modeling experience than boys, using significantly longer sentences and more conditionals in both postmodeling tests. It is well accepted that girls show more verbal facility than boys; thus, these data reveal that individual differences in language skill will affect children's reactions to a model's performance.

Social learning psychologists have recently begun to examine the effects of modeling on children's language comprehension. Brown (1976) found that young children who had little or no understanding of passive constructions acquired this rule via modeling. The gains in verbal modeling depended on the referential context in which a sentence occurred. In the strongest condition, a model enacted passive sentences while speaking them. In a substantially less effective condition, the experimenter showed pictures to the children as each sentence was modeled. In the weakest condition, passive sentences were verbally modeled without any referential aids. Brown suggested that the superiority of the enactive modeling procedure was based on its informativeness. If learning to understand the passive voice involved decoding the agent–object relationship, then overt demonstration of this relationship should prove optimal.

In sum, virtually all of the dimensions of children's speech studied to date have shown systematic changes resulting from modeling exposures. Included are passive verb constructions, prepositions, sentence structure, sentence length, and word content. These results seem generally compatible with psycholinguistic theory, although not readily predicted from it. Psycholinguists believe that the dimensions of syntax influenced in these studies have already been acquired by children of these ages. They would view such results as changes in *performance,* not competence; they allow that experience can affect performance. But Brown's (1976) recent study indicated that modeling also affects a child's basic competence or comprehension. In this study, children who showed no comprehension of a language rule were able to induce it from a model's performance. This vicarious learning process occurred when both the passive sentence and its nonverbal meaning were simultaneously demonstrated. It appears that the relative inability of modeling procedures to produce the language rule learning seen in some studies, such as those by Liebert and colleagues, may be attributable to the failure to demonstrate language in a fully meaningful referential context. The importance of the referential context in language learning is consonant with the emphases of many psycholinguistic scholars, such as Macnamara, who also spurn maturational explanations of language development.

THE OPERANT APPROACH

As was outlined in Chapter 1, operant and social learning approaches differ in both procedure and theoretical assumptions. In operant studies, speech patterns are usually modeled *after* a child fails to perform properly. Rewards for each correct response are presented immediately. Thus, both performance and reinforcement accompany a model's utterances. Language learning is assumed to be initiated by the reinforcing stimulus rather than by the modeling stimulus. Because single subject designs are typical, imitative learning treatments are adapted to the individual child studied. In contrast, social learning studies most often use group designs with treatment procedures specified a priori, and not tailored to specific individuals for research purposes. These group designs usually present the model depicting a relatively long series of responses before observers are asked to perform. This strategy was intended to assist the child in abstracting language rules without performance distractions between items, since learning is assumed to result from cognitive transforms of modeled information. Although considered inessential for learning, overt copying and rewards may assist the child to display knowledge in overt performance. In contrast to some psycholinguistic theories, both operant and social learning positions believe that language is learned from experience and does not arise via maturation; these approaches diverge, however, as to whether cognitive acts or reinforcement are required for acquisition.

Operant researchers have successfully taught a variety of generalized language forms via modeling and reinforcement techniques. This work has usually involved single-case designs in which very young or atypical children (often mentally retarded) learn to use linguistic rules. Methodologically, the emphasis has been on shaping the child's approximations to the model's language responses, with the gradual elimination of the model as a prompter, once the child can accurately produce rule-consistent statements. Operant researchers have stressed the need for reinforcement in conjunction with modeling.

In one such study, Guess *et al.* (1968) taught a 10-year-old retarded girl to use singular and plural morphemes appropriately. The girl was initially nonverbal; however, before the start of the research, she was taught to imitate vocal stimuli, and had developed a small repertoire of single words and simple phrases.

For a baseline, the child was asked to name common objects when they were presented alone or in pairs. Training was then initiated in three stages. First, the child was shown an object and asked to name it.

If she labeled the object falsely or failed to respond, the experimenter named (modeled) the stimulus, withdrew it for a brief period of time, and then reintroduced it. This procedure was repeated until the child labeled the object properly. Next, in stage two, the same procedure was followed with pairs of stimulus objects, but the girl was now required to give a plural response in order to be reinforced. As before, the experimenter modeled correct plural labels if the child responded improperly. Finally, in the third stage, a random sequence, consisting of single objects and pairs of stimuli, was presented, with reinforcement contingent upon appropriate labeling behavior. The experimenter supplied the correct verbal labels whenever the child erred. To establish the functional effectiveness of the training procedures, an experimental reversal was performed, during which plural responses were modeled and reinforced to single objects, and vice versa. This reversal test clearly eliminated maturation or general experience as explanations of the girl's progress, and disclosed that language output depended on the training contingencies.

Evidence from a variety of sources confirmed that the child had acquired a generalized syntactic rule: (*a*) During the second experimental stage, she was able to supply plural labels "spontaneously," unaided by modeling prompts. After the third pair of stimuli was presented, the girl correctly displayed pluralization and maintained proper usage for all succeeding pairs without having plurals modeled for her. (*b*) During the latter part of the study, the girl used the plural morpheme correctly when presented with three objects instead of the usual pair. (*c*) Generalization of plural skills was noted for words requiring irregular plural labels. For example, when shown a picture of two men, the subject responded *mans* rather than *men*, a response hardly expected from what she was typically exposed to outside the experimental setting. From data such as this instance of misapplied rule generalization, we earlier suggested that the "novel" mistakes of children may result from their attempts to transfer vicariously acquired rules to particular instances that fall outside the rule's boundaries. Whether for pluralization, syntactical word order, or tense, such misapplication of rules can explain how a child displays linguistic constructions that he never directly observed without recourse to any assumptions about innately determined language structures. (*d*) During the reversal, items for which the girl was trained to give plurals now required singulars. She was then retrained to give correct labels. After retraining, the reversal objects were again introduced and the girl then gave correct plurals consistent with the generalization hypothesis and contrary to her prior experimental experience with the particular stimulus objects. Thus, the researchers appeared successful in teaching the retarded girl to use a generalized plural morpheme rule, a skill entirely unavailable to her before training. This appeared to constitute *de nouveau* acquisition of a syntactic rule, an accomplishment attributable to a model's demonstrations and delivery of contingent reinforcement to the child. Taken together with the Kossuth (1972) and Malouf and Dodd (1972) experiments, the acquisition of different linguistic rules via modeling would therefore seem to be confirmed under laboratory conditions.

In the previous study, modeling and reinforcement were used conjointly to teach the child the singular–plural grammatical rule. However, in more recent research, there has been an attempt to distinguish the effects of these factors. Garcia, Guess, and Byrnes (1973) taught a 10-year-old retardate to respond in singular and plural declarative sentences. The experimenter first presented one or more objects to one adult model who composed a sentence in either the singular or plural form. The child was then queried and reinforced with candy and praise if she imitated accurately. Probes were interspersed among training trials. In separate phases, the child learned to use the singular and then the plural forms generatively. In an effort to separate the effects of reinforcement from modeling, two models were introduced, one who responded only on singular items, while the other modeled only plural items. During successive phases, reinforcement was contingent for only one model's responses. In general, the child imitated only the responses of the model who was reinforced, and these effects extended to nonmodeled items. However, after a reversal was performed, the experimenters were unable to recover near-perfect response levels, despite a large number of training trials. This finding indicates that once a plural rule was learned, reinforcment alone did not determine language performance.

Another natural syntactical construction that has been instated is verb tense. Schumaker and Sherman (1970) found modeling and reinforcement procedures to be successful in teaching past and present verb tenses to two retarded children who had initially displayed little or no evidence of using appropriate past tense forms in their speech. Three types of regular endings, or inflections, can be added to verb stems to denote the past tense: /-t/, /-d/, or /-ed/. Verb stems that end in voiced phonemes usually require the /-d/ inflection, for example, *climbed, played,* or *smiled.* Verb stems ending in either the /-d/ or /-t/ sounds require an /-ed/ inflection, for example, *graded* and *welded,* or *painted* and *taunted.* For experimental purposes, the /-ded/ and /-ted/ endings were separated to distinguish four different inflections: /-d/, /-t/, /-ded/, and /-ted/. In addition, the /-ing/ ending was used to produce present progessive verb constructions. Since the /-ing/, ending remains identical for all verb stems, four classes of present tense verbs were arbitrarily designated to correspond to the four classes of past inflections.

Schumaker and Sherman (1970) imposed two different experimental paradigms, training and probe. *Training* sessions were conducted by prompting the child as follows: *Now the man is painting. Yesterday he . . .?* or *Yesterday the man painted. Now he is . . .?* When the child erred or failed to respond, the experimenter provided the correct verb tense. Accurate responses were reinforced by praise and by dispensing tokens, which were exchangeable for toys or candy. A *probe* session was begun once the child had correctly produced both the present and past tense forms on successive trials without the modeling prompt. The probe sessions were designed to assess tense generalization to verbs not presented during training. In addition, some training words were interspersed among novel, untrained verbs whose stems required all four types of past tense inflection. Correct responses were reinforced as during training.

A multiple-baseline design was followed, and the different past tense forms were introduced successively. In the first phase, training was confined to one verb class; probe sessions then tested generalization to novel verbs from all four stem classes. Then, another class of verbs was trained and probe tested. Finally, a discrimination between the previously-trained verb classes was taught. The child's ability to keep the alternate classes separate was assessed in later probe sessions. The results showed that correct tense responses were performed to unfamiliar words drawn from the stem class of verbs undergoing training.

An interesting *overgeneralization* effect was observed after the teaching of the second stem class. The child responded to unfamiliar stimuli consistent with the inflection currently being taught and showed no evidence of having learned the preceding verb class. For example, the child was first trained with stems taking a /-ted/ ending. Later, when practice began on the /-t/ endings, the /-ted/ responses dropped to baseline levels. However, this faulty excessive transfer of /-t/ endings was rectified during discrimination training. Thus, overgeneralizations resulting from separate sequential presentation of each response class could be corrected by concurrent practice with two or more verb classes. These results were replicated in a study with a second child who was treated in identical fashion.

Clark, Sherman, and Kelley (1971) have found modeling and reinforcement effective in teaching past, present, and future tense rules. They studied eight retarded and four disadvantaged youngsters; all had failed to attain appropriate control over tense rubrics or to use noun suffixes. The children were otherwise able to adequately articulate and imitate verbal stimuli. For a baseline test, the experimenter pointed at a stimulus noun and said: *He is a baker. What did he do yesterday?* If the child responded with a past tense verb form, he was credited with a correct response. All the noun stems could take an ending to form the past tense verb, e.g., baked. Items assessing the child's control over the present (e.g., *He is a baker. What is his job?*) and future (e.g., *He is a baker. What will he do tomorrow?*) tenses were similarly measured. After baseline, training began with one verb category. The experimenter modeled each answer and the child was reinforced (with praise and consumables) only when he imitated all of the modeled words. Once the child could reliably duplicate single words, longer phrases were modeled, until complete responses were successfully reproduced. The experimenter then began to gradually eliminate (*fade out*) his display of the desired responses by making his words softer (lower amplitude), starting with the last parts of each sentence. In a manner that was much like the Cheshire cat's gradual disappearance, the experimenter continued removing verbal cues until all of his words had been eliminated and the child could verbalize adequately without modeling prompts.

Training involved a multiple-baseline design, and practice on each tense category was followed by probe sessions. As expected, instatement of the first tense class only influenced items requiring that verb ending but not the other syntactical classes. When training on the second class of verbs began, use of the first tense rule reverted to baseline frequency, just as in the prior study by Schumaker and Sherman (1970). However, subsequent discrimination practice, with both verb tenses presented in a mixed sequential order, once again corrected this overgeneralization. Training on the third tense also brought some decrease in accurate use of the two other tenses, but when discrimination training involved concurrent presentation of all three verb forms, the attenuation in rule use was again removed.

Using the same general reinforced modeling training paradigm, Clark and Sherman (1975) taught three retarded adolescents and four disadvantaged 3- and 4-year-olds to use the past, present progressive, and future verb tenses. All children could generalize the verb tense response to new stimuli. Some degree of overgeneralization was again noted as the second and third tenses were learned. As in previous research, this inaccurate transfer was corrected by discrimination training in which verb tenses were presented together in a mixed sequential order.

During the initial stages of training, *overgeneralization* of the syntactical rules was evident in all of the above studies. The latter three cases showed that introducing a new tense decreased the use of previously trained tenses. That is, transfer of the new rules was indiscriminate and extended to items requiring already-trained syntactic classes. In the Guess *et al.* (1968) study, the girl incorrectly applied the plural morpheme rule by adding an /-s/ to an irregular stem such as *mans* for *men*. As earlier noted, it has been argued by psycholinguists (e.g., Slobin, 1968) that children cannot acquire language, especially syntax, via modeling or "imitation." This position emphasizes that children display certain rule-consistent constructions that depart from the norms of English language use. Hence, such examples were probably never or quite rarely modeled for the child, for example, the use of *eated* instead of *ate*. The preceding evidence helps to support our suggestion that such deviant utterances might well be incomplete or inappropriate generalizations of language rules. Data to be discussed later clearly confirm that children can induce common governing rules from specific instances they observe, and can transfer such symbolic principles to new stimulus events without further training. It seems hardly amazing that when he is given considerable exposure to regular verbs that form the past tense by adding the /-ed/ inflection, a child should misapply the rule to verbs taking irregular endings. Thus, even if the child has never himself witnessed the use of *eated* he has observed *killed, pushed, marked, played,* etc., and may thus misconnect the /-ed/ past ending to *eat, run, bring,* and to other verb stems for which it is not legitimately grammatical. It further appears that such overgeneralization of a syntactical rule can be corrected by appropriate direct discrimination training and perhaps also by vicarious discrimination displays. The parallelism between the results of the three previous experiments and the data based on naturalistic observation of children's language behavior appears to lend additional weight to the social learning interpretation advanced here.

Recall that psycholinguists distinguish between *comprehension,* or unspoken reactions to language stimuli, and production, or actual overt speech. The plausible contributions of "imitation" have often been discussed and debated with regard to language production. Until recently, little attention had been directed to vicarious influences on children's comprehension of language. Guess (1969) studied the effectiveness of modeling plus reinforcement in teaching a discrimination between the /-s/ and /-z/ plural sounds to two retardates, both 13 years old. Initially, the adolescents were trained to respond nonverbally to orally presented stimuli. They learned to point to a single object (e.g., a cup) when the experimenter gave the singular form of the word, and to multiple stimuli when given the plural form (e.g., *cups*). This newly acquired symbolic facility did not transfer to the child's overt verbalizations. A reversal was successfully performed, in which the youngsters were taught to point to multiple stimuli when given a singular noun, and vice versa. It thus appeared that adequate verbal comprehension did not directly enable outward expression to show that syntactic elements are recognized. Given the rather large difference between the two response modalities, this finding is hardly surprising.

There is some evidence to suggest that these response classes are not independent. Mann and Baer (1971) found a relationship between comprehension and production in children's learning to associate nonsense syllable labels with unfamiliar objects. Two normal 4-year-olds were trained to point at stimulus objects when nonsense syllables were orally spoken. The youngsters were then taught to name these and other stimuli via modeling and reinforcement. The children's imitative utterances were tape-recorded and then coded for accuracy in a blind judgment procedure. The words that were subjects of comprehension training were imitated more closely than unfamiliar control words. Mann and Baer interpreted their results in accordance with a stimulus control hypothesis: Through comprehension training, overt verbal stimuli were discriminated and were thus copied better than control words later on.

However, in a recent study by Baer and colleagues, much less transfer between comprehension and production language modalities was observed. Guess and Baer (1973) studied language learning by four severely retarded boys who ranged in age from 11 to 21 years. The purpose of the study was to determine transfer from the receptive to the productive mode of plural morpheme usage. A complex design was used, in which the subjects were taught in one modality and were tested with probe items in the other. All boys showed generalization to novel items within the language modality being trained, but only one of the four subjects showed transfer to the opposite modality. Two of the boys showed partial transfer. Subsequent training for the three subjects who failed to spontaneously transfer effectively instated the response in the other modality.

Considering this study along with that of Mann and Baer, it appears that severely retarded subjects cannot spontaneously generalize from one modality to another as easily as children of normal intelligence. It is clear, however, that severe retardates can learn and generatively apply grammatical rules from modeling. Although these data are not conclusive, we will later discuss some definitive research conducted with young normal children, showing that acquisition of comprehension skills does indeed affect production. When taken together, such evidence might offer a partial explanation for a child's rapid acquisition of productive speech, a fact often cited by psycholinguists to support an assumption of innate language structures. And, as already mentioned, it is well established that covert comprehension skills are developed before the child displays his knowledge in overt speech. Since comprehension has been found to facilitate language production, rapid acquisition of productive speech can be expected once the child is capable of articulating sounds fluently. In other words, once a covert repertoire of verbal labeling and identification skills has been established, it should be easier for the child to coordinate these stored discriminations with overt language production. Typically, even when adults with well-established repertoires learn a *new* language, they find it easier to translate from the novel symbol system into their more familiar language than to "find" words in the new tongue that express their thoughts. It may take years of practice before the adult can transfer his "passive" comprehension of the newer language into facile, overt production. However, before such a covert repertoire is established, the adult may experience particular difficulty when attempting to directly write or speak the newer language, while he can read it (direction of translation from new to familiar language) with greater ease.

Further, one need not assume that comprehension of language rules is some innate endowment of the human species, even if the capacity to process symbols is part of our genetic legacy. Children learn to abstract such rules by observing the verbal and nonverbal response regularities displayed by adults, and, once learned, these rules may assist in the child's rapid development of overt speech. There is further evidence that vicarious and reinforcement variables can effectively influence comprehension of syntactic rules. Baer and Guess (1971) taught retarded boys (aged 12–13) and a 7-year-old girl to comprehend comparative (*-er*) and superlative (*-est*) adjective suffix endings. The subjects were first trained to point at stimulus pictures by discriminating polarized adjectives (e.g., *big–small*), and then comparatives (e.g., *bigger–smaller*) or superlatives (e.g., *biggest–smallest*) were introduced. Generalization of the adjective rule was found with novel probe items. The children also responded correctly to new composites of training stimuli, discriminating the relative properties of each combination rather than simply choosing the stimulus they had chosen during training. These results argue against views which assume that *discrete* responses are learned.

Lahey (1971) used modeling without contingent reinforcement to teach normal preschool children to use descriptive adjectives. The ten youngsters were first asked to describe the contents of boxes of toys, and the ratio of adjectives to nouns spoken was computed. Then, half of the children were exposed to a model who introduced number and color adjectives to describe the stimuli. The remaining five children observed the model name the toys without describing them. A marked increase in the incidence of descriptive adjectives, relative to the use of nouns, was found for the youngsters who witnessed the adjective-using modeling display. This changed pattern was maintained throughout three modeling and testing sessions, while the rate of adjective use by control children did not improve over baseline levels. Unfortunately, transfer of the altered style of description was not assessed. However, generalization of an adjective rule was demonstrated in a recent training study. Martin (1975) used modeling and reinforcement to teach this grammatical structure to two retarded children, a girl aged 6 and a boy aged 8. The youngsters learned to use size and color adjectives to describe animal pictures. Transfer of this linguistic skill to new pictures, to a new experimental setting, and even to a new examiner was noted.

Operant researchers have also modified the use of prepositions by modeling and reinforcement. Sailor and Taman (1972) studied the target constructions *in* and *on,* working with three autistic children whose language skills were impoverished. For two of the children, the same stimulus objects were initially exposed together with both prepositions. Later, the objects given in conjunction with *on* were changed from the materials that accompanied *in*. The third child received the reverse sequence, i.e., separate objects first differentiating the prepositions, with signals then being crossed by supplying the same objects for both prepositions. It was found that accurate use of prepositions only occurred when accompanied by demarcated objects. Under such conditions, practice appeared to improve performance when object–preposition pairings were confounded. However, there is reason to question whether a generalized rule was actually learned, since transfer to novel items was not assessed. However, generalization has been found to occur in children's receptive use of prepositions. Frisch and Schumaker (1974) taught three retarded children to respond to the prepositions *next, under,* and *on top of* by placing common objects, i.e., toy dolls and animals, in the appropriate relation to one another. The experimental setup was a multiple-baseline design (using probes) to teach each preposition in succession. Modeling and reinforcement procedures successfully instated generalized use of these prepositions with new stimuli. After the second preposition was taught, some degree of over-generalization was noted; however, this was corrected when a discrimination learning phase was inserted, in which the prepositions were presented in an intermixed fashion.

Research stimulated by a variety of theoretical viewpoints has shown that children may only partially imitate an adult's utterances. Incomplete copying is especially likely when the adult makes lengthy or complex statements (Clay, 1971; Lovaas, 1966; McNeill, 1970). For example, Clay (1971) presented sentences that exceeded the child's memory span for discrete words. The child's imitations depended on both the linguistic complexity of the modeled statements, and the subject's own linguistic facility, reflected in terms of age and sociocultural background. Grammatically complex sentences were reduced to simpler forms in the children's reproductions. Generally, psycholinguistic analyses have tended to reveal that imitative errors approach congruence with known grammatical rules. But what determines which segments within modeled utterances will be copied?

Risley and Reynolds (1970) were interested in verbal emphasis as a variable affecting differential imitation. To three disadvantaged 5-year-olds, they presented sentences (typically 8 to 12 words long) that differed in their proportions of emphasized words. The accuracy of copying was not contingently reinforced. Usually, the children only reproduced part of the statements, suggesting that complete recall was not possible. When relatively few words were stressed, so that these could be readily discriminated from the rest of the sentence, the stressed words were the most likely to be copied. Even entire phrases containing the emphasized words were imitated more often. This research raises a host of intriguing possibilities about mothers' differential patterns of emphasis when interacting with children. One might, for example, investigate maternal emphasis as a function of the child's age and the social background of the parent. In this study by Risley and Reynolds (1970), the dependent measure was sentence reproduction. It also would be interesting to pursue the modeling effects of emphasis on comprehension. Psycholinguistic research on phrase markers bears on this issue, assuming that emphasis and pauses are interrelated in natural speech. For example, the sentence *The President likes fighting wars* can be interpreted quite differently depending on whether *likes* or *fighting* is stressed, and hence followed by a pause. Although such a relationship seems plausible, the role of verbal emphasis in selectively influencing the comprehension of child listeners has not, to our knowledge, yet been addressed by researchers. Similarly, adult gestural cues (smiles, frowns, comforting, or abrupt motions) may qualify the impact of particular content categories favored or disliked by the speaker.

Wheeler and Sulzer (1970) helped an autistic and retarded 8-year-old speak in complete sentences. Initially, the child's English was "telegraphic," in that his sentences lacked most articles and auxiliary verbs. During training, he was given pictures and asked to describe them. If he failed to produce a complete sentence containing verbs and articles, the model would verbalize all or appropriate portions of the sentence for the child to imitate. When the child copied correctly, the next picture was introduced. These procedures were effective in teaching the child to use more nearly complete sentences, without further prompting by the model, both for the training and for the novel, untrained, stimulus pictures. Reversal again led to the production of more telegraphic utterances. A return to the former contingencies reestablished more nearly complete sentences.

Garcia (1974) taught two adolescent retardates who had very limited speech skills to respond to three simple questions. The children were shown a picture depicting common objects and were asked, "What is that?" The children learned to respond, "It's a [object name]." In response to the experimenter's second question, "This is a [object's name], what do you see?" the children were taught to answer, "It's a [object's name]." In response to the experimenter's third question, "Do you want the [object's name]?" the children learned to say, "Yes I do." Generalization of the question-answering responses to new stimuli and a new experimenter was assessed. These youngsters could transfer the question-answering responses to novel pictures when the latter were interspersed among pictures used during training. However, the response did *not* generalize to a new experimenter when he was introduced. As a result, the second experimenter reinstituted training and again successfully elicited proper question-answering. When a third experimenter was subsequently introduced, the response did generalize. These data indicated that if broad generalization to unfamiliar people is desired, several social agents should conduct training.

Fygetakis and Gray (1970) used modeling and reinforcement to instate use of the verb *is* with aphasic children, who had failed to make either descriptive or interrogative sentences containing *is* during a baseline "show and tell" game. In this study, the children were exposed to a model who progressively demonstrated portions of a sentence, and then complete sentences, for the child to copy. Finally, the child was required to produce *is* sentences without modeling prompts. Stars, which could later be exchanged for toys, were used as reinforcers. After training, the children exhibited an increased number of *is* questions when reassessed in the "show and tell" game. Similarly, Stevens-Long and Rasmussen (1974) used modeling, reinforcement, and time-out techniques to teach an 8-year-old autistic boy to speak in simple and compound sentences. Initially, his speech consisted of one- and two-word utterances. The child was shown pictures containing at least two actors performing various deeds. These investigators used a combination multiple-baseline and reversal design, in which simple sentences were first taught, extinguished, and then retaught. Finally, compound sentences were taught. The child was subsequently able to generalize his compound sentence formulation skills to novel pictures.

Most of the operant modeling research discussed thus far has either dealt with teaching language skills to mental retardates with limited verbal repertoires, or extending more complex syntactic rules to youngsters who already were able to communicate orally. Very few of these children were less than 4 years old and hence, were past the period during which, according to psycholinguistic accounts, most language is typically acquired. Other research confirms that modeling and reinforcement techniques can also influence the speech patterns of very young, normal children. Hursh and Sherman (1973) studied the effects of parental speech and praise on three toddlers, aged 15–20 months. None of the youngsters displayed an adultlike command of language. From each baby's spontaneous vocalizations, three sounds were selected as target responses. In an initial phase, the sounds were successively modeled and reinforced for the child through a mulitple-baseline procedure. For each class of sounds that was given, increases and decreases in its incidence were noted, when training of that category was respectively initiated and withdrawn. In the next phase of the study, four different combinations of treatments were compared for their effectiveness in modifying classes of sounds: modeling alone; praise alone; praise plus repetition of the baby's vocalization; and modeling plus praise. The amalgam of modeling plus praise was nearly twice as powerful as praise alone. Training by modeling only was moderately effective, but the addition of verbal repetition to praise failed to produce a discernable gain.

Hursh and Sherman (1973) added a fascinating final twist by recruiting three new parents and asking them to increase their child's production of a selected sound. The adults were given no training and were not directed to adopt any particular teaching strategy. Observation of their efforts revealed that the adults "spontaneously" adopted modeling techniques, but they seldom praised their children promptly (within 4 seconds) after a target response was emitted. Consequently, these parents proved less effective than the first set of parents, who were explicitly guided in the use of modeling and reinforcement interventions. Thus, when untrained adults were enjoined to stimulate production of a defined class of sounds, they resorted to extensive modeling, but failed to make any effective use of contingent praise. This experimental evidence indicates that under relatively unstructured conditions parents do readily elect modeling methods to teach their child.

Hursh and Sherman's finding is supported by recent research by

Moerk (1976) on parent–child interchanges. He found that parents actively taught their children using such procedures as didactic modeling, prompting, questioning, informing, answering, labeling, pictorial structuring, and accenting significant grammatical elements. Such evidence helps to bolster the importance and pervasiveness of naturalistic social learning processes in the acquisition of language and other symbolic skills by contemporary children. Other data, from studies that used modeling without incentive techniques, suggest that prolonged verbal demonstrations can promote speech production by very young toddlers (Nelson, Carskaddon, & Bonvillian, 1973). Indeed, Neihardt (1972) offers anecdotal data, suggesting that among the Oglala Sioux, observation was the typical mode for transmitting adult skills to children: "The boys of my people began very young to learn the ways of men, and no one taught us; we just learned by doing what we saw, and we were warriors at a time when boys are now like girls [p. 17]." Correspondingly, Molière's *bourgeois gentilhomme* was astonished to discover that he had been speaking prose all his life. It seems unfortunate that, for some, recognition of the role of social learning in the natural environment would still constitute an analogous revelation. The Hursh and Sherman (1973) study revealed that modeling and reinforcement can effectively modify the frequency of selected sounds already present in the child's vocal repertoire. Additional research suggests that the same techniques can promote learning of new sounds by very young children.

In a complex study on children's imitative acquisition of a grammatical rule, Whitehurst (1972) proposed a stimulus control hypothesis to explain transfer of the rule to novel stimulus instances: "While consequences may produce the motivation necessary to the process of responding, it is the child's attention to a stimulus attribute that allows him to produce new responses that have never been reinforced and that are appropriate [p. 503]." In this design, the learning of an adjective–noun syntactical rule was simulated through the use of nonsense syllables, analogous to such English fragments as *red car, red house,* and *red shirt.* Boys, 22 and 24 months old, both apparently normal and drawn from middle-class homes, served as subjects. For these babies, speech consisted of one-word labels plus a few multiple-word utterances. Each child was asked to name achromatic, free-form shapes with a nonsense syllable, and to label transparent, colored plastic sheets with another nonsense syllable. If the child failed to give a correct response, he was told, "No." The desired nonsense syllable was then modeled for him. Appropriate labeling was reinforced with food and praise. The children were trained to approximate an errorless criterion performance, first with the shape stimulus, then with the color stimulus, and then when the shape and color stimuli were presented on alternate trials. Finally, shape and color cues were simultaneously combined. Generalization was revealed by correct labeling on the first trial with the conjoint stimuli. Transfer of the labeling rule was successful with training sequences in which one color attribute was maintained across stimulus changes in shape. However, when both the color and form characteristics were varied, transfer was impeded. Whitehurst concluded that generalization was controlled by the portion of the stimulus display held constant across occasions, and that when this stimulus element was changed, generalization was impaired. Thus, modeling and reinforcement proved capable of instating a novel, languagelike rule for very young children; transfer was influenced by the stimuli denoting the class boundaries of the labeling rubric.

In further research with the same two boys, Whitehurst (1971) tested whether distinct grammatical sequences can exist as functionally separate response classes. Using free-form shapes and plastic transparencies similar to those just described, the children were taught to name various combinations of three colors and three shapes with six nonsense syllables. For all pairs of stimuli, the correct sequence required the color word first and the shape word second. If the baby erred, the experimenter said "No," and modeled the desired sequence for him. Proper labeling was reinforced with praise and edibles. After the child learned to name stimulus pairs fluently, one dyad was redesignated by a new rule: the original word order was reversed; the phoneme /-a/ was prefixed to the first nonsense syllable; and the phoneme /-e/ was prefixed to the second syllable. Thus, the former utterance *nug jit* became *a* ***jit*** *e* ***nug*** in the new syntax. This switch in grammatical paradigms is similar in pattern to an active-to-passive verb transformation; for example, *The boy lifts it.* would become *It is lifted by the boy*. When the child correctly applied the new syntax to the first (trained) pair of stimuli, he was given the remaining stimulus combinations as probes. This format, i.e., training followed by probe, was continued until both children could successfully manage all probe items. Some generalization (on approximately 25% of the items) was found during the first presentation of the probes. The children eventually attained criterion by following the new syntax for all of the probe stimuli. After criterion was achieved, a reversal was performed by reverting to the prior syntactical criteria. After only one training-probe session, reversal was successfully accomplished. The newer syntax was then reinstated, and the first syntax was then again reintroduced. Throughout all of these transformations, the children changed their verbal responding rapidly and accurately to agree with the syntax that momentarily governed reinforcement. Thus, the sequence of syllables could function as a grammatical rule, with training that was directly applied to one stimulus pair being transferred to other syllable instances. Further, a different ordering of the same components was discriminated as a functionally distinct response class, and even 2-year-old children proved able to shift flexibly between the alternative syntactical criteria in nearly errorless fashion. Whitehurst (1971) concluded that the syntactic properties of language could be taught to very young, essentially preverbal, children, and could be modulated through modeling and reinforcement.

Both of Whitehurst's studies were conducted under laboratory conditions using an artificial language. Although this research revealed the importance of modeling and reinforcement for instating generalized grammatical rules, it was still necessary to demonstrate that such training interventions would promote language acquisition in naturalistic situations. Accordingly, Whitehurst, Novak, and Zorn (1972) studied language development in a boy 3:3 years old who was diagnosed as speech-retarded but who appeared free of physiological impairment. The boy's mother administered training in the evenings, during dinner. Beforehand, the mother-son interaction patterns had been monitored for a month until it was possible to isolate several categories of the mother's behavior as relevant to the child's verbal responses: (*a*) imitative prompts, in which the mother modeled words for the child to emulate; (*b*) questions requiring answers; (*c*) the amount of general conversation; and (*d*) selective attention to the child's words or utterances. From these descriptive data, two categories, frequency of conversation and frequency of imitative prompts, were chosen for experimental study. This controlled research was performed in several steps. In the first, essentially baseline, phase, the mother restricted her conversation to answering the boy's requests *(low conversation)* and did not model new words for him to copy *(low prompts)*. In the two following phases, first *high conversation plus high prompting*, and then *high conversation but low prompting* conditions were established. The baseline, low conversation, low prompting maternal behavior was then reintroduced as an experimental reversal. Next, low conversation was combined with high prompting, and in a final phase, high levels of both conversation and prompting were introduced once more.

The results showed that when both conversation and imitative prompts were infrequent, the boy acquired new words very slowly. When high levels of either conversation or prompts were available, new words were added at a moderate rate. When both conversation and prompting were frequent, the child adopted new words at the fastest rate (6.8 words per session). This pace of new verbal learning at the end of the study contrasted dramatically with the near-zero baseline rate elicited by the mother during her unstructured interactions before the experimental procedures commenced. Further, the terminal rate attained was well above what can be expected for normal children at this age. The reversal abruptly halted the boy's acquisition of new material, and made a maturation or a general experience interpretation of the changes highly implausible. Analysis of the unstructured mother–son interactions provided interesting examples of how well-intentioned parents may fail to promote their children's language progress: The mother's questions did not stimulate the boy's speaking, because her queries were almost always phrased so that they could be answered by a gesture or nonlanguage vocalization, and thus did not require speech from the child. Although the mother directed much attention toward the boy, this did not stimulate new words because she was unselective in her visual reinforcing, and attended equally to nonverbal vocalizations and correct speech. It therefore appeared that parents' undifferentiated, noncontingent attention may do little to foster a child's acquisition of language.

In the main, these results revealed that the rate at which a child learns language can be substantially increased by improving the pattern of maternal interaction during routine daily activities, such as eating. These findings suggested that social learning features of a young child's linguistic environment, such as the frequency of speech displayed by adult models, and the nature of their efforts at eliciting imitative verbalizations, are significant variables that must be given due weight in theoretical explanations of how children come to acquire and use natural language.

Other evidence indicates that modeling and reinforcement procedures can teach syntactic rules to very young children before these structures emerge during normal development. Lutzker and Sherman (1974) studied two youngsters, both 30 months old. Neither child showed any evidence of consistency in subject–verb agreement of the verb *to be* in their spontaneous speech or in their verbal reaction to pictures of one or more stimuli. They were taught (along with three older retardates) to use the verb *is* with singular stimuli and *are* with multiple stimuli. All of the children could generalize the subject–verb agreement rule to novel pictures. The normal 2-year-olds learned this syntactic rule more quickly than the retardates.

In a recent theoretical paper, Whitehurst and Vasta (1975) attempted to reconcile the psycholinguists' objections to an environmental account of children's language acquisition with the existing data on language rule learning reported by social learning and operant psychologists. While ample evidence now appears to indicate that modeling plus reinforcement can create syntactically advanced speech in controlled training studies, there is reason to question whether these same techniques operate in the natural environment. These authors acknowledged that there is little evidence of systematic reinforcement of a child's grammar in studies of normal interactions between a mother and child (e.g., Brown *et al.*, 1969; Nelson, 1973).

Thus, Whitehurst and colleagues sought to determine if modeling alone could create language development. Whitehurst and Novak (1973) studied the relative effectiveness of modeling plus reinforcement for exact imitation of modeled utterances. In this study, four different types of language structures were investigated: participial, prepositional, appositive, and infinitive phrases. These investigators found that only the prepositional and infinitive syntactical structures, which were displayed to some degree during baseline, were influenced by modeling alone. The participial and appositive structures, which were seldom displayed during baseline, were not imitated accurately. These authors hypothesized that if the structure was not already known by the child, modeling alone was ineffective. However, if reinforcement was included with modeling, unfamiliar structures could be learned.

In subsequent research, Whitehurst, Ironsmith, and Goldfein (1974) attempted to test this CIP (comprehension → imitation → production) hypothesis experimentally. They planned (*a*) to demonstrate that 4- and 5-year-old children in their sample would not initially be able to imitate passive sentences, (*b*) to teach children to comprehend passives, and (*c*) to reexpose the children to a modeling experience that was expected to be successful. However, the second modeling phase was omitted when children in the experimental group demonstrated their ability to imitate passives during the first modeling phase. Whitehurst and colleagues found that the group exposed to modeling performed better on a comprehension posttest than did the nonmodeling group. Since comprehension measures were taken after modeling, the scores appear to have been affected by that treatment. Consequently, it cannot be determined from these results whether comprehension was necessary for language acquisition. The fact that comprehension was significantly improved from modeling alone implies that reinforcement is not necessary.

Recent research (Brown, 1976), showing that the referential context of language is a key factor in acquisition of comprehension skills, explains the limitations of modeling in Whitehurst's research. There, static pictures accompanied the model's utterances; however, Brown found such stimuli to be referentially inadequate. Considering all of these studies together, it appears that the additional information afforded by reinforcement can compensate for referentially impoverished modeling displays. Thus, adding rewards may increase the informativeness of the events, rather than fill any fundamental need for reinforcement per se.

From a social learning perspective, both comprehension and imitative performance are viewed as products of observational learning rather than as causally related (Bandura, 1977b). Children can learn to comprehend grammatical rules from referential modeling, and that understanding can aid later imitative performance. The Whitehurst *et al.* (1974) data indicate that reinforced imitations can also assist comprehension. It thus appears that the relationship between comprehension and imitative performance is reciprocal rather than linear. But this is not meant to imply that comprehension will automatically transfer to speech responses, since learning and performance depend on different subprocesses. To facilitate productive use of a rule, children must learn to convert knowledge into appropriate action. Given the importance of reinforcement in promoting overt response, language usage can best be taught using a modeling–performance–corrective feedback procedure.

A social learning account is consistent with psycholinguistic research and emphases. Both positions view comprehension skills as major factors in explaining linguistic competence, and both emphasize the importance of referential context in decoding meaning from modeled language. Finally, both standpoints accept that language is primarily *acquired* without much need for overt practice or social reinforcement. However, social learning theory also accounts for reinforced imitative practice gains in comprehension and language usage. Because of the functional character of a social learning approach, it is uniquely suited for organizing and guiding language instructional programs.

Whitehurst (1977) made a second attempt to experimentally confirm the CIP hypothesis. He studied acquisition of a direct–indirect object sentence rule by six normal 4-year-olds. He expected to find that modeling techniques would not elicit the productive use of a direct–indirect object rule which the children seemed unable to comprehend. Instead, the children proved able to reproduce sentences embodying the structure even though no reinforcement was provided. As a result, plans were altered and a reversal design was adopted in an attempt to impose greater experimental control. In this design, an incorrect direct-indirect object rule was learned in sequence with a correct rule. The sentences were formulated according to a series of pictures, with the referents reversed for incorrect rule statements. The child was first taught to comprehend one rule and, after observing a sequence of modeled examples, was then tested for productive use of the rule. During a second phase, the opposite rule was introduced for comprehension training. Finally, during a third phase, the first rule was presented again. These children were taught to comprehend (nonverbally respond to statements incorporating a rule) by modeling and reinforcement. After comprehension training, five of six youngsters could imitate the structural dimensions of the model's utterances on novel items not demonstrated before. Productive speech responses fluctuated as a function of the type of comprehension training the child received. Thus, it appears that comprehension skills did affect vicarious acquisition of productive speech.

Recent social learning research supports Whitehurst's conclusion that comprehension influences children's emulation of modeled speech. Morgulas and Zimmerman (1977) pretested 4- and 5-year-old children for their comprehension of passive sentences and then exposed them to an adult model who demonstrated that construction. The children were given no instructions to imitate but were simply asked to take turns with the model in composing sentences to picture cards. These youngsters thus performed only with transfer stimuli. A linear relationship was found between the children's comprehension and production of passive sentences, with low comprehenders displaying virtually no imitation of the passive rule structure in their speech.

Some recent normative evidence also suggests that comprehension typically precedes correct reproduction. Bloom, Hood, and Lightbown (1974) studied children while they acquired two-word utterances, and found that only utterances which were understood were imitated. Thus, descriptive data from the natural environment also support the preceding experimental results concerning the role of structural, cognitive factors as requisites for vicarious learning.

It may seem to the reader that Whitehurst's (1977) results conflicted with those of Guess and Baer (1973). However, there was a major procedural difference between these two studies: Unlike Whitehurst's design, Guess and Baer's subjects did not have the structure modeled for them in productive speech before being asked to use it themselves. Taken together, the data may indicate that generalization from comprehension to productive speech is not automatic, but rather requires social demonstrations once utterances are understood.

These results offer some resolution to the controversy regarding the role of imitation in speech development. It has been shown that a child can acquire productive speech from observation alone if he is able to comprehend or discriminate the speech structure. This finding unites the psycholinguists' emphasis (on comprehension preceding production) with the social learning emphasis (on cognition-regulating vicarious inputs). However, consistent with behavioral formulations of language development, it appears that comprehension can be taught. It was trained via modeling and reinforcement in the Whitehurst (1977) study, but was acquired from observation alone in the Whitehurst *et al.* (1974) and Brown (1976) studies.

A final caveat: It cannot be definitively stated that productive use of language cannot to some degree be learned observationally, even if comprehension is negligible. The Whitehurst *et al.* (1974) data are not clear on this point. Since comprehension can be learned from modeling, it seems dubious that there would be no imitative learning with sustained training, even if the CIP hypothesis were true. Nonetheless, there appears to be clear evidence that vicarious learning depends on the conceptual-linguistic rules available to observers. For subjects with very meager symbolic repertoires, reinforcement may be useful to sustain attention to social sources of linguistic information, and to draw attention to critical features of verbal displays.

WORD ASSOCIATES

The preceding studies on language development have mainly addressed the vicarious influences on children's acquisition of grammar. This thrust reflects the research emphases of the last two decades, by developmental psychologists, and by psycholinguists in particular. Undoubtedly the most significant impetus to psycholinguistic research on children's syntactic development was Chomsky's (1957) theory of transformational grammar. Even research on language learning conducted by behavioral psychologists centered on grammar, since a rebuttal of some of the psycholinguistic conclusions was sought. As mentioned earlier, only recently have psychologists begun to vigorously study semantic development in children. It is encouraging that many psycholinguists are giving attention to the environmental context, as well as to structural relationships, in their effort to determine developmental changes in word meaning. We have already cited evidence (Leonard, 1975) that social factors play a prominent role in semantic development. The following studies will illustrate the impact of modeling on an observer's coding of word meaning, in an attempt to explain some of the underlying psychological processes.

Levy (1968) studied a variety of training procedures for stimulating college students to create original word associates. The dependent measure in this study was the number of words that occurred with less than

5% frequency to stimulus words taken from Palermo and Jenkin's (1964) norms. Levy found that a combination of instructions to adopt the role of a "creative person" plus praise for original responses was the most effective. Ninety percent of all responses were original. Praise alone produced 71% originality, while role instructions alone yielded 74% originality. A protocol modeling procedure, in which creative responses were presented on a sheet of paper, produced 64% originality, but 46% of a control group's words were original. Note that for whatever reason, the control group displayed a rather high spontaneous output of these presumably rare responses. Transfer of uncommon usage was measured on a multiple-choice version of the Holtzman inkblots, where the students' selection of atypical (unpopular) percepts constituted "original" answers. On this task, only the role instructions plus praise groups picked more unusual options than the controls. Here then, symbolic modeling through instructions produced generalization of novel responses but the protocol model did not. Analogous results with children on a different task were obtained by Zimmerman and Dialessi (1973). Related research confirms that exposure to a model's spoken responses can substantially affect the adoption and transfer of a number of diverse inkblot percept categories (Rosenthal & Hertz, 1972).

Masters and Branch (1969) conducted two experiments in which instructions, modeling through examples, and social reinforcement were all used to prompt *syntagmatic* word associations, responses that might either plausibly precede or follow the stimuli in a sentence. For example, to the word *Watergate,* the associate *bugging* would be syntagmatic, since it might stand either before (e.g., *They were bugging Watergate*) or after (e.g., *The Watergate bugging made history*) the stimulus in a sentence. Such associations are quite typical for young children but not for older children, or for the adult college students who served as the subjects. The students were shown a word written on a card and were asked to say aloud another word related to the stimulus on the card. Subjects in an instructions group, who were asked to give syntagmatic words, produced the greatest number of these words. Modeling subjects, who had seen examples of syntagmatic responses, gave the second highest number of these words. Reinforcement subjects, who were praised whenever a syntagmatic response occurred, gave the next highest number of them. An originality set group, urged to "be as original as possible," failed to produce significantly more syntagmatic responses than the control group. All other conditions significantly outperformed the controls. On a transfer test, the instructions group showed relatively little transfer, but training through modeled examples and through reinforcement created stronger generalization effects.

These results suggested that *inducing* a rule from observing illustrations, or from direct experience plus feedback, may at times lead to more stable, generalizable learning than when the correct rule is provided through verbal means.

This bears on the point made earlier, namely, that it is most unlikely that instructions or exemplification will consistently prove superior. We will soon see research evidence favoring one or the other method, as well as cases in which both techniques bring comparable learning. Also, one must consider, as did Masters and Branch (1969), that transfer will not always correspond to the strength of acquisition. The respective merits of the alternative modes for conveying information will depend on many facets of the total situation, including the nature of the task and the characteristics of the subject population. For example, the concept of syntagmatic associations is typically neither self-evident nor familiar to most people. With verbally sophisticated college students, it was possible for instructions to effectively sponsor the desired responses. It would be interesting to apply the same procedures to less articulate adults, or to young children. On tests with these subjects, we would expect that exemplification would prove to be more efficient than verbal instructions alone. On the other hand, the concepts of synonyms and antonyms are relatively familiar. For such tasks, we would expect that normal adolescents and adults could be more efficiently guided by brief directions, especially if these instructions included one or two illustrations of the target behavior, than by lengthy (and, therefore more cumbersome) exemplification displays. When a concept is quite easy to grasp, instructions can produce results as good as or better than exemplication in much less time, even with young children (Alford & Rosenthal, 1973; Rosenthal *et al.*, 1972a). Similar considerations apply to the distinction between modeling and direct practice. Neither approach will always be the method of choice, and their respective merits will depend on numerous situational factors.

Rosenthal and White (1972a) performed a set of interrelated experiments that were designed to test whether children's word associate choices are better explained by "habit strength," linking stimulus with response, or by judicious selection based on active cognitive mediation. Many writers since Thorndike (1913), have favored an explanation of learning in which associative strength, based on the frequency of pairing, is assumed to govern which responses will be elicited by stimulus words (e.g., Pollio, 1968; Waugh & Norman, 1965). In contrast, social learning theory assumes that even young children can discriminate the appropriateness of a particular response in meeting verbal specifications like instructions, and normative and situational demands (Bandura, 1965, 1969a, 1977b). Symbolic coding and storage enable the child to respond in a manner congruent with his own and others' standards for social communication. From this, it follows that the usual frequency with which one word evokes another, or the number of times that any two words have been previously associated, will not necessarily control response emission. Particularly, if social and contextual demands are clearly switched, it would be expected that a child's language productions would rapidly reflect such changes in the situation. Instead of a slow relearning process, a rapid adjustment to the changed conditions akin to the shift of a set or *Einstellung* would be anticipated. The adaptability of children's utterances to a model's display has already been demonstrated by the research on syntactical constructions just discussed.

Rosenthal and White (1972a) used a task in which a standard word was presented along with three selection words. The response associates always included one high probability noun option, one relevant verb option of lower probability, and one quite arbitrary color word. Depending upon the experimental condition, the children watched a model select nouns, verbs, or color words. Some of these children were asked to repeat or rehearse the model's choices. The children were then asked to emulate the model. All of the observer groups followed whatever choice-rule they saw modeled with nearly perfect accuracy. A no-model control group picked words consistent with general probability norms.

After ability to imitate was assessed during posttesting, the children were allowed to go through the list and freely pick whichever associates they preferred. Relative to imitation phase choices, noun and color word selections decreased, while verb choices remained fairly constant. In a second experiment, children were not asked to emulate after modeling but instead were told to just play the game. With these permissive instructions, there was no sharp decline in color and noun responses from posttesting to free selection. Enforced rehearsal had no effect in the first experiment but did inhibit color selections in the second. It thus appeared that directive instructions and constrained rehearsal acted to reduce imitative adoption of the arbitrary color words.

These results clearly showed that the children were very responsive to the model's influence, but not in a slavish or automatic manner. Observing the model's performance led to increased use of his response choices during the imitation phase. Yet the nouns, most probable in baseline, did not lead to more stable increases than the verbs. Although of lower original probability, the verb class rose to a comparable level during the imitation phase and, unlike nouns, never declined from imitation to free preference. Therefore, an associative-strength viewpoint, which would assume that the greatest and most stable increases should occur with nouns, was not supported. Nor did rehearsal, by providing further S–R pairings, ever facilitate performance, as might be supposed from a habit-strength position. Rehearsal had no effect with strong instructions, and even *decreased* the maintenance of the color choices under permissive instructions. Since nouns, verbs, and color responses all approached asymptotic choice levels in the imitation phase, their differential maintenance under the free preference conditions cannot readily be explained by virtue of their differing "associative strengths" on the preceding trial. Instead, it appeared that the children were able to cognize the model's response choices and to emulate or abandon them flexibly, depending on their semantic appropriateness and the social demands of the situation, as occurred when color words were chosen less often given permissive instructions about following the model. Similar evidence from observational learning research, which questions associative pairings as the source of learning, is presented in Chapter 4.

Although overt practice might have been expected to add associative habit-links, enforcing choral repetition of the model's choices had only one effect. It reduced color selections when imposed in a context of permissive response instructions. This may well have resulted from the children either resisting or "boomeranging" against a format that was explicitly nondirective but that appeared, perhaps hypocritically, to demand adoption of the arbitrary color choices. Similar boomerang effects have been found when instructions and modeling cues are discrepant (Mischel & Liebert, 1966; Rosenhan, Frederick, & Burrows, 1968). For example, Bryan, Redfield, and Mader (1971) found a significant interaction among a model's deeds, exhortations, and actual delivery of social rewards. A model who advocated and demonstrated charitable behavior and who also reinforced children's self-denial elicited the greatest self-denial activity from the youngsters. In contrast, an inconsistent model, who appeared to speak with "forked tongue" by urging and displaying altruism, but who did not reward children's charitable actions, produced the lowest level of self-denial, even though children's charitable ratings of the model's *niceness* were determined by the adult's practices and preachings, rather than his delivery of reward.

In the Rosenthal and White (1972a) studies, the detrimental rehearsal effects were confined to the arbitrary color associates and did not influence selection of verbs or nouns. This specificity suggests that the rehearsal decrement was a function of the nature and appropriateness of the class of words chosen by the model, and was not simply the result of rehearsal groups verbalizing the model's choices aloud. In general, relative to the directive instructions of Experiment I, the permissive instructions of Experiment II were equally, or more, effective in creating stable response choices. If overt rehearsal itself may be considered as a constraint, the results generally favored the more permissive approaches as better means of instating stable word choices.

Subsequently, White and Rosenthal (1973) extended the word associates design to experiments with second-graders. The verb and color response categories were retained, but the children never observed a model select noun options. A *definition, no model* group was given an accurate description of the target (verbs or colors) word class, and was asked to choose some of these options, but without exposure to modeling. The *no definition, modeling* children watched a model pick verbs or colors without having these response classes defined, and a *rehearsal* treatment was conducted similarly, but here the children were also required to orally reiterate the model's selections. In a final variation, children received the definitions and also observed the model's word selections without rehearsal. As before, after the imitation phase measurements, a free preference phase was introduced and then, some 5 weeks later, a retention phase was conducted in a setting unlike that used for any previous procedures.

All of the modeling groups surpassed the nonmodeling, verbal definition subjects in greater selection of verbs during the imitation and free preference phases. Providing the definition, or imposing rehearsal, did not alone increase verb choices; neither operation added to the effects of simple observation of the model. Even after the delay interval, the modeling children exhibited a greater than baseline choice of verbs, and also surpassed the performance of an untrained control group.

With the color words, all of the modeling groups during the imitation phase outperformed the nonmodeling, definition children. In the free preference phase, however, only the modeling plus definition group scored higher than did nonmodeling, definition children. Rehearsal added nothing to vicarious training and, as before, seemed to slightly detract from the model-produced changes. Although the choice of color words in absolute number was greater during free preference than in baseline, increased color selections were not maintained over the delay interval. The reduction of target class word-choices after delay involved a sharper decline for the arbitrary colors than for the meaningful verb options.

Harvey (1973) compared the effects of stronger and weaker verbal rebuke to a model in suppressing selection of high probability word associates. In addition to vicarious punishment for the taboo response class, in some conditions the model was praised for choosing "correct" i.e., low probability, associates. Here, all of the stimulus words were nouns, and the response options included a high probability noun, and very low probability verb and adjective associates, based on the Palermo and Jenkins (1964) norms. Third-graders served as subjects, studied in same-sex groups of five. As before, the children circled their word choices during baseline, imitation, and generalization phases.

Both praising the model for low probability choices, as well as rebuking him for high probability choices, reduced children's selection of the to-be-inhibited options. Choosing the taboo noun class was not only significantly lower in the imitation phase than during baseline, but noun choices were also significantly depressed in the generalization phase with new word arrays. Thus, the children were able to discriminate the category of options to be avoided, and, without further training, could transfer this knowledge to a new set of word instances. However, strong rebuke to the model was no more effective than mild censure in suppressing noun choices by the children. Further, neither moderately nor highly restrictive directions had greater inhibiting effects than more permissive instructions, a result reminiscent of the previous outcomes (Rosenthal & White, 1972a).

SUMMARY

This chapter has presented evidence that diverse modeling procedures can be powerful influences on language and verbal behavior. Also discussed were psycholinguistic reservations about modeling influences on language acquisition. It appeared that many such concerns arose from misconceptions or narrow definitions of modeling, describing it as a limited process of mimicry or unit-to-unit matching. Recognition that modeling can transmit abstract, rule-governed patterns may resolve much of this controversy. Modeling displays were shown to be effective in promoting the adoption of numerous natural syntactic constructions including prepositional phrases, sentence arrangements, and verb tense forms. Modeling was also found to be effective in teaching language comprehension. Social cues appear to weigh heavily in young children's extraction of meaning from events. Acquisition of both natural language and arbitrary grammarlike rules through modeling was also seen in laboratory studies. It appears that language learning may occur in two separate phases. During the first, the child learns to comprehend or discriminate speech structures covertly. Then in a second phase, the child learns to use that structure in his own overt speech. Naturalistic data were also discussed, results which indicated that speech demonstrations by natural models, such as older children or mothers, greatly affect the acquisition and usage of language by young children.

Further, the combination of modeling techniques with other procedures, such as contingent reinforcement, proved valuable for instating rule-governed syntactical, vocal, and labeling performances in young normal children and in linguistically restricted older children such as retardates. Vicarious training was successful with sociocultural minority groups, as well as with children and adults from middle-class backgrounds, even without explicit reinforcement. Although reinforcement may *assist* the normal acquisition of language, there is presently no evidence showing that it is *necessary*. Word associate responses also proved amenable to human and symbolic modeling interventions given to college and child populations. Evidence casting doubt on a simple, associative strength, view of vicarious processes was also presented. The sheer frequency of previous stimulus response pairings failed to account for the results obtained. Instead, judicious cognitive mediation of organized categories characterized even the behavior of children.

3

Relational Judgments and Categorical Decisions

INTRODUCTION

Babies are born into a world permuted by social judgments and expectations. Adults may scrutinize the infant girl's movements and demeanor for signs of femininity; the baby boy's first grasping responses may be interpreted in terms of potential strength and self-assertion. As children grow older, the judgments of parents, kin, and peers will increasingly direct and constrain their behavior. Many social reactions are communicated directly ("Boys don't play with dolls"), but often judgments are conveyed by example or subtle behavioral cues. The prevailing climates of opinion guide the child in choosing from among the options available to him; with time, children gradually adopt these judgmental standards to regulate their own conduct. When others' judgments conform to some system of rules, the child will learn to discern the decisive cues and to induce the principles or criteria that dictate the reactions of others. This accomplishment is of major consequence. The child no longer needs others to exemplify decision guidelines in each new situation; he can now respond without prompting, applying the governing rule.

Although much evidence has shown that social factors influence the child's development of sex-typed roles (Mischel, 1970), only rather recently has study been directed at more complex categories of human judgment. Research now suggests that abstract decision rules for a wide variety of moral, perceptual, and cognitive judgments can be acquired and modified via modeling. The categories that govern response may be quite narrow, as is the case when a child must determine from the intentions of two persons which is the more blameworthy, or when, in making a psychophysical size judgment, a single word discloses that contextual stimuli have either been acknowledged or ignored. In contrast, the guiding principles may have broad limits, as long as a defined attribute, such as subjective value or practical utility, is addressed. In making judgments of conservation, and in related assessments, the decision is based on whether the original quantitative relationship between paired stimuli is thought to be either maintained or to be changed if one of the pair is physically altered. In the preceding examples, the decision principles are not *de nouveau* invented; rather, they are extracted from rules and social conventions met in everyday thinking. Yet, adopting a given judgment standard may be a novel accomplishment for an individual child. Whether or not the decision rules studied are initially familiar, the judge must interpret, sort, or organize the specific examples presented, in order to obey a set of categories. Sometimes, multiple guidelines clash, an event that strains the precise balancing of priorities. For example, although one may know the premise that all men are equal under the law, one may nonetheless believe that extralegal factors should be invoked to judge the guilt of a president or a star quarterback. Sometimes the relevance of a criterion is inobvious: One may know that maples, elms, and oaks all drop their leaves in autumn, without realizing that this deciduous feature is a valid basis for distinguishing them from pines and firs.

In making decisions in the natural environment, one is not often asked to learn new categorical rules, but rather, to decide which criteria should take precedence. Thus, to alter decision making, one may need to communicate *(a)* the defining features of a general standard; *(b)* information that selected instances obey a known principle; or *(c)* which of the multiple standards available should receive priority. It is rarely easy to determine what precise elements are contributed by a single training intervention. For some people, social guidance may create a novel understanding of plausible decision criteria, but for others, the *bases* for choosing among known rules are instead conveyed. The size of the gains will, in part, depend on the learners' previous standards, and their skills regarding the events to be judged. Yet, evidence confirms that modeling techniques can effectively modify previous judgment patterns, and can introduce a wide variety of abstract criteria used to regulate decision making. Included among these response classes are such symbolic tasks as moral and psychophysical judgments, conservation decisions, and abstract styles of inquiry. Because they are refined with age, these response classes have at earlier times been invoked to support structuralist theories of development.

The experimental data to be reviewed will question several key assumptions of structuralistic analyses, especially those that minimize the importance of experience on cognition. A competing interpretation, based on both laboratory and naturalistic research, will be proposed, and the possibility of some reconciliation between environmental and structural emphases will be considered.

Structuralistic Approaches to Cognitive Development

Earlier, we characterized Piagetian and other, closely related structural positions such as Kohlberg's view of moral development as basically nativistic, a conclusion drawn by other writers (e.g., Baldwin, 1967; Bruner, Olver, & Greenfield, 1966). Piagetians often object to such labels, claiming that their theory is interactional, and adding, that just as experience is interpreted in light of existing structures, new events can also reorganize cognition. However, the impact of experience is delimited by the child's prevailing logic, whose scope, in turn, is rooted in an assumed sequence of biological development. Furth (1969), a respected spokesman, is clear on this point: The form of the child's mental structure is neither induced by nor gradually evolves from the organization of experienced events; rather, it has biological origins. Piaget (1962) himself raised the same issue by denying that the logical features of thought can arise from experience; but while structures must exist before experience can be meaningful, experience cannot create or determine the form of the structures. Although new events can qualify structural content, the sequence of mental development is assumed to be invariant and irreversible. Further, a child at one developmental stage should not profit from, and may actively resist, guidance appropriate to a later stage.

Early efforts to teach conservation to preoperational children were largely failures and were interpreted as supporting structuralist theory (Beilin, 1971). However, Piagetians have been more reluctant to accept that the positive evidence of "precocious" response to teaching experiences calls for changes in their theory, or suggests that environmental events can move the child from one stage to the next, unless a "transition" is already underway. A transitional between-stage status has been used to explain successful teaching attempts. Those critical of this conclusion, therefore, have performed training studies with youngsters who showed no evidence of transition, as indicated by their zero scores on the task measures before training. Some Piagetian scholars, however, were led to deny that, prior to training, a child need evidence structural readiness at all, and, for example, to conclude that any 5-year-old should be regarded as in transition because some children of this age are trainable (Beilin, 1971). This seems circular, because evidence of learning becomes the proof of structural readiness. Another strategy used to discount precocious training data has been to require the most stringent structural criteria for evidence of changes. As summarized by Kuhn (1974), these added criteria include *(a)* that appropriate explanations accompany changed judgments; *(b)* the persistence of trained responses over time; *(c)* generalization of those responses to untrained stimuli; *(d)* resistance of "counter suggestion;" and *(e)* proof that structural development continues after training has ended, which, to our knowledge, was newly added, only to challange precocious training gains.

Besides the *precocious training* paradigm, there are other ways to test the validity of a structural stage theory. If several stages are proposed, the hypothesis of invariant order requires that the child pass through all of the stages in sequence. If it can be shown that the child can respond to guidelines two structural stages beyond his own, then the premises of stage theory would be damaged. Presently, we will find this *missing stage* paradigm has been applied to test Kohlberg's theory of moral development. The *reversal training* paradigm is perhaps the best means of assessing the value of a developmental stage theory. In a unidirectional sequence of developmental stages, it should not be theoretically possible to reverse the order of stages via environmental guidance, since it is assumed that later stages build upon and permanently alter prior structures. Any success in a reversal training design directly contradicts such structural postulates. Hence, three types of experiments bear upon the adequacy of structuralist explanations of age-related changes in children's cognitive organization: the precocious training study, the missing stage paradigm, and the reversal training design. This chapter emphasizes the impact of modeling influences on moral judgments and conservation decisions, response classes that other viewpoints frequently explain in structuralist terms.

Thus, stage theory formulations require data more exacting than mere age trends. These hypotheses assume *(a)* that there is uniformity in judgment at any given stage of development; *(b)* that individuals cannot display a particular stage level response without having passed through prior stages in an invariant sequence; and *(c)* that the structures of prior stages of thought are not available to an individual once he has advanced beyond these stages. As we will see, evidence suggests that thought is not uniform at any stage level, that multiple-stage "leaps" in thought can occur, that there are noteworthy irregularities in how well behavior follows the assumed stage sequence, and that people can flexibly shift stage-related rules, depending upon a variety of situational factors.

From a social learning standpoint, neither moral nor conservation judgments enjoy a privileged status. Both involve decision making in some context and are expected to respond to social influence, as are language and other classes of rule-governed behavior. In many cases, governing rules can often be abstracted from information conveyed by social exemplars. The cognitive gains will hinge on the observer's prior level of skill at related tasks, on the clarity of the teaching procedures, and on the learner's inferences about the value and relevance of the new guidelines modeled. Similarly, utilization of these rules will depend on the physical arrangement of stimuli, on the expected or perceived reaction of the social environment to alternative styles of conduct, and on related factors. The same variables will govern the regulation of covert understanding and overt performance, regardless of whether knowledge was first acquired vicariously, through overt experience, or from some combination of each.

MORAL JUDGMENTS AND BEHAVIOR

A Social Learning View of Moral Behavior

Social learning theory treats moral judgments as multidimensional social decisions. Many diverse criteria are utilized when an individual's responsibility for improper conduct is being determined. These criteria include such factors as the personal characteristics of the wrongdoers, the nature of the acts, the long-range as well as the immediate consequences of the acts, the setting in which the acts occurred, the precipitating conditions, the remorse of transgressors, the number and type of people who are victimized, and many other factors (Bandura, 1977b). By means of diverse social experiences, we learn which of these considerations are relevant in a given situation. The rules are gleaned from social encounters by means of modeling, tuition, or evaluative feedback. To learn from such complex experiences, a considerable degree of discrimination is required during the formation of moral judgment rules. It is not surprising that young children will err under such complex conditions. They may focus on obviously salient dimensions, such as consequences, before discerning more subtle dimensions, such as a protagonist's intentions. Thus, social learning theory treats moral decision-making as a highly intricate process, whose many interrelating factors must be considered and weighed in each situation for their relevance to be determined. Considerable situational variability in the use of ethical criteria is to be expected. Likewise, some age trends in moral reasoning are also expected, based on how children learn moral judgments. To control the conduct of a toddler who cannot fully understand language, parents may rely on physical means, such as corporal punishment. However, there are disadvantages to using these methods of control, as they require continual monitoring by the parent. One advantage of teaching a child moral rules is that transgressive acts are minimized outside the parents' presence. Thus, parents might cite public laws, ethical precepts, and their logical bases when guiding an adolescent, but to promote socially appropriate behavior in a preschooler, these same parents may exemplify very different tactics.

A social learning view rejects any sharp typology in moral development. Type approaches assume a high degree of moral homogeneity among individuals at every stage-type. These stances also assume that every individual fits nicely into one or another of the stage-type categories. There is little evidence to support either assumption. Moral decision making appears to be far too complex, conditional, and responsive to setting variations to be cast in terms of a single set of characteristics. As further research discloses the limitations of a static taxonomy of moral behavior and development, further subtypes must be devised to allow for more variation. However, as the number of categories for moral typing increases, the reliability of the typing process generally suffers. This situation compels advocates of fixed taxonomies to eliminate many individuals from the entire system when they do not clearly fit any single category (Turiel, 1966). Thus, social learning theory predicts that as children grow to social maturity, they will display increasing heterogeneity and discrimination in moral rule usage, rather than be confined to an irreversible sequence of qualitatively distinct stages.

A child's ability to learn or to correctly transfer moral rules may depend on his level of cognitive development. But in contrast to stage theorists, we believe that these achievements can be better explained in terms of prerequisite cognitive skills rather than by uniform mental structures. Social learning theory is wary of making inferences about the nature of underlying mental processes with respect to any age-related order of expected response emergence. Children typically walk before they swim; yet, this does not make walking a prerequisite for swimming. Conclusions about prerequisite skills are better based on evidence that learning one skill facilitates acquisition of another. Just such studies on the transfer of training often produce data that conflict with assumptions of uniform mental structures (e.g., Brainerd, 1974, 1977).

As we mentioned in Chapter 1, cognitive processes operate in a reciprocal fashion with the environment. For moral behavior, this means that social experiences are interpreted and acted upon in light of available moral judgment rules. Hence, older children, whose moral criteria are presumably more refined, may be more affected by some particular moral episode than a younger child who has less skill at integrating ethical information. The notion of reciprocal dependency also suggests that individuals will alter their moral standards based on how effectively a rule organizes their experiences. Thus, social learning theory expects "reversals" of moral stage under appropriate circumstances. In general, reciprocal determinism allows much more adaptability in moral reasoning than is permitted by assumptions of uniform cognitive-stage structures.

A unique feature of a social learning approach to morality is its capacity to explain the relationship between moral judgments and moral behavior. Social circumstances are assumed to influence the degree to which moral beliefs are displayed in actual conduct. As we indicated earlier, moral decisions are often made in complex and ambiguous situations. Further, individuals must often justify their *own* behavior to important others (such as a parent or boss) *after* an action has been committed. Moral rationales may have considerable survival value in such cases. For example, a child who tells his mother that he did not intend to hit a friend would probably be excused with a warning to be more careful in the future; however, a more candid child who admitted that he and his friend were intentionally fighting might well receive a spanking. Under these common conditions, sophisticated moral reasoning may be unrelated to actual conduct, and in fact may actually weaken moral inhibitions. On the other hand, moral rationales are less likely to excuse transgressions in more clear-cut situations, as, for example, when a person robs a bank. Thus, the social context and the consequences of both moral conduct and reasoning must be considered before discussing either class of responses or their interrelationship. Stage theories have devoted very little attention to the role of social factors in moral development.

Dichotomous Moral Judgments

As with cognitive evolution in general, Piaget (1948) proposed that moral development proceeds according to an invariant sequence of qualitatively distinct stages. Two stages are identified, and the movement between them is assumed to be largely independent of the norms and social influences present in the child's everyday environment. During the first period, *objective responsibility* determines moral evaluations. Presumably ignoring the intention that prompted the ill-fated deed, children in this stage judge an action by the harm or damage that it causes. At roughly age 7, this orientation supposedly gives way to the second, *subjective responsibility*, stage. Now, moral significance is decided by considerations of the anticipated meaning or intent that sponsored the injurious action. To assess children's moral status, Piaget presented youngsters with pairs of stories in which one character produces damage out of vindictive motives while another character unintentionally causes harm. The child must decide which protagonist is the more culpable. In Piaget's stories, intention and damage were mutually exclusive criteria, with evil plans leading to less material harm, and innocent motives producing considerable injury.

EXPERIMENTAL EVIDENCE

If brief social experience in the laboratory can alter a child's moral dispositions, it becomes difficult to accept the tenability of a stage theory. Perhaps the first experiment showing the influences of modeling on moral decisions was performed by Bandura and McDonald (1963), who studied boys and girls ranging in age from 5 to 11 years. In order for their initial moral dispositions to be assessed, the children were given pairs of stories, one of which portrayed maliciously intended actions as bringing minor harm, and the other depicting innocent motives that produced substantial material damage. For each pair of stories, the child was asked to judge which of the actors has been the more naughty, and then to justify the decision with a reason. This format was similar to Piaget's moral assessment procedures. According to their baseline judgments, children with either strongly objective or strongly subjective moral orientations were identified for further study, and boys and girls of each orientation were assigned to the following experimental conditions: *(a)* In the *model and child reinforced* group, stories were first presented to the model, whose judgment was always opposite to the child's baseline pattern, and then to the child. The experimenter always verbally praised the model's decisions, and would also praise the child's if the youngster had expressed the new moral stance. In effect, for initially subjective youngsters, the model's decisions followed a "judge material damage" rule, but for objective children, a "judge intentions" rule was modeled. *(b)* The *model reinforced child not reinforced* group was treated identically, except that no verbal approval was supplied when the child adopted the model's moral criteria. *(c)* In the *no model child reinforced* group, the model was eliminated. The experimenter presented the stories and would administer praise if the child's judgment shifted from the dominant baseline pattern. After these training and testing steps, generalization was tested in another room, where a different adult presented more stories, and then recorded the child's responses without praising or commenting on them.

The baseline results confirmed that while moral subjectivity was more common among older children, even the youngest, (ages 5 to 6:5 years), made some 30% subjective judgments before training. Most of the older children made many objective judgments. These baseline data did not reflect a sharp dichotomy in moral orientations. Instead, both subjective and objective judgments were seen across a wide range of ages, contrary to stage theory assumptions. Also, a child's judgments proved to be very stable predictors of verbal explanations: An objective judgment was usually followed by a material damage rationale, while a subjective judgment preceded an explanation based on intention.

The main results clearly showed that the children strongly adopted the moral standards modeled. The changes from baseline morality were generalized to the final story items, and were exhibited by both objective *(reversal training)* and subjective *(**precocious** training)* modeling groups. These same basic results were later replicated (Cowan, Langer, Heavenrich, & Nathanson, 1969). Adding verbal approval to modeling had little effect on the decisions of the children who were either originally objective or subjective. For children of both orientations (but less strongly for the subjective group, an outcome which better reflects naturalistic norms exemplified by adults and older peers), observing the model's judgments produced dramatically larger shifts than were found in the no model-child reinforced condition. This recalls prior evidence, namely, that for abstract tasks and with relatively normal, cooperative samples, modeling can promote rule-governed learning and transfer without external incentives (Rosenthal & Whitebook, 1970; Rosenthal & Carroll, 1972).

Objections have been raised about interpreting the preceding results as damaging to Piaget's stage theory (Cowan *et al.*, 1969). Discussing some points of contention will illustrate the communication difficulties that may arise when structuralist assumptions are confronted by the existing experimental data: *(a)* It was argued that reversing the presumed moral development sequence in the laboratory does not rule out that sequence as being typical in the natural environment. However, a laboratory study does not seek to recreate everyday life *in toto*. This experiment attempted to show that a child's moral orientations would promptly respond to social exemplars, and this in fact occurred. There are reasons for expecting adults and teenagers in our society to weigh intentions more heavily than accidental damage. This normative pattern neither confirms or refutes the developmental inevitability of

Piaget's stages. It is, however, doubtful that objective and subjective criteria are all-or-none, mutually exclusive patterns; witness that the baseline frequencies in this experiment ran counter to any simple dichotomy. *(b)* It was argued that Bandura and McDonald performed analyses on judgment scores rather than on explanations. However, since high correlations (*r*s of .88 for the pre- and posttest data) were found by Piagetians, it is difficult to understand the controversy surrounding this point. *(c)* Likewise, it was argued that children who in baseline consistently adhered to a moral stance might respond to modeling in different ways than those whose pretest dispositions were less extreme. Yet, initial extremity did not affect the magnitude of change, a result that cast further doubt on the assumption of exclusive stages. *(d)* It was argued that the original study did not address the maintenance of model-induced changes. Yet, in rejoining, Cowan *et al.* (1969) found that there was significant persistence of the new moral style after delay. But in the delayed test of this study, there was also some decline toward baseline levels. In research by Dorr and Fey (1974), model-induced changes in moral judgment were sustained over a 1-month delay. However, from a social learning standpoint, it would not be surprising to see the effects of one brief modeling session attenuate over time if the child returns to the environment that supported his original attitudes. If naturalistic norms were to change, and shift toward those that were modeled, then one would instead expect stronger adoption of the particular moral stance over time. *(e)* Finally, it was argued that in the original study, good intentions always covaried with major damage and malicious intentions always led to minor harm. This criticism seems puzzling, in light of Piaget's assumption that moral reasoning fits one of two dichotomous stages. Presumably, decisions made during the objective stage should always reflect the amount of material damage that results, while in the subjective stage, only the character's intentions should determine moral judgments—whether great or little harm results. At any rate, even when this covariation was controlled, the original results were confirmed. If the model's criterion was intention, the children abstracted that judgment rule regardless of the resulting damage. If the model's criterion was amount of harm, the children decided on that basis, regardless of the protagonist's intentions (Cowan *et al.*, 1969). In light of these empirical outcomes, there seems reason to question a theory proposing invariant moral stages.

This conclusion gains further support from two experiments by Schliefer and Douglas (1973). In Study I, 6-year-olds were assigned for instruction *(a)* by experimenter feedback, persuasion favoring intent criteria, and candy rewards for subjective judgments; *(b)* to a peer model who prompted and endorsed subjective moral decisions without using candy; or *(c)* to an uninfluenced control condition. Both guided groups shifted from their original positions toward intentional judgment criteria, with negligible difference between the two groups. Edible rewards did not exert a significant effect. The children were retested 4 weeks later, this time by a new adult. Most of the changes had endured, both for Piaget-type stories and for new scenarios that contrasted malicious with benign intent, when both led to heavy damage. Altered moral standards showed little transfer to the new story-pairs in which both characters had evil motives; few children recognized that the miscreants were equally blameworthy. Judgments thus proved easier with similar damage than with similar intent, showing the limits of a global dichotomy, whereby a child is assumed to evaluate all moral dilemmas by either objective or subjective criteria.

In Study 2, Schliefer and Douglas (1973) compared older (mean age = 5:7) and younger (mean = 3:8) nursery schoolers, and for both groups used children who were well below an age at which, in Piaget's theory, they should operate according to subjective moral standards. Instead of stories, brief films of ethical incidents were devised (with content overlapping Piagetian topics) and used for pre- and posttesting. Instead of a forced-choice format, this experimental design involved scoring responses to each incident for subjective versus objective morality. At each age level, an experimental group observed modeling skits performed using puppets and other props. If a child made subjective judgments, he received candy rewards; if material harm steered a moral decision, the adult modeled a subjective judgment and repeated the puppet episode. A control group received no training. Two weeks later, a new adult, blind to prior condition assignments, retested the children on the film items. For both ages, modeling significantly increased moral subjectivity as compared to the controls. The format differences between influence (with puppets) and testing (with films) signified the ethical changes as generalized measures of modeling effects, not tied to the teaching stimuli. According to Piaget's stage hypothesis, such young children should have firmly adhered to material moral standards. In fact, the modeling changes provide strong support for the Bandura and McDonald (1963) interpretation, which other studies with normal children have confirmed (Crowley, 1968; Durkin, 1961; Le Furgy & Woloshin, 1969). Similar outcomes have been found with delinquent teenagers. Although presumably past the material damage, objective stage, these youths did not favor subjective morality before being exposed to modeling influences. Live demonstrations as well as a symbolic modeling procedure, in which subjective judgments were illustrated by a printed text, proved effective in altering moral decisions immediately at posttesting, and similarly, on delayed generalization items. Since the youngsters were juvenile court charges, it is not surprising that they resisted the opportunity to reverse their attitudes on supplementary measures of "moral relativism." Shifts in the relativistic direction would have required them to endorse acts that violated legal sanctions while their beliefs were under scrutiny by an adult, presumably representing the court authorities (Prentice, 1972).

No violence is done by treating all of the preceding studies as cases of rule learning. The essential change was always a shift from an initial rule (e.g., "judge material damage") to the modeled rule (e.g., "judge subjective intentions"). Particular items were instances that could be construed to follow the modeled criteria. Yet, vicarious training did not create slavish rule adoption. Complete rule matching was not found. Instead, concept utilization depended on such additional factors as the discriminability of protagonists' motives (limited transfer when both characters had evil intentions) and situational threats (delinquents' avoidance of subjective criteria when legal sanctions were violated).

CONCEPTUAL IMPLICATIONS

Taken together, the data give little reason to cast moral development into rigid, dichotomous stages. Nor is it clear why developmental steps must be invariant, uniform, and mutually exclusive. Would the force of Piaget's contribution really suffer if a typical array of stagelike steps replaced an inevitable progression? Or if, within steps, more variability in response and more flexibility in adjustment to normative social influences were acknowledged? Where in psychology is there precedent for assuming an inflexible cognitive response to all instances of a problem category? That conceptualization is not required to account for observed regularities in the patterning and pacing of modal reaction styles. Very recently, hopeful signs of theoretical change have been coming from Geneva regarding points just raised (Beilin, 1976).

On the other hand, social learning psychologists have to date devoted relatively little research effort to detailed sequential regularities in the evolution of adult skill repertoires. However, Bandura (1977b) has described how sequential regularities in children's use of moral criteria can be explained on the basis of the way adults alter their teaching, modeling, and reinforcement in their dealings with children of different ages. As the child grows older and more adept, other sequential trends can develop, arising from progressive changes in environmental standards and expectations. Society may exemplify and reward baby-talk or belief in Santa Claus among toddlers, while not responding favorably to similar displays by adolescents. When earned by a scholastically derelict son, "B" grades may delight parents, but the same marks may bring grief if awarded to their honor student daughter. It is too facile to "explain" performance discrepancies in terms of individual differences and contrasting propensities *without* careful analysis of the conditions that may produce dispositional variations (Mischel, 1973).

In one of the few studies addressing this last point, Sax and Stollak (1971) selected young boys on the basis of teachers' ratings of their curiosity, prosocial attitudes, and aggressiveness. Interaction between the boys and their mothers was then systematically observed by trained raters. The results revealed that mothers of curious and highly prosocial boys displayed more positive feelings, levied fewer restrictions, and showed more attentiveness than mothers with aggressive sons, and were more rewarding than mothers of low curiosity boys (cf. Friedman, 1973a,b; Rosenthal *et al.*, 1969). Mothers' positive feelings (favorable affect) correlated with sons' levels of attentiveness, manipulation of materials, and offering of information. The boys' curiosity was most highly correlated with the curiosity exemplified by their mothers. Without such interaction samples, one might falsely conclude that classroom differences in curiosity resulted from innate determinants and were unaffected by the boys' social environments. Analogous modeling patterns have been found to influence children's aggressive tendencies (Bandura, 1973; Bandura & Walters, 1963). At least some progress has been made in the longitudinal study of social learning effects on conceptual strategies (e.g., Denney, 1972a; Gholson & Beilin, in press; Richman & Gholson, 1977) as we will see in the next chapter. Until more research along this line accumulates, it seems wise to withhold judgment about the extent to which environmental variables dictate a child's acquisition of stylistic or characterological attributes.

Bandura (1977b) has argued that parents initially rely on physical methods to control their child's inappropriate behavior. A young child's grasp of language is marginal at best; thus, efforts to explain complex concepts lacking clear referents, such as an individual's motives, to toddlers will not prove effective. In addition, Bandura has pointed out that moral reasoning is of functional value for children. For example, by citing his benign intentions, a child might disclaim responsibility for a socially disapproved act. This example raises another important point relative to the social context of moral reasoning: How likely is it that a parent of a preschool child would demand an explanation for a social transgression? Not very probable, we venture. But the reverse expectations are held for adolescents who are assumed to be facile speakers. Not only must adolescents speak, but their explanations had better be acceptable to Mom and Dad. Thus, there are grounds for expecting that, for a young child, moral reasoning might not be prompted, reinforced, or demonstrated to the same degree that it would for a youth. Once moral reasoning is expected of them, children will quickly adopt rationales to forestall punishment, such as asserting their benign intentions.

Bandura (1977b) has also described the way in which moral judgment rules are internalized, and how they guide an individual's behavior in environments where adverse consequences may not be present. After ethical and moral rules are adopted, they serve as a basis for self-condemnation reactions. Individuals usually avoid conduct that leads to self-condemnation, and thus behave morally. Moral inhibitions of behavior are the strongest under conditions where the causal relationship between deviant conduct and the injurious consequences is clear. However, ambiguity in social conflict situations permits a considerable degree of latitude for cognitive restructuring. One can reclassify culpable acts as moral by viewing the injured party as dehumanized or by comparing the acts to more outrageous ones. This explanation suggests an apparent paradox, one which is highly familiar: Individuals possessing the greatest sophistication in ethical reasoning also have the most resources to morally justify their immoral acts. Ultimately, however, whether one's moral explanations are treated as reasons or as rationalizations depends upon the reactions of the surrounding social groups, as amply evidenced by the Watergate scandal. Such a view implies that there may be considerable divergence between moral reasoning and moral behavior, and suggests that psychological theories focusing only on moral reasoning may have limited value in explaining moral conduct.

Bandura (1969c, 1977b) has emphasized the role of developmental factors and personal determinants in social learning analyses of behavior. However, he has discussed the limitations of developmental studies that lean heavily on age as an index of cognitive development. Although the quality of children's performance improves over time, sequential gains are not always orderly. To the degree that they actually occur, serial age effects can be explained by many factors other than cognitive maturation, such as the acquisition of subordinate skills, and by the alterations in social and environmental settings attendant on a child's age. Relating changes in functioning to a global index, such as age, does provide normative evidence but says little about the subprocesses that govern performance. Developmental research need not only address a child's mental functioning under naturalistic conditions. Experimental studies can yield precise information about the relative roles of component skills. It would seem more informative to explore how aspects of ethical situations influence and change both moral premises and conduct than to continue searching for idealized modal stage patterns.

In reality, culpability decisions of the intent versus damage variety are seldom easily made (Buchanan & Thompson, 1973; Costanzo, Coie, Grumet, & Farnhill, 1973; Gutkin, 1972). If an overriding stage distinction were adequate, children should consistently apply one moral standard with a single-mindedness that defies the ethical complexities of everyday life. In fact, the extremity of immoral deeds, as well as their antisocial direction, determines ethical evaluations (Leon, Oden, & Anderson, 1973). Diverse considerations may receive different weights in reaching a final decision (Sherif & Hovland, 1961). In judging the behavior of others, individuals are often influenced by social variables that should be extraneous to the logical requirements of the task. Identical cues may be differently perceived if the protagonist has high or low social status (Levy & Kahn, 1970); whether he has trustworthy or dubious credentials (Bergin, 1962; Bochner & Insko, 1966; Hovland, Janis, & Kelley, 1953; Rosenthal, 1976), if he appears personally "warm" or "cold" (Asch, 1946; Kelley, 1950; Rosenthal, Hung, & Kelley, 1977); and whether the protagonist is adorned with "hip" versus "square" garb and hair styles (Rosenthal & White, 1972b). Little has been done to bridge the gap between this area of social perception and the realm of moral judgments, even though their interface seems relevant.

DESCRIPTIVE EVIDENCE

Beyond the modeling experiments already discussed, considerable descriptive research bears on Piaget's two-stage morality conception. Some scholars have tried to determine if children can take account of subjective intentions at an earlier age than that anticipated by Piaget. Thus, Bearison and Issacs (1975) studied 6-year-olds' moral judgments in two testing formats: The traditional Genevan procedure, in which the intentions of the story's protagonist are not clearly labeled, and a contrasting format, in which intentions were explicitly designated. The explicit scenarios elicited significantly more judgments based on intentionality criteria. The children were able to utilize intent cues at an age much younger than would be possible to detect by the Piagetian test format. Thus, it appeared that although 6-year-olds may be less socially sophisticated in making inferences about characters' motives than older children, they can base moral decisions on subjective intentions once these are perceived. The procedural variations led to different conclusions about the child's moral propensities, illustrating a problem regarding much research performed by structural theorists: A focus on the logical dimensions of a child's cognition may lead to neglect of social and content variables affecting their procedures. For example, in the Piagetian method, two stories are presented to assess the child's moral orientation. Berg-Cross (1975) reasoned that the two-story format presents excessive information in a complicated logical paradigm, thereby straining the child's processing capacities. Two sets of intentions, story plots, and damage consequences must be considered simultaneously. The information processing burden, rather than the nature of the moral preference, might confuse a young child. When a simpler, one-story, format was instead employed, 6-year-olds proved readily capable of responding in accordance with the protagonist's motives. Thus, the child's moral responses were dependent on technical variations in the method, not on any general preference for material damage as a decision standard.

Likewise, putative morality may in fact depend on the order in which decision cues are presented within stories. The Piagetian format supplied intentions data first and damage consequences second. Might young children be more dependent on the last, that is, damage, cues, by virtue of memory limitations, implying a kind of recency effect? If so, the traditional format would act to artifactually depress the use of intentional criteria. Feldman, Klossen, Parsons, Rholes, and Ruble (1976) altered the content sequence by placing the intentionality cues last for some children and first for others. Six-year-olds proved incapable of easily recalling the initial moral cues. Their limited storage capacity seemed to explain their reliance on damage criteria in the usual Piagetian test procedures. Further, older children only considered intentions when a protagonist was punished. Their moral decisions were modulated by social response to the character, as well as by an absolute preference for one moral standard.

Such descriptive research on procedural variables taxes the notion of a moral dichotomy. Although Piaget's conception depends on the stage of a child's cognitive development rather than on absolute age, the use of intentionality criteria by such young children suggests that his stages are not highly distinct. Moreover, children, who by his assessment procedures will appear objective in morality, do respond to intentions criteria when tested by alternative methods. Older children did not show homogeneous reliance on the criteria presumably appropriate to their developmental stage. Instead, social reactions to the protagonist influenced their moral reasoning. There seems little basis, then, for accepting that stages are rigidly polarized. Instead, changes in moral development seem gradual at best, and moral criteria, instead of being mutually exclusive, are matters of relative frequency. The environment has a substantial impact. It may affect the moral reasoning that derives from the situation, the emphasis given to damage and intent as cues, their sequence within stories, and the social feedback that follows the protagonist's actions in the episode. To date unexplored, but certainly inviting study, are questions about the peer group norms encountered by the child, the relevance of moral discussion for various age groups, and the effects of moving from one social milieu to another with differing ethical standards.

Kohlberg's Six-Stage Theory

Kohlberg (1968) has extended Piagetian thinking into a theory of moral development spanning three major periods, each of which is divided into two stages. During the *preconventional period* (Stages 1 and 2), the child judges the propriety of a deed strictly by its consequences for the protagonist of the story. During the *conventional period* (Stages 3 and 4), moral reasoning is based on group norms, which are unquestioningly accepted as absolute standards. In the last, *postconventional period* (Stages 5 and 6), moral decisions are fully distinguished from situational outcomes and others' social influence as criteria. Instead, people reason according to such abstract ethical principles as the "Golden Rule." Kohlberg's views entail many structuralistic assumptions: children must advance through all of the stages in order, without skipping any. Moral and cognitive development are integrally related because common structures guide decision making in both spheres. Stages are assumed to be qualitatively distinct. Each new stage supplants its predecessor, whose structure is no longer available; hence, stage reversals are theoretically impossible. However, Kohlberg's stages require less homogeneity than Piaget's, since only half of a person's responses need fit a stage in order to show that it has been attained. Because a person manifests as much thought outside his moral stage as within it, this definition appears to be unusually generous, in light of Kohlberg's claim that the stages are qualitatively distinct. It seems highly misleading to ascribe such heterogeneous reasoning to a single stage designation. Kohlberg appears more willing to accept that social experiences such as modeling can bring structural advances without requiring the child to pass through some transition status. Since no stage can be bypassed, it is assumed that guidance toward standards two or more steps above a person's current level will be ineffective. Because the theory is more open to environmental influences, and because it proposes six steps for potential comparisons, the "missing stage" training paradigm has been widely used to test the validity of Kohlberg's formulation.

Kohlberg devised an interview technique using nine story dilemmas to assess children's level of morality. Rather than stressing decisions about which character was right or wrong, Kohlberg emphasized the style of reasoning a person offers to support whatever judgment is made. Thus, the theory seeks to explain the characteristics of moral thinking, rather than the particular decisions that are reached. At the same time, rather little is told about how moral reasoning style relates to overt conduct, such as altruism or resisting temptations. Although some covariation might plausibly be expected, this theory, like most structural accounts, makes few explicit predictions about tangible performance linkages.

Kohlberg's group has performed several studies to validate his assessment technique, whose psychometric properties are relatively unclear. Thus, a child's age is typically correlated with his moral stage, and trained scorers are reported to show close agreement on individual protocals (Kohlberg, 1968); however, little detail is usually provided about the overall accuracy of stage designations. Moral level correlates moderately (*r*s reaching the .50 range) with intelligence test scores. Does this suggest a relationship between moral and cognitive *development* or, rather, that any task testing verbal reasoning on complex problems will reflect general intelligence? While factor analytic data indicate that moral and intelligence test items load on different factors (Kohlberg, 1968), these data do not explain causation. For example, the common situational content of items can create a factor clustering (Mischel, 1968). Nor are the effects of intelligence typically removed from the correlations between moral level and age. The longitudinal correlations may well decrease if freed of the influence of nonspecific reasoning skill, which also covaries with age as an index of practice and expertise in solving problems of all types. The correlational research, using different individuals at each age level, does not address the more stringent assumptions of the theory, such as the sequential ordering, homogeneity, and irreversibility of stages.

Thus, a number of training studies have sought to validate these major premises. One attempt (Turiel, 1966) remains inconclusive because its statistical analysis was questionable (Kurtines & Greif, 1974), and because it involved assumptions, e.g., that teaching variations will affect children at diverse levels in similar fashion, that are hard to justify (Rothman, 1976). Nonetheless, despite controversial treatment of the data, Turiel's (1966) results at best gave weak support to the sequential stage proposal; furthermore, the control group behaved contrary to expectations derived from the theory. Unfortunately, related design issues, and evidence that Kohlberg's scale is unreliable, complicate the interpretation of other studies (Rest, 1973; Rest, Turiel, & Kohlberg, 1969). These studies claim to have found evidence suggesting that children fail to adopt moral rationales one stage below or two stages above their own. The fact that a brief exposure to conflicting moral judgments failed to produce negative or two-stage changes is not surprising. A fairer test of a child's resistance to moral arguments would be to consistently expose him to various examples over a sustained period of time. However, the conclusion drawn here, i.e., that two-stage changes in these studies failed to occur, is questionable. It was found that regardless of their initial moral stages, children would *select* the most cognitively sophisticated reasoning presented to them, but had difficulty in *restating* these arguments in phrases other than those appropriate to their initial moral level. These data, however, remain inconclusive. If the present stage reflects a cognitive structure refractory to guidance several stages more advanced, why should youth of all moral levels have preferred the most sophisticated arguments? Can inability to verbalize elegantly be taken as a failure to *comprehend* the chosen rationales, or is this merely a reflection of verbal skill, distinct from understanding? Indeed, do the higher levels of the Kohlberg scale reflect verbal fluency rather than moral or cognitive superiority?

Keasey (1973) studied the effects of social influence, and one- or two-sided rhetoric, in altering the moral judgments and reasoning of fifth and sixth graders. The children were exposed to adult confederates who drew arguments from the children's initial ethical levels or from the next highest stages. In one-sided conditions, the models only stated the advocated viewpoint, while the two-sided arguments also included the opposing stance. Based on previous findings by the Kohlberg group, it was hypothesized that when they are given arguments supported by reasoning one developmental step above their own ("plus one" reasoning), children would exhibit greater change than if the rationales were on their own level ("same-stage" reasoning). The prior empirical data actually question the necessity to assume discrete stages. For cognitive mechanisms at any given level, should not same-stage reasoning, presumably more appropriate, be required, or at least favored? Keasey found that both one-sided arguments and rationales from the later phase created more *opinion* (judgment) change. Children who started at Stages 1 and 2 changed their ethical *reasoning* more than the most advanced group, who began at Stage 3. How is this differential pattern of change to be interpreted? Considerable research on social influence processes involving diverse tasks suggests that the amount of induced change is a positive function of the possible room for change (e.g., Hovland & Pritzker, 1957; Rosenthal, 1963; White, 1975; Zimbardo, 1960). Thus, lower-level children had more latitude for upward shifts than higher-level children. Also, since the advanced ethical criteria were more adultlike, the child may have perceived the advanced rationales to afford more positive status connotations than the same-stage rationales, consistent with the data showing the preference for the most sophisticated arguments regardless of initial moral stage (Rest, 1973; Rest *et al.*, 1969). Hence, this reasoning, i.e., that the amount of change is a positive function of the room for change, seems plausible, and concurs with the experimental results. Another, related, possibility is that the Kohlberg scale may be subject to psychometric regression effects, with the relatively extreme (lower-stage) youngsters reverting toward the mean more than children at Stage 3, who are closer to the modal range. Keasey (1973) also found that the stage level of the confederates' arguments produced short-term differences in the children's reasoning, but the shifts were not maintained over a 2-week delay. However, some children spanned all three moral phases and gave some responses appropriate to each stage, data hard to reconcile with any postulate of discrete, stage-related cognitive mechanisms.

Working with children of comparable age, Tracy and Cross (1973) also studied ethical changes related to Kohlberg's stages. In order to socially alter judgments they used a role-taking procedure, with two adult confederates exemplifying the moral views intended to influence the child. Unlike Keasey, Tracy and Cross hypothesized that children with more advanced moral development would be *more* susceptible to higher level (same-stage) reasoning than would children at a lower stage—an inference that seems to follow more directly from a stage conception than the reverse prediction. The pertinent results showed that the models' role-taking successfully shifted the children's moral responses, as compared to uninfluenced controls. Again, socially induced change was a function of the child's baseline departure from the modeled viewpoint, with initially lower children making greater shifts toward more adult ethical standards. Indeed, without social influence, control children of low moral stage increased more than experimentals who began at a higher level, once again suggesting psychometric regression effects on the Kohlberg measures. Also, children whose inventory responses revealed that they were very concerned with meeting social desirability norms made significantly greater changes than less socially attuned youngsters.

The same pattern, i.e., of increasing change as a function of discrepancy between one's own and another's position (room to change), has also been found among college students who debated moral reasoning. Students were pretested on Kohlberg's scale and were then assigned in pairs such that their moral levels differed by one or more stages. Each partner was told to argue for the opposing views of one protagonist in the story, but then to jointly resolve the dilemma to their mutual satisfaction. Then, both participants were retested to assess shifts in moral orientation. Students whose partners reasoned at a higher stage earned significantly higher postdebate scores than those whose partners advocated lower-level moral criteria. Contrary to Kohlberg's assumptions, the greatest shifts occurred when the moral discrepancy between partners was maximal (differences of three and four stages), not when the partner advocated reasoning just one step higher (Arbuthnot, 1975). Thus, in a sample of people having superior verbal skills (and therefore no deficits in fluency), multiple-stage jumps emerged clearly. Likewise, the relationship between extent of shifts and room to change was again confirmed. Students who began at the lowest stages (2 and 3) later increased the most. Those starting at Stage 4 showed no change. The group initially highest (Stage 5), and whose partners necessarily espoused a lower-level viewpoint, moved *downward* in stage, arguing against the assumption of unidirectionality of moral sequences. Further, a general decline that was observed in a delayed test using different stories, suggested that the particular situational content of items affected the moral response, in contrast to Kohlberg's assumption that his scale only reflects the structural features of morality.

When room to change was held constant, adolescents' responses to modeling differed according to their initial levels of morality (Rothman, 1976). These data indict the practice, sometimes followed by the Kohlberg group in training studies, of combining subjects who start out at different scale intervals, and then measuring the effects of social experience across the aggregate group. But Rothman's (1976) results strain the theory still further, because her subjects were in the conventional period (Stage 3 or 4) when, presumably, responses to social cues should be most pronounced. In fact, influence effects depended both on the observers' starting levels, and on which of two competing models was heeded, in a rather complex fashion. If this result is replicated, it would seem that even when a child's measured stage does respond to social guidance, outcomes are more subtle than the theory would predict, and require clarification by additional experiments.

Several recent attempts have been made to validate Kohlberg's invariant sequence hypothesis, in research efforts involving longitudinal studies. In one study, the data were analyzed according to periods rather than their component stages, because the latter proved unreliable with both adolescents and adults studied over the course of 3 years Although the predicted sequence between the pre- and conventional periods was observed, it was not confirmed between the conventional and postconventional periods (Holstein, 1976). In other words, the expected improvements over time were found among subjects who had the most room to change (or whose initial assignment to the lowest period may have resulted from scale unreliability, so that subsequent "progress" may have stemmed from statistical regression, upward toward the overall mean). Movement from the middle to the uppermost periods was not found. Kuhn (1976b) tested children at 6 and 12 months following an initial moral assessment. As a group, the number of children who had regressed in measured stage at the second or third tests was greater than the number who failed to change or the number who progressed. The vast majority of those who advanced began initially at the two lowest stages, again suggesting the now-familiar "room to change" or "regression to the mean" interpretation. Despite these complications, the data were construed as supporting Kohlberg's hypothesis. Surely, some refinement in the precision or specificity of the theory (e.g., clarifying its boundary conditions for disconfirmation), is needed, in order for these results to be rendered supportive. Likewise, it is hard to judge the theory's capacity for revision through empirical feedback. Since it purports to describe moral competence rather than ethical performance (Kuhn, 1976b), what corrective role, if any, can be played by data showing unexpected relationships? Indeed, teacher's ratings of boys' moral and social adjustment proved unrelated or negatively related to moral development scores. Boys from divorced families were rated as more socially deviant, but earned higher Kohlberg scores than boys raised by widowed mothers. Little correlation has been demonstrated among the various measures of morality. A factor analysis has disclosed that although moral reasoning items cluster together, they remain distinct from ethical behavior items (Santrock, 1975). Despite Kohlberg's assumptions, stage level has been found to covary with preference for alternative modes of distributive justice (Gunzburger, Wegner, & Anooshian, 1977). It is difficult to determine the impact of this nonconfirming evidence on the theory as it is presently formulated. Related concerns have been raised about Kohlberg's testing methodology: Administration of the scale is unstandardized; responses are not scored objectively; scores are not stable over time; and inter-item consistency is unsatisfactory (Kurtines & Greif, 1974). Lack of intercorrelation among items suggests that the construct validity of the scale is poor, and that multiple variables can give rise to similar scores. If this is so, how can Kohlberg justify combining the points earned on each story into a summed score, or assigning a single stage level to the child's moral reasoning? There seems little basis for abandoning the view, held early (Hartshorne & May, 1928) and again more recently (Mischel, 1968), that morality depends on situation-specific determinants, rather than on a unitary ethical disposition.

Instead, the data indicate that people diverse in terms of age and assessed ethical stage are quite amenable to a wide range of social cueing operations. These operations have included observation of models' moral conclusions, the reconciliation of contrasting protagonist views as role-played with an interaction partner, and other forms of social influence. Once the criteria for new ethical reasoning are grasped, these decision principles are transferred to untrained test items; as well, despite the brevity of social guidance, people often preserve the new moral style after delay intervals. Structuralist views of moral development, like Piaget's and Kohlberg's, seem to assign far too little weight to these environmental influences. Further, the sequential patterning, invariant order, and irreversible progression of the proposed stages are strongly disputed by extensive research evidence. Moral judgments may well follow some loose developmental progression, based on the child's refinement of the prerequisite symbolic skills, and on the ethical criteria exemplified or encouraged by the social milieu. However, there seems no basis for isolating moral decisions and inferences from other categories of rule-governed cognition strongly affected by social norms, exemplary modeling, and environmental feedback.

CONSERVATION AND RELATED JUDGMENTS

Piaget (1952a,b) was the first to draw attention to the phenomenon of conservation. He noted such common examples as the following: When adjacent cookies are placed further apart, or when a ball of clay is squashed into a thinner pancake, the amount of either starting material remains unchanged. Only the perceptual features of the materials have been transformed. Yet, young children often fail to allow for this quantitative invariance. They confound instead the number of cookies with their spatial extension, or the mass of the clay with its appearance before and after modification. In Piaget's invariant sequence, the child's thought moves through four (sensorimotor, preoperational, concrete operations, and formal operations) qualitatively distinct stages. He proposed that the ability to perceive an amount as being intact even if stimuli are rearranged perceptually is an important facet of logical comprehension because it distinguishes stages of intellectual development: The concrete operational child should conserve; the preoperational child should not.

In the classical conservation paradigm, two identical stimuli (jars of sand or fluid; rows of objects, etc.) are presented and, if necessary, are adjusted until the child decides that both are equal. Next, one stimulus is altered perceptually (the contents are put in a container of different dimensions; objects are spread further apart or closer together, etc.), and the child is then asked if the unchanged and the transformed stimuli have equal amounts. By Piaget's criteria, to be credited as conserving the child must both (*a*) assert that the stimuli remain equal *and* (*b*) give an acceptable reason for so judging. Explanations stating that both stimuli had equal amounts to start with and nothing has been added to or removed from either, or that reversing the transformations would again make the stimuli identical, are taken as evidence that the child "really" understands the phenomenon. Sometimes, as in Piaget's method of assessing moral judgments, the child must also "stick to his guns" in the face of false social feedback. If told that other peers disagree, the child must maintain his decision despite the "countersuggestion" pressures, in order for his conservation responses to be accepted as legitimate, not ephemeral. Within specific dimensions like substance, number, volume, or space, it is also assumed that a child who comprehends the principles will judge correctly in all or almost all instances unless he is still in transition from an earlier stage of mental maturity. Assuming that conservation ability is stage-dependent has clear implications. As with moral judgments, stage reasoning suggests that environmental guidance to stimulate conservation should have negligible effect. Unless the crucial stage changes have been accomplished, or at least begun, conservation should not be manifested.

Training Studies

The first research that tested the impact of experience on conservation was performed by Piagetians who assumed that training efforts could not alter cognitive development (Beilin, 1971). Their attempts proved generally unsuccessful and, reviewing those early studies, Flavell (1963) characterized most of the guidance methods as plausible and sound, but concluded that "most of them have had remarkably little success in producing cognitive change." Yet, shortcomings in teaching procedures may explain the negative outcomes. Hatano (1971) and Brainerd (in press) have criticized the adequacy of the training methods used in the studies Flavell reviewed (i.e., Smedslund, 1961a,b; Wohlwill, 1959; Wohlwill & Lowe, 1962). In particular, these critics suggested that the children in the unsuccessful studies were not properly pretrained to understand and use the rather complicated experimental apparatus such as balance scales. Brainerd (in press) found that subsequent research using the same general methods, but not the complicated equipment, were successful. Thus, it appears that it was the ineffectiveness of the procedure rather than the resistance of children to teaching that hampered conservation gains.

Perhaps the first successful use of observational techniques was reported by Beilin (1965), who compared nonverbal reward, verbal orientation plus praise, demonstration plus rule provision, and "equilibration" methods to teach conservation of length and number to kindergarten children. Only the demonstration plus rule training succeeded. In this procedure, the experimenter modeled conservation responses and, if the child erred, stated the correct rule. Thus, the combination of exemplary plus verbal modeling broke the historical training impasse. Since then, progress has been more quickly made. Training to conserve weight then generalized to conservation of substance (Kingsley & Hall, 1967). Once kindergarten children had learned to conserve number, they transferred the principles to discontinuous quantity items (Rothenberg and Orost, 1969). Gelman (1969) conducted a very careful study that emphasized discriminations among relevant and irrelevant stimulus details, using feedback to help the child cognize and monitor critical cues, rather than practicing response skills. This guidance strategy fostered conservation of length and number.

Siegler and Liebert (1972) compared a feedback procedure similar to Gelman's under conditions of symbolic modeling through rule provision, rule provision plus feedback, and untrained control conditions, using kindergarten children who failed to conserve liquid quantity during a pretest phase. While the feedback-only technique brought some improvement during training, rule provision led to stronger gains. On perceptually discrepant inequality items, rule provision aided performance, whereas knowledge of results did not; however, the best scores were earned by the rule-plus-feedback group. On a retention test 1 week after training, the rule-only and rule-plus-feedback groups surpassed the controls in conserving liquid quantity with equal stimuli. The feedback-only children did not perform better than the controls. On liquid inequality items, the combination of rule provision plus feedback prompted superior performance; children of no other trained groups outperformed the controls. There was also a tendency for more children (35%) of both rule groups to generalize conservation to amount of solid substance (clay). In contrast, only 10% of the feedback-only and the control children displayed this transfer. These results illustrate the rather narrow generalization across stimulus dimensions typically found even in successful attempts to train conservation. Further, most effective techniques have required extensive application before progress can be made. Piagetian scholars point out that in studies like the preceding one, transfer appears so dimension-bound that the results merely reflect the preoperational child's limited ability to profit from experience. Yet, note that the items used for training were drawn solely from a single stimulus dimension. From the standpoint of rule learning strategies, little transdimensional generalization might be expected unless training procedures sample instances from a greater variety of stimulus dimensions. For this purpose, the next set of studies was undertaken.

Rosenthal and Zimmerman (1972b) explored the effects of demonstration, rule provision, and positive feedback to the model on the acquisition and generalization of multidimensional conservation, using the Goldschmid and Bentler (1968a,b) scales. Forms A and B each contained items representing the conservation dimensions of number, area, substance, weight, and continuous and discontinuous quantity. Four related experiments were conducted. In each, the child performed in baseline and acquisition phases on Form A items, which were also presented to the model for training. The new, Form B, items served to assess generalization. For the first two studies, first-graders were randomly selected and baseline-tested. The one-fifth who consistently conserved were assigned to Experiment II. The nonconserving majority was studied in Experiment I. In this experiment, the children were taught by observing the conservation performance of an adult female. In one condition, the model stated for each item both a correct judgment of equality and an explanatory rule ("because they were the same in the first place"). In the alternative treatment, the model merely gave correct judgments (e.g., "There is the same amount there as there is there.") and did not offer reasons. Within each modeling variation, while half of the children witnessed the experimenter supply feedback (e.g., "That's right" or "Correct") to all of the model's answers, praise to the model was withheld when the remaining children observed. Neither feedback, praise, nor rewards were applied to the child's responses, which were scored by two criteria: correctly judging conservation relationships (judgments only), and also giving an adequate explanation for so judging (judgments plus rule).

On the judgments-only measure, observing the model prompted strong increases in conservation from baseline to acquisition and generalization tests, with no decline between the trained (Form A) and transfer (Form B) items. The control group scored significantly lower in both postbaseline phases. Praise to the model, and her stating or withholding explanations, had no effect on these results. To assess experiential effects among children giving no evidence of being "in transition" to the concrete operations stage, the same analyses were performed for those in the modeling groups who utterly failed to conserve (zero judgments-only scores) during baseline. The same pattern of results was obtained (see Table 3-1). One should note that, (with 6.0 the maximum possible score), although the postmodeling means rose sharply over baseline, they did not nearly approach perfect conservation.

On the judgments-plus-rule measure, the modeling children again surpassed the controls in both acquisition and generalization phases. Feedback to the model had no effect but, with explanations now required for response to be correct, the children who heard the model give reasons for her judgments outperformed the no-rule modeling subjects. Thus, providing the rule improved verbal rationales later, but did not aid in decisions about stimulus equality. Both with-rule and no-rule modeling groups exceeded their own baseline scores in each later phase, and the no-rule experimentals significantly outscored the controls in acquisition, although not in generalization. At least for the acquisition test, these data suggested that observing an adult who judges stimuli without giving explanations led children to *induce* cor-

TABLE 3-1
Mean Conservation Instances by Phase for Modeling and Control Groups on Judgments-Only and Judgments-Plus-Rule Criteria[a]

	Criterion of dependent measure					
	Judgments-only phase			Judgments-plus-rule phase		
Group	Baseline	Acquisition	Generalization	Baseline	Acquisition	Generalization
Total sample						
No rule, no feedback	.50	4.90	4.50	.25	2.45	2.10
No rule with feedback	.50	4.90	4.30	.35	1.60	1.55
Rule, no feedback	.50	4.20	3.90	.20	4.10	3.35
Rule with feedback	.85	4.20	4.10	.45	3.35	3.00
Control	.65	.90	1.20	.45	.65	.95
Zero baselines						
No rule	.00	3.64	3.36	.00	1.79	1.65
With rule	.00	4.52	3.93	.00	3.37	2.81

[a]Control subjects did not observe a model but were given the acquisition and generalization tests to assess "spontaneous" changes. [Table adapted from Rosenthal and Zimmerman, 1972b. Copyright © 1972 by the American Psychological Association. Reprinted by permission.]

rect reasons, consistent with their altered judgments. As before, when the data were reanalyzed for children with zero baseline (judgments-plus-rule) scores, the results were very similar to those for the total sample (see Table 3-1). This experiment showed that modeling could promote multidimensional conservation. The effects of adding verbal explanations to the model's routine depended on which conservation criterion was invoked. The model's reasons did not affect the accuracy of the children's judgments, but improved the judgments-plus-rule scores. Commending the model for her answers, which might make her appear a more authoritative source of information and heighten the situational demands to adopt her decisions, did not influence the children. For both response criteria, those who never conserved in baseline made gains comparable to those able to correctly judge some baseline items.

In light of the effects of a facilitating model, what would happen if initially conserving children observed a consistently *non*conserving adult? An invariant stage view might expect that these social cues would be resisted or ignored. This was tested in Experiment II with the children whose baseline conservation had either been almost or entirely perfect. For each item of a pair, the model alternately judged the left-hand or the right-hand stimulus as greater, but gave no explanations to justify her nonconservation answers and received no praise from the experimenter. Essentially, except for the direction of the modeled judgments, the procedures were the same as for the no rule provided-no feedback condition of the first study. The model's impact was pronounced. On both response measures, the children reduced their post-modeling conservation. The judgments-plus-rule data provided some evidence for significantly *reversed* inferential processes, because the child's original explanations no longer fitted the changed judgments and were therefore altered as well. This interpretation was supported by the reasons offered by the children. After watching the model, pro-conservation rationales were usually dropped and replaced by various nonconservation arguments, e.g., "because it's heavier (or taller, larger, etc.)."

We wanted to study a group of economically disadvantaged youngsters for whom English was not the language spoken at home, and also to compare the effectiveness of demonstrations versus instructions in teaching these minority group children. These were the goals of Experiment III, whose subjects were Chicano first graders from a *barrio* community. Half of the boys and girls received demonstration training identical to that for the with rule provision no-feedback condition of Experiment I. The remaining children received verbal instructions training similar to classroom lecture methods. After establishing a baseline, the experimenter presented items to instructions subjects, using stimuli already transformed, e.g., both a ball and a cylinder of clay were shown. The child was told that both items were equal in mass and was told the reason for equality, i.e., that both had the same mass in the first place. Hence, both the instructions and the demonstrations groups were told that the transformed and untransformed items were equal, and heard the same reasons for stimulus equivalence. The two groups differed in only two respects: (*a*) Instructions children saw the stimulus pairs after the transformation had been performed, while the demonstrations children watched the experimenter modify one member of each stimulus pair. (*b*) The instructions group heard the experimenter give a monologue containing a paraphrased judgment i.e., the assessment of equality, and the rationale justifying this judgment. The demonstration group instead observed the model respond to the experimenter's inquiries, so that the adults enacted a question-and-answer dialogue. Apart from these differences in the format of training, children in the two conditions were treated identically. Yet, on both dependent measures, the demonstration group outperformed the instructions group in every posttraining test. In addition, while the demonstration children significantly surpassed their own baseline scores on acquisition and generalization, the instructed group failed to benefit from their form of training. These results offered rather striking evidence that, for certain populations and conceptual tasks, exemplary modeling may be much more efficient as teaching devices than presenting equivalent information in an exclusively narrative format. Other research suggesting the same conclusion will be discussed later.

According to Piaget's theory, children do not reach the stage at which conservation is possible much before age 7 (Inhelder & Piaget, 1958). Thus, it was of interest to test modeling techniques with a group of very young nursery schoolers (median age = 4:6 years). Pilot exploration had shown that this age group could not watch attentively during the model's six consecutive training performances, as had the 6-year-olds. The length of the model's performances seemed to exceed the preschool child's willingness or capacity to maintain attention, without which observational learning suffers. Hence, an alternation format was substituted. The model demonstrated the first item, after which it was presented to the child; the model performed the next item, then the child's turn came, etc. Except for this alteration, which kept the children involved in the experimental events, all procedures were just as in the modeling-alone condition of Experiment I. On the judgments-only measure, modeling significantly increased conservation scores, which surpassed baseline levels comparably in acquisition and generalization phases. The judgments-plus-rule data were more equivocal, because the children failed to state scorable reasons, instead offering various unscorable rationales, e.g., "That one was a ball." or "That one was a block and that one is." These oracular pronouncements must have met the child's own standards for shared social communication. When asked to explain further, the child typically gazed at the adult with perplexity, and then repeated the prior cryptic revelation, as if hoping that the adult would prove less dense the second time. Such attempts to elicit more information were futile. Viewed qualitatively, it seemed that either the *linguistic* skills or the norms of specificity needed to state an adequate conservation rationale were not yet a part of the children's verbal repertoires. Despite successful discrimination of stimulus equality on judgments alone, the children's verbal efforts failed to express the bases for their reasoning. With the first graders of Experiment I, those children's scores on the judgments-only and judgments-plus-rule tests correlated substantially ($r = .83$). One would expect an even higher correlation between teenagers and adults. Conversely, it has been noted (Kendler & Kendler, 1967; Morris, 1970) on various tasks that young children's abstract grasp may show a low correspondence to their skill in verbalizing inferences, making it hazardous to weight spoken language too heavily in measuring the level of their thought. A child may be able to learn and transfer instances of a concept, while still unable to state the principles that govern his reasoning. It is easier to devise operational tests that enable a child to display comprehension than it is to illuminate the covert symbolic processes which regulate understanding. For example, psycholinguists, to explain the psychological processes underlying language, have trusted comprehension tests as being reliable prototype measures of skill. But any definition that coordinates all thinking to verbal indices must exclude important symbolic feats (e.g., musical virtuosity, the ability to draw spatial analogies) from the corroborating evidence.

The conservation studies revealed prompt progress by the observers after receiving socially mediated guidance. Children with zero baseline scores profited about as much as other learners. Although it did not alter the effects of modeling on judgment responses, providing a verbal rule aided the production of scorable reasons. Among children who only observed judgments, there was some spontaneous increase in correct rationales making their scores fit the judgment shifts in both directions, i.e., toward stimulus equality and toward difference. Feedback praising the model's responses had no effect on conservation, a finding not expected if children are assumed to passively yield to adult influence. Exemplary modeling was quite successful, but a verbal narration technique presenting similar information failed to aid *barrio* children. In this instance, too, if the observed conservation changes in fact were based on uncritical compliance to situational and social demands, the experimenter's overt propaganda should have swayed the instructions group.

No single set of studies can do more than make a small contribution, and spur further inquiry. To validate the notion that modeling can teach conservation, we felt that four points required further exploration: (*a*) Retention had not been tested. Would the children's gains resulting from brief modeling be maintained after some time had elapsed? (*b*) The children had always spoken their judgments and reasons. Could they generalize to a purely nonverbal conservation measure? (*c*) Feedback to the model did not affect performance, and rule provision only improved the judgments-plus-reasons outcomes. Yet, Beilin (1965), Gelman (1969), and Siegler and Liebert (1972) had all found that when the *child* received feedback, rule provision, or both, his learning was aided. How would a form of verbal correction training that combined rule provision with positive feedback to the child compare with demonstration, and would combining both methods prove best? (*d*) Perhaps most crucial, the previous tasks only used equivalent stimuli, to preserve Goldschmid and Bentler's (1968a,b) standard formats. Hence, all correct responses were in the direction of equality judgments. This might have created a summary set for the child to report equality even when unsure of an answer based on the stimulus quantities. If this occurred, it would inflate the scores earned. What would happen when both equal and unequal stimulus instances were displayed, so that neither response set would fit more than half of the items?

Zimmerman and Rosenthal (1974b) set out to address these issues. By freely adapting items from the Goldschmid and Bentler tasks, three different 12-item stimulus sets were developed. In each set, conservation of number, length, and two-dimensional space were assessed by a quartet of items, two of which were equalities as before, and two were inequalities. On inequality tests, a pair of unequal stimuli was presented, and the larger was indicated for the child. The experimenter next transformed the appearance of the larger or smaller stimulus, asking the child if the transformed stimuli were now equal or unequal, and also requesting the child to explain his judgment. Inequalities tested whether the child could preserve the original unlike amounts after one stimulus was perceptually altered. By counterbalancing, half of the inequality items were veridical, with the actually larger stimulus appearing larger; the remaining inequalities were nonveridical, e.g., an array of five poker chips was spread out to span more space than a six-chip array. Stimulus Set I was used for baseline and again to test retention some 10 days after training. Set II served for training purposes and to measure immediate acquisition. Set III was used only to assess immediate generalization.

The rationales the children provided to justify conserving the main items were classified as *invariant quantity* explanations by Goldschmid and Bentler (1968b), who treated *reversing transformations* as a qualitatively distinct conservation index. To assess reversing, after the child completed the generalization (Set III) items, the experimenter showed the child a blue and a green rod of equal length, arranged in parallel. The experimenter transformed the rods into a sidewise "T" shape, and then asked the child to judge the rods' respective lengths. If equality was judged correctly, the child was asked how he would show a friend that the sticks were still the same length. Correct response required the child to nonverbally meet the reversibility criterion, by returning the rods to a parallel spatial format. Kindergarten students (mean age = 5:7 years) from lower middle-class homes, who could not conserve equality before training (failure on all six baseline equality items), served as subjects.

Four training conditions were established. In the *modeling only* group, the model demonstrated a correct judgment and supported it with an invariant quantity explanation. In the *correction only* group, the child judged items as in baseline, but on correct judgments was told "That's right," and on false judgments was given an appropriate invariant quantity rationale, e.g., "No matter what they look like, they don't have the same amount because that one [pointing] had more in the first place." In the *model-plus-correction* group, the model performed as above. Then, when the child attempted to assess the item, he received positive feedback if he was right, and if he erred, he was instructed as in the correction-only group. *Control* children neither observed a model nor obtained any feedback about their responses. After training and the test for emulative acquisition, all later (generalization, reversal, and delayed retention) tasks were given without any feedback or added guidance.

Both modeling and correction training significantly improved conservation, with the correction method producing somewhat more substantial gains on the primary measures. The modeling group surpassed their own baseline levels at each later phase and outperformed their nonmodeling counterparts on each individual training and retention test. The corrections group also surpassed their own baselines *and* at all later phases outperformed the noncorrection children. The model-plus-correction group was slightly stronger, tending to score better than the correction-only condition only during acquisition. The untrained controls changed little, continuing to fail *all* equality items given after baseline. On the nonverbal, reversibility task, there was also evidence that training had instated conservation. The four groups differed significantly, largely because the controls *never* reversed correctly. The training conditions did not differ statistically but, as was the case with the main items, the direction of results showed modeling-plus-correction best, correction-only next, and modeling-only last. These nonverbal transfer data support our prior conclusion that real *learning*, not superficial yielding to adults' views, was imparted by the information conveyed in brief teaching exposures: Once the child had witnessed and discerned the adults' judgmental standards, the same criteria were then used as anchors, guiding the child's later conservation decisions.

This study confirmed the prior results and helped to answer some previously posed questions: (*a*) *Conservation learning was retained with untrained items.* How long might this retention persist, given the brief transaction between the adults and the child? Although the answer depends on the importance of conservation skills in daily living, many factors could affect the child's competence. Active practice, tangible rewards and social praise, continued guidance and feedback from others, and discussing or comparing judgments and reasoning with peers, would all promote further skill if the interpersonal milieu encouraged the child to excel at conserving. The typical *saliency* of conservation for 4- to 8-year-olds, unless they are subjects in psychological research, is a moot point. Few if any childhood games, hobbies, or peer group actions seem to hinge on conservation acuity. Hence, it was striking that short-lived training promoted retention over the interval studied. If conservation was not made salient by periodic environmental demands to elicit the concept, retraining might be needed to refresh it. Conversely, suppose the Parker Brothers devised an enthralling new game, requiring conservation skills, which was enthusiastically adopted by this age group. Or suppose that conservation miraculously became a criterion for social popularity and prestige. One would then expect long-delayed retesting to show increases in aptitude. The same variables as apply to any intellectual skill should also apply to conservation. Based on its value for a particular child, as largely determined by the social environment, competence may be refined by further experiences or diminished by neglect. This occurs because the salience of a skill will affect the coding, storage, and retrieval strategies that are applied to organize and maintain it (Bower, 1974; Pressley, 1976; Rosenthal & Bandura, 1978; Royer & Cable, 1976).

(*b*) *As an index of comprehension, conservation was generalized to a task requiring nonverbal behavior.* All unguided control children failed this task, but many trained youngsters spontaneously grasped the fact that replacing the rods in parallel array could show a friend that the sticks were still the same length. Children coordinated the concept of equivalent lengths to moving the rods, a feat not easily explained by classical views of stimulus or response generalization. In essence, children abstracted the idea of equality and the reversal movements as related, that is, as instances that belong to a category of similar events. In doing so, they again illustrated that in conceptual social learning, people typically gain information in terms of symbolic attributes and relationships, rather than accumulate discrete stimulus–response connections (Rosenthal & White, 1972a; Rosenthal & Zimmerman, 1976; Zimmerman & Rosenthal, 1974c).

(*c*) *Conservation could be taught.* Once more, "precocious" conservation was instated by verbal correction techniques (Beilin, 1965; Gelman, 1969; Siegler & Liebert, 1972), by demonstration (Rosenthal & Zimmerman, 1972b), and by the combination of these two techniques, which generally brought the strongest gains. In this study, the correction method seemed more efficient. In the prior study, youngsters who had a more limited English language facility learned far better from exemplary modeling than from a narrative verbal technique. The relative merits of verbal correction and demonstration as instructional formats would depend on the nature of the tasks and their complexity for the children, and on the consequences of error. In complex rule-governed behavior such as learning linguistic rules, it would be exceedingly difficult to produce generative grammatical speech by correction without modeling. Also, where errors in performance exact high prices correction procedures will not be optimal. Under less taxing conditions, or when children must refine already-familiar knowledge, verbal correction might prove to be relatively more effective. As yet, research results are too tentative to attempt broad theoretical classifications. Particularly needed are empirical analysis and organization of the key components of important scholastic tasks. The more clearly stated the criterion goals of teaching, the easier it becomes to compare alternative means of implementing them. Hopefully, continued research will supply useful guidelines for practical teaching efforts in the relatively near future. But more evidence is still needed to inform the working educator about the pros and cons of technique variations, and how to best sequence them, for effective learning.

(*d*) *Conservation of both equal and unequal quantities was acquired, generalized, and retained.* Children did not display knowledge by a set that required the same judgment direction always be followed. The training benefits persisted when each conservation subtype was analyzed separately, showing that conservation learning transcended specific stimulus dimensions.

Sequential and Social Considerations

The role of developmental skill acquisition needs further comment. Once a child has mastered part of a symbolic domain, related knowledge can be added with relative ease. Refining existing paradigms into more elaborate forms is easier than instating basic abstract components. Consider the difficulties encountered in operant attempts to introduce simple language responses in preverbal children. Although it proved less taxing to expand limited but extant language repertoires than to instate language use, diligent efforts did succeed. This suggests the limitations of age-based "readiness" for teaching purposes. Within an age range, such as the school years, during which most children have at least mastered simple symbolic skills, precise age should not be an especially critical factor in learning (e.g., Rosenthal & Zimmerman, 1972a). The situation is reversed with younger, preschool children. During the earliest years, when the foundations of abstract proficiency must evolve from scratch, age becomes a much more powerful indicator of the child's basic repertoire. All else being equal, age variations index differential opportunity to gain experience with symbolic and cultural conventions. The younger the child, the less stable and well practiced his abstract skills, the fewer or more limited his repertoire of accomplishments, and the more rudimentary his covert organization of information.

The system of cognitive categories should then, be relatively simple, encompassing fewer elements within hierarchically arranged superordinate and subordinate classes (Aaronson & Scarborough, 1976; Mandler, 1967a; Posner, 1973; Spoehr & Smith, 1975). In addition, the child will have access to a sparser network of interconnections among separable but related concept ladders. For example, under the broad heading of "animals" would be fewer illustrations of particular species, with fewer and less inclusive functional (e.g., domestic, edible, dangerous) or morphological (e.g., feline, reptile, vertebrate) groupings. One would expect less facility with crisp distinctions (e.g., real versus cartoon) among animal categories, and less skill in extracting correspondences across classes, for example, the parallels to be drawn from examples of fish swimming, birds flying, and gazelles running as characteristic means of locomotion. Also, the young child will have had less chance to become adept at transforming a grasped abstraction into adequate spoken language. One would expect a greater discrepancy between the child's ability to recognize facts or relationships, and his ability to express that understanding verbally, than would be evidenced by an older child or adult.

These longitudinal aspects of skill development are important phenomena for study. In a social learning framework, they would be analyzed and explained in terms of (*a*) shared component skills (Gagné, 1970); (*b*) the amount of exposure, familiarity, and practice available; (*c*) the meaning and importance assigned to specific concepts by the social environment; (*d*) the utility of the knowledge for earning tangible and symbolic rewards; and (*e*) the evolutionary history of each individual's covert rules for organizing and storing information. All of these considerations suggest some greater proficiency for older children. Older children will have wider contacts with assorted events and more chance to apply their learning to subsequent conduct. They will have more familiarity with multiple demands met in diverse social situations, and in interpreting cues from a wider sample of social partners. They will be more adept at judging others' expectations and foreseeing the consequences of meeting or violating norms. They will also have learned to better harmonize, revise, cross-index, and shift among their own categorical storage units (Bell & Handel, 1976; Hawkins, Reicher, Rogers, & Peterson, 1976). None of these accomplishments requires any assumption that innate forces determine the learning or management of information. The same variables, operating in unique historical combinations, will create individual differences among specific children. One does not expect novice learners in an experiment or a course to display great skill early in training. With experience, mental rehearsal, and feedback, competence will improve. Yet, some people may then profit or suffer from atypical personal backgrounds and thus either greatly surpass or lag behind their peers. The same variables that govern learning may favor the older child and, like other abstract skills, conservation should also reflect such differences. But there is no reason to assume that even quite young children *cannot* learn to conserve. On the contrary, the social learning view, which emphasizes the reciprocal interaction among cognitive, behavioral, and environmental determinants, suggests that the weaker the initial repertoire, the more urgently guidance is needed. Additional systematic teaching may help compensate for deficiencies in spontaneous learning. Even when these children receive additional training, generalization may at first remain more limited than for children who command a more diversified system of stored abstract guidelines. Limitations such as these are expected if conservation is treated as but one of many cognitive skills. If, however, conservation is taken to mark the attainment of a new, discrete developmental stage, continuity of progress may be masked by setting a threshold for learning that ignores *relative* advances.

In this way, some of the disputes between structuralist and enviromentalist stances are reduced to questions of how conservation is to be defined. Thus, in the previous studies, 4-year-olds were taught to make correct judgments (but not scorable explanations) to equality (but not inequality) "displays." Judgment gains were measured within a single session, but were not tested for durability over time. Do these results constitute "conservation" by 4-year-olds? The answer depends on interpretive premises rather than fact. Which aspects of conserving should and should not be taken as critical remains a matter of preference among dependent measures.

Zimmerman and Lanaro (1974) tried to circumvent the labeling problems by including both equality and inequality items, and by testing generalization after delay. They studied conservation of length, and its transfer to two-dimensional space tasks, among children drawn from low-income homes whose ages ranged from 4:1 to 4:9 years. Since children so young could not sustain attention unless modeling displays were kept very brief, each conservation item was divided into separate steps, for teaching judgments and reasoning. Under modeling conditions, an adult demonstrated the correct response by taking turns with the child but did not do so for the controls. On the judgments-only measure, the trained children showed significant acquisition and retention of length conservation, while the control children did not. The judgments-plus-rule results were even more pronounced, with the modeling children surpassing the controls in learning and maintaining length conservation for both equality and inequality items. However, on the delayed transfer test, significant generalization to spatial items was limited to the judgments-only measure.

What do these results tell us? Since conservation was tested on items different from those used for training, the acquisition and retention data on length were themselves generalized measures of conceptual learning. Modeling procedures effectively promoted adoption and maintenance of the decision criteria exemplified. Unlike the previous research with 4-year-olds, observers clearly acquired verbal rationales to accompany their changed length judgments. Since both equality and inequality tasks were included, social learning gains were confirmed under conditions that ruled out the possibility of response sets determining children's decisions. Since the children had never heard the model give verbal rationales for two-dimensional space, it was of considerable interest that cross-dimensional transfer from length to space was only found on the judgments-only criterion. By their failure to generalize reasons, they behaved like their age-mates in the prior study, who also had not observed modeled explanations. Although judgment changes were found in each case, unguided verbal reasoning did not significantly improve. In contrast, when the present observers repeatedly witnessed explanations accompanying the model's length judgments, they were able to learn the skill and apply it correctly to new length conservation items. The results support several points already discussed. Quite young children learned abstract response patterns as the result of socially mediated guidance. Learning was retained after delay; judgment changes also generalized to new spatial items at a later time. Unlike the slightly older groups in the previous modeling studies, 4-year-olds could not, unaided, spontaneously integrate their verbal explanations with their judgments. These results, and the procedural adjustments needed to sustain the child's attention, underscore the more rudimentary nature of skill repertoires in younger children. Nonetheless, these children were quite amenable to, and clearly benefited from, social learning experiences.

Likewise, Denney, Zeytinoglu, and Selzer (1977) taught 4-year-olds to conserve length and number through demonstration and feedback. Although transfer to substance conservation, using material very different from the training stimuli, proved nonsignificant, the results prompted further study of transfer effects to check hypotheses based on Piagetian theory. In their next experiment, children were taught to conserve length and mass, and transfer was tested with number, a dimension that is typically conserved before those trained, and with weight, a dimension that occurs developmentally after those trained. If structural development follows a fixed sequence, then guidance that is effective at a particular stage (able to teach the intermediate, i.e., length and mass, dimensions) should also assist in tasks involving earlier stages (number) but not in those that emerge later (weight). In fact, delayed posttesting revealed significant transfer on both weight and number dimensions, counter to fixed-stage deductions. Thus, significant learning and transfer were again obtained with children presumed to be some years from the onset of concrete operations. The second study, unlike the first, assured the salience of the materials used in assessing transfer, even though the principles tested were not demonstrated during training. It appeared that both situational context cues (material composition) and modeled rules affected observers' conceptual performance.

The role of setting stimuli was also addressed by Rose and Blank (1974), who argued that cognitive processes cannot be isolated from their defining context without distorting the conclusions. In other words, the connotations of inquiry, as well as the content, will steer behavior. For example, in the traditional conservation test, the pattern of questioning has evaluative implications not usually acknowledged by structuralists. The child is first asked to judge two perceptually equal stimuli, e.g., glasses of water. Then, one stimulus is transformed into a different shape, e.g., the contents of one glass are poured into a flat pan, and the child is again asked the same question. The task stimuli aside, how would you react if, after a common, everyday event occurs, the same question is promptly repeated? One might well be suspicious and guess that either one's first answer was wrong or some critical metamorphosis had transpired. In either case, one might very well change the second answer, even though believing the first to be correct, through confusion or a desire to satisfy the examiner. This hypothesis was tested by comparing children's performance in the traditional format with another that assessed conservation by a single question. Rose and Blank showed that conservation judgments doubled under single-question conditions, and concluded that context cues strongly influence this class of decisions. Unless these situational factors are taken into account, the respective weights of conceptual reasoning and implicit social demands remain ambiguous.

Because he was concerned with the prototypic growth of abstract thought, Piaget paid little attention to situational influences in either theorizing or devising and validating his task procedures. But neglect of such methodological factors as those just illustrated, raises serious questions about the data base on which sweeping, fixed-stage claims have been made. In fact, there are reasons for questioning whether studies that have been interpreted as supporting stagelike effects in conservation learning actually do so. Brainerd (1977), for example, has argued forcefully that correlational patterns, often used to bolster stage interpretations, suffer from psychometric artifacts. In reanalyzing the data from a series of studies to correct these shortcomings, Brainerd found no evidence that conservation guidance aided "transitional" more than "preoperational" children.

Most teaching studies conducted from agnostic viewpoints have chosen to treat conservation like any other conceptual behavior. The classical criterion for confirming rule learning is evidence that knowledge generalizes to new examples and settings where it is relevant. Concessions have been made to Geneva by also undertaking to examine the types of reasons given by children to justify their conservation judgments. However, it seemed that the criteria for "true" conservation expanded as the number of successful training studies grew. This culminated in Kuhn's (1974) review, which dismissed all training research because it failed to satisfy all Genevan (Inhelder & Sinclair, 1969) criteria. Besides the usual requirements of appropriate explanations, transfer, retention, and resistance to counter suggestion, Kuhn added a yardstick seldom invoked before: Guidance methods must create continued "mental reorganization" after teaching ceases.

A recent modeling study appears to meet even this most stringent criterion. Charbonneau, Robert, Bourassa, and Gladu-Bisonnette (1976) exposed first-graders to an adult's 10-minute demonstration of conservation judgments. Children were then tested immediately after training, after a week had elapsed, and after 3 months, using a wide variety of transfer items as well as the training stimuli. While untrained controls failed to conserve at any time during the initial or later testing, children exposed to modeling displayed significant learning and transfer, even to the most novel generalization items. Conservation was not only retained, but was also significantly improved across the 3-month interval. In contrast to the controls' performance, this continued improvement by the modeling group would seem to meet the requirement for structural reorganization progressing after training. Whether viewed as a change in the patterning of thought, or as a gain in cognitive skill, the impact of social guidance now seems beyond dispute. Moreover, cognitive advances, including "mental reorganization" are not purely intrapsychic, autistic events that suddenly cross some fixed threshold of skill during a discrete period of time. Whether or not socially initiated changes in conservation continue will depend on reciprocally interacting factors. Children who begin conserving after modeling may be selectively exposed to additional people and circumstances that either support or work against conservation reasoning. For example, the child may actively seek opinions about conservation principles from adults or peers after initial teaching experiences. Such altered salience can sway events in the child's environment, serving to sustain and further develop expertise in conserving (or other cognitive skills).

Actually, in Piaget's theory, social forces play an equivocal role. Although the sequence of stages is assumed to be innately fixed, events that spur mental disequilibrium can bring advances. Thus, transitional children may derive some gain from social conflict situations. A research paradigm to test this possibility has involved combined groups of conserving and nonconserving children who were required to decide on a common judgment for conservation items. In a first study, a nonconserving child was placed with two conservers to agree on joint answers. The group could manipulate the stimuli and discuss their disagreements. Although this method limits the experimental control over training, it has the great virtue of creating a peer microculture charged with reconciling its divergent views. The nonconserving child found himself in a minority, communicating with peers about socially acceptable standards for defining reality (Festinger, 1950; Schachter, 1951). In making group decisions, social influence processes would be expected to sway the deviant, nonconserving child. But compliance pressures were removed when children were individually tested on both the original and novel generalization items a week later. At that time, significant numbers of former nonconservers shifted toward conservation both on the original and on the transfer tasks. This outcome is in contrast with stage premises: Children who gave no pretraining evidence of conserving gained as much as those, presumably transitional, who had shown some conservation in baseline tests. Further, those children initially classified as conservers also improved after the modeling episodes, showing that increased saliency of cognitive standards can affect the majority, as well as the minority (Murray, 1972). In later work, Miller and Brownell (1975) paired one conserver with one nonconserver to discover whose judgments would dominate. Although the two-children groups rendered more conservation than nonconservation decisions, there was no unidirectional shift toward conservation, which was presumably the more "logically necessary" standard. Also, the pretest data suggest that conservers were, from the start, more confident in their judgments than the nonconservers; owing to the peer conflict paradigm, it cannot be determined which of the range of competing judgment standards was the most "logically necessary." A better test of the logical necessity of conservation would entail exposing children who display conservation to opposing social standards. If conservation is truly a mark of stage attainment, its logic should hold in the face of divergent social demands. If, instead, conservation is the product of self-regulatory criteria drawn from past social experience, it should respond to new events like other socially mediated standards (Bandura, 1977b; Rosenthal & Bandura, 1978).

This hypothesis was tested by Miller (1973), who studied the acquisition and extinction of weight conservation among three groups: fifth-graders who always conserved; third-graders who always conserved;

and third-graders who never conserved weight. Children less than perfectly consistent (partial conservers) were considered to be transitional, and were excluded from the sample. Children were taught to measure relative weights using a balance scale that would give distorted feedback when the experimenter activated a hidden electromagnet, or accurate feedback when the electromagnet was turned off. After pretesting, the child received a set of conservation problems on which feedback clashed with original beliefs. Thus, nonconservers observed proconservation outcomes, and conservers received anticonservation feedback. During feedback, each child's facial reactions were videotaped. After these events, the child received another set of problems, some familiar and others novel, with no feedback from the scale. The younger children readily and substantially altered their final judgments to conform to their prior feedback. The older, fifth-grade conservers were no more resistant to disconfirmation than the third-graders; both groups showed similar propensity to revise their judgments to fit the earlier feedback. Perhaps the most unexpected finding, according to Piagetian assumptions, was the low level of surprise among all of the children. The conservers showed no more evidence of arousal, nor any greater resistance to change in the face of disconfirmation, than their peers. Thus far, attempts to rebut these results have been hampered by procedural shortcomings, e.g., in selection of the sample and because of the use of a single extinction item (Strauss & Liberman, 1974). On the surface, conservation, like other forms of conceptual behavior, appears responsive to new information, and is not a rigid structural product impervious to experience.

The need for assuming that some form of motivational arousal, such as a state of conflict, is a prerequisite for cognitive change has also been challenged by further work. Some groups of children reached common solutions under social conflict conditions in which one conserver and two nonconservers were forced to reconcile their differences. Other children merely observed the leader of a conflict group report their final decision. The results of the more and less stressful modeling variations proved comparable; in each, significant, but similar, levels of acquisition and transfer of the conservation principle were attained. The nonconflict observers gave quite a different pattern of explanations from those that were modeled, in justifying their conservation judgments. Although acceptable by Piagetian criteria, their rationales showed spontaneous evidence of new cognitive ("structural") changes following social experience (Botvin & Murray, 1975). Hence, it would seem that while socially mediated guidance was just as effective without obvious conflict arousal, guidance alone was sufficient to induce complementary shifts in spontaneous reasoning once the judgment standards were altered. Nor were "natural conservers," clearly not in transition, refractory to anticonservation criteria (Miller, 1973).

Our concern with the social mediation of cognitive activities includes both the instructional and normative aspects of modeling. One is hard-pressed to imagine a case of conceptual social learning in which models do not "influence" observers (Simpson, Rosenthal, Daniel, & White, 1976). As social figures who respond in some coherent manner and exemplify performance criteria for stimulus events, the models assert a norm for behavior. The same social forces operate when a teacher instructs a class by any method, and when an experimenter–scientist guides child or adult subjects in any nonvicarious, traditional learning procedure. In all cases, the tutoring source has relevance for the learner, whether the advisor is informal, such as a fellow human being i.e., friend, or more pointedly specified by role labels like teacher and psychologist. Typically, the learner seeks to please and cooperate with the instructor. Adapting per se, to such implied or overt social demands does not constitute "compliance." Compliance may be said to occur when people overtly perform or endorse behavior they would avoid if free to act differently. Children do not adhere to dubious criteria even when apparently favored by authority figures (Rosenthal & White, 1972a). Instead, people use current events, past conclusions, and predictions about the future to construct meaningful standards to guide their present conduct (Bandura, 1977a,b; Rosenthal & Bandura, 1978). In the social conflict research, when tested alone after group decisions, children under no pressures to comply, still followed what they had learned in their social transaction (Murray, 1972). This is typical in normal living. Long ago, Festinger (1950), Kelley and Thibaut (1954), and Deutsch and Gerard (1955) pointed out that social influence has *information* value, i.e., to share and foster the knowledge of group members. Contemporary social learning theory assumes that a myriad of guidance cues and judgment standards are used by the person to construct meaningful systems and mnemonic strategies steering overt conduct (Bandura, 1977a; Rosenthal & Bandura, 1978). Social cues, pressures, and demands are forms of information that people may either follow, take into limited account, or completely ignore. Yet, there are very few situations in which decisions are made unmindful of social precedents from the past, or their current and future implications. This responsiveness mirrors the general human situation, and does not represent a slavish yielding to arbitrary or coercive norms.

The Logic of Conservation

Any decision rules will have limits if pushed far enough. Euclidian theorems, for example, must alter if assumptions switch to a Riemannian space. The logical necessity of conservation too is limited: Empirically, because "formal operational" adults do not always adhere to it; and conceptually, because its principles sometimes lead to illogical conclusions.

Russell (1976) compared conservation of area with groups of 6-year-olds and adults. The task involved deforming a 5 × 5-inch square into a rectangle by making adjustments that appeared to spatially equalize one another. In fact, although the rectangle was smaller, the adults accepted it as being equal in area to the square. Their reasoning, although using logic, was faulty, showing that conservation is not self-evident, even to mature judges. In contrast, children based their judgments on perceptual cues. As physicists have noted (Feynman, 1965), conservation is not a fact of nature, but rather, involves logical subrules appropriate for certain phenomena and human purposes but not for others. In Piagetian terms, the truly conserving child must understand all of the three justifications for conservation: invariant quantity, reversibility, and compensation. But it was the latter, i.e., compensation, rule that led the adults astray. This shows that contextual factors determine the relevance of conservation in general and the pertinence of its underlying subrules, despite the ontogenic mystique that many have attributed to conservation tasks.

There is also dispute as to whether the various subtypes of conservation are learned in the invariant sequence proposed by Piaget (Flavell, 1970). Although some studies confirm the expected ordering, others do not (Beard, 1963; Hyde, 1959; Uzgiris, 1964). Goldschmid and Bentler (1968a,b) found conservation subtypes to be largely intercorrelated, rather than distinct, and their items have not shown dimensional sequence effects when used by other investigators (Murray, 1972; Rosenthal & Zimmerman, 1972b; Zimmerman & Rosenthal, 1974b).

Although there seems to be some regularity in the order of acquisition of conservation subtypes, the sequence is hardly invariant and may depend on children's social and cultural experiences (Price-Williams *et al.*, 1969), as well as on stimulus parameters that make it either harder or easier for the child to infer and apply guiding rules. The relative ease of conserving various dimensions will hinge on several factors. First, the *frequency* of social modeling and reinforcement differ among types of conservation. Frequency itself indexes the *saliency* and *importance* of a class of events. Thus, number relates to many recurrent naturalistic activities, perhaps starting with finger games in infancy. From determining the number of quarters needed for the movies, or the span of days until Christmas, to keeping score of home runs and touchdowns, the child continually uses counting in daily experience. But other dimensions, such as weight, are cued by far fewer stimuli and are met in a narrower set of situations. These differences in importance and incidence enable some dimensions, and the social communication norms for dealing with them, to be more easily conserved than others. *Verifiability* is another distinguishing feature. Anyone able to count can determine the number of apples in a pile, and can readily compare stimulus groups in this regard. Determining small weight differences is much harder without access to a scale and knowledge of its use. Because of these disparities in properties and incidence of encounter, the child would be expected to develop more refined and stable conceptions of some dimensions than others. This should help in distinguishing regularities and changes for more familiar classes of attributes, as compared to rarer events, which are less meaningful and not well categorized. Particular item characteristics, for example, the novelty or interest value of materials, and the child's personal history of relevant experiences, will naturally qualify the importance, salience, and verifiability of dimensional attributes.

Cross-culture research supports the present interpretation. Greenfield (1966), Maccoby and Modiano (1966), Goodnow (1962), and Goodnow and Bethon (1966) all found that children raised in Western societies tend to conserve earlier than children from Third World nations, as a result of dissimilar cultural experiences. Formal education may spur certain cognitive skills, such as conservation, because these covary with the onset of schooling many cultures; however, in other societies, adults may never adopt "abstract" thought patterns: Adults of the African Wolof tribe seem unable to understand conservation of liquid (Bruner *et al.*, 1966b). Thus, certain cultural conditions may accelerate, delay, or prevent the acquisition of cognitive skills such as conservation. Local milieu variables also affect development. Illiterate potters' children, while adept at judging the quantity and character of clay, were otherwise unexceptional in other cognitive skills, which were neither exemplified nor reinforced because of parental occupation (Price-Williams *et al.*, 1969). In short, conservation seems to be acquired in a manner similar to other conceptual rules, readily to respond to teaching experiences, such as modeling, to be retained after delay and to be generalized to new stimuli, and does not appear to result from innately programmed growth processes.

The logic of the conservation response is another matter. Is it *logical* that functional equivalence or difference be subordinate to weight, or area to number (as when one set of objects is spread farther apart)? If conservation expresses an inherent logic, then the "extinction" studies discussed earlier would seem to imply that originally conserving children surrendered the logic they had already attained through development. Instead, it seems more plausible that children generalized from and adjusted to shifts in social conventions. Implicitly, these usage norms affect all conservation acting as boundary demands.

Conservation appears to depend both on *socially defined* reality, and on the nature of particular tasks. The dimension of number may offer the least ambiguous criteria. However arranged, seven diapers equal seven diapers, *as long as* numerosity remains the only decision standard. Seven diapers positioned far apart comprise a *Gestalt,* whose perimeter spans a much wider area than do seven stacked diapers, which in turn have greater apparent height. Stitched together, or variously decorated by infant use, seven diapers have functional and aesthetic properties quite distinct from seven pristine, unmodified diapers (Avant & Lyman, 1975; Banks, Clark, & Lucy, 1975; Clark & Brownell, 1975). If one cuts some of them into swatches, their sum still weighs the same. But do the cut nappies actually satisfy the grouping criteria for "diaperness?" This question can be answered in terms of social convention, but not by logic. People endow moving geometric forms with human properties as a function of contextual cues (Bassili, 1976); these judgments reflect situational standards rather than egocentric thought. One can define a diaper as whatever started as a diaper, however transformed, if its mass is unchanged. It is no less plausible, and probably more socially compelling, to base definition in part on whether a thing can be *used* as a diaper, hence, excluding the cut swatches. Even if he can easily reverse a transformation, the experimental subject may not feel free to judge in terms of that possibility since he was not invited or instructed to do so. In addition, while the child may know that it is quite possible to reassemble Daddy's fishing reel or Mom's hair dryer, he may have learned to expect unrestrained parental indignation if these items are dismantled. The same cautions would apply to many daily events, such as reworking a delicate pastry dough even if it remains quantitatively constant.

Multiple and conflicting categories for ordering events apply to all conservation stimuli. It is the child's actual task to first identify, and then follow, the criteria deemed socially germane. Criterion ambiguities are worse for dimensions other than number. Consider the example of two balls of Play-doh or clay. After one is squashed into a pancake, the child is asked if it contains "as much clay" as the other. For the quantitative attributes of height and area, the clay lumps are logically *unequal.* By verbal implication and according to social usage, the child may be expected to ignore these dimensions, but is this a matter of logic? Even adults have difficulty attending to one realm of cues while trying to ignore related events (Bregman & Rudnicky, 1975). When transferring a solid quantity, such as sand or salt, one may visibly spill a grain or incompletely transfer the contents of the first container. The sticking problem is much more of a complication with liquid quantity. Rarely if ever, no matter how hard or long one shakes, can all of the fluid be poured from the first container. Some drops invariably adhere to the first container, and remain where the child can see them. Logically, then, the stimuli have been made to be unequal. Indeed, rather than trying to free the residue, one's shaking efforts are more aimed at showing the child that one is earnestly attempting to transfer all of the fluid. A child's judgments of equality, it thus can be seen, are determined by context, usage, and convention. The child is expected, and after sufficient socialization, expects himself, to *ignore* the sinful droplets and judge as if all the liquid had been poured. In effect, the boundary demands are: "Ignore those trivial drops or assume they flowed out when I tried to shake them loose. Now decide if the water amounts are essentially equal." Likewise, there seem to be semi-implicit rules for all of the subtypes of conservation, rules which comprise the actual criteria for what must be discriminated and ignored. Although logical clarity would require it, we do not tell the child, "Exclude this, this, and this criterion, but follow the weight (or length or substance) dimension that I have in mind." Instead, we ask if stimuli are equal or have the same amounts, and expect children to infer our categorical boundaries from the norms of verbal usage and from the task context. We ask the child to follow a rule, not to display logic per se.

In fact, the operations used to assess conservation almost always confound several quantitative dimensions, any of which alone may admit or exclude equality. If several items are spread apart, a larger hand or a longer string would be needed in order to span them. The child can maintain identity between a solid array of elements and a larger hollow rectangle only by ignoring the amount of space enclosed by either stimulus. If sand is poured into a tall, narrow container, its area, circumference, and diameter all change. Although it could initially float in a shallow pan, a boat will not even fit on the surface when the fluid is poured into a slender bottle. Practical effects such as these must be ignored. In all of the examples given, conserving also requires the child to disregard the adult's motor acts, a demand violating the typical socialization norm that close attention must be paid to the examples of grown-ups, and that their demonstrations must be taken into account. In fact, most transformations seem to be visual and involve cues that draw attention to divergent stimulus properties. But in most cases, a child receives no guidance telling him to ignore what happens to the material and to make his decision only on the basis of quantity. To intuit these boundary conditions is neither more nor less logical than to ignore them. In both cases, the child must infer the social standards appropriate at the moment, as well as judge quantity. Analyzing these issues, Haygood (1972) and Siegler and Liebert (1972) drew similar conclusions.

Thus, although it is representative of rule learning, conservation does not reflect a child's inherent logical skills. Instead, the child is asked to perform tasks that may contain irrelevant dimensions (area, volume, pragmatic function) which, although they are legitimate, must be ignored in order to make correct responses, as defined by the experimenter and as socially expected. This is no different than the case of a sorting task, in which the subject must retain the dimensions of size and shape while ignoring color and composition in order to correctly match a governing concept. It is psychologically convenient, and of the utmost importance for rational thought, to be able to hold extraneous categories in abeyance while being guided by a given set of decision criteria. Yet, as with the recalcitrant droplets in the task of conserving liquid quantity, if logic were rigorously exercised, nominally correct answers would prove false guides. "Real" understanding would require responses like: They are the same in respect to substance, weight, color, and potential function, but are unequal with respect to area, volume, height, shape, and immediate utilitarian properties.

Judging Class Inclusion and Exclusion

One can see that conservation bears a strong family resemblance to the discrimination of sameness (equality) and difference (inequality) cues, whose importance was emphasized by Miller and Dollard (1941). Using groups of 3- and 4-year-olds, Zimmerman and Rosenthal (1974b) studied the effects of modeling and verbal correction in teaching recognition of sameness (class inclusion) and difference (class exclusion). Both types of guidance significantly enhanced sameness–difference judgments. Among these very young children, the 4-year-olds outperformed the 3-year-olds by a wide margin, and the correlation between judgments and verbal reasons proved much lower ($r = .44$) than had been previously found with first-graders ($r = .83$). As was previously noted, age differences are more critical at the very young end of the scale, and the ability of toddlers to integrate verbal response with their other reasoning skills is particularly fragile as a result. These sameness–difference results were among the first to confirm that modeling can improve the conceptual discriminations of very young children; however, some of the most interesting data were anecdotal. It proved very difficult to devise any techniques that would keep these youngsters attending to the teaching events for very long. This should caution against conclusions of limited capacity for abstract *thought* among toddlers. The quality of these children's responses may in fact depend on the vicissitudes of attention and motivation during teaching procedures. Temporal limitations on focused endurance, rather than structural constraints on the nature of information processing, may account for cognitive thresholds among preschoolers.

Also, very young children may lack expertise in flexibly selecting and shifting among alternative judgment criteria, rigidity akin to the Gestalt notion of "functional fixedness" (Duncker, 1945; Luchins & Luchins, 1950). Piaget has characterized such inflexibility among toddlers in terms of their limited abilities at *decentering*. The preoperational child is assumed to be unable to shift categorical focus because of limits imposed by biologically determined mental maturity. Hence, Zimmerman (1974) studied dimensional groupings among 3-, 4-, and 5-year-olds. He found that modeling improved the children's ability to follow new dimensional cues, and exemplary explanations helped children to transfer, retain, and verbally elucidate judgments; however, adding tangible incentives brought no additional benefits over symbolic guidance alone (cf. Rosenthal & Carroll, 1972; Rosenthal & Kellogg, 1973; Rosenthal & Whitebook, 1970). Age created an interesting pattern of results. While it did not affect the number of correct judgments, the youngest group gave fewer adequate reasons than 4- or 5-year-olds, who did not differ. When the teaching routine was further expanded for an additional group, the children's ability to flexibly shift among judgment dimensions improved further, was generalized to new stimuli, and enhanced skill that endured over time delays. Thus, brief social guidance assisted toddlers in decentering from one focal dimension to another.

If young children are assumed by their parents or teachers to be in a state of "unreadiness," then rigidity may be fostered inadvertently. When strenuous efforts at teaching skills, using various complementary methods, are applied, even preschoolers may reveal very surprising aptitudes. All too easily, the child's "readiness" can become a convenient excuse for the adult's laxness, especially since many relationships between the environment and abstract skills are obscure. Behavioral limits may seem to be rules of nature, unless nature is prodded, tickled, and juggled, to improve the status quo. The traditional conclusions about stable age limits on conservation are a case in point: Skill is refractory if age trends are simply described, but not when addressed by suitable modes of guidance.

The interface between social and cognitive variables has been studied far too little. Considerably more information is needed to clarify the ways in which interpersonal sources affect the adoption and utilization of cognitive norms. In daily life, a child is exposed to multiple—and often conflicting—live and symbolic models, and must reconcile these diverse influences in order to develop a personal cognitive framework. Ordinarily, one is not given the simple choice of invoking purely one's own or purely others' standards. One may start with a tentative bias, find that peers disagree, and thus alter one's views, believing that the revised stance represents a marked improvement. Usually, face-to-face groups select some focal norms as relevant for members to follow. When tested privately, people may show that they have interiorized these standards (Botvin & Murray, 1975; Murray, 1972; Sherif, 1935, 1936), recognizing that violations of dominant norms invite warnings, censure, or sterner reprisals (Adair, 1955; Bandura, 1977b; Homans, 1950; White, 1975; Whyte, 1943). But outside these relatively specific spheres, most groups condone plentiful variations in beliefs and conduct. Even within rather homogeneous social units, supervisors, colleagues, and intimate friends furnish a counterpoint of contrasting standards. We are bombarded by implied appeals and overt exhortations in the name of patriotism, honor, rationality, good fellowship, and bowel regularity. Who in a society become heroes and villains largely depends on which members of a polyglot society serve as the beholders. Social reasoning is a coat of many colors. Usually, an individual is aware of a range of diversified criteria that are partially overlapping and partially conflicting. It takes active effort to construct a workable synthesis from among the thoughts, convictions, expectations, and the behavioral standards exemplified by various others. Hence, the processes governing the cognition, selection and utilization of social cues as points of reference for conceptual performance deserve much more vigorous research attention.

Anchoring and Relational Judgments

Just as a human model can set performance standards for observers by adopting more or less stringent criteria for self-reward (Bandura, 1974, 1977b; Watts, 1973), and can even alter phenomenological experience (Coyne, 1976; Craig, Best, & Ward, 1975), other social and physical events are psychologically referenced by the range of values in which they occur. Psychophysical judgments serve as prototypes for all judgmental phenomena. Abstract responses such as opinions, attitudes, and preferences can be ordered relationally, in much the same way that serial weights can be judged relative either to one another, or to some standard stimulus, as are instances from other sensory dimensions, e.g., length, loudness, etc.

Piaget (1928) doubted that young children are capable of relational thought, but assumed that they make judgments independent of the frame of reference established by surrounding, contextual stimuli. These youngsters are believed to be incapable of grasping that certain concepts (e.g., hard and soft, heavy and light) involve a relationship between at least two stimulus values. In this view, the perception of a tennis ball should not be changed whether the ball is accompanied by marbles or by basketballs. The same size label should be thought to be suitable whether a teddy bear sits alone on a table, is seen adjacent to toy soldiers, or is cradled in the arms of a giant snowman. Piaget's later writing (e.g., 1968) holds to the pessimistic view that toddlers cannot manage even rudimentary relativism in thinking. Some research on weight judgments appeared to support this stance. Five-year-olds proved incapable of either seriating weights or showing awareness of an anchor value (O'Reilly & Steger, 1970). However, that study involved indirect procedures (pulling levers joined to unseen weights and expressing weight judgments via spatial analogs). Would less complex, more direct methods allow the child to show comprehension of relative stimulus differences?

Social judgment (e.g., Helson, 1964; Sherif & Hovland, 1961) and social learning (Bandura, 1969a; 1977b) theories maintain that abstract judgments are made in relation to both the stimuli presented and internal norms based on past experience. Given these assumptions, changing the stimulus frame of reference should alter judgments in the same way that a live model's deeds set a new guidance standard for observers (cf. Brickman, 1975). If one's past level of adaptation is based on very short or faint stimulus values, then presenting longer or louder anchors should create relational judgment shifts, with the largest prior stimuli being perceived as smaller, due to the introduction of the new larger anchors. Such relative displacements are expected for any dimension, whether physical or social in nature.

Hence, Rosenthal, Kelley, and White (1974) conducted a set of experiments with young children to test anchoring effects on the cue dimensions of brightness, texture, visible facial happiness, height, and weight. All of the studies were then replicated with a group of severely retarded adults and adolescents. In three phases, spaced some weeks apart, the child received a first pattern of anchors (some strong, others weak) for comparison, a second pattern of anchors (reversing the strengths of those given prior), and an unanchored exposure to the quite small intensity differences among the test stimuli. The results were dramatic. When exposed after *smaller* anchors, the same test stimulus was judged as more intense (taller, heavier), but when judged after anchors of greater magnitude, the test stimuli were interpreted as diminished. The children made relational shifts consistent between phases, showing that differential judgments hinged on anchoring values. There was evidence that these relational adjustments resulted from cognitive mediation through memory, because the presence or absence of an overt anchoring value at the time of judgment made no difference. Both the children's sex and age level (older—4:6 mean years—versus younger—3:8 mean years) had trivial impact on the results. Further, even with relatively small variations among test stimuli, the children's judgments showed a strongly relational pattern during the final (no anchors) phase. Related research with preschoolers led to similar conclusions (Kelley, 1974). The retarded judges, a decade or more older, performed in much the same fashion as the children of nursery-school age. These studies strongly confirm that very young children can discriminate relationally if procedural formats are simple and straightforward. With gross differences between anchor and test stimuli, and with more subtle disparities among the test stimuli, judgments disclosed relativistic thinking. This held for the physical dimensions of height, weight, length, and texture, and for the social attribute of happiness as depicted in outline faces. Children consistently evaluated events by reference to the range of stimuli available for comparison, and showed continuity in how they cognized the physical and the social cue dimensions. This illustrates how guidance derived from contextual stimuli, and from the exemplary precedents of social models, activates common psychological processes that underlie terminal decisions and behavior (Bandura, 1977b; Rosenthal & Bandura, 1978).

QUESTION FORMATION

In the research discussed thus far, a rather narrow range of judgment dimensions and explanatory verbal rationales proved to be responsive to social guidance. The child can communicate moral decisions simply by stating which of two actors was naughtier, or reflect conservation by uttering a few words to convey quantitative equality and difference. These circumscribed productions are taken as evidence of grasping the more elaborate symbolic relationships under study. Often, however, in giving examples of an abstract class, the particular instances and their expression in language are of entirely our own choosing. We need only provide an example that satisfies the governing principles. We may phrase answers as we choose, and it is a matter of conceptual indifference if, when asked to name a famous film, we offer *Gone With The Wind, Deep Throat,* or *King Kong.*

Skill in posing questions is an important means of acquiring new information, and its benefits are so pervasive that one is apt to lose sight of the myriad services that inquiry can provide. By asking appropriate questions, one can monitor physical phenomena, rather than learn by trial and error, e.g., without having to get wet in order to learn that it is raining. One can detour around poison ivy, hostile dogs, and washed-out bridges, and need not wander about super-market aisles to locate the right brand of starch. One is spared futile trips to banks and gas stations already closed for the day, and can also prepare for a wide range of social phenomena by asking what is fashionable in clothing, opinions, and underarm hygiene. One can avoid repacious merchants, shady lawyers, boring guests, corrupt politicians, demanding instructors, and long-winded clergymen. One can assess acquaintances' reputed generosity in dispensing lawn mowers, recipes, alcohol, baby-sitting aid, monetary loans, stock market tips, and sexual favors. Proficient questioning can usually determine all of these facts without the tribulations of trial and error experience. As with modeling itself, information-seeking skills enable the vicarious acquisition of much useful knowledge. Directly performing terminal responses is not necessary to obtain cues for guiding effective action. Well-conceived questions control social feedback, by designating which aspects of the world are appropriate topics for response. One need not wait and hope for one's companions to spontaneously demonstrate or discuss erotic, economic, or child-rearing techniques. Instead, the question can specify the content boundaries for answers, setting rather sharp limits on the information that is solicited and supplied. These features make questions a highly efficient means for exposing oneself to selected parts of others' stored knowledge. To gain prompt access to socially mediated information, one must be able to decide on the gist of interest, identify the scope of related points needing mention, and by oneself formulate questions that elicit sufficient coverage of the relevant category. Any samaritan who has struggled to answer diffuse, ambiguous, and seemingly aimless questions will know that information-seeking skill is not to be taken for granted.

From such considerations, Rosenthal *et al.* (1970) set out to show that, through modeling, children could adopt a range of distinct abstract standards governing questions that were produced according to a set of stimulus pictures. The criteria for inquiry were never directly stated, and had to be induced from the model's questions. Separate groups of children observed inquiries that followed different superordinate rules: For the *nominal–physical* class, the model asked questions about the perceptual or object status of the stimuli, e.g., "What shape is that?" For *functional uses,* modeled questions involved the possible pragmatic applications of the stimuli, e.g., "What do you use it for?" *Causal relations* questions addressed how stimuli might affect one another or the larger environment, e.g., "How come the guitar makes music?" *Value judgments* questions concerned a liking or a preference for stimuli, e.g., "Which do you think is the prettiest?" These contrasting styles of inquiry illustrated how widely diverse were the types of questions that might apply to the same pictorial stimuli; these styles of inquiry were also related to Piaget's (1959) descriptive grouping of children's questions.

In baseline, the child made up a question for each picture, and then observed the modeled style of inquiry. Next, the pictures were again presented to the child for question construction, after which new, generalization stimuli were introduced. Half of the children were explicitly told to try and emulate the model's question-asking strategy, while the remaining youngsters were spared any demands to emulate. After modeling, children substantially increased their production of questions in the style of inquiry observed. Although some question classes were much more frequent than others during baseline, all of the experimental groups significantly surpassed their own baseline levels, and the scores of a control group as well, both with the familiar pictures and with the untrained generalization items. Directions to emulate had a limited impact, and only increased scores of the simplest, i.e., nominal–physical, class of questions. However, the alternative instructions led to quite different amounts of mimicry or exact copying of the model's questions. Overall, mimicry was rare. Less than 12% of all responses were exact imitations, and more than 70% of all children never once copied the model's precise words. Of the limited amount of mimicry that was observed, a large proportion (74%) was given by the group instructed to phrase their questions like the adult's. This pattern recalls the similar findings involving a syntactical task (Rosenthal & Whitebook, 1970); in both cases, while strong directions to emulate a model increased the repetition of discrete word content, these instructions had minor effects in the learning of categorical standards governing the model's demonstrations.

Some question classes, e.g., causal relations and functional uses, seem phenomenologically closer. If the child could not maintain stable boundaries between those styles, perhaps observing functional questions would increase causal but curtail nominal–physical and value responses. It was hence interesting to note that the child's observation of one question standard never increased the production of another categorical criterion. These studies showed that the children were able to abstract from modeled examples a range of categorical features whose boundaries and rules were never stated. Children induced the organizing principles from the displays they witnessed, and promptly applied the rules to new, transfer stimuli. Acquisition and generalization of these abstract configurations seem to mandate assumptions of active inference and self-guided decision-making by the child. The classroom potential of modeling as a teaching method was also enhanced, because all of the children were from economically disadvantaged backgrounds, and many were from Spanish-speaking homes.

In a sequel, Rosenthal and Zimmerman (1972a) compared verbal prompts as modeling supplements, using only the value judgments questions with a sample of younger children. After determining baseline, the *implicit* directions group was merely told to be attentive to the model; the *explicit* directions additionally asked the child to attempt to learn and emulate the adult's questions; the *pattern* directions added that the child should try and discover the similarity among all of the model's questions; and the *mapping* directions added three examples of the type of question the adult would ask, thus alerting the child in advance to the common aspects of the modeled inquiries. In each group, half of the children were given a positive expectation of their ability to learn the game, cueing that was omitted for the remaining children.

Observing the model led to strong increases in value judgments questions. All of the instructions groups surpassed their baseline scores in both acquisition and generalization phases; however, giving favorable, as opposed to neutral, expectations utterly failed to affect any response measure. The main contribution of the alternative verbal prompts was observed during acquisition, when the implicit directions led to the lowest, and the mapping prompts to the highest scores. But these differences were not maintained during generalization, when children in all of the instructional conditions performed comparably. Demonstration alone seemed to foster more rule learning than the verbal aids. With respect to acquisition, the "pure modeling," implicit directions group earned over 57% of the maximum performance obtained, and later, with the new, transfer stimuli, scored almost as high as the groups receiving any composite of demonstration plus instructions (cf. Blanchard, 1970; Mann, 1972). The individual children were also asked to estimate how well they had performed. Although there was some difference among children of the various directions groups, with the mapping group reporting the most success and the explicit group the least, there was scant correlation between children's perceptions of success and their actual scores. This disparity is reminiscent of other data (e.g., Kendler & Kendler, 1967; Morris, 1970) evidencing the limited relationships between young children's inferential skills and their verbal labeling. It is also of interest to examine the results in terms of the vicarious establishment of novel behavior. In both of the preceding studies, baseline production of value judgments questions was very low, with all means less than 0.4 responses. After demonstrations, the lowest cell mean was 4.4 responses, an eleven-fold increase from brief observational guidance. Some writers (e.g., Wallach & Kogan, 1965) have considered acceptable but unusual behavior to be evidence of creativity. The question formation data can be viewed in this light, and as we will later discuss, modeling has been shown to effectively promote several other classes of original behavior. More generally, it seems important to note that social learning techniques can, with unusual rapidity, instigate novel action patterns, for both average and disadvantaged learners.

A practical teaching analog was studied by Zimmerman and Pike (1972), with second graders from a Chicano *barrio* community, who were clearly deficient in question-asking skills. Repeated, brief instruction sessions took place in classlike groups of six children, and were conducted first by one and later by another Anglo-American woman. After training, a stringent generalization test was performed by an Anglo man. This format has obvious relevance for practical pedagogy, in situations where teachers engage in repeated interactions with students, and where minority groups are often taught by middle-class members of the ethnic majority. In addition to unguided controls, two training methods were compared. In the *praise-only* group, all of the questions asked by the children were praised and answered by the adult. The incidence of praise was high, as it was given about once every 1.5 minutes, making this a viable example of verbal reinforcement procedures. In the *modeling-plus-praise* group, the teacher demonstrated the process of asking questions and, although praising the children's questions, she did not answer them.

The results demonstrated no change for the controls over time, despite increased familiarity with the stimuli. The praise-only group made very limited gains and never significantly surpassed the control group. In contrast, the modeling-plus-praise children showed clear evidence of learning and transfer in question-asking skill. They outperformed both of the other groups in learning and generalization tests. The data, obtained through group instruction, confirmed the value of vicarious techniques to promote question formation by young children from poverty homes in which Spanish was the language spoken. The limited benefit of praise by itself, when not joined to informative guidelines, supports the earlier research, in which incentive operations failed to improve observational learning (Rosenthal & Carroll, 1972; Rosenthal & Kellogg, 1973). However, Garcia and Zimmerman (1972) provide further reasons to doubt the value of verbal approval when, as in the present case, an ethnic boundary must be crossed. They found that verbal reinforcement administered by Anglo adults was a less effective reward for Chicano children than were similiar compliments from a fellow Chicano. Very possibly, the praise-only group was handicapped at learning because of the ethnic status of the adults who bestowed the praise. If so, the successful achievements of the modeling-plus-praise children become especially impressive.

SUMMARY

A process of matching conceptual orientations unifies this discussion of judgment and category adoption. Whether tasks are relatively familiar, like discerning magnitude and asking questions, or comparatively novel, like resolving ethical dilemmas, the human judge must fit a particular example to a more general standard. This view of matching does not merely involve the copying of concrete details. In repeated instances, modeled criteria were maintained with entirely new stimuli and in altered response contexts. For this to occur, salient attributes must be abstracted and appropriate boundaries must be inferred. What is matched in these instances is a governing rule, whether based on subjective intentions, value-laden styles of inquiry, or the preservation of like amounts. In each case, discrete specifics were quickly subordinated to broad categorical criteria, envelopes which subsume constant common attributes. Such prompt superordinate classification suggests that abstract information is stored in organized categories. Even young children could recognize, retain, retrieve, and utilize patterned symbolic arrangements. In effect, successive stimulus instances were matched to a principle or paradigm that itself underwent further refinement during additional decision-making trials. This conception supposes that related events are grouped into concept ladders, and maintained with the aid of mnemonic summary codes (Bandura, 1969a, 1977b; Rosenthal & Bandura, 1978; Zimmerman & Rosenthal, 1974b).

Although grouping may reflect physical similarities in stimuli and responses, cognition is not confined to discrete sensory attributes. Instead, including (generalization) or excluding (discrimination) instances within or from a given category depends on how well a new example matches the superordinate criteria governing that class. Likeness in propriety, function, and meaning, are as important as similarity in size or pitch, and probably are more representative of our dominant norms for organizing information.

This chapter has surveyed modeling influences on the selection and utilization of abstract judgment standards. The basis of ethical decisions, originally emphasizing material damage, was shifted to subjective intentions criteria. Some limitations of nativistic assumptions and rigid stage distinctions were discussed, and the powerful role played by social exemplars was demonstrated. Models were shown to effectively guide children's choice of question patterns when specific stimuli and responses varied without constraint. Primarily, children acquired question-forming rules, but rarely reproduced the particular utterances they observed. Style of inquiry was generalized to new examples without rewards or further training. The phenomenon of conservation was considered in terms of experimental evidence and conceptual status. In a variety of formats, social influences successfully promoted conservation by children younger than would be possible according to current stage-dependent theories. The ability to conserve in cases of equal and unequal stimuli to generalize principles to new situations, and to retain the judgmental rules over time was observed among the trained groups. Common features and overlapping responses were found to bridge the nominally distinct conservation dimensions. Implicit social demands to match experimenter-defined properties, but to ignore other cogent aspects of quantity and pragmatic function, complicate the logical inevitability of conservation reasoning. It instead appeared that conserving is just one of a family of rule-governed symbolic skills. Data illustrate a case where exemplary training proved quite effective but equivalent verbal guidance utterly failed to instate conservation. Examples favoring rule provision over demonstration, and in which the alternative techniques were comparable, were also given. A social learning analysis suggested that the age variable should index general concept repertoires for the very young child, but should tell much less about abstract facility once at least rudimentary skills are available. The need to make earnest teaching efforts, rather than presuming inward unreadiness or incapacity was stressed. Reliance on age as an index of cognitive skills may have some normative value, but it tells us little about subprocesses governing cognitive performances. Cited were data to support this age interpretation and to show that persistent teaching could bear unexpected fruits.

Observing a model's decision criteria led both preschool and older children to adopt these criteria, on tests with new items and after time lags had intervened. The categorical nature of judgment phenomena was discussed in regard to abstraction and inferential reasoning. The need to distinguish between comprehension and verbal fluency was noted. Evidence showed that even children less than 4 years old can judge relationally if procedures are kept simple and clear. On diverse sensory and social dimensions, young children, as well as retarded adults, made consistent relational shifts in response to stimulus anchors. Cognitive relativism was as great when the test and anchor stimuli were separated in time, thus requiring mediation through memory, as when the child could simultaneously compare test stimuli with an anchor. The importance of information and guidance provided by social agents and usage norms was discussed as an integrating framework for the development of cognitive standards.

4

Concept Attainment and Problem Solving

Man has always been fascinated by his own problem solving. The ability to reason is taken to establish mankind's sovereignty over all other creatures, a dominance which is strengthened by the adaptability of human behavior. This flexibility stems from man's skill at manipulating symbols and generalizing from one event to another, allowing rapid adjustments to environmental change. Rather than merely accepting altered conditions, man can influence the forces of natural selection. Almost casually, we level woods, cut roadways across the land, and dam rivers, transforming other animals' habitats. We have decimated the wolf and brought prosperity to the dog, shaping evolution. All because a rather puny biped can conceptualize and plan. No wonder that psychology has emphasized learning processes more than any other topic. Whatever theories or viewpoints one favors, they must deal with the same facts: People are thinkers. New ways are invented to meet new problems. Better ways to solve enduring problems are devised and welcomed. Honor and coin still await the person who improves the mousetrap.

The most important types of learning are categorical. If obstacles, hazards, or other stimuli can be properly grouped, skills and principles drawn from even limited overt experience can be applied to their common features. We need not approach each zipper, skunk, or ethical dispute as if it were our first. Generalizability and memory improve when a summary rule replaces the unique aspects of separate examples. A thorough understanding of a principle, or even only a partial grasp, allows facile transfer from previous knowledge to related cases never before encountered. Selecting and grouping events into cogent categories spares repetitive exploration. One ignores the discrete details, acting instead on the relevant constancies shared by a class of events. The time, effort, and grief saved can be vast. Learning by observation also minimizes the need for overt trial and error practice. Even elaborate concepts and cognitive strategies are vicariously acquired. Also, most of our cultural heritage is socially transmitted. If it were not, each generation would need to reinvent algebra and the means to harness electricity. Witnessing others' actions at solving problems, and the environmental effects so produced, together foster observational learning. Information acquired vicariously greatly aids problem solving in natural settings. From a Darwinian perspective, consider a hypothetical example.

Imagine being suddenly abandoned on a mythical island. One finds oneself amid lurid vegetation, weird fauna, and surrounded by burbling streams and geysers of many colors. What can one do? The intrepid but unwary castaway might try direct experimentation to gain sustenance, hoping that experience will be a successful teacher. This would be fine if blind guesses were rewarded, and if one example could aid one's inferences about the still-untested alternatives. But hasty trials with unknown contingencies also invite the punishing, perhaps fatal, effects of permanent time out. The more cautious adventurer could greatly improve prospects by observing the exotic animals. What do they eat? Where do they drink? How do they behave toward one another? Direct action would be better postponed until one could classify at least some facets of the new milieu as either probably wholesome or sinister. The modeling exposures would suggest that some options were better bets than others. While the green and yellow globes and the tawny canes seem to be relished by many creatures, the red pods and purple tubers earn consistent avoidance. One's guidelines would be imperfect, yet this observationally gleaned information is far safer than reckless gamble. Once one developed some lexicon of cues to distinguish potable from noxious waters, edible from deadly plants, and docile from hostile beasts, one is well on the way toward survival. Premature overt practice instead shifts the odds in favor of calamity. Of course, if the area were populated, watching or asking the local inhabitants would be still more informative, provided that one did not end up as their main course. Closer to home, failure to properly classify nutritive and toxic fungi every year claims the lives of rash epicures seeking wild mushrooms. Or consider the brave and canny souls who first mastered the artichoke and manioc plants. If one just transfers the familiar acts of peeling and slicing before eating, one finds these plants to be the most punishing of morsels. They are best savored by techniques that have been socially evolved and transmitted. In all such cases, trial and error learning is not recommended to aspiring gourmets.

Whether the concept instances are gustatory, or reflect subtle abstract categories, conceptual rules can be learned, generalized, and remembered purely from vicarious exposures. Modeling is especially effective if the needed response patterns have little chance of occurring spontaneously. Behavior can be organized into complex ensembles, to fit novel abstract principles. Relatively complete or perfect solutions can be instated and maintained. Learners are spared tedious fumbling and avoidable errors. These modeled examples, because they narrow the alternatives, reduce the number of false hypotheses that are tested, or the acts that are ordered into futile configurations. Overt efforts can be minimized, and confined to realistic approximations of terminal goals.

In Chapter 3, we discussed how diverse judgment criteria respond to vicarious influences. Material damage must often be ignored, when subjective intent is emphasized, and area must be subordinated to number. These conflicting vectors, continuously in operation in daily life, must be overcome. In the present chapter, we will be concerned primarily with problems that have explicit, unambiguous solutions; most of the tasks discussed were devised for research purposes. The advantage to this approach is that cognitive functions can be studied under conditions less bounded by prior social mores and naturalistic precedents. Prompting observation with supplemental guidance does not always prove to be a boon. Covert symbolization and storage can be aided by supporting information, e.g., mnemonic rule summaries. But verbal coding and other acts performed by models and observers can also interfere, such as when an observer engages in complex tasks; these efforts may distract the learner's attention, or disrupt his efforts to construct stable representations of crucial features. In solving problems and exemplifying concepts, models often modify the environment so that observers can examine the target patterns to be learned. Terminal arrangements of conceptual stimuli also convey useful knowledge. Observing the desired end-products aids the learners, helping them to infer the relevant solution. Even when all of the material aspects of stimuli change, observers can maintain relational rules intact. Cognition is aided by analogies and similes, in operations to organize information (Royer & Cable, 1976). Guidelines are abstracted from training events and promptly transferred to new cases, whose literal details, although all novel, allow ordering by the same principles. Storage mechanisms need not be isomorphic with their referents. Reductive codes can condense elaborate data into succinct symbols, arbitrary in form, which preserve information economically until it is needed to guide conceptual endeavors. Whatever the mode or source by which knowledge is acquired, symbolic operations regulate its processing. Vicariously derived concepts are mediated just like those acquired from any other learning method. The same rules can be acquired from direct practice, though often less efficiently, or from statements of principles to verbally adept observers. In other cases, demonstration will teach better than verbal directions. Often, combining modeled examples with verbal guidance will surpass either technique used alone.

OBSERVATIONAL LEARNING OF NOVEL BEHAVIOR

When can it be concluded that new learning has occurred? If it is reasonable to assume that abstract rules or language patterns are met in daily life, then there is no way to assure that extralaboratory familiarity was never influential. Teaching might strengthen skill, but not create it anew. Sometimes, vicarious changes are best viewed as social facilitation rather than as new acquisition. Thus, Kanfer, Duerfeldt, Martin, and Dorsey (1971) exposed second-graders to a model who illustrated the concept of oddity: Always choose that item in a set that is unlike all the others. Experimental observers adopted the solution far more often than controls, who had not been made privy to the teaching examples. If the classification rule was new for some youngsters, probably many others had encountered and used the concept in natural settings. For these latter youngsters, the model assisted in the choice, but not the grasp, of the oddity principle. At the other extreme, one can define new learning according to criteria too severe for realistic use, insisting that all the elements of cognition must be novel. Very few concepts, if any, are freshly minted in so rigorous a fashion. Understanding calculus demands some conversance with numbers, algebraic symbols, and the operations they signify. This familiarity with mathematics is not the same as the knowledge of calculus. Shakespeare and Faulkner wrote in English, Dostoyevski in Russian. Competence in their native tongues does not explain the originality of their fiction. Novelty stems not from their coining new words, the individual response elements of language, but from their unique *use* of commonly known words.

Psychology has no operational definition of "novelty," let alone standard metrics to quantify it. Actually, units of newness would be convenient to determine how varying degrees of novelty affect other situational variables. A continuum might be constructed from the probability of an event's occurring in the environment, or from comparative judgments of pairs of options drawn from an array of items to be scaled. Such precise measures may be feasible, but we must await their development. Bandura (1969a) has proposed a working criterion to assess whether a response sequence or arrangement of events not earlier available as an organized configuration may be considered novel. If, under appropriate stimulus conditions, baseline responding fails to suggest prior knowledge, or if naïve controls score close to zero, or both, subsequent gains can be credited to training for two reasons: The task stimuli did not initially govern the desired abstract response class; the myriad impacts of uncontrolled variables did not lead people to spontaneously infer the correct rule. In associative terms, no evidence alludes to prior connections between input and output events. The ability of "nonresponse" vicarious guidance to establish new learning has often been doubted by reinforcement theorists (Gewirtz, 1971a,b; Miller & Dollard, 1941; Thorndike, 1911, 1913). Hence, it seems germane to show how modeling can generate nonverbal concept attainment in a stricter sense than implied by relative gains after baseline.

Rosenthal *et al.* (1971) studied the acquisition and transfer of a novel coordination rule, i.e., that for every disk stimulus, a three-marble triangle should be constructed in the same color. Thus, if two blue disks are presented, correct response requires two blue triangles, etc. A model demonstrated the stimulus–response conjunctions for observers, either silently, or by verbally describing the examples as they were performed. Control children responded to the stimuli without training. The mean numbers of correct responses appear in the top section of Table 4-1. One can see that all groups approached zero scores in baseline and, at each age level, the controls maintained almost total ignorance in the later-phase tests. Modeling brought significant understanding of the solution. While unprompted observers performed on the same level as children who also heard descriptive statements, verbal cues did aid transfer for the older groups. There was further evidence of partial concept attainment not reflected in the tabulated scores, which give a conservative picture of the abstract gains created by brief modeling.

These basic results were confirmed by later research (second study in Table 4-1). From baseline means close to zero, which were maintained by the controls in later tests, silent demonstrations again produced appreciable concept learning and transfer. As expected, the results were comparable when a separate adult served as the model, and when both roles were played by the experimenter (Rosenthal *et al.*, 1972b). The outcomes were similar with severely retarded adolescents and adults,

TABLE 4-1
Mean Correct Responses by Phase in Three Marble—Triangles Studies[a]

Condition and sample	Phase: Baseline	Acquisition	Transfer
First study: Children			
Middle class, age 3:5 years			
Silent model	.00	3.11	.00
Model plus cues	.00	3.10	1.20
Controls	.00	.00	.00
Disadvantaged, age 5:0 years			
Silent model	.00	1.28	0.00
Model plus cues	.00	3.71	2.36
Controls	.14	.28	.00
Middle class, first-graders			
Silent model	.05	7.58	2.53
Model plus cues	.00	7.42	4.58
Controls	.00	.00	.00
Second study: Children			
Disadvantaged, first-graders			
Silent E − M format	.03	6.06	2.16
Silent E + M format	.00	5.00	2.66
Combined silent modeling	.02	5.53	2.41
Controls	.09	.06	.03
Third study: Retardates			
Adolescents			
Demonstration	.00	5.00	.00
Instructions	.00	.75	.00
Work skills			
Demonstration	.00	5.25	1.50
Instructions	.00	.25	.00
Prevocational			
Demonstration	.00	11.00	9.00
Instructions	.00	4.75	4.50

[a] Adapted from Rosenthal, Moore, Dorfman, and Nelson (1971), Rosenthal, Feist, and Durning (1972), and Rosenthal and Kellogg (1973).

who failed on every baseline item (third study in Table 4-1), but who learned to apply the principle after solutions were demonstrated (Rosenthal & Kellogg, 1973). Hanson (1972) showed that kindergarten and first-grade students could retain the concept without further practice; they performed just as well 1 week later as when tested immediately after modeling. Oddly, a delay of 1 day led to weaker retrieval than the longer and shorter retention intervals. As a group, these studies included individuals divergent in age, socioeconomic and ethnic backgrounds, and residential communities. Various adults of both sexes served as models. Yet, the results were very consistent. Despite baseline scores of virtually zero, observing correct demonstrations generated learning, transfer, and retention of the disk–triangles concept.

Abstract conceptualization hinges on isolating the relevant aspects of objects or events and then grouping them into useful categories (Bourne, 1966; Winters & Brzoska, 1976). Once learners derive a general principle, it can be applied to new examples, never before met, without serious performance loss (Bourne, 1970). Despite the variability among aspects of specific instances, dimensional classifications govern the organization of input. Modeled guidance can introduce precepts enabling learners to structure events in novel ways, e.g., by altering children's use of dimensions in concept identification problems (Kobisigawa, 1968). Ryan and Kobisigawa (1971) imposed an unfamiliar conceptual rule by having a model sort stimuli to highlight attributes formerly ignored by the child. The model's choices were always praised. Observers later discriminated new items to reflect the exemplary classifications.

Concept attainment does not require rewarding observers or mentors. A stringent case of vicariously acquired grouping rules is illustrated by research on clustering (Alford & Rosenthal, 1973; Rosenthal *et al.*, 1972a). The conceptual task entailed combining different kinds of colored objects into triads, so that all color and identity attributes were represented once per cluster. Size, texture, and detail features varied considerably within each class of items. Entirely distinct colors and types of objects were later introduced to test generalization. The stimuli gave no hint of cueing proper configurations before training: In baseline, despite over 3150 response opportunities, no child ever produced a correct cluster. Further, on all later phase tests, control groups in both studies maintained their total failure. No trace of "practice effects" resulted from sheer continued exposure to the task materials. Yet, modeling techniques promptly established rule learning and generalization to dissimilar stimuli. Significant concept attainment and transfer were evident in the groups trained just by silent demonstrations. Retention 5 weeks later depended on the adequacy of encoding aids supplied by the model.

In other experiments, adult observers have demonstrated acquisition of intricate movement sequences, which were never once successfully performed by controls. When the patterns were not modeled, familiarity with the component motor elements utterly failed to aid guessing of configurations. Here too, the retention of novel patterns depended on the availability of, and strategy for utilizing, effective mnemonic symbols (Bandura & Jeffery, 1973; Bandura *et al.*, 1974; Jeffery, 1976). The preceding data are based on extralinguistic tasks and responses, but are consistent with prior evidence that wholly arbitrary syntactical rules can be taught by modeling (Kossuth, 1972; Malouf & Dodd, 1972). Taken together, this research confirms that new concepts can be formed from vicarious experience. Contrary to the assumptions of reinforcement theories, novel learning occurred without overt activity or the provision of any rewards.

Incentives and Expectancies

Although reinforcement can enhance the frequency and vigor of performance, and can provide cues as to desired behavior in ambiguous situations, it is not crucial for acquisition. In experiments on novel abstract learning, a range of incentive procedures had trivial effects. This was probably because the tasks were akin to the meaningful endeavors of normal life, thereby motivating the learners to excel without goads. If an activity holds intrinsic interest or promotes valued competencies, people do not need incentive props to monitor and execute behavior (Bandura, Grusec, & Menlove, 1966; Garbarino, 1975; Yussen, 1974). Thus, supplementing informative feedback with candy rewards failed to improve concept mastery (Rosenthal & Kellogg, 1973). This was consistent with language modeling results. Promising small (Rosenthal & Whitebook, 1970) or large (Rosenthal & Carroll, 1972) rewards did not augment children's syntactic learning. Adults as well may not improve their efforts to preserve modeled information when reinforcers are anticipated or dispensed (Berger, 1966). Unnecessary incentives can be harmful (Haddad, McCullers, & Moran, 1976). If subjects attribute their participation to external rewards, then once the inducements are removed, the subjects' spontaneous interest in a task may be reduced (Ross, 1976). Children who expected and worked for later rewards were much less drawn to an activity than unrewarded subjects or those whose bonuses came as unexpected surprises (Lepper & Greene, 1975; Lepper, Green, & Nisbett, 1973). However, apart from children's attribution of causation to their own behavior, there are many other reasons that might cause them to reduce their interest in previously rewarded activities (Bandura, 1977b). These include children's perceiving the administrator of rewards as being manipulative; inferring that they were being punished since previously rewarded activities later produced no rewards; becoming bored with the task or satiated by the reward as a result of extensive participation, or being "turned off" if rewards were dispensed in a coercive or noncontingent manner. Any one of these contextual factors can affect the way children extract meaning from rewards.

In any case, rewards themselves do not engender learning. Thus, giving positive and negative reinforcement to models need not affect abstract progress by observers. These vicarious motivators, although helpful in one setting, may add little if the total context is altered (Harvey, 1973). Self-reliant observers were unaffected by both contingent and noncontingent prizes to a model, while more dependent children interpreted the rewards as cues or demands to emulate (Geshuri, 1975). Rewarding a model did not improve attention to concept examples. The children's scrutiny of the modeled examples did not increase when the information was relevant to forthcoming demands; however, if the content was extraneous, observers attended less. Indeed, self-exposure defied utilitarian concerns. Youngsters seemed more eager to use the vicarious data for evaluating completed actions than to assist them with impending decisions (Kanfer *et al.*, 1971).

Expectancies dictate the way in which individuals process upcoming information, which is cognized in light of future plans (Bender & Levin, 1976; Meltzer, Martin, Mills, Imhoff, & Zohar, 1976). Positive or negative expectancies often count more than overt consequences (Mischel, Ebbesen, & Zeiss, 1976). But expecting a later test on one's knowledge may or may not prompt greater diligence during acquisition. Neither forewarning (Berger, 1962) nor anticipated rewards (Bandura *et al.*, 1966) will enhance participation if vicarious displays are lucid and compel attention, as shown with adults and children on a range of tasks. When the task was interesting, concept utilization was not altered, whether premodeling directions created a definite, an ambiguous, or no expectation of later testing (Hanson, 1972). Other youngsters, urged to remember newly learned rules, retained no better weeks later than without any retest expectation (Rosenthal *et al.*, 1972a). However, when training demonstrations must compete for attention with tempting distractions, the balance shifts. Then, the expectation of a test can increase scrutiny of the modeled events, hence, aiding later recall. Praising or scolding the model did not assist attention and memory among observers who expected that they were required to reproduce the behavior witnessed. Yet, the more vivid, i.e., approval and censure, formats better overcame distracting lures for children who were not forewarned that a test was coming. This naïve group attended and recalled better when the model was reinforced (Yussen, 1974).

When teaching displays hold learners' attention, positive expectations about their ability do not necessarily aid active concentration.

Told that they had special talents for grasping an equivalence rule (Rosenthal *et al.*, 1972b), or for constructing abstract questions (Rosenthal & Zimmerman, 1972a), children scored no higher than when not exhorted by pep talks. These aggregate results suggest that when teaching contexts instill adequate motivation, extra inducements offer little. But if tasks are boring or arduous (Benowitz & Busse, 1976), or if they tax learners' information-processing capacities (Liebert & Fernandez, 1969, 1970), violate social mores, or must compete with other diversions, incentive supports can enhance attention (Yussen, 1974; Yussen & Levy, 1975) and inhibitions about executing taboo deeds can be overcome (Bandura, 1965). While reinforcers may amplify, curtail, and otherwise color modeling results, they are not necessary for observational learning. As the data on novel concept attainment demonstrate, conceptual relationships are learned, transferred, and remembered without giving incentives. These results call into question assumptions that modeling is dependent on, and governed by, reinforcement consequences (e.g., Baer, Peterson, & Sherman, 1967; Gewirtz, 1968, 1971a,b; Gewirtz & Stingle, 1968). The rather slight effects of incentives, hedged by interacting corequisites, evident when rewards and skill expectancies were provided, also challenge views that predicate social learning on affective conditioning (Aronfreed, 1969; Mowrer, 1960). If emotional components underlie the matching of input to cognitive templates, then more arousing guidance formats should lead to better performance. Motivating cues play key roles in determining whether observers attend, and where, when, and how they express their knowledge in action. Incentives do not control the processes by which information is acquired from modeling and how it is covertly stored. In many natural settings, observers are informed by live, filmed, and televised exemplars. New problem solutions, styles of dress and conduct, and other complex human guidelines can be discerned and adopted (Rosenthal & Bandura, 1978), although neither the models nor the spectators receive any reinforcers.

Matching to Sample

Operant scholars have been concerned with the way in which emulative activity develops. In their view, a skill or disposition toward generalized imitation evolves from reinforced practice aimed at matching the models' overt acts. Thus, Baer *et al.* (1967) suggest that behavior is imitative if (*a*) it temporally follows the model's responses and (*b*) if the topography of modeled deeds controls the form of learners' overt acts. These criteria emphasize imitative matching aptitude rather than the information conveyed by example. No allowance is made for abstract inference or other human mediating processes. Yet in the previously described clustering studies, for example, a newly acquired rule was generalized to totally new items, which were distinct from training stimuli on all sensory and object–class attributes: Although transfer examples were never modeled, observers, with no additional teaching, preserved and applied the grouping rules long after they received exemplary guidance.

Gewirtz (1971a,b; Gewirtz & Stingle, 1968) equates social learning with the matching-to-sample paradigm of operant research. In such designs, stimulus examples are displayed, and the child must choose from these examples those instances that match the sample on all or selected attributes. A study by Sherman, Saunders, and Brigham (1970) illustrates the approach. They wanted to measure generalization from training to new items when reward was given for either matching or mismatching the sample. The children were shown either various geometric forms or lines tilted from the vertical. Marbles, which were exchangeable for treats, were given as reinforcers. During baseline, the child's choice of stimulus examples was assessed, and noncontingent reward was given for all responses. Then, reinforcement, i.e., receiving marbles, was made contingent on adopting the originally unpreferred response style. The results showed that the rewarded behavior pattern was usually transferred to the new probe items. When the incentive contingencies were reversed, children switched their actions accordingly, confirming that the reinforcers controlled the matching acts. These data suggest that people modulate their behavior to meet situational demands. Reinforced matching can induce subjects to discriminate among an array of choices, whose relevant features must be grasped, and to select the option that shares a common property with the sample. But little light is shed on how learners actually cognize the events. The bases for integrating stimulus cues with response deeds remain nebulous, or sometimes are seen as unimportant (Gewirtz, 1971a,b). In terms of *learning*, reward necessitates overt matching acts, the motor execution of which can interfere with cognitive processes (Mims & Gholson, 1977). The child's symbolic feats are neglected except as they are indexed by matching responses. Covert efforts at refining categories, formulating principles, and developing mnemonic strategies are ignored, since all learning is assumed to reflect a history of reinforced instrumental conditioning. In fact, there are ample grounds to contest such premises (Farnham-Diggory & Gregg, 1975; Rice, 1976). In addition, the matching paradigm lacks ecological validity as a prototype of human learning.

There is a tremendous difference between the matching of stimuli and the reproduction of response patterns. One can easily match a recording of an operatic aria while unable to sing one modeled by a Wagnerian. The match-to-sample paradigm is notably deficient in providing evidence about novel *response* acquisition, since terminal responses are usually available before vicarious learning and need only be linked to particular stimuli. In this regard, matching represents a marked departure from the usual conditions of observational learning in the natural environment. There, a model's response elements must be discriminated, translated into action patterns, and performed when appropriate as signaled by important contextual cues. In these situations, observers do not merely choose from a fixed array of stimulus options.

Doubtless, many concepts taught by modeling could be learned in the course of matching-to-sample trials. But the abstract information acquired in this manner is distinct from the overt matching steps in both form and meaning. When no rewards are supplied, concepts can be attained by interpreting static exemplars that express abstract rules (Alford & Rosenthal, 1973; Hull, 1920; Robert *et al.*, 1975; Woodson, 1974). The examples themselves, and not the acts of matching, are the source of knowledge. Conceptual gains can be made as well or better if correct samples are provided with no array of discrimination options. Instead of teaching the range of correct instances by adding cues to a series of samples, an instructor could utilize a subtractive format. In this approach, positive concept instances would be presented consecutively, along with comparison examples containing an error in a single dimension, different each time. On each trial, the learner would choose between the two stimuli, receiving feedback as to the correctness of the choice. These conditions offer no overt target to match. For learning to occur, there must be successive testing and refining of the concept rules until positive instances are selected consistently. Yet, similar tactics prompt concept attainment with no explicit sample (Haygood & Bourne, 1965; Hull, 1920). In some cases, such as teaching conditional rules, concepts are acquired faster by presenting only negative instances (Bourne & Guy, 1968b). Matching to sample may be one method of conveying abstract knowledge but, like modeling, it is just a means of transmitting the information that guides the covert symbolic activities.

In terms of *performance*, the matching-to-sample analysis over-simplifies the response integration that is critical in many practical, applied endeavors. If trained by the matching paradigm, people need not construct novel response ensembles: Uniting separate elements into complex molar wholes would be a slow and toilsome process, and would rarely, if ever, occur. Integration costs would be the steepest for consecutively organized acts, which are not easily disected into discrete, static fragments. Thus, envision a child learning to tie shoelaces by picking the option that best matches a sample segment of the entire serial behavior episode. Similar frustrations await instructors who apply the matching paradigm in teaching beauticians to style hair. Students might possibly learn to recognize tonsorial chic, while not acquiring dexterity in fashioning it. Demonstrating the full sequence of skilled hairdressing would benefit the student beauticians' patrons. Many abstract skills, such as computer programming, building or machine design, and conversing in sign language, require intricate response coordinations. Matching to sample is unrepresentative of these common human tasks; it neglects the activities required for conceptual competence to be exercised. Although it shares certain general features of the social learning model, the matching paradigm becomes merely a truncated, scarcely applicable analog of the theory when vicarious acquisition entails using the alphabet of the deaf (Berger, 1966; Gerst, 1971); synchronizing complicated movement chains (Bandura & Jeffrey, 1973; Bandura *et al.*, 1974; Jeffery, 1976); constructing organized response configurations (e.g., clusters and triangles) to index comprehension; reproducing tenuous visual signal patterns (Rosenthal *et al.*, 1974), or earning the benefits of muscular skill training (Rosenthal & Bandura, 1978). It is equally hard to apply the matching paradigm to language modeling (Chapter 2), because syntactic categories are adopted without literal duplication of the specific words modeled. Although they adhere to rules for using constructions, observers themselves must integrate the behavior by selecting verbal components and arranging them into meaningful composites. The same considerations apply when functional classifications of language, such as styles of inquiry, are modeled (Chapter 3).

MODELING, OVERT PRACTICE, AND INTERFERENCE

Direct practice can be very useful in consolidating and finalizing principles learned from modeling, particularly if response integration requires postural adjustments that are regulated by proprioceptive feedback cues, information not readily acquired by observation. But often the main role of practice is to acquire information about how events are arranged. Producing overt responses is not necessary to gain this type of knowledge, as opposed to what is required in attempting to refine or synthesize intricate motor skills like playing the violin or swatting a golfball. Performance is not impeded by inhibitions or clumsiness. One need only know where, when, or how often to execute the behavior, and seek cues to guide appropriate decisions. For this type of learning, observing situational patterns is a shortcut from learning by actual toil.

Maze Learning

Among both adults and children, modeling is effective in transmitting cognitive maps of the correct routes in mazes. Poliakova (see Aronfreed, 1969) showed that youngsters learned a maze more efficiently after an adult demonstrated its pathways. Mastery of this task requires direct performers to endure lengthy motor exploration. But the vicarious learner instead enjoys the luxury of observing the visual cues and feedback available to the overt searcher, who is hampered by motor chores largely irrelevant to the cognition of proper choice points. The earliest research comparing vicarious with overt practice was spiced with serendipity. Hillix and Marx (1960) used an elaborate switch-maze, with direct performers learning complex switch patterns. Their response attempts were modeled, at a later time, for yoked observers who were required to call out the numbers of each switch thrown, allowing observers the elective strategy of coding and storing routes by numerical mnemonics. Although they bore no physical similarity to the switch patterns, the numbers provided a terse symbolic map of switch sequences. In an initial study, observers erred less often than direct learners. Still cherished during that era was the dictum that overt experience was mandatory for learning (Chapter 1). Alone, "imitation" was assumed incapable of generating new responses. Dubious about their unexpected results, Hillix and Marx repeated the study with other adults; again, the observers excelled, leading Hillix and Marx to suggest that the demands of decision making, and the movements of throwing switches may have hampered the direct performers.

Giving number designations was not a crucial ingredient for successful learning. Omitting that step, Rosenbaum and Hewitt (1966) used a simpler maze and confirmed the results of Hillix and Marx, namely, that vicarious exposure is superior to overt practice. Craig (1967) obtained the same results when yoking was abandoned, using naïve observers and performers working simultaneously in pairs. Shock feedback for errors was given to some groups in both studies, but had inconsistent effects: While shock interfered with the performance of Rosenbaum and Hewitt's adult males, and had the same effect on Craig's women, it assisted the performance of Craig's men. This illustrates how supplementary events (shock, motor acts, overt verbal coding) of the same class, depending on how they are cognized, can produce contrary impacts on modeled content. Motor demands usually handicap the storing of information, but the reverse has been found with some response equipment (Rosenbaum & Schultz, 1967). But these conditions, i.e., those required for movement acts to be facilitating, are little known. With verbal adjuncts, however, the picture is clearer. Meaningful statements usually enhance exemplary gains unless cueing distracts attention from ongoing demonstrations (Zimmerman & Bell, 1972), intrudes on covert symbolizing processes (Bourne & Bundersen, 1963; Coates & Hartup, 1969), or is too cumbersome for concise storage (Alford & Rosenthal, 1973; Rosenthal *et al.*, 1972a). Rosenbaum and Schultz (1967) showed that choosing which options to test also interfered with maze learning. They compared overt with observational learners, giving the judgment chores to one member of each pair. Decision makers retained correct locations less well than their peers who were spared the executive duties. Observation proved superior to direct efforts only when performers were forced to use an unwieldy device to make manual responses.

The preceding research involved college adults. Rosenbaum (1967) then confirmed the virtues of vicarious acquisition with students of various grammar school levels. Access to numerical coding props had varying effects, depending on overt conduct and attention. Children who heard partners speak the numbers at correct choice points learned best. For them, number cues were made salient. Yet overt scanning and stating of the numbers were not required. The group who spoke numbers aloud did not profit from forced attention to the symbols. Oral reporting burdens disrupted the potential gains afforded by preserving maze locations by numerals. The scores of these children were equal to those of their peers to whom numbers were made available but not emphasized. When not alerted to the informative value of digits, children of all age levels ignored them. Other data support the virtues of making concept attributes more salient for learners (e.g., Fishbein, Haygood, & Frieson, 1970; Hull, 1920; Schvaneveldt, Meyers, & Becker, 1976). Thus, to obtain the benefits of coding, two things were required: Social facilitation to make digits relevant; but exemption from public verbalizing.

These results challenge associationist views of the learning process. If antecedent stimuli were contiguously linked to terminal responses, rehearsing S–R coordinations should be an optimal means of stabilizing learning. Yet, repeating conjunctions between input and output terms may have minor or negative effects (Ferguson & Bray, 1976; Rosenthal & White, 1972a). Likewise, if observational learning depends on instrumental conditioning, then supplemental overt task practice should be very useful. However, rehearsing symbolic codes, quite different in form from terminal conduct, is more effective in promoting acquisition and retention of complex response patterns than reproducing target responses themselves (Bandura & Jeffery, 1973; Jeffery, 1976). The typical superiority of observation to direct task practice also argues in favor of a symbolic explanation. Instead of improving performance, pertinent overt activity was generally less helpful than pure observation (Craig, 1967; Hillix & Marx, 1960; Rosenbaum, 1967; Rosenbaum & Hewitt, 1966). For this to be the case, the witnessed events must be covertly represented in forms enabling the patterns to be later utilized. Since no overt gross muscle movements are required of spectators, it is difficult to explain vicariously derived competence in terms of connections between stimuli and response acts. Instead, the integration of information occurs independently of the direct execution of terminal conduct, except when overt activity interferes with cognition.

Concept Acquisition

In the teaching of concepts, overt practice also fares poorly when pitted against modeling. Kessler, White, Rosenthal, and Phibbs (1973) compared vicarious guidance with a variety of direct methods: Some overt performers were told when they made errors; others were also allowed to correct their mistakes; another group was prevented from executing terminal responses until their arrays had been properly organized. The concept required children to adjust number and content attributes in accordance with new ordering rules for changing serial patterns. Despite the complexity of the task, demonstrations were superior to all approaches based on direct practice. With a similar task, Macri (1976) showed that the scope of modeled scenarios is a key variable in concept attainment; illustrating how to plan for, and monitor, solution steps far surpassed less comprehensive exemplars. Since the breadth and coherence of modeled event structure is a crucial determinant of vicarious guidance, the inefficiency of trial and error formats is in glaring contrast with the facilitating effects of impoverished modeling strategies. Time spent on direct concept practice led to error rates twice those arising from exposure to just one correct demonstration amid two false examples (McLaughlin & Brinley, 1973). Adding 2 minutes of filmed modeling significantly boosted transfer and retention compared to active practice alone (Borkowski, Levers, & Gruenenfelder, 1976).

These results presuppose that the briefly modeled guidelines alert observers to relevant features of the task, and help them exclude irrelevancies, thus simplifying problem solving alternatives on subsequent trials. If this is the case, vicarious gains should be the sharpest early in acquisition, before learners can infer similar information from protracted overt efforts. This was demonstrated by Chalmers and Rosenbaum (1974), who first exposed adult performers and observers to a multidimensional concept. Then, on a transfer problem, either reversal (intradimensional) or nonreversal (extradimensional) shifts were required for solution. Most notably under reversal shift conditions, error rates were lower for observers than performers, who, unlike observers suffered negative transfer losses. The greatest advantage for modeling was evident early in transfer, when prior training contrasts were sharpest. As both groups continued their direct performance of the new task, the vicarious edge diminished and the achievements of the groups converged. Zimmerman and Rosenthal (1972a) used a difficult, multidimensional concept task in which proximity to a reference item and number-coded directionality designated correct instances. Distracting attributes of color, shape, and notching burdened the identification of target forms. Before training, all of the children heard the correct rule clearly stated twice. One group then was engaged in direct task practice, and received positive feedback for proper responses. This was analogous to instrumental learning by trial, error, and social reinforcement. Two modeling techniques were also grafted onto the practice-plus-feedback format: symbolic guidance from hearing the rule repeated; and demonstration of correct target selection. Both versions of modeling were superior to reinforced practice in terms of rule acquisition and were especially favorable for transfer, with their combination yielding the best scores. In generalization, combined modeling was three times more effective then purely instrumental learning.

Children who heard the recurrent rule summary could state the concept far better than groups receiving scant exposure to the rationale (cf. Chapter 3). Likewise, Gholson and his colleagues (Gholson, Theobald, & Thomas, 1977; Richman & Gholson, in press) have used modeling to teach solution principles for multidimensional hypothesis problems. In one study with first-graders, gestural demonstrations—particularly if linked to rule summaries—far surpassed overt practice and feedback (Tumblin, Gholson, Rosenthal, & Kelley, 1977). It seems clear that overt trials and feedback are usually less informative than more symbolic guidance methods. Viewed in isolation from competing learning techniques, reinforced toil may seem an efficient method of teaching abstract competence. When judged in contest with methods that support cognitive mediating skills, a very different conclusion may result.

This point was further confirmed in research involving the mastery of an elaborate dial-reading concept, a task which demanded that children do more than identify positive instances. To signify their comprehension of principles, children also had to construct response composites by assembling materials in proper colors and numbers; this task thus imposed a response integration hurdle that had to be overcome in order for credit to be earned. Some children were trained by guided practice that elicited only correct overt responses; all errors were prevented during training trials. Viewed from an S–R contiguity stance, adding this direct task experience should improve on the usual instrumental learning format: Only pairing stimuli with correct responses should reduce interference from cues being connected to errors during practice. Other learners saw a model silently construct proper response ensembles for each dial item. Since only correct examples were demonstrated, observers were also spared false pairings while being taught: Interference from error-producing actions and recall of self-produced mistakes is routinely minimized in vicarious guidance. Here, acquisition was much better with exemplification than with direct guided practice. Vicarious training accounted for more than twice as much variance as guided rehearsal, and was equally effective for third- and fifth-graders, despite their skill differences. Modeling produced comparable learning and transfer among older as well as younger children; in contrast, grade level qualified the gains due to overt practice. Thus, adding practice to modeling did little to boost knowledge, but adding modeling to practice significantly improved concept attainment (Rosenthal & Zimmerman, 1973).

These outcomes defy explanations based on unmediated pairing, because errorless overt response, i.e., practice, should greatly assist the chaining of input to output. Yet, silent observation of modeled examples proved superior. An informational view of social learning suggests that the observers discerned the crucial abstract relationships, and transformed the key gist into symbolic representations (Posner, 1973; Pressley, 1976), while spared any need to perform distracting motor acts during learning. To be sure, direct responses are vital for effective conduct in many situations, including skilled motor acts regulated by internal feedback cues not easily accessible to observation. If people must apply and extend general principles to specific milieux, firsthand efforts are also needed. Rarely can learners make transitions between school, laboratory, or clinic and more natural settings without testing and refining competence on concrete challenges not met during symbolic guidance (Bandura, 1977b; Rosenthal & Bandura, 1978). In some types of problems, internal relationships seem to be best mastered after direct exploration has supplied a "feel" for the task (Kirby, Rosenthal, & White, 1973); however, little research exists to classify these cases. Hence, opportunities to practice may vastly augment vicarious guidance, but not when overt responding distracts attention from cognizing the essential abstract gist.

Interference and Concept Maintenance

Intuitively, it seems plausible that stronger immediate acquisition would produce better transfer and retention. Factors that interfere with grasping information should also handicap applying and maintaining the knowledge. In S–R views, such conclusions follow from the premise that stimulus cues are linked to responses; hence, the more connections that are formed initially, the more correct chains that exist to support later utilization. In purely functionalist terms, eventual retrieval should parallel the strength of prior learning, but at a lower level, adjusted to allow for decrements in transfer and retrieval. Both accounts imply an ordinal relationship between levels of acquisition and utilization. This reasoning does not always square with empirical data. Instead, it seems that greater initial learning will be preserved only if it is converted into meaningful and stable representations to guide later applications, which in turn influence the cognitive processing of new content (Aaronson & Scarborough, 1976). Even though interference may limit the level of acquisition, paradoxically, knowledge garnered despite obstacles may be relatively resistant to transfer decrements and temporal decay.

Much abstract modeling research bears upon these points. Superior maze learning did not hold up on a related transfer task (Hillix & Marx, 1960). Various instruction aids helped initial adoption of question-asking rules, but initial benefits did not transfer to new stimuli (Rosenthal & Zimmerman, 1972a; Rosenthal *et al.*, 1970). In these studies, net learning was powerful. All of the modeling groups earned transfer scores far superior to baseline and to those of the untrained controls. Yet, the surplus learning, cued by supportive directions, was lost by the generalization phase. Similar results were obtained for the clustering concept. Some information aids that boosted learning did not similarly benefit transfer or retention, although order of testing (with transfer items preceding or following training stimuli) did not affect the results. Yet, the modeling gains were substantial, and proved to be robust over time and with transfer alterations. In other studies, it was found that while added helping cues might work initially, their extra gains were sometimes short-lived (Alford & Rosenthal, 1973; Rosenthal *et al.*, 1972a). Indeed, orienting sets, intended as aids, can have the same effect as distracting events, expected to interfere (Malouf & Dodd, 1972; Tsujimoto & Liebert, 1971; van Hekken, 1969). Likewise, while pictorial coding and narrative descriptions assisted prompt reproduction of complex motor patterns, the initial benefits waned fast. After a 15-minute delay, those groups performed no better than observers trained with enforced interference (Gerst, 1971). Likewise, manual and symbolic aids that bolster original performance may be very vulnerable to rapid forgetting if the behavior is not coded into meaningful forms. Symbolic codes combining meaningfulness with retrievability produced superior memory performance (Bandura & Jeffery, 1973; Bandura *et al.*, 1974).

There are two distinct aspects to these aggregate results: (*a*) Why do the initial benefits of some supportive measures extinguish so soon? (*b*) What might explain the relative stability of learning established under intellectually demanding conditions? Exactly how profitable aids to modeling will eventually be seems to depend on what happens as the result of acquisition bonuses. If an initial advantage entails restructuring the gist into economical and durable covert transforms, benefits endure for later utilization (Shimmerlik & Nolan, 1976). Instead, if augmented acquisition fails to establish concise and meaningful mnemonics to stabilize storage, the gains are negligible. Both the memory codes and their capacity to enhance retrieval will soon dissipate (see below).

The question of why conditions that strain cognition may lead to more stable knowledge requires a separate explanation. While the degree of concept mastery does not necessarily *increase*—a lower level of skill may result—learning seems especially robust. It generalizes to new conditions with minor loss, and persists in large part after delay. From related paired-associate data, Battig (1968, 1972) proposed a broad theoretical premise: "Intratask interference represents an important source of intertask facilitation." His basic point is that introducing some "noise," heterogeneity, malorganization, or other interference into training arrays can have positive effects. It may force the learner to make sharper distinctions and to cognize events more diligently to grasp their principles. Perseverance at learning, despite distractions, may ultimately be of assistance in new but related transfer problems, and increase the durability of learning. In this connection, Bourne and Guy (1968a) showed that heterogeneous training aided concept transfer. The more diversity in rules during practice tasks, the better was performance when a new transfer rule was later introduced. In this view, encountering some adversity in training may lead learners to actively concentrate and to refine information. If interference spurs vigorous mental rehearsal and symbol construction, more enduring comprehension may plausibly result (Hiller, 1974).

TASK STRUCTURE AND INTERFERENCE

The data just cited suggest that knowledge earned under conditions of relative strain may be particularly durable. Other research also shows the value of subjective organization. Classifying gist into hierarchical categories aids storage and utilization (Bourne, 1970; Carson & Abrahamson, 1976; Mandler, 1967a,b). Personally meaningful content relationships boost retrieval (Begg & Anderson, 1976; Tulving, 1968). In light of the positive effects of *subjective* organization, one would naturally expect orderly external structure to aid information maintenance. This is true if well-organized gist is easier to integrate with covert categories, e.g., when rules subsume a multiplicity of separate instances. Intuitively, one would expect better-organized input formats to promote more enduring gains. Yet, Battig's interference—transfer hypothesis suggests that the relationship between external organization and the ultimate stability of knowledge is not necessarily so simple (nor monotonic). This was shown by Gavurin and Donahue (1961). They found that although it took longer to instate a scrambled learning program than a well-ordered program, the levels of retention by the structured and scrambled groups were equal when the subjects were retested a month later. Research involving a dial-reading concept also questions whether abstract mastery is merely a positive function of input structuring. For training stimuli that were random or low in structure, there were no transfer losses between familiar and novel items. Although it led to better acquisition, full structuring also resulted in significant transfer decrements. With orderly sequences for testing generalization, 50% external organization was at least as good as 100%. With random testing formats, 50% structure in training yielded poorer results. Yet, when all items were randomized within sets, varying the between-sets order of presenting the familiar training and transfer items, and the new tasks, had no effect on delayed retrieval (Rosenthal & Zimmerman, 1973, 1976; Zimmerman & Rosenthal, 1972b).

Aggregately, these task structure and concept stability data confirm that utilization is not a linear correlate of measured acquisition. Reducing the external order of teaching content need not weaken transfer or retention. A nominal amount of interference may slow or decrease immediate learning, while still leading to eventual mastery as good as intuitively preferable teaching formats. All of this defies explanations based on one-to-one connections between abstract stimuli and terminal responses. The results depart from what should occur if instrumental conditioning or S–R chaining assumptions were prototypes of cognition (i.e., monotonic S–R linkage). Instead, the data suggest that what is truly critical, i.e., what governs storage, are the central organization and symbolic mediators constructed by the learner.

The evidence implies that some long-run benefits are derived from overcoming strains on comprehension, a point less relevant for the teaching of circumscribed skills or rules that will be sharpened by everyday use. Especially at first, structuring to minimize errors will probably aid progress toward such goals. To establish more inclusive mediators, some disorder or "noise" in training may be better. This applies if knowledge must be extended to new situational contexts, novel task formats, or to temporally remote retention episodes without intervening rehearsal. There, error-making may aid one in distinguishing key from peripheral aspects. Ambiguous or less-than-ideal cases can aid in clarifying boundary conditions not met in exposure to modal examples. When, for instance, does a dubious plant specimen qualify as poison ivy, or a faltering apology as a socially adequate response? If teaching only includes perfect exemplars, one may falsely exclude minor deviations. One can better assess normative standards after testing the variations that are tolerated and rejected in diverse social settings. Heterogeneity and marginal cases can be added to modeling displays once basic rules are grasped. The same reasoning suggests that overt trials can refine principles learned vicariously. To conceptualize skillfully, one must judge when to bend or respect nominal criteria. Chances to make and correct errors from practice with taxing examples can prepare learners for the imperfect structuring and borderline cases of natural settings (Bandura, 1977b; Martin, Burkholder, Rosenthal, Tharp, & Thorne, 1968).

STRUCTURING THROUGH RULES

The prior data revealing some uses for adversity concerned *external* structure. More heterogeneous content may force attention to limiting conditions; organizational "noise" prepares one for transitions to less orderly arrangements. Another type of structure concerns the internal criteria for grouping or segregating instances. People assemble events into larger units bridging shared attributes, and store organized classifications, rather than strings of discrete associations (Bourne, 1970;

Carson & Abrahamson, 1976). If a spate of particulars is subsumed by common rules, vast cognitive savings result. This entails assigning events to a category and knowing how to address the class or type. Labels like "apple" reduce countless examples to one class of edibles. New instances are treated in ways that were rewarding in prior apple encounters. The term "tornado" or cues to its approach can guide precautions suiting that hazardous species without overt contact. For abstract concepts conforming to rules about shared functions (knife, ax, scissors), relationships (cities larger than their respective state capitals), and other criteria (all ships named for women), sensory cues do not govern class membership. Whatever the defining rules, concept attainment requires that instances be grouped together, and that one react adeptly to their common features. When this is possible, performance is far more efficient and robust than if events are cognized discretely and dealt with in piecemeal fashion. Research confirms that enhancing rule structure augments vicarious concept formation.

Liebert and his colleagues have studied various means of graduating the structure underlying modeled demonstrations. In initial tests, verbal aids brought closer emulation of a model's criteria for self-reward, with children who met those standards engaging in more self-praise (Liebert & Allen, 1967). On the same task, but with high, moderate, or low levels of structure, the clarity of rule cues dictated how well guidelines were adopted. Violating the reinforcement criteria was inversely related to the degree of structure provided (Liebert, Hanratty, & Hill, 1969). Verbal emphasis helped first-graders to recall a model's choices of paired silhouettes, forms that defied natural grouping dimensions. Thus, labeling gains were specific to prompted items, and were not transferred to uncued choices. Verbal structuring proved a rather weak strategy, of limited benefit for other, younger learners (Tsujimoto & Liebert, 1971). When correct answers involve discrete elements that lack an organizing framework, memory strains increase, with the increase in the content to be preserved. Recall drops sharply under these conditions, as the amount of data expands. Boosting attention by rewarding a model can assist memory: Vicarious incentives were of most assistance to observers who were shown many items, were some aid when amounts of content were moderate, but when given few data to store, learners retained equally well with and without incentive props. Both overt and vicarious rewards may bolster recall (Liebert & Fernandez, 1969, 1970). The preceding designs varied structure indirectly, by means of devices to focus attention. One can also adjust the internal features of the task to support cognitive organization. A constant color attribute helped children to match exemplary choices; if color cues varied across modeled decisions, the task was harder to learn (McDavid, 1962). In a similar vein, intrinsic structure was tested. The task involved a model's choosing between paired commodities which shared a common element (e.g., one large versus two small things). Observers who could discern and apply a rule such as "always the big object" had a simplified map for organizing modeled responses. Observers' retrieval of commodity preference was compared with and without a common decision rule available to subsume the model's binary choices. Children able to follow a unifying principle displayed much better recall. The common rule group made fewer errors, earned perfect recall scores more often, and responded faster than their nonrule counterparts. Further, when rule structuring was possible, the length of list to be stored had no effect, but with unsystematic modeling, errors were a positive function of the amount of information presented. The same results were found among black and Caucasian children (Liebert & Swenson, 1971a). Next tested was the ability to predict or infer a model's commodity preferences on new items (i.e., transfer), as well as retention of prior choice. The data bespoke the merits of categorization. Youngsters observing the common dimension made fewer errors, more perfect scores, and faster judgments than children shown an arbitrary choice pattern. Consistent modeling helped learners induce and generalize the witnessed criteria. More of the common rule group predicted perfectly how new items would be selected, showing abstraction of the decision rules; even though judgments were more quickly made, they were more accurate (Liebert & Swenson, 1971b). In both of these studies, a uniform preference style simplified cognition. There was little need to store item details. Retrieval was harder when there was no conceptual regularity between objects and choices. Nonrule observers were forced to try and remember the specific items chosen, requiring them to spend more time and causing more memory strain. In this commodity preference task, grasping of rule structure is akin to *Einstellung* formation: Once the modeled pattern was cognized, the same response served for all items. Modeling can establish problem-solving sets. Observing indirect solutions to water–jar problems led to emulation of the cumbersome strategies (Rosenbaum & Arenson, 1967).

However, the advantages of organizing rules are not confined to uniform terminal examples or to dichotomous stimulus options. In one concept task, a child displayed knowledge when he constructed proper output ensembles to index a range of shifting number and color values. Many false response combinations were possible. For half of the learners, the sequential steps were arbitrary, making it hard to infer the key principles. Other children observed a better structural paradigm, involving a consistent serial progression. The clear rule produced superior retention and generalization after delay, with no transfer losses between immediate and later tests; however, initial learning declined significantly for the rule-deprived group (Zimmerman & Bell, 1972).

One standard for successful rule acquisition is that new concept instances can be handled with only minor decline in performance (Bourne, 1970). In terms of this criterion, most of the concept modeling research already discussed reveals category formation. With no extra guidance, significant transfer was found on the disk–triangles coordination rule (Table 4-1). Immediate and delayed generalization without transfer losses have resulted with the clustering concept and various versions of the dial-reading concept (see p. 224), as well as for abstract verbal categories (Chapter 3). In all of these studies, modeling techniques sponsored stable adoption of symbolic paradigms. Instead of linking discrete, overt acts to concrete cues, the observers induced governing principles, which were then extended to heterogeneous but rule-consistent transfer stimuli. Most of these generalization tasks were totally unlike the teaching instances in literal attributes, e.g., shape and color. Yet, the concept rules were correctly interpreted and applied to novel transfer examples by inferential reasoning. The observers cognized symbolic relationships, such as structural analogies (Rosch, 1975; Rosch *et al.*, 1976), and mediated, fitting abstract criteria rather than sensory dimensions.

Adequate conceptual rules integrate and preserve knowledge economically. But imperfect and tentative principles also serve important response-regulating functions. Until a concept is fully attained, fragmentary hypotheses are used as temporary guides, subject to refinement when newer information forces revisions (Duncker, 1945; Haygood & Bourne, 1965; Meltzer *et al.*, 1976; Miller *et al.*, 1960; Mims & Gholson, 1977; Richman & Gholson, in press; Schvaneveldt *et al.*, 1976). Indeed, learners may actively develop, follow, and strive to verify guiding rules even though the structure of events is purely random from the experimenter's standpoint (Estes, 1975; Rogers & Haygood, 1968). In one study, although given directions to the contrary, most of the subjects persistently sought conceptual patterns to solve a nonexistent abstract problem. Most of the learners seized on accidental regularities, constructing sequential hypotheses which were at times "confirmed" by coincidence. From an external vantage point, the pattern classification was "superstitious" behavior; but for the person, it represented an attempt to organize experiences into a sensible framework. After many trials, only 19% of responses indicated acceptance of the stated task rationale (Rosenthal *et al.*, 1975). Thus, even in situations designed to study rule-free associative conditioning processes, learners are usually self-instructed to approach the task in more personally meaningful terms (Banks *et al.*, 1975; Battig, 1968; Perlmutter & Meyers, 1976; Tulving, 1968). Although entirely spurious for adequately specifying concepts, false rules still can actively regulate overt behavior. It is therefore risky to assume that poor performance or insoluble problems assure that abstract mediation has been excluded. More likely, people will interpret happenstance events as informative guides and will reason in defiance of the experimenter's task definition (Bower, 1974; Clark & Brownell, 1975; Gholson, O'Connor, & Stern, 1976).

Demonstration or Narration?

Rule structuring supports cognition, whether the information comes from direct practice, witnessed demonstrations, or from symbolic modeling. Under what conditions is one social learning technique favored over another? Example *can* teach better than precept. This is most likely to be the case if the learners' language skills are not adequate for utilizing information cast in language symbols, or if the requisite patterns cannot be easily captured in words. In many cases, such as in learning to ride a bicycle, verbal directions may be too cumbersome, since quick and intricate coordinations must be made. In mastering certain concepts, diverse subroutines must be integrated serially. Here too, demonstration may impart a working grasp of the consecutive steps faster than narrative modeling, even if the head start does not persist after extensive training. Reciprocally, instructions that boost short-term progress may add gains no more durable than those due to pure exemplification (Lepper, Sagotsky, & Mailer, 1975; Rosenthal & Zimmerman, 1972a). If the content is difficult and unfamiliar, lengthy lecture presentations can tax comprehension and satiate the discerning attention of the learners. In these cases, and also when learners are of limited verbal facility, demonstration offers advantages over undiluted narration. However, if verbal symbols can be easily stored and adeptly translated into their action referents, symbolic modeling should be much more efficient than enacting actual illustrations for observers. Research evidence supports these contentions.

For young Chicano students accustomed to speaking Spanish at home, modeled demonstrations have been shown to instate conservation skill; the children acquired the judgment principle and generalized it to new items without transfer decrement. Another group received equivalent decision guides by directions in English, which they used routinely at school. Not only was narrative teaching weaker than demonstration, but the instructions children evidenced no trace of any learning. When cast in the less familiar language, these difficult rules failed to be grasped by the children, even though the youngsters had been shown all of the relevant physical stimuli during training (Rosenthal & Zimmerman, 1972b). Retardates are a population whose verbal skills are impoverished. Severe, resident cases were studied on the disk–triangles concept. A demonstration group observed silent modeling of correct solutions. For instructions subjects, identical gist was instead stated in words. The response means appear in the final section of Table 4-1. Exemplification was a much better teaching device than directions for all levels of handicap tested. Aggregately, the demonstration group showed significant learning and transfer, surpassing the instructions subjects in both of the posttraining tests. Narration led to concept acquisition, but comprehension was not maintained on transfer items (Rosenthal & Kellogg, 1973).

In light of these results, then, exemplification should be of value for applied pedagogy. Yet, little research bears upon this topic, despite the popularity of "show and tell" presentations. One pertinent study compared the impact of radio and television for children's newscasts. The video format, which presents information both auditorily and visually, proved superior (Barrow & Westley, 1960). To approach scholastic realities more closely, White and Rosenthal (1974) performed a field experiment with normal third-graders, studied in their own classrooms. A 10-lesson curriculum drew on college-level psychology as novel abstract content, material previously unknown to children of this age group. The topics included sensation and perception, discrimination and transfer, shaping and classical conditioning, and cognition. Baseline knowledge and learning gains were assessed by a factual content test. Table 4-2 lists some of these items, to illustrate the scope of information coverage.

Few concessions were made to the youngsters' age level. Some terms were simplified, and test items were read aloud so that preliterate youngsters could understand by means other than reading. Questions were prohibited during training, and the regular teachers had no exposure to the procedures or content of the study. Otherwise, the training contexts typified classroom settings. In both the demonstration and lecture classes, all key terms were emphasized orally and printed on the chalkboard during teaching. For the lecture group, information was conveyed by narration. In the demonstration format, some material was instead taught by simple modeled illustrations. The demonstrations did

TABLE 4-2
Ten of the 40 Factual Test Items[a]

#3. Pitch depends on the ______ of sound vibrations
amplitude *height* *length* *number* *shape*

#11. The measure of learning based on how LONG it takes for a response to BEGIN is called ______
amplitude *errors* *latency* *rate* *trials-to-extinction*

#13. The measure of learning based on HOW MANY responses occur in a minute or an hour is called
amplitude *errors* *latency* *rate* *trials-to-extinction*

#16. Language is an important aid to people because it helps them to ______ events
conditional *organize* *practice* *recognize* *reinforce*

#18. The word that means we get accustomed to, or stop noticing, stimuli that do not change is ______
adaptation *aversive* *pleasant* *strong* *weak*

#23. It is easier to recall words that can be ______ together
chunked *heard* *measured* *spoken* *welded*

#28. Unlike smell or touch, we learn about TASTE from receptors that are in special ______
frequencies *patterns* *places* *sizes* *waves*

#30. Fear may come from attempts to ______ a response
count *observe* *punish* *satiate* *stimulate*

#35. The SERIAL POSITION effect means that we learn the first and last stimuli
by chance *in pairs* *the best* *the same* *the worst*

#39. Usually, on changing schedules the response rate is more ______ than on unchanging schedules
elastic *fast* *uneven* *unpredictable* *weak*

[a]Adapted from White and Rosenthal, *Journal of Experimental Education*, 1974, *43*, 91–92. Copyright © 1974 by Heldref Publications. Reprinted by permission.

not rehash concepts also contained in the lectures; rather, they replaced narration as a method for teaching suitable content. Thus, in one lesson, both groups were told: "In a partial schedule, it takes more than one response to earn a reinforcement. Say, for example, we could only pay reinforcement for every other response." Then, in the demonstration format, the model nodded slowly, and received coins on alternate nods. The lecture format instead continued: "Then, if a man nods, nothing happens; but if he nods again, he gets a penny. Then he nods and nothing happens; but if he nods again, he gets a penny, and so on." Lessons were held biweekly over a 5-week period, so that for any gains to be attributed to training, knowledge had to be retained over time.

The results were quite clear. All of the classes were comparable before teaching, but diverged at later testing, depending on the method of guidance. Untrained controls' scores progressively declined from the first to the final test. The lecture group made a nonsignificant gain, and the lecture and control children failed to differ. The demonstration group showed significant improvement, surpassing control performance. Illustrative modeling also generated more positive attitudes than narrative teaching. The demonstration group rated the science topic as easier and more fun than youngsters who were lectured alone. These outcomes confirmed that exemplification can offer special advantages when acquiring a basic foundation in difficult subject matter. Most of the training syllabus concerned new concepts and nomenclature for learners with minimal prior knowledge. Similar results have been found with adults given graphic illustrations to teach electrochemistry (Rigney & Lutz, 1976), and analogies or illustrations to exemplify hard prose content (Royer & Cable, 1976). Exemplary guides often boost clinical outcomes (Rosenthal & Bandura, 1978).

In contrast, when learners can grasp abstract concepts cast in words, narration will be a far more efficient technique than demonstration. This implies some greater familiarity with the material, and that learners' verbal skills enable them to extract and utilize meaningful information from concise language cues. Thus, symbolic modeling through brief rule directions led to concept learning, transfer, and retention equal to that prompted by much longer guidance by exemplification plus coding supports (Alford & Rosenthal, 1973; Rosenthal *et al.*, 1972a).

In most cases, there is no reason to confine guidance to just one mode. With pure demonstration, learners must construct all rule summaries on their own; however, their spontaneous efforts may not produce or achieve stable representational guides. If rule statements help condense a barrage of details, or organize symbolic mediation, concept mastery will improve (Bandura & Jeffery, 1973; Bandura *et al.*, 1974; Clinton & Boyce, 1975; Forehand & Yoder, 1974). Likewise, observing illustrations can make input more vivid and clarify the sequential structure of events (Macri, 1976; Rohwer & Matz, 1975; Tumblin *et al.*, 1977; Zimmerman & Rosenthal, 1974a).

Usually, teachers can best introduce new principles by combining examples and narration. Thus, Beilin (1965) found demonstration plus verbal correction the only effective conservation training technique among a range of methods tested. Zimmerman and Rosenthal (1972a,b) showed that rule provision plus exemplary modeling surpassed each technique alone in fostering concept mastery. Sometimes, merely summarizing rules orally is not enough. Rule practice by covert rehearsal or overt reviews can assist the integration of principles far better than briefer access. This depends on how readily narrative information is transformed into the faithful and stable representations that guide utilization. When meaning is easily extracted from verbal messages, brief directions may suffice. When it becomes harder to translate verbal discourse into summary codes, mnemonic systems, or terminal deeds, rule narration can be augmented by repetition and mental rehearsal, by illustrative demonstrations, and by guided practice with supplemental feedback.

Individual Differences

In principle, observer differences on any defined continuum may influence a host of dependent measures. In fact, trait characteristics have not proven very useful predictors of diverse forms of emulative learning (Akamatsu & Thelen, 1974; Mischel, 1973). Various self-report measures of one's personality, need for social approval, and self-esteem have generally been shown to be relatively unrelated to terminal performance (e.g., Finch, Rickard, & Wilson, 1970; Herbert, Gelfand, & Hartman, 1969; Tasch, 1971). However, when state and situational determinants have been *manipulated,* observer variables may aid prediction. For example, experimentally created competence or failure, as well as arousal can affect observational outcomes (Akamatsu & Thelen, 1974; Bandura & Rosenthal, 1966; Gelfand, 1962; Rosenbaum, Chalmers, & Horne, 1962; Walters & Amoroso, 1967).

Evidence is still scanty on the way in which specific conceptual modeling tactics relate to person variables. In recent work, adults having high and low levels of test anxiety faced a difficult anagrams task. Separate groups were taught by silent observation alone, and with attention statements or strategic principles also being supplied. Learning varied according to the type of guidance employed, with the best results obtained for principles; following, in descending order, were attention aids, silent modeling, and control groups. Arousal level interacted with tuition format in a complex fashion. When they were given rules, the less emotion-prone subjects earned their *lowest* scores, but their best performances were produced with attention guides. Hence, although there may have been subtle interference effects related to arousal thresholds, these unfortunately were not clearly isolated. Later, on a memory task, learners with low levels of test anxiety had better overall scores than highly test-anxious learners. Yet, given a model who provided an appropriate counterarousal strategy, the high-emotion observers recalled more than any other group (Sarason, 1973, 1975). These results invite further inquiry into the personal and task characteristics that can dictate social learning benefits. It is important to clarify the developmental and dispositional factors that enter into modeling processes (Bandura, 1977b).

AGE AND GROSS OUTCOME IN ABSTRACT MODELING

In explanations of children's learning, however, chronological or mental age has all too often been looked upon as all-important, while potentially more informative individual factors have received less emphasis. No doubt age is a global index of evolving cognitive skill, and has gross value in predicting young children's performance after conceptual modeling. Even so, it can distract attention from other concerns, such as parental encouragement of intellectual efforts (Bradley & Caldwell, 1976). Age-related differences are likely to be most common in the years before children begin their formal education. Thus, age has covaried with performance when abstractions are demonstrated to very young learners (Zimmerman & Rosenthal, 1974a), when school-age groups are compared to preschool samples (Coates & Hartup, 1969; Hanson, 1972; Yussen, 1974), and when language fluency in the primary grades is crucial to success (Vasta & Liebert, 1973). Compared to teenagers, much younger children earn lower scores on syntactical modeling of novel linguistic constructions (Kossuth, 1972; Liebert *et al.*, 1969b), or when lengthy sessions with stringent problems tax youngsters' endurance (Gholson & Danziger, 1975; Richman & Gholson, 1977). Nonetheless, age may not affect relational thought by nursery schoolers (Rosenthal *et al.*, 1974a) or their grasp of abstract categories apart from verbal justifications (Chapter 3). Each year, new results confirm the semantic and categorical abilities of children younger than had previously been thought possible (Steinberg & Anderson, 1975; Westman & Youssef, 1976). Socioeconomic disadvantage has proven to be more of a handicap than age disparities in several cognitive tasks, namely, concept learning by preschoolers (Rosenthal *et al.*, 1971), and category adoption by disadvantaged sixth-graders, who scored somewhat below middle-class third-graders (Rosenthal & Zimmerman, 1972a). If task demands are eased and clarified by supporting guidance, age trends otherwise likely may become negligible (Coates & Hartup, 1969; Geis & Hall, 1976; Siegler, 1975). In one study, kindergarten and second-grade groups were comparable, when serving as untaught controls and when a model added verbal facsimiles to overt distinctions. With silent demonstrations, the elder group made *more* concept errors (Ryan & Kobisagawa, 1971). Once children enter school, age becomes a weaker predictor of abstract modeling gains, although individual *skill* differences remain important (Gholson, O'Connor, & Stern, 1976; Keating and Caramazza, 1975). Pattern associates were retained better by sixth- than by fourth-graders (Williams & Willoughby, 1971). Yet, no differences were found between the abilities of second- or third- and fourth-graders to adopt modeled grammatical features (Harris & Hassemer, 1972; Rosenthal & Whitebook, 1970), or between the ability of third- and fifth-graders to master a complex concept (Rosenthal & Zimmerman, 1973). In designs involving children whose ages ranged more widely, linear trends were not observed. There was no difference between children in grades 3 to 4 and 5 to 6 with respect to remembering a maze, although they surpassed a group selected from grades 1 to 2 (Rosenbaum, 1967). No age effects emerged on a sorting concept when observers were tested on the training stimuli. Although sixth-graders had the best performances on a harder transfer task, second- and fourth-graders scored alike (McLaughlin & Brinley, 1973). Collectively, these results suggest that age loses predictive power after the preschool years. As a gross index of nonspecific cognitive socialization, age becomes less informative than situational variables in estimating observational learning gains. Even when age does relate to terminal proficiency, the underlying determinants still need clarification.

Shortcomings of Age Interpretations

Overconcern with the age variable invites similarly global explanations when differences occur. Rather than explaining age effects in terms of process analyses of causal factors, theorists have postulated discrete types of mediation. This theoretical tendency is exemplified by the "production deficiency" hypothesis that older but not younger children will self-produce and utilize verbal codes during problem solving (Flavell, 1970; Miller, Shelton, & Flavell, 1970). According to this view, verbal mediators appear to operate in a manner dichotomously related to age, either clearly available or playing no role; however, it seems more plausible that many gradations of skill would fall between the polar extremes. The dichotomous view was tested in a modeling study, in which age differences failed to resolve the issue: 7-year-olds outperformed 4-year-olds, who gained the most from verbal structuring; but both groups improved when guided by adult statements. The older group was hampered by self-generated phrases, as compared to their performance when verbally guided and when they observed silent modeling. Those results should not be obtained if older children necessarily construct more effective verbal codes. The preschoolers benefited from their own statements, a technique which facilitated retrieval (mean = 9.92) as compared to silent observation (mean = 6.25); however, adult coding exemplars led to the best scores (Coates & Hartup, 1969). Self-coding should not have helped if the preschoolers could not mediate verbally. Similar theoretical problems arise if dichotomies based on global cognitive readiness replace age as predictors (van Hekken, 1969). All-or-none distinctions are insufficiently refined for mapping cognitive development.

Likewise, generic age trends are of little use in elucidating underlying cognitive processes. Age levels, task demands, types of stimulus items, and verbal coding formats may interact in a complex fashion. While giving verbal labels does not fill a conceptual void, it may replace preschoolers' faulty codes with more efficient mnemonics (Mowbray & Luria, 1973). Much recent evidence suggests a picture of youngsters mediating quite actively, although they may be hampered by correctable flaws in their strategies (Harris & Bassett, 1976; Tighe, Tighe, & Schechter, 1975). Guidance to screen out irrelevant cues has been shown to improve children's conceptual performance, with no differences between 4- and 7-year olds (Casey, 1976). If younger children are less discerning in what they cognize, irrelevant attributes will burden their processing efforts (Kemler, Shepp, & Foote, 1976). Perceptual distractibility and overattention to extraneous content can then impair their causal reasoning, because inferences will be based on irrelevant information (Siegler, 1975). Thus, demonstrating abstract solution responses may not assist observers unless they are helped to grasp the critical solution principles (Whitehurst, 1976). Modeling displays which clarify the necessary steps in decision-making have been observed to improve concept reasoning, in comparison to formats providing less guidance in analyzing task demands (Macri, 1976). All too often, particular children are stigmatized by age norms and the presumed level of their intellectual maturity. Indeed, if there were effective tests for categorizing children into stages, then abuses might be even greater than those resulting from IQ designations (Bandura, 1977b). "Readiness rationales can exact high human prices if age, or failure on a limited work sample, are prematurely used to conclude that a child cannot handle a multitude of problem-solving challenges. Diverse conceptual activities may have very different thresholds and require distinct skills (Carson & Abrahamson, 1976; Finkel, 1973; Sheingold, 1973). Even related tasks can have surprisingly disparate outcomes (Rosenbaum & Schultz, 1967; Rosenthal & Zimmerman, 1976; Tversky & Teiffer, 1976). If data from remote, age or "readiness" criteria were not extrapolated to global cognitive competence, and children were instead graded according to their known skills, greater clarity would then result. Then, successive levels of specific aptitude could be compared in response to various coding formats and guidance techniques. Relationships between available skill repertoires and teaching methods could shed light on global age trends in concept learning. Age mainly attracts interest as a basis for inferences about underlying differences in information processing. Comparing children who have clearly defined symbolic skills on various task competencies would yield clearer individual difference relationships than are possible from extrapolations from the indirect age measure, which serves to roughly index ability variables (Keating & Caramazza, 1975). Thus, mastery of a family of concepts might require spatial analogies skills only crudely reflected by age norms. Comparing groups of subjects with known levels of spatial competence would provide a sharper picture of how skill differences contribute to solutions, strategies, and types of errors. In turn, these data could then guide the design of teaching programs (Furth & Milgram, 1973; Siegler & Atlas, 1976).

SOCIAL LEARNING BASES OF AGE EFFECTS

During the first years of life, the foundations of abstract proficiencies must be developed from scratch. At this level, the child's age reflects his opportunities to acquire familiarity with symbolic and social conventions. Generally, the younger the preschool child, the less robust and diversified his repertoire of conceptual skills, and the more rudimentary his covert organization of information. Cognitive classifications will be simpler and less precise; they will encompass fewer elements in hierarchical categories, with a sparser network of interconnections among separable but related concept ladders (Cramer, 1973; Liberty & Ornstein, 1973; Winters & Brzoska, 1976). One would expect the child to exhibit less facility at distinguishing categories, to be less able to both perceive correspondences across groupings, and to shift sets flexibily to meet contextual changes (Cole, 1973; McFarland & Kellas, 1975; Rogers & Johnson, 1973; Rubin, 1973; Westman & Yussef, 1976). Also, young children will be far less adept at converting their grasp of an abstraction into public language. More discrepancy would be found between the child's comprehension of facts or relationships, and his ability to express the knowledge verbally, than would be observed for an older person. Reciprocally, the young child should have greater difficulty interpreting and processing the information contained in verbal messages (Chapters 2 and 3).

Such longitudinal aspects of cognitive development are important phenomena requiring study. In a social learning framework, they would be analyzed in terms of (*a*) prerequisite skills and shared components common to related tasks; (*b*) the amount of exposure and practice, and the quality of guidance, given to the person; (*c*) the salience, importance, and meaningfulness of specific abilities in terms of the social environment; (*d*) the value of particular knowledge in earning tangible and symbolic rewards; and (*e*) the personal evolution of the child's covert rules and strategies in his structuring, storage, and application of information. All of these factors point to a global assumption of greater proficiency in older children. Older children should be more adept at judging situational demands, and in foreseeing the consequences of meeting or violating social norms (Costanzo *et al.*, 1973). They will have acquired more knowledge, and will have learned how to better harmonize, revise, cross-index, and shift among their own categorical storage units than younger children (Ciborowski & Cole, 1973; Danner & Taylor, 1973; Tenney, 1975). When the child reaches school age, the number of years of normal socialization becomes a less informative index of symbolic competence. Four-year-olds will outperform 2-year-olds more often than fourth-graders will surpass second-graders.

Conceptual development is spurred by the child's educative transactions with the social environment (Stewart & Hamilton, 1976). These contacts introduce data and pose problems that the child must solve. By his attempts at coping and exploration, the child gains expertise in manipulating and refining symbolic skills. The child's knowledge expands, as he observes how others deal with events and organize information, and from feedback about his own efforts that the child receives. Facility is not assumed to stem from the ripening of preprogramed, innately specified mental growth processes or structures. Rather, recurrent situational forces shape intellectual capacities and styles. One's history of success and failure in problem-solving endeavors may govern how one approaches learning challenges. Children with little self-confidence in solving problems, such as retardates, may be especially responsive to external social cues and seek intervention or hints from models in order to preempt their own expected failures (Yando & Zigler, 1971; Zigler & Yando, 1972). Once the child has acquired some foundation of cognitive skills, further age-related opportunity for nonspecific practice becomes less important. Because of redundancy with what is already known, the molar age variable yields diminishing predictability for common tasks (Clarkson, Haggith, Tierney, & Kobasigawa, 1973; Geis & Hall, 1976; James & Miller, 1973; Perlmutter & Meyers, 1976). Instead, the particular content of a task and the adequacy of the child's educational experiences will have a stronger impact on the rate and course of later progress. Moreover, age differences in measured competence need not reflect ability differences in *comprehension*. Age trends can be the result of relatively high-level, molecular, component skills which support, but are distinct from, understanding. For example, young children process information less efficiently than older groups whose cognitive strategies and mnemonic labels are more appropriate and akin to those of adults (Drummond, Williams, & Aiken, 1973; Nelson & Earl, 1973; Posnansky & Neumann, 1976; Smith, Kemler, & Aronfreed, 1975).

DEVELOPMENTAL TRENDS IN COMPONENT PROCESSES

A child's skill at paying effective attention to stimulus events shows longitudinal gains. This progress stems in part from cumulative rehearsal of monitoring plans and increasing self-controlled endurance (Doyle, 1973; Smith *et al.*, 1975), and from the developing ability to discriminate and organize conceptual categories (Tighe *et al.*, 1975; Tenney, 1975). Older children more adroitly ignore irrelevant cues which distract their scrutiny from attributes essential in meeting the main task demands (Kemler *et al.*, 1976; Pick & Frankel, 1973; Wheeler & Dusek, 1973). Such data recall Gelman's (1969) emphasis on teaching attention and cue discrimination in order to promote conservation learning. Attentional strains can underlie molar age differences. A kindergarten group could sustain cumulative monitoring just two-thirds as long, and could tolerate half as many visual recognition items, as third- and sixth-graders (Mowbray & Luria, 1973). Preschoolers are less persistent in attending to modeled events, and their motivation to perform in similarly limited (Aronfreed, 1969; Rosenthal & Zimmerman, 1972b; Zimmerman & Lanaro, 1974; Zimmerman & Rosenthal, 1974a). Even when monitoring time is comparable, older children are more discerning. Second-graders scrutinized crucial modeling cues more often, and thus remembered better than preschoolers. Although both age groups spent comparable time watching items, older children were observed to monitor more adeptly (Yussen,1974).

Short-term memory provides another instance of age-linked competence (Sabo & Hagan, 1973). Finkel and Smythe (1973) compared children of four different age levels on their ability to recall arrays of geometric forms. Despite the simplicity of the inputs, a kindergarten group showed by far the poorest recall. Third-graders were intermediate, but sixth-graders and college adults displayed almost perfect retention. Similar results, suggesting that poor coding and rehearsal strategies hamper the young child's memory, have been found with various other tasks (Kellas, McCauley, & McFarland, 1975; Kelly, Scholnick, Travers, & Johnson, 1976; Ornstein, Naus, & Liberty, 1975; Varley, Levin, Severson, & Wolff, 1974). Component skills such as these may require extensive practice before they are fully acquired. Hence, they would influence many conceptual performances, yielding age trends that were not based on underlying differences in ability to understand principles or to reason abstractly (Harris & Bassett, 1976; Moynahan, 1973; Odom & Corbin, 1973; Westman & Yussef, 1976). While various limits on terminal competence may be falsely ascribed to symbolic weakness in young children, these limits may actually stem from primitive molecular skills.

AGE AND ABSTRACT COMPREHENSION

Longitudinal evolution of component skills can arouse false pessimism about the younger child's ability to grasp complex abstractions. Important research based on hypothesis theory illustrates this point. These studies involve elaborate hypothesis-formation tasks, spanning multiple stimulus dimensions and often permitting analyses of the learner's reasoning strategy by means of specially constructed probe items. One test followed the premise of earlier work—no memory aids were used—which suggested that young children could not attain a demanding concept. Using the prior "standard" format as his control condition, Eimas (1970) then explored second-graders' comprehension when recall was supported by access to items already completed. One group was only able to examine correct prior instances; other groups had full access to both positive and negative prior examples. When memory was aided, all groups showed learning, with the full access groups far surpassing the other techniques, and reaching almost perfect efficiency in an elegant hypothesis-focusing strategy (Bruner, Goodnow, & Austin, 1956). Thus, children extracted the abstract information when spared memory strains. The "standard" control group had the poorest performance of all groups, and learners who had been deprived of prior error items were hampered relative to full access techniques. These results were then extended downward, to children of lower age levels. With memory aids, first-graders also exhibited almost perfect hypothesis focusing. If helped by mnemonic guides, they systematically applied very abstract concept rules. Thus, the patterning of available cues, and not limits on understanding, had led to failure with the standard format. Eimas concluded that apparent intellectual deficit might instead stem from weakness in component skills that prevented the youngsters from having access to relevant information for cognitive processing. This conclusion, consistent with a social learning approach to developmental changes in conceptual learning based on prerequisite cognitive skills, is in conflict with the uniform structure assumptions of stage theories. Data from related hypothesis tasks confirm that children can apply rather sophisticated problem-solving strategies if memory strains are reduced (Gholson, Phillips, & Levine, 1973). Analogous training gains were observed among adults reared in a non-Western, tribal society (Ciborowski & Cole, 1973).

Likewise, when helped by reward and feedback cues on difficult matrix tasks, youngsters detected pattern changes which had been assumed to entail discriminations far beyond their ken (Gaines, 1973). Indeed, under the proper conditions, children display many abilities which, until recently, had been thought impossible for their age level. These achievements include: (*a*) selective attention by second-graders (Smith *et al.*, 1975; Yussen, 1974); (*b*) observational learning of meaningful verbal labels by babies 30 months of age and younger (Stewart & Hamilton, 1976); (*c*) abstraction of visual prototypes by second-graders (Posnansky & Neumann, 1976); (*d*) semantic regulation of memory in 4-year-olds (Perlmutter & Meyers, 1976); and (*e*) utilization of abstract categories and hierarchical classes by children age 7 and below (Steinberg & Anderson, 1975; Tighe, Tighe, & Schechter, 1975; Westman & Yussef, 1976). Across wide age ranges, children profit from aids for recoding information (Schadler, 1973; Schonebaum, 1973), and construe feedback adaptively to correct their hypotheses (Gholson, Levine, & Phillips, 1972).

A major gap in present knowledge concerns the subskills that are common or unique to mastery of particular concept tasks. For some abstract tasks, IQ scores predict the performance of younger children better than that of older children (Kuhn, 1976a); however, empirical bases are lacking to explain why the strength of the relationship diminishes with age. We badly need an explicit, objective framework by which solution demands on one problem class can be weighted and compared with those on another. Otherwise, appraising underlying abilities remains speculative. What may seem to be individual differences in global cognitive readiness may actually be the manifestation of the relative mastery of molecular skills that assist, but do not signify, comprehension. Thus, children below age 5 are able to imagine themselves in a new position and can reason according to their new perspective. Their spatial errors stem from inept utilization of the changed orientation, not from the inability to conceive the transformations (Harris & Bassett, 1976). While such teachable skills as conservation, categorical grouping, and hypothesis testing covary to some degree, the sources of their measured correlation remain obscure: Mutual as well as distinct skill elements, and their respective roles in learning, need to be analyzed and applied in order to help individual children. Additionally, measured proficiency is not the same as potential achievement. Since the concepts used to study hypothesis formation are often stringent and intricate, it is not surprising that a child's initial skill on the same or related problems may predict how much he will gain from teaching under rather brief laboratory conditions (Gholson & Danziger, 1975; Gholson *et al.*, 1976; Haynes & Kulhavy, 1976). If continued regularly, as in natural educational settings, guidance might well benefit even the more refractory learners. By and large, recent results are optimistic about the knowledge young children can acquire, and call for vigorous attempts to further our understanding.

Modeling programs and other systematic methods can bring substantial conceptual gains not expected by readiness or maturational views of learning ability. Training to screen out irrelevant cues aided concept performance equally for 4- and 7-year-olds (Casey, 1976). Help at discerning connections among stimuli improved free recall by pupils from kindergarten to fifth grade (Tversky & Teiffer, 1976). Given stepwise guidance at monitoring fewer cues at one time, and aided at reviewing their content, 6-year-olds equaled untrained adults in concept learning (Rydberg & Arnberg, 1976). Likewise, vicarious tuition has been shown to aid observers ranging widely in age, from babies who were taught verbal symbols (Nelson *et al.*, 1973; Stewart & Hamilton, 1976), to middle-aged adults, who were taught study skills and new concepts (Kunce, Bruch, & Thelen, 1974; Rosenthal & Kellogg, 1973). Task procedures must remain lucid to prevent the observers from becoming confused (Rosenthal *et al.*, 1974a; Rosenthal & White, 1972a). Given this precaution, demonstrating language and decision rules (Chapters 2 and 3), or elaborate concept strategies (Macri, 1976; Richman & Gholson, in press; Rosenthal & Zimmerman, 1976; Tumblin *et al.*, 1977) can clarify the structure of abstract events. Guided in this fashion, youngsters typically display greater cognitive sophistication than would be expected from assumptions of age-inferred competence. Without earnest teaching efforts, it is wasteful and unjustifiable to assume that a child lacks the ability or "readiness" for symbolic activities. By extrapolating a child's capacity on the basis of age and other normative standards, one ignores the progress attainable when appropriate teaching methods are diligently applied (Bandura, 1977b; Bruner, 1966; Rohwer, 1972).

Sex of Child

When models exemplify sex-typical actions, sex differences plausibly related to cultural role definitions have been observed (e.g., Bandura, 1965; Cook & Smothergill, 1973; Harris & Siebel, 1976). However, in conceptual modeling research, sex differences have been demonstrated relatively infrequently and do not fall into coherent patterns. This is probably because the procedural settings and target deeds mesh with children's expectations about learning from teacherlike adults, and because conceptual tasks are unlikely to be highly sex-typed. Usually, the cognitive exemplars studied have no differential relevance for boys and girls; both sexes are accustomed to similar abstract guidance at school. When sex effects have been observed, they have arisen most often when adults of only one sex conducted all of the experimental procedures. When the experimenter and model were both male, boys outscored girls (Rosenthal & Carroll, 1972). When women occupied all of the teaching roles, girls twice performed better (Kossuth, 1972; Liebert & Swenson, 1971a). Yet, using much the same task, Liebert and Swenson (1971b) found boys to be superior when taught by women. In one case, boys excelled with adults of each sex (Rosenthal *et al.*, 1972a). Most other sex effects were interactions of negligible importance (Rosenthal *et al.*, 1974a; Rosenthal & Zimmerman, 1976; Yussen, 1974; Zimmerman & Rosenthal, 1974a). For example, in one of six studies, sex differences that occurred primarily with regard to a single phase seem best treated as chance events (Rosenthal & White, 1972a). Otherwise, regardless of the sex of experimenters and models, girls and boys of various ages have learned comparably well on tasks involving syntactical constructions (Bandura & Harris, 1966; Brown, 1976; Harris & Hassemer, 1972; Rosenthal & Whitebook, 1970), other verbal classifications (Carroll *et al.*, 1971; Rosenthal & Zimmerman, 1972a), and a range of distinct conceptual requirements (Alford & Rosenthal, 1973; Denney, 1975; Howie, 1975; Roberts, Santagrossi, & Thelen, 1976; Rosenthal *et al.*, 1971, 1972b; Rosenthal & Zimmerman, 1973; Zimmerman & Bell, 1972). If abstract tasks were cast into sex-linked formats, e.g., in terms of what must be learned by mothers or nurses versus generals or pugilists, perhaps the sex variable would assume greater importance. By the same token, when tasks do not imply an obviously correct solution, but involve elective preferences, the sex of the child may become more relevant. Thus, with configural modeling of stylistic approaches to solving problems, it is not rare for boys and girls to differ (e.g., Barnett & Andrews, 1977; Debus, 1970; Denney, Denney, & Ziobrowski, 1973; Zimmerman & Dialessi, 1973).

SYMBOLIC PROCESSES

Like all other stimulus events, modeling displays are only potentially informative for learners. The fate of the external cues will depend on how people scan, interpret, represent, and organize content. This processing will in turn be jointly governed by the semantic and structural features of witnessed events, and by the symbolic operations adopted by the learner. Typically, data that are personally meaningful are easily apprehended. Stimuli arranged to support categorical organization enhance one's ability to cognize and store information. Transfer is easier when tasks follow the same principles than when new dimensions or unordered events must be processed (Campione & Brown, 1973; Cole, 1973; Rosenthal & Zimmerman, 1976). When items are stored within a class, they can be reached faster than when the boundaries of separate categories must be crossed (McCauley & Kellas, 1974; Patterson, Meltzer, & Mandler, 1971; Rosch *et al.*, 1976). Illustrations and contextual cues can help to integrate storage, to overcome interference, and to facilitate retrieval (Anderson & Bower, 1972; Brown, 1976; Nelson & Brooks, 1974). The learners' biases in selecting features of input dictate priorities for information processing (Kraut, 1976; Odom & Corbin, 1973; Rogers & Johnson, 1973; Rollins & Castle, 1973). For example, learners of all ages have more- and less-preferred dimensions for ordering multifaceted events. When personally salient attributes are relevant, problem solving is greatly simplified. However, dimensional biases can impede solutions by reducing concern with other pertinent categories. Expertise in devising, selecting, and executing cognitive strategies also plays a major role in how content is perceived, rendered durable, and utilized (Conroy & Weener, 1976; Cramer, 1972, 1973; Drummond, Williams, & Aiken, 1973; Rubin, 1973; Rydberg & Arnberg, 1976).

Science is just beginning to understand what goes on in the head during thought. The inventiveness and flexibility of human cognition are not easily described by deterministic analyses in which overt stimuli are mechanically linked to external responses. Numerous cultures have been regulated by such purely hypothetical agencies as witchcraft, magic, and sorcery (Evans-Pritchard, 1937; Kluckhohn, 1944; Whiting, 1950). Fantasy solutions may be adopted as communal fact, even though the actual events have never been experienced by anyone. Indeed, a dramatic belief pattern has been found among geographically dispersed, persecuted minorities the world over: namely, that the honored dead will shortly reform and join forces with the living to expel the oppressors (Rosenthal & Siegel, 1959). Although consoling to disenfranchised populations, one must strain to account for such beliefs on the basis of pairing, contiguity, or any prior experience.

Explanatory problems are compounded if one assumes that some master formula must exist. It is unlikely that any precise series of mental maneuvers are carried out in a linear chain. More optional linkage of mechanisms and more circularity of processing steps seem called for (Ambler & Proctor, 1976; Clark & Brownell, 1975; Gruen & Poll, 1973;

Osler & Madden, 1973; Posner, 1973). If several causes can separately or jointly produce the same effects, scientific superegos often twitch. Yet, the same vicissitudes in fact characterize most overt molar acts. Redundant subsystems overlap and combine in a somewhat haphazard fashion, to produce ultimate functional outcomes. As an animal is learning a maze, one counts time or errors until the proper goalbox is entered. One rarely worries about which paw does the most work. Yet, one could record whether the animal runs smoothly, or whether it lurches, hops, or pauses to scratch its rump. All of these various movements govern ambulation. There would be little controversy about a theory which assumes that response integration proceeds through multiple, recursive steps that operate intermittently. William of Occam does not leap from his grave brandishing a razor. However, if our concern is shifted to cognition, we view a different situation. In the name of rigor, we are asked to seek a definite series of conceptual steps, ideally unfolding like the cycles of the internal combustion engine. Very likely, cognition will defy such hoped-for parsimony. Stimuli can trigger a myriad of cue-producing, mediating events. These events can be further selected, elaborated, and organized in various ways, and still produce similar outcomes. Their topographies may differ; their courses wend back and meander. Recursive feedback cycles may intervene, to monitor and guide progress. A relatively palpable example of information processing episodes which differ in form but which are functionally equivalent can be found in geometry, where the same theorem can be validated by a variety of proofs. Elements are deployed in distinctive formats, but reach identical logical goals (Aaronson, 1976; Bower, 1974; Yuille, 1973). Sometimes the position is taken that attempts to map covert operations stand outside legitimate inquiry (e.g., Gewirtz, 1971a,b; Parton, 1974). Evidence already cited and forthcoming demonstrates that abstract mediation governs conceptual performance, which adjusts to the changes affecting intervening symbolization. Social learning theory views cognition as regulated by multiple and often recursive processes (Rosenthal & Bandura, 1978). For convenience, these processes are discussed in schematic, but globally typical, input-to-output sequence.

Attention

In order for vicarious benefits to accrue, information must reach the learner. This is absolutely essential. The observer must perceive and attend to the modeled display. Conditions which obstruct the perception of ongoing events, or divert attention to other matters, will impair learning (Bandura *et al.*, 1966; Clark & Brownell, 1975; Gerst, 1971; Rosenbaum & Schultz, 1967). Subjective distractions can also limit registration of the epitomized information. If observational content is distressing (Faw & Nunnally, 1967, 1968, 1973), seems unrelated to personal needs (Kanfer *et al.*, 1971), or must compete with other distractions (Haddad *et al.*, 1976), monitoring is reduced. Conversely, if scrutiny is directed to pertinent features of the task, discriminative attending improves. When displays permit interpretive clarity, modeling is more effective than when exemplary cues are difficult to organize in meaningful terms (Bandura & Jeffery, 1973; Spiegler & Liebert, 1973; Zimmerman & Bell, 1972). Sometimes, motivational supports will enhance attention to modeled routines (Durrell & Weisberg, 1973; Dusek & Dietrich, 1973; Geshuri, 1975; Yussen & Levy, 1975). However, extrinsic inducements do not necessarily augment scrutiny if demonstrations are already graphic and compelling (Rosenthal & Kellogg, 1973; Thelen, McGuire, Simmonds, & Akamatsu, 1974). In all types of teaching situations, effective information processing requires the learner's attention. Research with children of various age levels has shown that children's attentiveness is positively related to their school achievements (Cobb & Hops, 1973; Samuels & Tenure, 1974). The intimate connection between attention and observational learning was clearly shown in a study by Yussen (1974). He used incentive and instructional sets to vary the degree to which children monitored a model's activities while being tempted by attractive competing events. The sheer duration of scrutiny, as well as the number of times the child watched at key points, were measured. Subsequent recall of the vicarious content was shown to be dependent on prior attention. The relationship between discerning observation and memory was very substantial ($r = .79$), but the time spent in gross scrutiny covaried more weakly with retrieval ($r = .55$). These results confirmed that the retention of modeled information is directly linked to the attentiveness of the observers. However, more than perceptual exposure is necessary. The time spent observing was a poorer predictor of knowledge gained than the judicious sampling of crucial moments.

Even when cues are presented by tachistoscope for only microseconds, meaningfulness steers attention and dictates eventual symbolic priorities. Judgments of whether an arrow was pointed up or down were faster when "up" arrows were high and when "down" arrows were low within their surround; the spatial thrust of the "up" direction was more readily detected if it was congruent with the semantic thrust of higher elevation (Clark & Brownell, 1975). Likewise, the patterning of cues alters processing. Attention to focal content can be disrupted if the structure of extraneous signals competes with the learner's efforts to monitor and organize key elements (Bell & Handel, 1976; Bregman & Rudnicky, 1975). When observers can regulate perception through inferential guidelines, both the speed and the adequacy of cognition improve (Kobasigawa & Orr, 1973; Liebert & Swenson, 1971a,b). Attentive scrutiny to all steps in modeled episodes is less efficient than emphasis on critical events, even though the capacity to scan is surprisingly stable as the number of perceptible elements increases: Watching while meaningless spatial patterns unfolded was less of an aid than comparable access to the terminal configurations (Rosenthal *et al.*, 1974b; Shiffrin, McKay, & Shaffer, 1976). These would not be the expected results if sheer visual contiguity, rather than interpretive constructions, determined vicarious learning. Serial scanning on a sensory level does not appear to account for the speed and efficiency of conceptual modeling. Instead, people perceive input selectively in terms that have personal meaning, even during the earliest moments of cue perception (Avant & Lyman, 1975; Berry & Baumeister, 1973; Sabo & Hagan, 1973). Decision-making processes guide the extraction of cues for storage and utilization. Although they may notice specific details, learners most often judge relevance in view of the categorical features that usually organize experience. If a set of messages maintains semantic continuity, but varies in discrete aspects, the general meanings attract greater attention (Banks *et al.*, 1975; Carson & Abrahamson, 1976; Paris & Carter, 1973). When informative passages were repeated with the details varied but the core meaning kept constant, free recall was improved. Learners discriminated and stored the gist of the content, although the changing details interfered with their memory for fine-grained specifics (Bower, 1974). Similar results are obtained for visual patterns (Rosch *et al.*, 1976) and memory for sentences, which improves when common concepts and gist continue across successive instances (White & Gagne, 1976). Even for toddlers, semantic relationships integrate serial tasks (Suppes, 1974). Despite molecular variations in form, the substance of discourse dominates and regulates cognition (Anderson, 1971, 1974; Barclay & Reid, 1974). Conceptual meaning, rather than frequency of word use, governs children's acquisition of polar adjectives (Klatsky, Clark, & Macken, 1973). In numerous studies on paired associate learning, storage and retrieval improve when items are perceived as linked by comprehensible relationships (e.g., Begg & Anderson, 1976; Danner & Taylor, 1973; Kerst & Levin, 1973; Yuille & Catchpole, 1973).

Similarly, interpretive perception takes place during abstract modeling. Inferential, rather than rote, monitoring is suggested by studies in which concepts and structural categories have been spontaneously transferred to new stimuli (e.g., Alford & Rosenthal, 1973; Rosenthal & Zimmerman, 1973, 1976). Although they are perfectly capable of discerning the many novel features of generalization tasks, observers typically ignore those molecular changes. Instead, people attend to the abstract constancies; this monitoring permits meaningful extrapolations from principles already cognized. Examples provide cues to guide inferential standards, not rote mimicry, such as when demonstrations serve to refine qualitative constructions like titles for plots (Stratton & Brown, 1972). Performance models can improve the quality and quantity of the abstract hypotheses formulated by adults who are free to choose and fashion the microstructure of their answers (Fredericksen & Evans, 1974). Indeed, children directed to emulate a model may be no more faithful to concept categories than uninstructed observers who adopted concepts spontaneously. Requests to duplicate modeled response styles usually prompted observers to copy peripheral details, while these requests did not generate more adherence to abstract criteria (Rosenthal & Whitebook, 1970; Rosenthal *et al.*, 1970). Observers predominantly attend to classifications, demonstrating a rather low frequency of matching discrete, literal features (Carroll *et al.*, 1972; Robert *et al.*, 1975; Zimmerman & Dialessi, 1973). Exhortations to emulate a model rarely clarify, or draw attention to, the conceptual principles that govern the solution.

In contrast, instructions can be designed to help support careful monitoring and task involvement. When directions focus learners' active attention and provoke their attempts to fathom the regularities in modeled classifications, performance is improved (Bandura & Harris, 1966; Rosenthal & Carroll, 1972; Rosenthal & Zimmerman, 1972a). Instructions can alert the observer to structural features of the input, as can labeling to enhance selective perception (Abravanel, Levan-Goldschmidt, & Stevenson, 1976; Ellis *et al.*, 1974; McCauley & Kellas, 1974). Likewise, various meaningful guides can highlight and elaborate the relationships among task items (Conroy & Weener, 1976; Koenigsberg, 1973; Nelson & Earl, 1973; Rand, 1973). When attention is drawn to categorical dimensions or to connections among stimuli, learning improves, and becomes superior to what is observed in rotelike formats (Frederiksen & Rohwer, 1971; Liberty & Ornstein, 1973; Moynahan, 1973; Schvaneveldt *et al.*, 1976).

AFFECTIVE CUES IN SCANNING AND ENACTING

Affective factors probably play their greatest roles in observational learning by luring attention toward or away from modeled events, and by influencing the willingness to execute what has been acquired. Although certain characteristics of the model will captivate attention, others will repel scrutiny or will engage it only listlessly (Bandura, 1977b). Models who are charming, warm, or trustworthy (Fugita, 1974; Yussen & Levy, 1975), who are comparable to the observer in relevant respects (Kazdin, 1976), and who point the way to valued goals (Bandura *et al.*, 1963; Geshuri, 1975) will normally be watched and emulated more closely. Attention and receptivity to stimulus persons will depend on whether models are perceived as modish or unkempt (Rosenthal & White, 1972b); reliable or hypocritical (Midlarsky, Bryan, & Brickman, 1973), fastidious or indiscriminate (Walster, Walster, Piliavin, & Schmid, 1973), and beautiful or homely (Landy & Sigall, 1974). Pronounced discrepancy from one's own position has arousal properties that alert observers (Festinger, 1950; Sherif & Hovland, 1961). While perceived deviance can make a model highly salient, whether or not the model is accepted and emulated depends on still other variables, especially the meaning and valence of the behavior epitomized. Vividly deviant portrayals may rouse attention to subsequent information even when models are viewed with repugnance and their standards are strongly repudiated (Coyne, 1976; Rosenthal, Rogers, & Durning, 1972). Conversely, deviance may strike a sympathetic chord, depending on the values and needs of the observers. In a technological society, social concerns and newsworthiness bring audiences into contact with remote but compelling events. Media and word-of-mouth communication can instigate emulation of rioters, hijackers, and violent criminals (Bandura, 1973, 1977b), or more sanguine deviants like streakers and geneology buffs. Since affectively arousing displays often compel attention, they enjoy privileged status as *potential* cues for vicarious learning. However, alertness to exciting but noxious portrayals may elicit grief, censure, or disgust, emotions which could inhibit storage and utilization. In most cases, the impact and valence of demonstrations will depend on the particular viewpoint adopted by the observers (Kanfer *et al.*, 1974). When prepared to empathize with a model, observers interpret the same events very differently than when personally detached from the modeled scenario (Aderman, Brehm, & Katz, 1974). Thus, arousal of the observers' affect ensures neither learning nor zeal to perform. Few visitors to Skid Row undergo drastic bohemian transformations. Spectators may independently recall a model's conduct regardless of whether they approve of or adopt it (Spiegler & Liebert, 1973). In most conceptual modeling studies, abstract learning occurs largely without any identifiable emotionality. Strong or redundant motivators can actually hamper proficiency and decrease intrinsic satisfactions (Ross, 1976). The potency of inducements will vary according to the observers' cognitive plans and preparations (Moore, Mischel, & Zeiss, 1976; Patterson & Mischel, 1976). When children labeled a problem-solving task as easy, they performed it longer when the affective context was neutral or negative in tone. But when the task was judged as difficult, a positive tone led to greater persistence. A different pattern of self-regulation results was found with a motor task (Masters & Santrock, 1976).

The role of affective cues is highly dependent on the cognitive and situational variables as construed by observers. Feedback in the form of material rewards can impair performance (Haddad *et al.*, 1976). The personal meaning of rewards, and one's standards for accepting them, can be altered by appropriate modeling (Bandura, 1974; Lepper *et al.*, 1975). Especially when tasks are repetitive, rotelike, or require actions that violate social norms, there is evidence that arousal through rewards may aid terminal performance, although it is not a necessary condition for vicarious learning (Bandura, 1965; Benowitz & Busse, 1976; Thelen *et al.*, 1974). Further, the relevance of modeling displays to one's own prospects dictates the extent to which positive incentives will or will not bolster attention and learning (Yussen, 1974). Perceiving events as painful can elicit emotional reactions in observers (Berger, 1962). Sometimes, the intensity of vicarious arousal is as strong as or stronger than what is actually experienced in overt duress (Rosenthal, Rosenthal, & Chang, 1977). Yet, often the result of strong arousal is avoidance. Observers may spontaneously devise cognitive strategies that will actively divert attention from the arousing events (Bandura & Rosenthal, 1966). In contrast to the predictions of affective-feedback explanations of modeling (Aronfreed, 1969), attentive observation and purely representational rehearsal of conceptual patterns can introduce responses whose form is totally novel (e.g., Alford & Rosenthal, 1973). Indeed, vicarious exposures can change observers' thresholds for tolerating noxious arousal itself, with the inferred magnitude of distress exhibited being more influential than the presumed intensity of pain the model receives (Craig & Neidermayer, 1974; Hygge, 1976).

There is another sense in which affective components may well influence abstract accomplishments. Incentive contingencies convey much information about the desires and foibles of the social environment. Ambiguity is often aversive or stressful and can increase one's susceptibility to modeling cues. The reduction of uncertainty has rewarding properties (Feldstein, 1973; Geshuri, 1975; Jones, Bentler,& Petri, 1966). Valences enter into the meanings of events, and meaningfulness itself may have positive affective qualities (Bell & Handel, 1976; Rychlak, Duc

Tuan, & Schneider, 1974). The evidence already considered demonstrates that semantic and structural lucidity greatly aid selective perception and learning. In this vein, there is no wish to deny that attending to and discriminating significant content or well-structured displays may have positive valence for the observer. Those meaningful features are, in large part, responsible for the efficiency of modeling as a teaching method. There is probably no way, and surely no need, to undermine the contributions to vicarious guidance made by such personal "Aha" reactions (Rosenthal *et al.*, 1975). Nevertheless, even when stimuli are purposely degraded and cast into arbitrary, random patterns, surprising observational learning has been demonstrated (Rosenthal *et al.*, 1974b; Shiffrin *et al.*, 1976).

Coding and Storage

To be useful, observational data must be cognized and stored in a durable form. Covert representations and mnemonics provide the records and index keys that allow witnessed events to guide subsequent conduct. Content may be retained as the retrievable images of sense impressions. Auditory cues (Abravanel *et al.*, 1976; Doyle, 1973), and even tactile data (Hunt & Fitzgerald, 1973; Rydberg & Arnberg, 1976) can guide symbolic operations. Visual memories preserve many features of past experiences (Paivio, 1971). Iconic (i.e., pictorial) imagery may be particularly effective when people need only recognize previous material without demands to retrieve or reproduce it on their own (Rychlak, 1975; Von Wright, 1973). Together, both the structure and meaningfulness of stimuli affect visual recognition. But categorical content frameworks may be less important for recognition than for other memory feats such as free recall (Perlmutter & Meyers, 1976; Schvaneveldt *et al.*, 1976; Tversky & Teiffer, 1976). If the data to be identified are physically present, there is less dependence on storage mechanisms that file knowledge into organized groupings. When the task instead is to retain and deliver previous content in the absence of external retrieval cues, images provide informative links among verbal and motor stimuli, as well as pictorial items. The value of imaginal coding depends on specific features of the task, such as the background context, the complexity, and the concreteness of the stimuli (Brown, 1976; Lefton & Fisher, 1976; Randhawa, 1973). For example, visual processing of pictorial items, such as landscape scenes, is sometimes better than verbal symbolization; in other contexts, verbal and iconic images may affect cognition equally (Chow & Murdock, 1976; Entwisle & Huggins, 1973; Rohwer & Matz, 1975).

However, with complex modeled ensembles in which similar elements are recombined into diverse configurations, it becomes harder to maintain distinct pictorial images. Iconic coding is more suitable for brief memory spans. Learners who visualized novel modeled patterns in detail produced highly accurate immediate reproductions; however, after only a brief delay, they had forgotten almost all of what had been learned. Forming more vivid images did improve later recall (Gerst, 1971). When action sequences are easily grasped, and contain familiar, interpretable steps, imaginal representations of modeling sequences can have strong facilitating effects (Kazdin, 1976). Repetitive events permit stable pictorial mediation more readily than transitory, isolated exposures, particularly if subtle variations of cues have different implications. For example, while the letters *b, d, p,* and *g,* support images readily discriminable for users of English, these same letters would challenge speakers accustomed to Chinese or Persian characters. Under naturalistic conditions, both recurrent exposures to visual referents, and the periodic rehearsal of covert images can refresh iconic mediators. Thus, imaginal connections may be as useful as actual exposures for relating familiar events (Cautela, Flannery, & Hanley, 1974; Clarkson *et al.*, 1973; Rosenthal & Reese, 1976; Yuille & Catchpole, 1973). It is an oversimplification to envision images as enduring fixedly, as if preserved in amber. In fact, imagery may undergo myriad evolutionary transformations before it is utilized, and peoples' styles of coding may shift drastically as task requirements alter, even if the same external stimuli are presented (Aaronson & Scarborough, 1976; Bundesen & Larsen, 1975). In daily life, people are free to combine pictorial with lexical mnemonics. Such a union can make relatively evanescent images much more durable. Verbal representability enhanced the visual storage of complex motor patterns (Gerst, 1971), as did numerical coding aids (Rosenbaum, 1967). Provision of arbitrary but convenient letter props boosted retention, even though the modeled stimuli were impoverished, composed of overlapping elements, and defied semantic regulation (Rosenthal *et al.*, 1974b).

For most abstract information, perceived events are best coded into condensed, mnemonic shorthand by means of various symbolic transformations. The main ideas and features are abstracted and reduced to items of manageable magnitude. Extraneous details are deleted. It is rarely necessary to recall that the model had a wart on his nose or smelled of garlic, no matter how vivid the earlier cues. The selected content is actively mapped by constructing concise mediators that can withstand attrition due to disuse and competing activities. The learner may resort to conventional symbols like verbal labels if these are appropriate and available (Clinton & Boyce, 1975; Furth & Milgram, 1973; Wheeler & Dusek, 1973). Lexical encoding is the most efficient when the categorical or semantic structure of knowledge is easily cast into words (Levin, Davidson, Wolff, & Citron, 1973; Stewart & Hamilton, 1976). But reductive verbalizations also have merit for preserving more elusive displays, if the linguistic coding allows terse, retrievable mnemonic symbol patterns (Bandura & Jeffery, 1973; Bandura *et al.*, 1974).

If shared terms and classifications do not fit the structure of information, people may construct new symbolic codes to retain the core gist of what has been perceived. They may adopt language cues to map essentials in the form of analogies and similes (Gerst, 1971). Or, they may contrive acronyms whose letters signify key steps, details, or principles to be remembered (Bandura *et al.*, 1974). Culturally useful facts are sometimes embedded in rhymes to assist memory. Such verses specify the lengths of months *(30 days hath September . . .)*, lore about weather *(Red sky at night, sailors' delight. Red sky at morning, sailors take warning)*, and rules for spelling *(**I** before **E** except after **C** or when sounded like **A** as in **neighbor** and **weigh**)*. As a coding device, rhymes can function like conceptual categories to integrate knowledge (Nelson & Brooks, 1974). Some representations, such as flow charts, anatomical diagrams, and graphs, exploit spatial structures to clarify and condense information (Price, Martuza, & Grouse, 1973; Rigney & Lutz, 1976). Various illustrations, such as line drawings and conceptual analogies, can link difficult new content with more familiar knowledge (Royer & Cable, 1976). Diverse imagery strategies seek to interrelate content elements with favorable results; guidance to make new information become more personally meaningful by paraphrasing or restructuring can improve encoding and memory (Andre & Sola, 1976; Begg & Anderson, 1976; Pressley, 1976). Categorical prototypes serve the same functions, by subsuming the core meaning of conceptual envelopes and by compressing this meaning into suitable exemplars. When a prototype typifies its surrounding category in structure or gist, learning and covert organization are aided (Rosch *et al.*, 1976). Children classify better when categories contain typical rather than atypical examples (Carson & Abrahamson, 1976). Likewise, when semantic classes are stored in memory, it is easier to search related categories than to search dissimilar ones (McFarland & Kellas, 1975). Even second-graders can form these symbolic prototypes from a set of similar stimuli (Posnansky & Neumann, 1976). Depending on the realm and the pattern of the information, either configural Gestalt, familiarity, or representativeness may dictate which instances will be chosen as models to exemplify the larger category. Rehearsing figural mnemonics or class prototypes, and further reducing them to coded symbols, can economically maintain complexly organized relationships (Jeffery, 1976). These types of cognitive mediating stratagems work to sustain knowledge derived via any sensory channels and methods of guidance.

Research has begun to clarify some of the variables that determine how perceived events are coded. Familiar cues are processed faster and more easily than unfamiliar stimuli (Kraut, 1976). Previous experience with a task setting was shown to increase the recall of modeled actions, because it was easier for observers to discern and encode the pertinent cues and to ignore irrelevancies (Roberts *et al.*, 1976). And, while they may emulate a model's communication style, younger children may still fail to encode key facets of unfamiliar content (Whitehurst, 1976). Likewise, simple structures or episodes are easier to discriminate and code than more complex events (Jeffery, 1976). In part, the form of coding depends on the specific nature and concrete attributes of the information. For example, the cognitive representations of color names may include data used to encode physical color stimuli. These cognitive representations are analogs of color categories: They parallel the internal structures of color groupings and are organized so that they reflect the prototype hues which exemplify and distinguish various color categories (Rosch, 1975). There seems no reason to expect coding processes to differ between vicarious and overt forms of guidance. Whether information is derived from observing human models, from symbolic renditions, or from direct task practice, essentially the same cognitive mediating events should operate (Estes, 1975).

SYMBOLIC SUPPORTS DURING MODELING

Encouraging observers to describe witnessed events in words can enhance storage, as can externally provided verbalizations (Bandura *et al.*, 1966; Rosenthal & Zimmerman, 1972a). However, access to spoken facsimiles does not assure better mediation for several reasons. If spontaneous narration is poorly phrased, if it neglects key content, or if external statements are misinterpreted, then noise, rather than clarity, may be introduced. Giving verbal supplements that seem intuitively superior may help storage less than coding aids seemingly more barren (Alford & Rosenthal, 1973; Rosenthal *et al.*, 1972a). The need to integrate overt descriptions with ongoing thought can distract learners' attention and interfere with their covert symbolization (Coates & Hartup, 1969; Zimmerman & Bell, 1972). This suggests that the time relations between verbal guides and coding intervals may be an important variable. The same statement, when spoken at various times before, during, or after demonstrations, can have different positive or negative effects on processing (Andre & Sola, 1976). Likewise, concurrent activities such as decision making and speaking aloud can intrude upon cognitive processes. Interference has also been observed when motor rehearsal was compared with undisturbed observation (see the section entitled "Maze Learning," p. 220). There is a trade-off, needing further clarification, between the benefits and strains created by specific adjuncts to spontaneous coding. Probably, the more demanding, unfamiliar, and intricate the modeled ensembles, the more likely that systematic mediating codes will prove to be assets. With such difficult task demands, reducing events to concise ciphers has advantages over encoding strategies seeking to rehearse and maintain the entire fabric of witnessed episodes. Verbal summaries that extract focal regularities are more valuable than mental reproductions of observed scenarios. This has been demonstrated both when attempted duplicates were pictorial, and when they were in the form of verbal recountings (Alford & Rosenthal, 1973; Gerst, 1971; Rosenthal *et al.*, 1972a).

A series of modeling studies, in which intricate motor compounds were demonstrated, illustrates the value of reductive coding in preserving complex information. Gerst (1971) asked one group to devise summary labels and phrases that might be based on analogies between the novel input patterns and more familiar events. These observers far surpassed others who strove to retain the patterns as iconic and narrative copies. Since the summary coders recast and stored their knowledge in a succinct, convenient form, they were able to overcome item differences in content representability, unlike the other groups. Response accuracy was dramatically better with patterns for which people could recall their prior codes (52%) than on patterns for which the code was forgotten (7%).

Bandura and Jeffery (1973) showed that symbolic keys need not maintain any literal isomorphism with their referents. One group reduced movement sequences to letter ciphers, another to number compounds, by following organized rules to translate external patterns into covert mnemonics. Both types of systematic coding improved memory, as compared to a *laissez faire* group, who were asked to develop their own mediators on the spot. The virtues of a reductive coding system were the most pronounced after delay. While the impromptu plans of the spontaneous coders were cumbersome and vulnerable to forgetting, the digit and letter codes proved durable. Despite their distinctive and different topographies, letter and number symbols differed little in helping to conserve information. There were striking relationships between the accuracy and availability of codes and immediate and delayed performance. Over 85% of the correct terminal responses corresponded to instances on which learners were able to maintain their coding symbols intact. Observers very rarely reproduced patterns when their codes were lost or faulty. Hence, access to covert mediators closely paralleled the extent of overt retrieval. By measuring the retention of mnemonic keys, as well as target reproductions, their interdependence was graphically confirmed. Bandura *et al.* (1974) next showed that narrative summaries can suffer attrition unless they are condensed into reductive ciphers, while arbitrary symbols, in turn, are vulnerable to loss unless they are embedded in personally meaningful structures. One group was instructed to create sentences to map the crucial features of modeled patterns. Another group of subjects reduced motor sequences to letter keys. A third group, dual coders, instead used a combined strategy: They first condensed the modeled acts into letter ciphers, and then devised meaningful sentence acronyms to preserve the letters in sequential order. Although immediate learning was similar for all coding formats, this comparability was short-lived. After delay, dual coders far surpassed both other groups in remembering patterns. As before, terminal scores depended on code availability. When correct mnemonics were retained, the likelihood of accurate responses was very high. The letters group, however, forgot their ciphers significantly more often than did dual coders, who were aided by lucid acronyms. Thus, people need more than an economical shorthand in order to condense voluminous information. This unsuccessful retrieval is analogous to what happens when a diligent but idiosyncratic secretary retires from her office job. The filing system may be efficient and well-organized, but only if one knows how to plumb its mysteries. But without guides to reconstruct the arbitrary storage rules, retrieval attempts are liable to remain frustrated.

It is of interest that intelligible encoding strategies can aid observers when learners generate their own mnemonic representations (Bandura *et al.*, 1966; Gerst, 1971), when models supply coding schemes (Alford & Rosenthal, 1973; Bandura & Jeffery, 1973; Rosenthal *et al.*, 1972), and when self-produced meanings elaborate on ciphering rules given by others (Bandura *et al.*, 1974). The author of coding keys seems to be less important than the adequacy of the keys for mapping the content to be stored, and for remaining accessible over time. One need not invent mnemonics to make them one's own. As with human language, symbolic conventions can derive from cultural usage, but still serve to represent knowledge personally. Research with primates suggests the same conclusions. Chimpanzees will execute activities long after observing exemplary models. Once taught a useful set of mediating skills, the animal can store and apply them for its own purposes. Thus, after a chimp has learned a vocabulary of signs, it may utilize the signs flexibly to communicate with humans, and may even teach the acquired symbol system to other primates, as a means for conversing with peers (Fouts *et al.*, 1973; Melgren *et al.*, 1973).

Even with laboratory constraints, it is not unusual for observers to adopt spontaneous coding strategies that further simplify or change the task as originally conceived by the researchers (e.g., Bower, 1974; Goldberg, 1974; Hunt & Fitzgerald, 1973; Meltzer *et al.*, 1976). In natural learning situations, people are not confined to brief teaching exposures. We can repeat guidance episodes, ask questions of tutors, and discuss issues or resolve misunderstandings by social communciation. There is opportunity to scrap inefficient symbols in favor of more suitable guides. Sometimes the culture will provide ready-made concise codes (UNESCO; 5 × 2 ANOVA; QP to KB3; X-rated), or other abstract guides, useful as assists in traversing conceptual labyrinths. Sometimes learners will devise their own mnemonics. Further, they can activate and practice storage keys whenever needed, not just at isolated stages. Because of this latitude for self-tuned refinement, mediators can be honed to greater precision. Thus, symbolic codes should be even more powerful and durable guides during routine thinking than when orchestrated by the necessities of experimental design.

Rehearsal and Cognition

The continued practicing of mediating codes and abstract principles is an important means of stabilizing information. Repeated efforts enable learners to refine mnemonics and sharpen categorical distinctions. Extending problem-solving trials helps learners construct more adequate performance rules and hypotheses. Sufficient experience confirms an individual's sense of being able to master task demands and instills confidence about meeting future tests of his skill (Bandura, 1977a). If target activities require delicate motor adaptations, practice will also add finesse to the execution of responses (e.g., Rand, 1973). Rather than serving to imprint mechanical associations, rehearsal is largely a means of coordinating behavior. Sustained experience does not automatically raise the topographic fidelity between internal "templates" and external models (Aronfreed, 1969), nor does it strengthen behavioral matching skills (Gewirtz, 1971a,b). Further practice can either help to codify abstract demonstrations (Whitehurst & Novak, 1973), or add nothing to competence (Kennedy & Miller, 1976). Enforced drill and familiarity before training had little effect on how closely children matched a model's choices of word associates (Rosenthal & White, 1972a). When plans were clear and appropriate, having the child practice executing them to modeled examples offered no rehearsal benefits (Patterson & Mischel, 1975). If conceptual properties are adequately grasped from informative displays, periodic experience may help sustain the saliency and retrievability of the information, without changing the level of original understanding (Meacham, 1975; Nelson & Kosslyn, 1975). Approaches that assume any literal isomorphism between central events and teaching demonstrations run into difficulty when the content of rehearsal is quite distinct from modeled stimuli and terminal deeds. As already noted, practicing cognitive mediators such as acronyms, or mnemonic letter and number tags, can bolster conceptual acts that are very different in form. Also, the observer's patterning of intervening and terminal deeds will often depart from the structure of modeled examples, even when duplication is possible. Cognitive processing involves interpretive decisions about how to maintain abstract guidelines, not facility in matching exemplars. For these reasons, views which treat observational learning as "imitation" do not adequately allow for the elective judgments and reasoning that enter into symbolic processing (Boykin, 1977; Safer & Leventhal, 1977). Research confirms that rehearsal promotes the integration of knowledge. Repeating the categorical structure of information improves retrieval even when lexical details are varied (Bower, 1974; Robinson, 1977; Yuille, 1973). Emphasizing attribute organization has facilitating effects similar to additional practice (Klatsky *et al.*, 1973; Tversky & Teiffer, 1976). Repetition of items led to the evolution of higher-order categorical clusters, much like those constructed when observers grouped words by means of images or linguistic connectors (McCauley & Kellas, 1974; McFarland & Kellas, 1975).

Reviews can help to refine functional classifications. When tasks involve relatively novel dimensional groupings, learners make more frequent errors in maintaining class boundaries (Ornstein *et al.*, 1975). Offering general strategies, or algorithms, for analyzing content is the most helpful when students are properly initiated. Experiences with the use of rules can acquaint the learner with information-regulating techniques, and can assist problem solving (Dodd, Kinsman, Klipp, & Bourne, 1971; White & Lindqust, 1974). Rehearsing organizational sets that are initially of low priority can improve one's ability to utilize subsequent guidance (Rollins & Castle, 1973). Gains from preparatory orientations are similar to the benefits from extended problem-solving exposures. Further experiences engender familiarity with the task and provide feedback. This access to expanded information allows the student to delete errors and to sample new hypotheses and strategies (Gholson & O'Connor, 1975; Mims & Gholson, 1977).

Circumscribed modeling formats can impede abstract progress simply because not enough trials are provided (e.g., McLaughlin & Brinley, 1973). It is unclear how much modeling is optimal for teaching different concepts and for different populations of learners. This topic needs further study if vicarious approaches are to be harnessed for applied pedagogy. Sometimes, rather brief exemplification can be as effective as demonstrations of much longer duration (Zimmerman & Rosenthal, 1972a), but often protracted demonstrations may be crucial. If lessons are too few or too short, insufficient rehearsal may give the false impression that vicarious techniques are inadequate. By sufficiently expanding teaching efforts, modeling episodes can stimulate toddlers' syntax acquisition and infants' vocabularies; however, such important gains will not be evident when guidance is minimal (Nelson *et al.*, 1973; Stewart & Hamilton, 1976).

CONCRETE AND SYMBOLIC REHEARSAL

In a general sense, isomorphic response matching views are weakened by the ability of purely observational experience to teach new concepts. Inferential mediation is demonstrated in these cases, since principles are immediately applied to totally changed instances never seen during teaching (Alford & Rosenthal, 1973; Rosenthal & Zimmerman, 1973, 1976). Theories doubting or denying the importance of abstract representations are also strained when manipulations of mental processes determine results *before* overt performance occurs. Yet, operations aimed to modify inferred mediating acts can cause major changes. This is even shown by simple studies on preparatory set and reaction time. Different processing expectancies can modify an individual's response latencies. When subjects are told to anticipate enacting the response, performance is swifter than when they are told to concentrate on detecting the stimulus (Dashiell, 1949). Purely mental rehearsal can enhance motor feats in a fashion akin to the improvements in motor performance after physical exercise (Mahoney, 1974b). Kindergarteners who mentally planned to perform motor acts both soon or in the future learned as well as those who rehearsed overt movements (Bender & Levin, 1976). Likewise, children who were told to practice mentally by thinking about the stimuli showed improved storage of pictorial content (Sabo & Hagan, 1973). Demonstrating a serial rehearsal strategy proved beneficial, although covert rehearsal was more efficient than overt review (McCauley, Kellas, Dugas, & DeVellis, 1976). Repetitive, rote rehearsal will usually be far less valuable than both meaningful orientations, and integrative mnemonic strategies (Arkes, Schumacher, & Gardner, 1976; Raugh & Atkinson, 1975).

These results are similar to the gains discussed earlier, where reviewing imagery links improved the learning of verbal and pictorial content (e.g., Andre & Sola, 1976). Since information can be extracted from multiple symbolic channels and cues, and can follow alternative routes for processing, it is not surprising that a host of interpretative revisions can help stabilize knowledge. Semantic and structural regularities can be divined by means of socially conveyed exemplars as well as by self-probes (Ross & DiVesta, 1976), just as people can themselves apply organizing skills learned from others (Gruenenfelder & Borkowski, 1975; Kennedy & Miller, 1976). Particular tactics for mental rehearsal seem less important than their common functions: They require the individual to activate conceptual networks, to identify parallels and relationships, to discern and reconcile deviant cases, and to organize continuities into meaningful frameworks and storage codes. Comparisons between practicing terminal acts versus reviewing symbolic keys provide the clearest tests of whether rehearsal helps to synthesize knowledge lucidly or is simply a means of forging conditioned links between stimuli and action. Bandura and Jeffery (1973) studied people who were either taught to apply concise reductive codes or left to improvise their own rehearsal techniques. Different types of immediate review took place. Some people again rehearsed their symbolic ciphers, some overtly practiced the correct target action patterns, and others were prevented from rehearsing. After a time lapse, learners who refreshed their cognitive mediators retained patterns better than those who practiced behavioral matching. In fact, as compared to no review, direct motor rehearsal did rather little to stabilize learning. Boosts from overt practice were mainly confined to individuals whose encoding keys were inefficient. Naturally, reviewing of faulty mediators did not aid eventual performance. Prompt symbolic practice only assisted retrieval if people had adopted an economical coding strategy earlier on. Semantic factors had strong effects. Target arrays that converted to meaningful serial codes were remembered better than patterns which reduced to unfamiliar compounds, and the gains from familiar sequences progressively rose over time. Permitting deferred reviews after the delay interval did not aid utilization. By that point, forgetting had already taken place. Further practice merely expressed, but did not magnify, the individual's knowledge. One storage mechanism was clarified, since prompt repetition helped people to recall their mnemonic keys. Without immediate recitations, more summary mediators were forgotten.

Thus, timely rehearsals do not only enhance final emulation. They also help to sustain the central representations that enable cognition to regulate terminal acts. This conclusion was supported by other research on vicarious learning, using tasks of high and low complexity. Symbolic practice surpassed motor rehearsal for learning and remembering both the hard and easy tasks. Covert reviews helped to stabilize people's grasp of the organizing principles involved in the stimulus configurations (Jeffery, 1976).

Even when all learners are familiarized with the essential components, *cumulative* rehearsal usually is needed to better store, retain, and implement complex symbolic exemplars. This was demonstrated by Bandura *et al.* (1974), who encouraged or prevented symbolic rehearsal for various coding formats. At first, the opportunity for mediating practice did not affect learning. All groups initially reproduced the modeled configurations equally well. After brief delay, multiple code reviews during exposure led to better storage, depending on the serial position of items. Patterns observed early in the series of items were retained better with rehearsal, but practice did not aid retention of later items. However, a week later, aggregate memory was shown to be assisted by the prior reviews. Coding that combined reductive storage keys with lucid aids for retrieving those keys brought the most durable long-term gains. Once again, target patterns that converted to semantically and structurally familiar mnemonics were remembered best. In essence, all of the three preceding studies suggest that mental events are more important than the frequency of S–R pairings: Overt matching practice was less valuable than symbolic reconstructions. Rehearsal benefits also depended on how promptly review followed exemplary modeling, on the complexity of tasks, on the organization of mnemonic systems, and on the familiarity of reductive codes.

Factors in Utilization

After the original scanning and classification steps of processing, sustained experience is usually necessary in order for new information to be optimally represented and understood. If a series of analogous problems is given, the cumulative exposures will aid interpretive refinements and recoding into more suitable mediators. Practical implementation will depend on how well cognitive organization maps knowledge and simplifies information search. Likewise, presenting correct summary rules does not ensure that observers will grasp or symbolize the prototypes adequately. This point may be all too evident for novices who have tried either to follow recipes in advanced cookbooks or to assemble complex prefabricated merchandise from the "simple, step-by-step" directions on the carton. Continued effort and redundant exposures may be needed to comprehend and apply guidelines in personally useful terms. Sometimes, stable concepts can be just as well taught by terse statements of the essential rules as by much longer exemplary modeling (Alford & Rosenthal, 1973; Rosenthal *et al.*, 1972). If principles are harder to interpret, or to integrate with task operations, prolonging rule repetitions brings cumulative benefits (Zimmerman & Rosenthal, 1972a, 1974b).

If allowed to self-pace rehearsal, people can better adjust the span of review to suit their individual needs and tolerances. These conditions are operative in much of formal schooling—during homework assignments, preparing for tests, and with programed instruction. Opportunity to self-regulate periodic reviews should be a major asset for stabilizing knowledge. McCauley and Kellas (1974) showed that placing content practice under students' control can encourage reviewing, which in turn aids later utilization. Some pupils were directed to organize word stimuli by pictorial imagery, others by forming unifying sentence frameworks. A third group instead developed classifications by freely repeating items. The experimental method enabled the temporal flow of information to be monitored. Although all types of encoding led to conceptual chunking, the repetitive coders took far longer to process the information because they performed cumulative reviews: These learners spontaneously rehearsed prior items and established stronger relationships among word clusters. As a result, transitions across categories were simplified and eventual retrieval surpassed that of the other groups. These self-directed integrating activities affect the acquisition and mastery of environmentally prominant conceptual skills. One advantage of modeling as a teaching method is that relatively complete and serially organized ensembles are depicted and conveyed (Bandura, 1977b). Thus, the learner is spared the considerable drudgery that arises when piecemeal segments must be harmonized and sequenced by means of overt attempts and their feedback consequences. This saving allows observers to devote later practice to refining meaningful structures instead of uniting discrete, lower-order components (Kessler *et al.*, 1973; Macri, 1976).

GUIDED LEARNING

External aids to mediation and memory are important in supporting practical retrieval. Dictionaries, almanacs, encyclopedias, and systems for cross-referencing information are classic cultural examples. Performance guides often accompany teaching in natural settings. The same variables that enhance attention, such as emphasis through vivid formats, make it easier for students to discern, and hence to integrate, the main gist of new knowledge (e.g., Chandler, Greenspan, & Barenboim, 1972; White & Rosenthal, 1974). Various illustrations that clarify meaning and require people to vigorously study selected data have similar helpful effects (Brown, 1976; Rigney & Lutz, 1976; Royer & Cable, 1976; Woodson, 1974). Announcing that key facts or concepts are likely to appear on exams is one means of emphasizing prime content for students to self-rehearse later (Duell, 1973). Stating educational objectives aided prose learning, with covert rehearsal proving equal or superior to overt review (Kaplan, 1976). Supplied plans to steer rehearsal are often superior to children's impromptu efforts (Ornstein, Naus, & Stone, 1977; Sheingold & Shapiro, 1976). Organized rehearsal strategies typically assure better sampling and integration of content than unsystematic practice. Thus, in one study, although mere repetition and labeling did not assist cognition, ordered reviews improved children's learning and subsequent rehearsal patterns (Ferguson & Bray, 1976). If questions are interpolated within textbook discussions, the reader may better interpret and organize the content to satisfy the didactic probes. Queries that stimulate covert answer seeking can benefit immediate and delayed retrieval of prose material (Boker, 1974; Sanders, 1973; Swenson & Kulhavy, 1974). This enforced review effected by means of questioning or written reports, is routinely used in classroom teaching. Likewise, note-taking assists the extraction and synthesis of knowledge. Learners who took notes while listening to prose selections remembered more ideas and earned better test scores after delay. Prompt rehearsal further aided retention (DiVesta & Gray, 1972, 1973). Using a lecture format more typical of classroom settings, Fisher and Harris (1973) found that the activities of formulating, as well as reviewing, written memoranda bolstered retrieval. It appeared that taking notes both sharpened organizing processes and provided external memory aids. Having to recode or reconceptualize information enhances understanding. Students who revised the structure of prose by taking notes in a modified order remembered more than peers whose notes paralleled the sequential outline of the material. Paraphrasing content by taking notes most aided the less gifted pupils, who were not as likely to rework new information spontaneously (Shimmerlik & Nolan, 1976). Likewise, summarizing content is a useful retrieval strategy, and can be acquired vicariously. Observing a partner's summary was roughly comparable in value to one's own summary of text material. However, observers were spared the stressful arousal reported by the children who epitomized the content aloud and in public (Ross & DiVesta, 1976). Such results suggest the potential applications of modeling for classroom pedagogy. By selecting skilled pupils who are comfortable when scrutinized, or by conducting videotaped demonstrations under private conditions, instructors could exemplify many conceptual strategies and study skills for student audiences.

A myriad of other techniques to stabilize knowledge are cultivated in applied pedagogy. Teachers conspicuously post maps, tabular charts, and schematic diagrams on the walls of classrooms. They provide impromptu demonstrations and sketches, as well as replicas, scale models, and commercial audio–visual aids. Role-playing through debates or mock trials, field trips, and other group projects seek to embed course material in meaningful naturalistic frameworks. While many of these educational tactics are vivid and plausible, specific devices need to be further validated and compared with respect to their relative utility. Teachers often furnish students with self-guidance aids such as organized content outlines for study. Structured manuals that set forth serial programs for the learner are helpful in regulating progress. Handbooks that specify the appropriate steps for attaining terminal goals steer action and are accessible records for prompting memory. Such codified plans orient learners to organized programs, reducing confusion and variability in making transitions from one step to the next (Martin *et al.*, 1968; Rosenthal & Bandura, 1978). One can expect that the evolving data on self-management techniques will promote novel methods of fortifying concept utilization (Mahoney, 1974b, Mahoney & Thorensen, 1974).

SOCIAL PRIORITIES AND SETTINGS

The social context factors in implementing learning have received limited attention. The approval or censure expected from others can determine people's willingness to express available knowledge (Bandura, 1965; Harter & Zigler, 1974; Rice, 1976). Institutional reinforcement practices and peer usage norms may have important effects on children's scholastic behavior (e.g., Garbarino, 1975; Maratsos, 1973; Rosenthal *et al.*, 1969; Ulrich, Stachnik, & Mabry, 1974). However, far too little research has addressed the social forces governing the mediation and execution of conceptual prototypes. People typically have access to feedback, correction, and advice from others while important competencies are being developed. Research is particularly needed with respect to the teaching of new abstract principles in comparative social contexts. The designs should allow for the monitoring of the social exchanges that surround information integration and cumulative performance until proficiency has stabilized. Thus, under brief laboratory conditions, pairs of college students allowed jointly to discuss and share problem solving strategies had the best performances on tests of concept attainment. Poorer scores, in descending order, were earned by individuals who reasoned aloud to a confederate or to the experimenter, serving as a silent partner, or who did not express their thought processes orally. Showing the poorest grasp were student pairs who, unable to share ideas with one another, merely advanced hypotheses without joint discussion (Durling & Schick, 1976).

These results call for closer scrutiny of social processes in cognitive development. Variables such as group discussion and reciprocal sharing need to be traced using representative content in natural learning environments. There is a great need for explorations of the role of interpersonal transactions in normal problem solving. Especially with children, the ecology of symbolic progress has been neglected. How do socialization milieux influence personal interpretations and mastery of abstract mediators? For example, spontaneous note-taking, content reviews, and self-questioning attempts may depend on how well various study aids or cognitive plans are exemplified by classmates and teachers. Although they may favor certain modes of solution, group sanctions and social comparison processes may discourage other, equally useful, conceptualizations. Thus, the structure of communal arrangements was shown to determine children's attitudes about social science lessons and collaborative learning; how students perceived behavior modeled by peers depended upon the form of classroom organization (Wheeler & Ryan, 1973). Topics of these sorts deserve intensified study.

Target Modeling

In most social exchanges, meanings are conveyed by cues deriving from multiple sources. Vicarious learning requires neither a human model, nor the exemplification of entire sequential episodes. People learn from charts, diagrams, and other target replicas. Observers are guided by more than the activities they watch or which are described to them. Inferential processes allow learners to extrapolate from the environmental consequences which are left as clues by completed deeds. Reasoning can also proceed in reverse, moving backward from the final stages of perceived events whose origins were not observed. The sight of another vehicle stopped beside a police car along the highway typically sponsors cautious reactions. Drivers reduce their own speed without knowing how or why the motorist was apprehended. They rarely construe the scene as a chance family encounter between the patrolman and his traveling in-laws. Motorists instead infer some prior violation and slow down to avoid a similar fate. The briefly glimpsed roadside spectacle supplies partial data, which passers-by enlarge and reconstruct in guiding their own conduct.

Life would be vastly more hazardous if conclusions were only drawn after events unfolded in their historical sequence. The hornet would always have had to sting before one dodged. Fortunately, categorical scanning and storage permit valid deductions from fragmentary exposures. Indeed, vicarious processes would be trivial guides if they required point-to-point correspondence between cues and behavior. The gist of events will come across despite many variations in the precision and patterning of demonstrations. Often, information conveyed by human models can be transmitted by other channels as well (Alford & Rosenthal, 1973; Dubanoski & Parton, 1971; Parton & Geshuri, 1971; Rosenthal *et al.*, 1974b). Having a person transport stimuli does not assure that movement displays become social occasions (Parton, 1974). However, people in action draw attention, and alert observers to other content features. Neutral events may seem more relevant or meaningful if people participate; the neutral events, as a result, acquire interpersonal significance greater than their literal content. Observers even attribute human characteristics to the motion cadences of geometric forms (Bassili, 1976; Heider & Simmel, 1944). With abstract concepts, students' role expectations are very well-suited for guidance by teacher like models akin to their adult mentors at school. Conceptual modeling research has built upon this parallel by using task formats reminiscent of formal education (Bandura & Harris, 1966; Rosenthal & Carroll, 1972; Rosenthal *et al.*, 1972b; White & Rosenthal, 1974; Zimmerman & Pike, 1972).

In any case, observers monitor and code selectively (Yussen, 1974; Yussen & Levy, 1975). They focus on what is relevant for them, whether or not it is social in nature or historically organized. This was demonstrated in research comparing three degrees of human and background elaboration in fostering retention. Some children heard a story in which a model actively arranged toys in novel ways. Others were told that the model had found the toys already organized in the same patterns. In a third group, while the story described the unusual toy placements, this time no person was mentioned. Children emphasized the key spatial data in all versions of the story. Including a human protagonist, and recounting the movement details of shifting toys, added little to just telling the final locus of objects. All cue conditions reproduced the target placements with almost equal accuracy (Masters & Driscoll, 1971). In other situations, human teachers will improve performance even when terminal demands are clearly understood. Watching models execute target deeds can stimulate interest, focus attention, and invite emulation through social facilitation (Grusec & Skubiski, 1970). As with any other information, the utilization of exemplary modeling will depend on many factors of particular tasks, contexts, structural clarity of guidance episodes, and social characteristics of models (Klein, 1976; Santrock, 1976).

ABSTRACT MEDIATION THROUGH EXEMPLARS

People can induce cognitive principles from the final effects created by others' solutions. If lucid enough, these terminal exemplars can guide concept attainment without any demonstration of the problem-solving process events (Alford & Rosenthal, 1973; Robert *et al.*, 1975). How well particular output specimens will themselves guide conceptual progress depends on the learners' ability to properly interpret both target samples and the rules governing their construction. One determinant of inference from target replicas will be the vantage point of the observer. In many modeling episodes, learners perceive visual stimuli and subsequent feedback in much the same fashion as they would during overt performance. Usually, moderate departures in visual angle and distance from task materials are minor considerations. As long as vicarious cues support accurate covert representations, they convey most of the available data to overt learners, without distracting movement demands. When sensorimotor coordinations are subtle, differences in postural and perceptual orientation become more critical. It would be taxing to learn a jigsaw puzzle viewed in reverse configuration, bottom side up, across a table. By standing before it, with the pieces arrayed in natural topside-up fashion, one can more readily translate visual images into spatial guides used for eventual placement. Thus, observers fared better if a model's stance approximated their own perspective during testing. There was less divergence between the sensory cues first perceived and those available later. People whose initial viewpoint departed from that taken during performance had a harder time (Greenwald & Stuart, 1968).

The more that task success depends on conceptual understanding, the less important the specific positioning of concept instances. When familiar, meaningful objects were stimuli, no effort was made to precisely control spatial placements. Although arranged rather freely, items were placed within boundaries in order to segregate organized units. Despite this visual latitude, children were able to acquire and generalize a novel clustering concept merely from studying target ensembles (Alford & Rosenthal, 1973). Even esoteric cognitive specimens can guide sophisticated observers to self-generate lofty abstractions.

Presenting college students lists of hypotheses reflecting high-quality or prolific answers led to proper inferential constructions. More gifted students were better able to integrate, and hence profit from, the illustrative samples (Frederiksen & Evans, 1974; Klein, Frederiksen, & Evans, 1969).

At times, merely supplying terminal exemplars may be the technique of choice. Results of this kind seem most plausible if customary or simple information must be reproduced or enacted with scant interpretation. The decision-making and organizing demands involved are minimal. In such cases, serial modeling may depict functionally superfluous or distracting elements. Deleting surplus context by target modeling can then bring results as good (Masters & Driscoll, 1971) or better than those obtained with cinematic displays (Rosenthal *et al.*, 1974b; Shiffrin *et al.*, 1976). More often, verisimilitude between witnessed and tested activities will aid observers in grasping abstract relationships (Macri, 1976). If component elements must be integrated, access to demonstrations that clarify the distinctions among stimuli and the links among compound responses will be preferable to merely observing target examples (Bandura & Jeffery, 1973). Exposure to step-by-step demonstrations spares learners the necessity of synthesizing all information from spontaneous inferential reasoning. Even with simple rules, adults benefit from serial modeling when the task demands selecting and organizing multiple components. With many possible options, target modeling may invite learners to consider and test irrelevant cue dimensions while comparing the sample with the item pool; however, serial modeling can reduce information search by contrasting key with extraneous features during the model's choices. In cashing checks, for example, while net value is relevant, denominations of coins and bills are more optional. An observer naïve to this convention might grasp it sooner by watching tellers make change than by examining the particular arrays of money disbursed. Conditions such as these were studied with college students who had to infer and apply the rule that response item values should add to twice the sum of dot stimulus numbers. Serial modeling proved to be by far the more effective technique with both easy and harder item arrays. Live demonstrations socially facilitated solutions much more than knowledge drawn from target exemplars; however, with both modeling variants, array complexity had parallel effects (Robert *et al.*, 1975). Likewise, changing the order of the acquisition and transfer tests, and various coding permutations, all led to parallel results between live and target modeling (Alford & Rosenthal, 1973). These consistent failures to find interactions between enactive and target modeling formats, and other facets of guidance, suggest that both serial and target concept modeling are regulated by similar cognitive processes. However, there are several reasons for distinguishing the serial process from the target products observed. First, target examples can guide reasoning that is falsely ascribed to observing the instrumental actions of people or human surrogates. Respective contributions are best assessed if the guidance value of target prototypes is also known. Second, differences between competing forms of enactive vicarious guidance can be obscured by common target samples. These different teaching methods can be compared more precisely if final ensembles are not left available to continued scrutiny. When, for example, purely narrative modeling is compared to demonstration, it is often found that the latter supplies visual target prototypes that may or may not be made available to the narrative observers. Unless both groups either have access to target facsimiles, or a separate control group is included to assess target modeling contributions, differences between narration and demonstration may be harder to interpret. Third, successful concept attainment from target prototypes themselves has some important theoretical implications.

INFERENCE OR TOPOGRAPHICAL MATCHING?

Certain views of modeling propose that observers acquire a generalized response-matching skill. At times, problems about how informational variables preside over cognition are redefined and lose their identity as a result. Thus, rats' latent place learning, infants' trial vocal cadenzas, and school children's or adults' abstract problem solving may be lumped together because all may involve some common learning factors. These theories go further, erasing distinctions between the modeling of simple movements and symbolic guidelines. All forms of elementary and abstruse vicarious benefits are reduced to "imitation" as an experimenter-imposed category for analysis. The upshot is to deny the value of studying cognitive progress. Observational concept learning and inferential transfer are treated as if no different from the matching or mismatching of rudimentary acts (Parton, 1974). According to this legerdemain, the molar pilgrimage of spawning salmon would be explained merely in terms of the factors affecting the first navigational strokes of newly hatched fry. The efforts that culminate in launching a space probe would be treated in terms of their final button-press, as instances of button-pressing skill.

Related views seem to assume that the functional control of matching repertoires depends on a topographical isomorphism between the observed action sequences and the terminal responses (e.g., Baer *et al.*, 1967; Gewirtz, 1971a,b). An *informational* analysis of modeling processes instead assumes symbolic mediation and inference (Bandura, 1971b, 1977b). There is no reason to confine a cognitive stance to tasks in which observers mainly copy the overt movement acts they have watched. When children rapidly acquire new concepts from studying target exemplars, and correctly transfer the relational principles to novel stimuli, there is little concrete isomorphism between the exemplars and behavior. Formal correspondence is even weaker when purely symbolic guidance teaches concept utilization faster than tangible matching exposures (Alford & Rosenthal, 1973; Rosenthal *et al.*, 1972a). Even when it was easy for adults to duplicate the specifics of modeled solutions, there was little concrete matching (12.7%). Instead, although they inferred and adopted the rules governing the cue events, the adults avoided copying literal details. Mimicry was equally low among learners who saw live serial modeling (allowing greater chance for matching all steps of response execution), and among learners who just observed target exemplars (Robert *et al.*, 1974). Indeed, people may be somewhat reluctant to copy simplistic exemplars (Rosenthal & White, 1972a). Abstract emulation was stronger for novel transfer stimuli than for those viewed by adults during training. It was also stronger with subtle but rare stimuli than with obvious but banal modeled prototypes (Rosenthal & Hertz, 1972). These data fit well with the premise that modeled events are cognitively transformed and processed based on the focal meanings that observers extract. Isomorphic response-matching views are now even harder pressed: Inferential conclusions were drawn from static target ensembles; the mode of vicarious guidance affected retrieval; but similarity in form between observed and terminal behavior did not produce conceptual or copying results that would support an isomorphic basis for integrating knowledge.

The main facts which argue for a cognitive, information exchange approach to abstract social learning have now been set forth. At this point, it may be helpful to review the evidence in summary form:

1. Without direct practice, serial and target modeling can teach new conceptual patterns, never intuited before guidance nor spontaneously constructed by control subjects.
2. Abstractions acquired vicariously are promptly generalized with substantial accuracy to topographically distinct test items, and are retained after delay intervals. This transfer suggests that conceptual principles, and not discrete S–R connections or matching responses, were learned. These durable concept gains resulted without giving observers (or models) any inducements to learn or perform.

3. Direct practice, which is considered the predominant source of new learning by mechanistic conditioning analyses, is often less effective than observational guidance. In fact, rehearsing abstract storage codes is superior to behavioral matching practice.
4. Verbal guides and other symbolic aids to modeling do not simply operate like response-strengthening trials; more frequent recitations may not be the best teaching technique. Instead, abstract supplements either add or detract, depending on their structure, meaning, temporal pacing, and context, in conjunction with other information-processing variables. Interpretations constructed by the learner often dominate the content intended by the teacher.
5. Like other ensembles of information, modeling episodes respond to differences in rule structure during presentation, and to the arrangement of content formats. Guidance that allows observers to organize information in clear form will produce better learning.
6. Modeling benefits reflect cognitive subprocesses. Observational learning depends on selective attention. Conceptual progress is governed by the formation of symbolic categories and by inferential reasoning, rather than by rote matching, "imitation," or copying.
7. Mnemonic mediators, such as symbolic keys or meaningful summaries, assist the storage and retrieval of modeled content as a function of how well the cognitive guide can maintain stable covert representations. There is good correspondence between the durability of symbolic codes and terminal concept utilization. Remembering mediators, in turn, depends on how economical their organization and how lucid their meaning, rather than on how often they are contiguously paired with their referents.

It may also aid the reader to have an organized outline of the experimental references that support these propositions. For each preceding numbered conclusion, some of the research data from which it was drawn are cited in Table 4-3.

In light of this evidence, it seems difficult for nonmediational views of modeling to survive without major revisions. Prospects appear brighter for Aronfreed's (1969) affective coupling, cognitive template theory. It is not clear whether (or why) his position *requires* incentive operations in order for learning to take place, and there is no reason to dispute that reinforcement benefits sometimes accrue. The status of templates is more puzzling. At times they assume the appearance of automatic conditioned linkages. At other times templates do not seem to be necessarily isomorphic with cue or response events, and might

TABLE 4-3
Illustrative Research Supporting the Main Conclusions Favoring a Cognitive Interpretation of Abstract Modeling

1. *Observation can teach novel concepts.*
   Alford & Rosenthal, 1973; Bandura & Jeffery, 1973; Hull, 1920; Kossuth, 1972; Macri, 1976; Rosenthal, Alford & Rasp, 1972; Rosenthal, Feist, & Durning, 1972; Rosenthal & Kellogg, 1973; Rosenthal, Moore, Dorfman, & Nelson, 1971.
2. *Concepts learned vicariously are promptly generalized and are retained over time.*
   Alford & Rosenthal, 1973; Hanson, 1972; Rosenthal & Hertz, 1972; Rosenthal & Zimmerman, 1972b, 1973, 1976; Zimmerman & Bell, 1972; Zimmerman & Rosenthal, 1972a, b, 1974b.
3. *Observational guidance often teaches better than direct practice.*
   Bandura & Jeffery, 1973; Bandura, Jeffery, & Bachicha, 1974; Chalmers & Rosenbaum, 1974; Craig, 1967; Hillix & Marx, 1960; Jeffery, 1976; Kessler, White, Rosenthal, & Phibbs, 1973; Rosenbaum, 1967; Rosenbaum & Hewitt, 1966; Rosenthal & Zimmerman, 1973; Williams & Willoughby, 1971.
4. *Abstract aids to modeling depend on their information value, not on associative pairing.*
   Alford & Rosenthal, 1973; Bandura, Grusec, & Menlove, 1966; Bandura, Jeffery, & Bachicha, 1974; Brown, 1976; Coates & Hartup, 1969; Gerst, 1971; Jeffery, 1976; Rosenbaum, 1967; Rosenthal, Alford, & Rasp, 1972; Rosenthal & White, 1972a; Rosenthal & Zimmerman, 1972a; Ross & Di Vesta, 1976; van Hekken, 1969; Zimmerman & Bell, 1972; Zimmerman & Dialessi, 1973.
5. *Modeled guidance depends on rule structure and content organization.*
   Brown, 1976; Kobasigawa & Orr, 1973; Liebert & Swenson, 1971a, b; Macri, 1976; Spiegler & Liebert, 1973; Rosenthal & Zimmerman, 1973, 1976; Zimmerman & Bell, 1972.
6. *Cognitive subprocesses such as selective attention, categorical grouping, and inferential reasoning determine the gains from modeling.*
   Carroll, Rosenthal, & Brysh, 1972; Robert, White, & Rosenthal, 1975; Richman & Gholson, in press; Rosenthal & Whitebook, 1970; Rosenthal, Zimmerman, & Durning, 1970; Yussen, 1974; Yussen & Levy, 1975.
7. *Memory for modeled events depends on symbolic mediators rather than overt behavioral matching trials.*
   Bandura & Jeffery, 1973; Bandura, Jeffery, & Bachicha, 1974; Gerst, 1971; Jeffery, 1976; Kaplan, 1976; McCauley, Kellas, Dugas, & DeVellis, 1976; Rosenthal & White, 1972a.

rather be compatible with symbolic mediating processes. Greater elaboration would be required to allow really critical comparisons between the template account and the symbolic events proposed by social learning theory.

In contrast, radical operant and reductionist analyses seem weakened by the evidence we have surveyed. Since concern is confined to overt stimuli and responses, these approaches are seriously questioned, because central processes dominate over the external aspects of input and enactment. Possibly, reinforcement theorists could tolerate a viewpoint more like Bourne's (1970), in which hierarchical organization becomes a stimulus property. Greater allowance would then have to be made for discerning and generalizing categorical attributes. One would need to acknowledge and study cue patterning variables that influence matching. Even if judgmental events are ruled out as explanations, their measurable effects must still be explained. When scrutiny of a target ensemble leads observers to generalize the internal structure of the array, discrimination has been highly selective. The standards for maintaining parallel analogies with new items are not given by the physical stimulus cues. Some substitute construct must account for inferential decisions. Rather than just asserting that stimuli control responses, the determinants of category boundaries would need to be addressed. Stimulus-control analyses would have to embrace the functional relationships between the cue and response events that determine symbolic feats without recourse to cognitive mediation. Adopting reasoning of this general type would force rather drastic changes in the traditional epistemology used in conditioning explanations of modeling. Currently, however, some operant scholars seem to favor a broader view of vicarious phenomena (e.g., Epstein, Peterson, Webster, Guanieri, & Libby, 1973; Whitehurst, 1976).

CONCEPTUAL STRATEGIES AND STYLES

The research already reviewed shows that observation can teach or refine a host of conceptual categories. Modeling can also modify the stylistic patterning of abstract deeds. With behavior that begins at very low frequency, exemplary symbolic guidelines can alter the adequacy of encoding and hence, the accuracy of later retrieval. Orienting directions can steer the manner in which learners address and process the data of modeled problems. In effect, this form of social guidance transmits strategies for learners to follow. If complex operations require stepwise activities, it may be best to divide vicarious teaching into progressive stages. This can be accomplished by scenarios that accentuate the optimal sequencing of separate steps. In addition to illustrating the principles to be grasped, this temporal ordering also helps observers to analyze the progressive elements of serial skills (Macri, 1976). Likewise, demonstrating stylistic priorities can alter the structural contours of response enactment. A wide spectrum of texturelike response features and abstract solution strategies can be altered by configural modeling.

Response Pacing

Speeding up or slowing down a model's behavior can bring parallel changes in the rate at which witnesses perform simple responses (Borden, 1973; Borden & White, 1973). This variable, reaction tempo, has also been studied with conceptual tasks. Debus (1970) selected children who were typically impulsive, responding very rapidly to problems without sufficiently pondering them. Different groups watched a peer model who was either consistently reflective, consistently impulsive, or who switched from a hasty to a more deliberate judgment style while working on visual discrimination items. In a final test condition, dual models contrasted prompt and more sluggish judgments for observers. Reward was given when the model pored over the stimuli before answering, and verbal cues further capsuled the response strategies that were demonstrated. While variants of reflective modeling helped girls to slow their immediate decision times, only the consistently reflective peer affected the rapidity of boys' performances. Although the type of scenario did not directly alter error making, learners who adopted a slower decision tempo judged more accurately. After some weeks, the brief training session only continued to influence the girls whose model had changed from rapid to deliberate decision making. Thus, a model's performance altered the tempo, but not the accuracy, of the children's decision making.

However, similar research by Ridberg *et al.* (1971) met with greater success. For impulsive boys, decision times increased after deliberative modeling; these tempo changes endured a week later. Verbal cues, and emphasis on visual scanning, had effects that varied according to the observers' intelligence. While brighter children could profit from limited aids, less gifted students gained most if broad supporting guidance amplified the model's routine. Thus, individual differences in scholastic skill altered the merits of specific teaching formats. Witnessing a contemplative response style also significantly reduced visual errors. In contrast with other results (Denny, 1972b) impulsive modeling decreased the speed of judgments, perhaps because the reflective boys were in conflict, torn between their usual intellectual style which had worked well in the past, and the model's rapid tempo. This group did show poorer judgment accuracy after impulsive modeling. The data indicated that the perceptual accuracy of boys who were initially reflective deteriorated when they were induced to perform more hurriedly. Impulsive boys showed relatively little improvement in their perceptual accuracy even though their responding slowed. However, inaccuracies in perceptual discrimination can stem from the *quality* of the modeled decision-making strategy as well as from its speed of execution. Both criteria are used to define reflective and impulsive styles of performance.

Debus (1976) concluded that the qualitative features of the reflective model's strategy were not very evident in the above studies. To better convey them, the covert dimensions of the process needed to be made more overt so that children could discern and adopt them. Debus incorporated some informative refinements in the modeling display. The model demonstrated an elimination strategy by gesturally comparing each response option to the standard, and by deleting incorrect options with a marking pencil. While he performed, the model explained his reasons for eliminating each incorrect option and for choosing correct alternatives. The child took turns with the model. As the youngster became more proficient in using the decision-making strategy, the model gradually eliminated the adjunctive modeling cues until the child was able to execute the strategy without assistance. This guidance sequence, which resembled participant modeling procedures used in clinical studies, produced stable learning, comprehensive in scope, which was retained over a 4-month delay. Yet, follow-up testing was conducted by an unfamiliar experimenter, using a transfer task substantially different from that given in training.

This evidence again underscores the critical role of component skill elements in achieving molar competence. Performance gains resulted when strategic modeling was aided by a clarification of the covert dimensions governing response, and by active familiarization with response execution. Likewise, giving impulsive children explicit guidance in a strategy for responding slowly reduced response speed, as compared to teaching that omitted this planning. Children who were aided in verbalizing their own strategies gained more than those hearing equivalent directions spoken by a tutor (Bender, 1976). Other research on teaching mediational strategies to children suggests that active involvment can facilitate progress. The best results were obtained when peer demonstrations were combined with informative personal involvement (Borkowski *et al.*, 1976). The preceding research supports a point made earlier. Initially, children appeared refractory to guidance experiences. Their failure to benefit from instruction might have been interpreted as confirming a stable personal trait, e.g., an impulsive or reflective cognitive style. Following trait assumptions, one would be led to abandon further efforts to assist impulsive youngsters, since by definition traits resist change through new experience. Yet, when the demands of the conceptual tasks were analyzed in terms of their subprocess elements, highly effective guidance procedures could be devised and successfully implemented.

Originality

The latitude separating literal stimulus features and response topography is further revealed when sample displays serve as the impetus for creative thinking. The governing concern of this research is to teach learners to choose or create exemplary instances of uncommon or inobvious rules. Hence, the logic of the oddity concept is reversed. Exemplification becomes a means of stimulating atypical reasoning.

Simon, Ditrichs, and Jamison (1965) showed that children increased their novel word associations after a model gave remote associates. Observers also produced rare responses more often than controls on a transfer test of unusual uses for familiar objects. Praising the model and instructions to select unique or customary words did not affect performance. In contrast, the model's stylistic exemplars promoted originality. With more facile audiences, simply presenting target samples has proven to be quite effective (Hudson, 1968). Directions to take the role of a creative person plus approving feedback for novel responses can be more potent than illustrations alone (Levy, 1968). Related to the data on role taking is considerable evidence that modeling techniques help constricted people to adopt more spontaneous, expressive personal styles (Rosenthal, 1976; Rosenthal & Bandura, 1978).

Harris and Evans (1973) gave college students written protocols containing banal or unusual uses for a brick. The obvious (convergent) array involved construction responses, e.g., building a patio. The imaginative (divergent) exemplars included such potential functions as an anchor and a bookend. Despite the brevity of target modeling, the type of exemplar determined the students' choice of convergent or divergent response styles, with appreciable transfer to other stimulus objects. Demonstrations have been used clinically, along with other methods, to influence covert regulators and improve self-control among both adults and children (Mahoney, 1974b; Rosenthal & Bandura, 1978). In one study, protracted cognitive modeling of self-statements that favored expressive spontaneity heightened the creativity of adults. The modeling plus symbolic practice regimen generalized to a myriad of dependent measures. Gains were made in the frequency, variety, and originality of answers given on an unusual uses test (Meichenbaum, 1973).

Using a similar task, Zimmerman and Dialessi (1973) studied children in groups. Modeling tapes varied both the number of "ideas" (fluency) and the number of qualitatively distinct categories (flexibility) presented to observers. A prolific model increased both the quantity and flexibility of uncommon uses on a transfer problem. Paradoxically, modeling very heterogeneous uses reduced the fluency and categorical diversity of response on transfer and stringent generalization tasks. The sex of the child further complicated the unexpected handicaps wrought by highly variable examples. This evidence thus suggests that there are possible information processing limits to the stylistic diversity that youngsters can manage per display. Despite this evidence, namely, that the task was challenging, very little exact imitation (2.1%) was found. Although children could easily have copied the teaching examples (the modeled answers also fitted the transfer problem), in reality, negligible mimicry was demonstrated. These data further confirm that vicarious techniques usually guide discerning inference, as already discussed, and not slavish or literal matching. However, display variations did affect the likelihood of what little copying was displayed. Most duplications were made in situations with a fluent but low flexibility model. When only a few—but categorically distinctive—answers were modeled, there was no mimicry. This suggested another possible basis for the paucity of creative answers with highly variable examples. If children inferred that vastly diverse answers were demanded, they may have set overly high standards for response originality (Bandura, 1976). The result may have been to dampen their confidence about stating answers that were only moderately novel (Hiller, 1974; Parnes & Meadow, 1959).

These configural modeling studies open new paths for research by testing the nuances of behavior which observers can discriminate and apply. Cognitive performance is transformed because stylistic criteria are inferred, and then dictate revised priorities for structuring action (Rosenthal & White, 1972a). Once the guidelines defining systematic features are grasped, observers can thoughtfully select and reorganize known components to construct a broad range of new configurations. While responses match the abstract constraints of categorical examples, detailed response forms remain highly diversified. This was shown earlier, in the discussion of how words are flexibly chosen to follow syntactical patterns (Bandura & Harris, 1966; Brown, 1976; Carroll *et al.*,

1972), and various sentence structures (Rosenthal & Carroll, 1972; Rosenthal & Whitebook, 1970). Whether with alternative styles of inquiry (Rosenthal *et al.*, 1970), or selective perception of images (Klinger, 1967; Rosenthal & Hertz, 1972), subtle class boundaries are maintained; variegated stylistic elements, however, are promptly transferred to entirely new stimuli. The scope of cognitive modeling is especially broad because general strategies for extracting information and attacking families of problems can be taught.

Frameworks for Problem Solving

The prime test of a teaching method is how well it equips learners to handle cognitive demands like those met in everyday experience. Observing the way in which others meet intellectual challenges has guided both children and adults. Consider, for example, a model who exemplified indirect, circuitous solutions to water jar puzzles. Witnessing the cumbersome strategy led adults down the primrose path. When solving test problems on their own, the observers followed the indirect routes, and as a result, took a longer time (Rosenbaum & Arenson, 1967). Like Sarason (1973), Harris and Fisher (1973) studied college students on an anagrams task. One group watched a model arrange letters flexibly, in diverse orderings, to build solution words. Other groups saw peers construct rigid answers in which a constant letter series was repeated. While flexible patterns did lead people to devise more diversified ensembles, rigid modeling also conveyed task guidance: Those learners actually proved to be more inventive than controls deprived of any target illustrations. Observers reinterpreted the exemplars imaginatively, rather than falling into their model's rut. Once again, target samples did not enforce slavish "imitation," but rather, allowed perceptive observers to infer and apply appropriate strategies (see above section entitled "Abstract Mediation through Exemplars"). The specific work samples were interpreted and revised, not matched uncritically.

Denny (1972b) used modeling to change biases in categorizing. An *analytic* conceptual response predicated selection on a visible attribute shared by all class instances. A *relational* choice instead reflected functional connections among category members. To alter conceptual styles, typically "analytic" children watched a relational videotaped model, and typically "relational" children viewed analytic modeling. Both types of grouping demonstrations led to significant adoption of the strategy witnessed, and the altered styles endured at a delayed follow-up. The tempo of modeling did not affect how well either strategy was utilized. These shifts in the organizing principles of categories recall data discussed earlier: Vicarious guidance has changed the grouping criteria used by preschoolers (Zimmerman, 1974) and dimensional priorities on concept identification problems (Ryan & Kobasigawa, 1971).

Modeling effects on information search have been studied with a modified "20 questions" game. The child must ask questions to discover which, among alternative stimuli, is the correct target. Laughlin, Moss, and Miller (1969) had an adult exemplify either an *hypothesis scanning* pattern, in which specific items were tested piecemeal, or a *constraint-seeking* strategy, in which categorical features were systematically extracted to efficiently narrow options. The constraint-seeking model helped children to pose more informative queries and to expend fewer total questions in reaching the solution. Reciprocally, the hypothesis scanning model led to more discrete, long-shot questions than were asked by unguided controls. The results were the same whether the stimuli were pictures or words. The main aspects of this study were replicated and confirmed by Lamal (1971); in addition, after both types of strategic modeling, observers took less time in reaching the solution than did naïve controls. Evidently, even marginal exemplars may clarify task demands (cf. Harris & Fisher, 1973). These results further illustrate how people can derive information vicariously without necessarily matching inept models. This is hardly surprising since, in daily life, one observes myriad contrasting styles epitomized by others. We adopt a cafeteria approach: to abstract helpful tidbits, and to avoid the mistakes we can discern if others act and err. Since the crux of behavior depends not on literal, external aspects of cues, but on how the cues are cognized, various overt display formats can guide acute observers to adopt similar strategies (McConkie, Rayner, & Wilson, 1973; Rosenthal & Bandura, 1978).

Denny (1972a) used the 20-questions task to study strategy modeling effects as a function of age. Although older children profited from constraint-seeking demonstrations without adjunct guidance, 6-year-olds failed to grasp the strategy. These results did not prompt premature conclusions that young children are either incapable of complex observational learning, or unready to handle such tough abstract demands. Instead, reasoning in line with Eimas' (1970) research approach (use of memory aids) was adopted: Would supportive guides aid preschoolers in learning the crucial principles?

Thus, Denny *et al.* (1973) studied three new composite methods with 6-year-olds. In all teaching variations, the experimenter and child took turns at problem solving. Such alternation formats have generally helped to sustain the attention of younger learners (Bandura & Harris,

1966; Rosenthal & Zimmerman, 1972b, Exp. III; Zimmerman & Rosenthal, 1974b). For the basic modeling group, the adult clarified constraint seeking by stating the need to consider all items in the choice array, while pointing at them with his finger, explaining that one must seek common attributes among stimuli, and illustrating how "yes" or "no" feedback from answers can further aid correct inferences about the options. For the modeling-plus-graduation group, the preceding techniques were combined with exposures to small sets of items before shifting to full-sized arrays. For the modeling-plus-elimination group, rather than a graduated format, after questions the adult instead concealed those items which could be logically eliminated by properly interpreting the feedback.

Relative to unguided controls, all modeling groups significantly increased their use of a constraint-seeking strategy. Compared to basic modeling with full-sized arrays, the graduated format was slightly less effective, and aided boys more than girls. Concealing the logically discredited items brought strong gains. The modeling-plus-elimination method proved far superior to both other techniques, especially for girls. Overall, vicarious guidance significantly reduced the number of questions children needed to reach solution. Girls' information-processing efficiency was particularly enhanced by the teaching session. Hence, increased adoption of a constraint-seeking strategy, and the resultant economy during information search, were evidenced by preschoolers, when adjunct guidance assisted demonstrations of the strategy.

Denny (1975) then compared several teaching formats with children 6, 8, and 10 years old. Some observers watched a model only exemplify constraint-seeking questions. Others also observed the model state her guidelines for devising proper questions and for integrating information. In addition to observing modeling and guidelines, another group was given self-rehearsed repetition trials. Neither the least nor the most embellished teaching plan proved to be optimal. The combination of exemplary modeling plus explanatory rationale from the model was the maximally efficient method. It was a particular boon to the youngest children, although there were *no* overall age or sex differences in learning the constraint-seeking style. The failure of sheer repetition to assist cognitive modeling is consistent with other evidence: Generally, when planning principles supplement exemplification, comprehension is enhanced; however, repetitive practice may not add to, and can even detract from, understanding (Rosenthal & Bandura, 1978). Our knowledge is still primitive with respect to the best specific means to support complex information processing with defined tasks. Various forms of clarifying guidance, in addition to those already mentioned, and diverse individual difference variables may or may not aid strategy attainment, depending on the precise context. Thus, cues signifying positive feedback to the model bolstered children's grasp of a constraint-seeking style in both immediate and delayed tests; internal versus external personal orientations also affected the results (Howie, 1975). As yet, systematic rules for choosing the best types and organization of adjunct guides for teaching must await further research on strategic modeling.

However, it is encouraging that vicarious methods are being applied to even rigorous, multidimensional hypothesis-formation problems. These techniques allow careful scrutiny of the solution strategies learners adopt. Typically, such stringent problems are introduced by a phase of pretraining, in order to orient the learners to the ground rules and dimensions of the task. Gholson and his colleagues are exploring observational methods to improve children's problem-solving strategies. A brief modeling film aided preschoolers to varying degrees, depending on their prior skills. It taught the most adept group a subtle conceptual strategy; an intermediate group needed oral rule provision, as well as demonstrations, to grasp the solution principles; the least skillful group, while not attaining strategies from brief modeling, did reduce their errors and futile response stereotypes (Gholson *et al.*, 1977). Likewise, 10 minutes' filmed modeling of alternative strategies was utilized in accordance with the competence of the observers. Although 7-year-olds gained the most from exposure to a moderately complex hypothesis-testing plan, 11-year-olds were best aided by an elegant, sophisticated focusing strategy. Indeed, when given a focusing model, the older group adopted that strategy with a frequency comparable to that spontaneously used by college students (Richman & Gholson, in press). Omitting the customary pretraining, narrative and exemplary teaching were compared with first-graders, using an alternation format whereby model and child took turns. Purely verbal instruction brought no conceptual gains. The same content conveyed by demonstration led to strategic benefits. The sharpest progress was made by a group given exemplary plus narrative modeling, although the information cast in one mode was nominally redundant with that in the other. It was as if alternate versions of the difficult gist enhanced the meaning of their core content. The dual modeling group performed best on multiple concept measures, succeeded on extremely hard (eight-dimensional) transfer problems, and generally increased their use of systematic strategies across successive items (Tumblin *et al.*, 1977). It seems evident that continued lessons, and supplying adjunct guidance to further clarify strategic principles, would yield still better abstract mastery. Since on these very abstruse problems, vicarious methods can help young children to improve the planning and efficiency of their reasoning, optimism about future applications seems in order!

Some Glances Forward

The preceding results on strategy learning highlight important directions for future research. The detailed event structure of modeling episodes must be examined more closely (Rosenthal, 1976). We need to determine which specific arrangements can best utilize social learning in transmitting abstract knowledge. The configurations that make a display more appealing, accessible, and helpful to the learner need investigation. Accordingly, the outcomes were very different when preschoolers did and did not receive guidance in interpreting and planning from constraint-seeking demonstrations. Greater meaningfulness led to better utilization. Likewise, models can do far more than just emit proper abstract examples. They can also emphasize the analytical steps helpful in cognizing information. If organized sequential operations are made prominent, the underlying logic is better communicated (Kessler *et al.*, 1973; Macri, 1976). Further clarifications through symbolic guidance, timely reviews, and informative feedback during or after demonstrations promise major advantages (Bandura & Jeffery, 1973; Bandura *et al.*, 1974; Jeffery, 1976; Zimmerman & Rosenthal, 1974b). The variables governing the optimal structure and pacing of elaborations need greater study. We have now shown that modeling methods are viable by themselves. Yet, in practical terms, surely cognitive modeling will make its greatest educative contributions when observational and traditional learning techniques are adeptly united. We hope to play a role as brokers to such marriages.

Most important for pragmatic teaching and utilization, is to determine which recipes are the *best,* and to less worry whether ingredients are of a vicarious or participatory nature (Rosenthal & Bandura, 1978). Learners might be allowed to take notes during displays, to ask questions of the models, or to direct them to repeat and summarize segments not clearly grasped. Practice on subskills can be given before advancing to more subtle steps. These kinds of unions should enhance understanding, retrieval, and the confidence of the pupils about their subsequent preformance (Bandura, 1977a). Modeling is rarely stressed in courses on pedagogy and lesson planning. The time seems ripe for such efforts. Practical applications offer vast research opportunities. As one conjecture, the same natural curriculum topic might be taught in traditional and modeling formats to different classes, but involving the whole range of potential teaching devices favored by instructors as legitimate adjuncts in all conditions. Comparisons would not be made in terms of the medium for conveying items of knowledge, but rather, would be drawn with respect to alternative classroom organizations. For example, the modeling teacher might confine guidance efforts to one student at a time, while the other pupils observed all pedagogical exchanges during each lesson. The classmates would take turns as the "formal pupil," but the instructor would have free recourse to any device that seemed appropriate for each student's understanding. After peers observed one another's information-processing styles, noncritical class discussions could further emphasize the range of optional reasoning strategies exemplified by various class members. These research comparisons would pit the attention-holding value and relative freedom from direct performance demands, against the virtues of more customary educational practices, even though specific teaching interventions were not further constrained. Likewise, individual students or teams of peers could be charged with preparing demonstrations of how they address problems, plan assigned projects, or organize required papers as if called upon to create an educational television program, with the rest of the class serving as the audience. The social and structural permutations in which cognitive modeling might be applied to natural educational settings are, paradoxically, almost limitless, although virtually unexplored by research to date.

One may object that our present suggestions would invite a mélange of tactics, within which the contributions of modeling would be diffused. The special character of "imitation," as historically debated, would be lost. One main concern of this book has been to show that, while no panacea, modeling can stand on its own merits within the larger family of instructional methods. Another main goal of our writing has been to urge that conceptual modeling be given its rightful place in the psychology of cognition and learning. No disputes ensue when incentive operations or the dimensions of stimulus classification are studied in conjunction with overt trial and error paradigms. By the same logic, modeling is neither a leper nor a vestal virgin. As with any other method for conveying information, social utility, and not arbitrary distinctions, will eventually determine which tinctures of vicarious with other techniques will serve people best in reaching selected educational goals.

References

Aaronson, D. Performance theories for sentence coding: Some qualitative observations. *Journal of Experimental Psychology: Human Perception and Performance,* 1976, *2,* 42–55.

Aaronson, D., & Scarborough, H. S. Performance theories for sentence coding: Some quantitative evidence. *Journal of Experimental Psychology: Human Perception and Performance,* 1976, *2,* 56–70.

Abravanel, E., Levan-Goldschmidt, E., & Stevenson, M. B. Action imitation: The early phase of infancy. *Child Development,* 1976, *47,* 1032–1044.

Adair, J. A study of cultural resistance. Abstract in B. J. Siegel (Ed.), *Acculturation: Critical abstracts, North America.* Stanford, California: Stanford Univ. Press, 1955. Pp. 19–24.

Aderman, D., Brehm, S. S., & Katz, L. B. Empathic observation of an innocent victim: The just world revisited. *Journal of Personality and Social Psychology,* 1974, *29,* 342–347.

Aichhorn, A. *Wayward youth.* New York: Viking, 1935.

Akamatsu, T. J., & Thelen, M. H. A review of the literature on observer characteristics and imitation. *Developmental Psychology,* 1974, *10,* 38–47.

Alford, G. S., & Rosenthal, T. L. Process and products of modeling in observational concept attainment. *Child Development,* 1973, *44,* 714–720.

Allport, F. H. *Social psychology.* Boston: Houghton-Mifflin, 1924.

Allport, G. W. The historical background of modern social psychology. In G. Lindzey (Ed.), *Handbook of social psychology.* Vol. 1 (1st ed.) Cambridge, Massachusetts: Addison-Wesley, 1954. Pp. 3–56.

Ambler, B. A., & Proctor, J. D. The familiarity effect for single-letter pairs. *Journal of Experimental Psychology: Human Perception and Performance,* 1976, *2,* 222–234.

Anderson, J. R., & Bower, G. H. Recognition and retrieval processes in free recall. *Psychological Review,* 1972, *79,* 97–123.

Anderson, R. C. Encoding processes in the storage and retrieval of sentences. *Journal of Experimental Psychology,* 1971, *91,* 338–340.

Anderson, R. C. Concretization and sentence learning. *Journal of Educational Psychology,* 1974, *66,* 216–224.

Andre, T., & Sola, J. Imagery, verbatim, and paraphrased questions and retention of meaningful sentences. *Journal of Educational Psychology,* 1976, *68,* 661–669.

Arbuthnot, J. Modification of moral judgments through role playing. *Developmental Psychology,* 1975, *11,* 319–324.

Aristotle. *The poetics of Aristotle.* (P. H. Epps, translator) Chapel Hill: Univ. of North Carolina Press, 1942.

Aristotle. *Aristotle's the poetics.* (P. Wheelwright, translator) New York: Odyssey Press, 1951.

Arkes, H. R., Schumacher, G. M., & Gardner, E. T. Affects of orienting tasks on the retention of prose material. *Journal of Educational Psychology,* 1976, *68,* 536–545.

Aronfreed, J. The concept of internalization. In D. Goslin (Ed.), *Handbook of socialization theory and research.* Chicago: Rand McNally, 1968. Pp. 263–323.

Aronfreed, J. The problem of imitation. In L. P. Lipsett & H. Reese (Eds.), *Advances in child development and behavior.* Vol. 4. New York: Academic Press, 1969. Pp. 209–319.

Asch, S. E. Forming impressions of personality. *Journal of Abnormal and Social Psychology,* 1946, *41,* 258–290.

Avant, L. L., & Lyman, P. J. Stimulus familiarity modifies perceived duration in precognition visual processing. *Journal of Experimental Psychology: Human Perception and Performance,* 1975, *1,* 205–213.

Baer, D. M., & Guess, D. Receptive training of adjectival inflections in mental retardates. *Journal of Applied Behavior Analysis,* 1971, *4,* 129–139.

Baer, D. M., Peterson, R. F., & Sherman, J. A. The development of imitation by reinforcing behavioral similarity to a model. *Journal of The Experimental Analysis of Behavior,* 1967, *10,* 405–416.

Baer, D. M., & Sherman, J. A. Reinforcement control of generalized imitation in young children, *Journal of Experimental Child Psychology,* 1964, *1,* 37–49.

Bahn, E., & Bahn, M. L. *A history of oral interpretation.* Minneapolis, Minnesota: Burgess, 1970.

Baldwin, A. *Theories of child development.* New York: Wiley, 1967.

Baldwin, J. M. *Mental development in the child and the race.* (3rd rev. ed.) New York: Macmillan, 1906.

Bandura, A. Social learning through imitation. In M. R. Jones (Ed.), *Nebraska Symposium on motivation.* Lincoln: Univ. of Nebraska Press, 1962. Pp. 211–269.

Bandura, A. Influence of a model's reinforcement contingencies on the acquisition of imitative responses. *Journal of Personality and Social psychology,* 1965, *11,* 587–595.

Bandura, A. *Principles of behavior modification.* New York: Holt, 1969. (a)

Bandura, A. Social learning theory of identificatory processes. In D. A. Goslin (Ed.), *Handbook of socialization theory and research.* Chicago: Rand McNally, 1969. Pp. 213–262. (b)

Bandura, A. Social learning of moral judgments. *Journal of Personality and Social Psychology,* 1969, *11,* 275–279. (c)

Bandura, A. (Ed.) *Psychological modeling--conflicting theories.* Chicago: Atherton/Aldine, 1971. (a)

Bandura, A. *Social learning theory.* New York: General Learning Press, 1971. (b)

Bandura, A. *Aggression: A social learning analysis.* Englewood Cliffs, New Jersey: Prentice-Hall, 1973.

Bandura, A. Self-reinforcement processes. In M. J. Mahoney & C. J. Thoresen (Eds.), *Self-control: Power to the person.* Monterey, California: Brooks-Cole, 1974. Pp. 86–110.

Bandura, A. Self-reinforcement: Theoretical and methodological considerations. *Behaviorism,* 1976, *4,* 135–155.

Bandura, A. Self-efficacy: Towards a unifying theory of behavioral change. *Psychological Review,* 1977, *84,* 191–215. (a)

Bandura, A. *Social learning theory.* Englewood Cliffs, New Jersey: Prentice-Hall, 1977. (b)

Bandura, A., The self system in reciprocal determinism. *American Psychologist*, in press.

Bandura, A., & Barab, P. G. Conditions governing nonreinforced imitation. *Developmental Psychology*, 1971, *5*, 244–255.

Bandura, A., Grusec, J. E., & Menlove, F. L. Observational learning as a function of symbolization and inventive set. *Child Development*, 1966, *37*, 499–506.

Bandura, A., & Harris, M. B. Modification of syntactic style. *Journal of Experimental Child Psychology*, 1966 *4*, 341–352.

Bandura, A., & Huston, A. C. Identification as a process of incidental learning. *Journal of Abnormal and Social Psychology*, 1961, *63*, 311–318.

Bandura, A., & Jeffery, R. W. Role of symbolic coding and rehearsal processes in observational learning. *Journal of Personality and Social Psychology*, 1973, *26*, 122–130.

Bandura, A., Jeffery, R. W., & Bachicha, D. L. Analysis of memory codes and cumulative rehearsal in observational learning. *Journal of Research in Personality*, 1974, *7*, 295–305.

Bandura, A., & McDonald, F. J. Influences of social reinforcement and the behavior of models in shaping children's moral judgments. *Journal of Abnormal and Social Psychology*, 1963, *67*, 274–281.

Bandura, A., & Perloff, B. Relative efficacy of self-monitored and externally imposed reinforcement systems. *Journal of Personality and Social Psychology*, 1967, *7*, 111–116.

Bandura, A., & Rosenthal, T. L. Vicarious classical conditioning as a function of arousal level. *Journal of Personality and Social Psychology*, 1966, *3*, 54–62.

Bandura, A., Ross, D., & Ross, S. A. A comparative test of the status envy, social power, and secondary reinforcement theories of identificatory learning. *Journal of Abnormal and Social Psychology*, 1963, *67*, 527–534.

Bandura, A., & Walters, R. *Social learning and personality development*. New York: Holt, 1963.

Banks, W. P., Clark, H. H., & Lucy, P. The locus of the semantic congruity effect in comparative judgments. *Journal of Experimental Psychology: Human Perception and Performance*, 1975, *1*, 35–47.

Barclay, J. R., & Reid, M. Semantic integration in children's recall of discourse. *Developmental Psychology*, 1974, *10*, 277–281.

Barnett, M. A., & Andrews, J. A. Sex differences in children's reward allocation under competitive and cooperative instructional sets. *Developmental Psychology*, 1977, *13*, 85–86.

Barrow, C. L., & Westley, B. H. Exploring the news: An experiment on the relative effectiveness of radio and tv versions of a children's news program. In W. Schramm (Ed.), *The impact of educational television*. Urbana: Univ. of Illinois Press, 1960. Pp. 143–150.

Bartlett, F. C. *Remembering*. New York: Cambridge Univ. Press, 1932.

Bassili, J. N. Temporal and spatial contingencies in the perception of social events. *Journal of Personality and Social Psychology*, 1976, *33*, 680–685.

Battig, W. F. Paired-associate learning. In T. R. Dixon & D. L. Horton (Eds.), *Verbal behavior and general behavior theory*. Englewood Cliffs, New Jersey: Prentice-Hall, 1968. Pp. 149–171.

Battig, W. F. Intratask interference as a source of facilitation in transfer and retention. In R. G. Thompson & J. F. Voss (Eds.),*Topics in learning and performance*. New York: Academic Press, 1972.

Beard, R. M. The order of concept development, studies in two fields II. Conception of conservation of quantity among primary school children. *Educational Review*, 1963, *15*, 228–237.

Bearison, D. J., & Issacs, L. Production deficiency in children's moral judgments. *Developmental Psychology*, 1975, *11*, 732–737.

Begg, I., & Anderson, M. C. Imagery and associative memory in children. *Journal of Experimental Child Psychology*, 1976, *21*, 480–489.

Begg, I., & Paivio, A. Concreteness and imagery in sentence memory. *Journal of Verbal Learning and Verbal Behavior*, 1969, *8*, 821–827.

Beilin, H. Learning and operational convergence in logical thought development. *Journal of Experimental Child Psychology*, 1965, *2*, 317–339.

Beilin, H. The training and acquisition of logical operations. In M. F. Rosskopf, L. P. Steffe, & S. Tabock (Eds.), *Piagetian cognitive development research and mathematics education*. Washington: National Council of Teachers of Mathematics, 1971. Pp. 81–124.

Beilin, H. Constructing cognitive operations linguistically. In H. W. Reese (Ed.), *Advances in child development and behavior*. Vol. 2. New York: Academic Press, 1976. Pp. 68–102.

Beilin, H. Inducing conservation through training. In G. Steiner (Ed.), *Psychology of the 20th century*. Vol. 7. *Piaget and beyond*. Zurich: Kinder, in press.

Bell, H. H., & Handel, S. The role of pattern goodness in the reproduction of backward masked patterns. *Journal of Experimental Psychology: Human Perception and Performance*, 1976, *2*, 139–150.

Bender, B. G., & Levin, J. R. Motor activity, anticipated motor activity and young children's associative learning. *Child Development*, 1976, *47*, 560–562.

Bender, N. N. Self-verbalization versus tutor verbalization in modifying impulsivity. *Journal of Educational Psychology*, 1976, *68*, 347–354.

Benowitz, M. L., & Busse, T. V. Effects of material incentives on classroom learning over a four-week period. *Journal of Educational Psychology*, 1976, *68*, 57–62.

Berg-Cross, L. G. Intentionality, degree of damage, and moral judgments. *Child Development*, 1975, *46*, 970–974.

Berger, S. M. Conditioning through vicarious instigation. *Psychological Review*, 1962, *69*, 450–466.

Berger, S. M. Observer practice and learning during exposure to a model. *Journal of Personality and Social Psychology*, 1966, *3*, 696–701.

Berger, S. M., & Johanson, S. L. Effect of a model's expressed emotions on an observer's resistance to extinction. *Journal of Personality and Social Psychology*, 1968, *10*, 53–58.

Bergin, A. E. The effect of dissonant persuasive communications upon changes in self-referring attitude. *Journal of Personality*, 1962, *30*, 423–438.

Bernard, L. L. *An introduction to sociology*. New York: Crowell, 1942.

Berry, F. M., & Baumeister, A. A. Paired-associate learning by normal children and retardates with relevant compound stimuli. *Journal of Experimental Child Psychology*, 1973, *15*, 63–76.

Bettelheim, B. Individual and mass behavior in extreme situations. *Journal of Abnormal and Social Psychology*, 1943, *38*, 417–452.

Black, A. H. The extinction of avoidance responses under curare. *Journal of Comparative and Physiological Psychology*, 1958, *51*, 519–524.

Black, A. H., Carlson, N. J., & Solomon, R. L. Exploratory studies of the conditioning of autonomic responses in curarized dogs. *Psychological Monographs*, 1962, *76* (29, Whole No. 548).

Blanchard, E. B. The relative contributions of modeling, information influences, and physical contact in the extinction of phobic behavior. *Journal of Abnormal Psychology,* 1970, *76,* 55–61.

Bloom, L. M. *Language development: Form and function in emerging grammars.* Cambridge, Massachusetts: MIT Press, 1970.

Bloom, L., Hood, L., & Lightbown, P. Imitation in language development: If, when, and why. *Cognitive Psychology,* 1974, *6,* 380–420.

Bochner, S., & Insko, C. A. Communicator discrepency, source credibility, and opinion change. *Journal of Personality and Social Psychology,* 1966, *4,* 614–621.

Bok, S. T. The development of reflexes and reflex tracts. *Psychiatrische en Neuroligische Bladen,* 1917, *21,* 281–303.

Boker, J. R. Immediate and delayed retention effects of interspersing questions in written instructional passages. *Journal of Educational Psychology,* 1974, *66,* 96–98.

Borden, B. L. Resistance to extinction as a function of schedules of direct or vicarious reinforcement and amount of acquisition training. Unpublished doctoral dissertation, Tucson, Univ. of Arizona, 1973.

Borden, B. L., & White, G. M. Some effects of observing a model's reinforcement schedule and rate of responding on extinction and response rate. *Journal of Experimental Psychology,* 1973, *97,* 41–45.

Borke, H. Piaget's mountains revisited: Changes in the egocentric landscape. *Developmental Psychology,* 1975, *11,* 240–243.

Borkowski, J. G., Levers, S., & Gruenenfelder, T. M. Transfer of mediational strategies in children: The role of activity and awareness during strategy acquisition. *Child Development,* 1976, *47,* 779–786.

Botvin, G. J., & Murray, F. B. The efficacy of peer modeling and social conflict on the acquisition of conservation. *Child Development,* 1975, *46,* 796–799.

Bourne, L. E., Jr. *Human conceptual behavior.* Boston: Allyn and Bacon, 1966.

Bourne, L. E., Jr. Knowing and using concepts. *Psychological Review,* 1970, *77,* 546–556.

Bourne, L. E., Jr., & Bunderson, C. V. Effects of delay of informative feedback and length of postfeedback interval on concept identification. *Journal of Experimental Psychology,* 1963, *65,* 1–5.

Bourne, L. E., Jr., & Guy, D. E. Learning conceptual rules: I, Some interrule transfer effects. *Journal of Experimental Psychology,* 1968, *77,* 432–439. (a)

Bourne, L. E., Jr., & Guy, D. E. Learning conceptual rules: II, The role of positive and negative instances. *Journal of Experimental Psychology,* 1968, *77,* 488–494. (b)

Bousfield, W. A. The occurrence of clustering in the recall of randomly arranged associates. *Journal of General Psychology,* 1953, *49,* 229–240.

Bower, G. H. Selective facilitation and interference in retention of prose. *Journal of Educational Psychology,* 1974, *66,* 1–8.

Boykin, A. W. Verbally expressed preference and problem-solving proficiency. *Journal of Experimental Psychology: Human Perception and Performance,* 1977, *3,* 165–174.

Bradley, R. H., & Caldwell, B. M. Early home environment and changes in mental test performance in children from 6 to 36 months. *Developmental Psychology,* 1976, *12,* 93–97.

Braine, M. D. S. The ontogeny of English phrase structure: The first phase. *Language,* 1963, *39,* 1–13.

Brainerd, C. J. Training and transfer of transitivity, conservation, and class inclusion of length. *Child Development,* 1974, *45,* 324–334.

Brainerd, C. J. Cognitive development and concept learning: An interpretive review. *Psychological Bulletin,* 1977, *84,* 919–939.

Brainerd, C. J. Learning research and Piagetian theory. In L. S. Siegel & C. J. Brainerd (Eds.), *Alternatives to Piaget—critical essays on the theory*. Hillsdale, New Jersey: Erlbaum, in press.

Bregman, A. S., & Rudnicky, A. I. Auditory segregation: Stream or streams? *Journal of Experimental Psychology: Human Perception and Performance*, 1975, *1–104*, 263–267.

Brickman, P. Adaptation level determinants of satisfaction with equal and unequal outcome distributions in skill and chance situations. *Journal of Personality and Social Psychology*, 1975, *32*, 191–198.

Broadbent, D. E. *Perception and communication*. New York: Pergamon, 1958.

Brown, I., Jr. Role of referent concreteness in the acquisition of passive sentence comprehension through abstract modeling. *Journal of Experimental Child Psychology*, 1976, *22*, 185–199.

Brown, R. The development of why questions in child speech. *Journal of Verbal Learning and Verbal Behavior*, 1968, *7*, 279–290.

Brown, R. *Psycholinguistics*. New York: Free Press, 1970.

Brown, R. W., Cazden, C., & Bellugi, U. The child's grammar from I to III. In J. P. Hill (Ed.), *Minnesota Symposium on Child Psychology*. Vol. 2. Minneapolis: Univ. of Minnesota Press, 1969. Pp. 28–73.

Brown, R., & McNeill, D. The "tip of the tongue" phenomenon. *Journal of Verbal Learning and Verbal Behavior*, 1966, *5*, 325–337.

Bruner, J. S. On perceptual readiness. *Psychological Review*, 1957, *64*, 123–152.

Bruner, J. S. *Toward a theory of instruction*. Cambridge, Massachusetts: Belknap, 1966.

Bruner, J. S., Goodnow, J. J., & Austin, G. A. *A study of thinking*. New York: Wiley, 1956.

Bruner, J. S., Olver, R. R., & Greenfield, P. B. *Studies in cognitive growth*. New York: Wiley, 1966.

Bryan, J. H., Redfield, J., & Mader, S. Words and deeds about altruism and the subsequent reinforcement power of the model. *Child Development*, 1971, *42*, 1501–1508.

Buchanan, J. P., & Thompson, S. K. A quantitative methodology to examine the development of moral judgment. *Child Development*, 1973, *44*, 186–189.

Bühler, C. *Kinderheit und Jugend*. Leipzig: S. Hirzel, 1931.

Bundesen, C., & Larsen, A. Visual transformation of size. *Journal of Experimental Psychology: Human Perception and Performance*, 1975, *1*, 214–220.

Campione, J. C., & Brown, A. L. The role of contextual cues in mediating transfer. *Journal of Experimental Child Psychology*, 1973, *16*, 217–224.

Carr, H. Teaching and learning. *Journal of Genetic Psychology*, 1930, *37*, 189–219.

Carroll, L. *Alice's adventures in wonderland and through the looking glass*. New York: E. P. Dutton, 1964.

Carroll, W. R., Kossuth, G. L., & Rogers, C. A. Observational learning of a verbal discrimination. *Psychological Reports*, 1971, *29*, 1047–1050.

Carroll, W. R., Rosenthal, T. L., & Brysh, C. G. Social transmission of grammatical parameters. *Journal of Educational Psychology*, 1972, *63*, 589–596.

Carson, M. T., & Abrahamson, A. Some members are more equal than others: The effect of semantic typicality on class-inclusion performance. *Child Development*, 1976, *47*, 1186–1190.

Casey, M. B. Blocking of incidental information in young children. *Journal of Experimental Child Psychology*, 1976, *22*, 468–477.

Cautela, J. R., Flannery, R. B., & Hanley, S. Covert modeling: An experimental test. *Behavior Therapy*, 1974, *5*, 494–502.

Chalmers, D. R., & Rosenbaum, M. E. Learning by observing versus learning by doing. *Journal of Educational Psychology*, 1974, *66*, 216–224.

Chandler, M. J., Greenspan, S., & Barenboim, C. Judgments of intentionality in response to videotaped and verbally presented moral dilemmas: The medium is the message. *Child Development*, 1973, *44*, 315–320.

Charbonneau, C., Robert, M., Bourassa, G., & Gladu-Bissonette, S. Observational learning of quantity conservation and Piagetian generalization tasks. *Developmental Psychology*, 1976, *12*, 211–217.

Chatterjee, B. B., & Ericson, C. W. Cognitive factors in heart rate conditioning. *Journal of Experimental Psychology*, 1962, *64*, 272–279.

Cherry, L., & Lewis, M. Mothers and two-year-olds: A study of sex-differentiated aspects of verbal interaction. *Developmental Psychology*, 1976, *12*, 278–282.

Chomsky, N. *Syntactic structures*. The Hague: Mouton, 1957.

Chomsky, N. Formal discussion. In V. Bellugi & R. W. Brown (Eds.), The acquisition of language. *Monographs of the Society for Research in Child Development*, 1964, *29* (1, No. 92), 35–39.

Chomsky, N. *Aspects of the theory of syntax*. Cambridge, Massachusetts: MIT Press, 1965.

Chow, S. L., & Murdock, B. B. Concurrent memory load and the rate of readout from iconic memory. *Journal of Experimental Psychology: Human Perception and Performance*, 1976, *2*, 179–190.

Christie, A. *The secret adversary*. New York: Bantam Books, 1970.

Ciborowski, T., & Cole, M. A developmental and cross-cultural study of the influences of rule structure and problem composition on the learning of conceptual classifications. *Journal of Experimental Child Psychology*, 1973, *15*, 193–215.

Clark, D. L. *Rhetoric in Greco-Roman education*. New York: Columbia Univ. Press, 1957.

Clark, H. B., & Sherman, J. A. Teaching generative use of sentence answers to three forms of questions. *Journal of Applied Behavior Analysis*, 1975, *8*, 321–330.

Clark, H. B., Sherman, J. A., & Kelley, K. Use of modeling and reinforcement to train generative sentence usage. Paper presented at the meeting of the American Psychological Association, Washington, D. C., September, 1971.

Clark, H. H. & Brownell, H. H. Judging up and down. *Journal of Experimental Psychology: Human Perception and Performance*, 1975, *1*, 339–352.

Clarke-Stewart, K. A. Interactions between mothers and their young children: Characteristics and consequences. *Monographs of the Society for Research in Child Development*, 1973, *38*(6–7, Serial No. 153).

Clarkson, T. A., Haggith, P. A., Tierney, M. C., & Kobasigawa, A. Relative effectiveness of imagery instructions and pictorial interaction on children's paired-associate learning. *Child Development*, 1973, *44*, 179–181.

Clay, M. M. Sentence repetition: Elicited imitation of a controlled set of syntactic structures by four language groups. *Monographs of the Society for Research in Child Development*, 1971, *36(3*, Serial No. 143).

Clinton, L., & Boyce, K. D. Rule-governed imitative verbal behavior as a function of modeling procedures. *Journal of Experimental Child Psychology*, 1975, *19*. 115–121.

Coates, B., & Hartup, W. W. Age and verbalization in observational learning. *Developmental Psychology*, 1969, *1*, 556–562.

Cobb, J. A., & Hops, H. Effects of academic survival skill training on low achieving first graders. *Journal of Educational Research*, 1973, *67*, 108–113.

Cofer, C. N. On some factors in the organizational characteristics of free recall. *American Psychologist*, 1965, *20*, 261–272.

Cole, M. A developmental study of factors influencing discrimination transfer. *Journal of Experimental Child Psychology*, 1973, *16*, 126–147.

Conrad, R. Acoustic confusion in immediate memory. *British Journal of Psychology*, 1964, *55*, 75–84.

Conroy, R. L., & Weener, P. The development of visual and auditory selective attention using the central-incidental paradigm. *Journal of Experimental Child Psychology*, 1976, *22*, 400–407.

Cook, H., & Smothergill, D. W. Racial and sex determinants of imitative performance and knowledge in young children. *Journal of Educational Psychology*, 1973, *65*, 211–215.

Cook, S. W., & Harris, R. E. The verbal conditioning of the galvanic skin reflex. *Journal of Experimental Psychology*, 1937, *21*, 202–210.

Costanzo, P., Coie, J. D., Grumet, J. F., & Farnhill, D. A re-examination of the effects of intent and consequence in children's moral judgments. *Child Development*, 1973, *44*, 154–161.

Cowan, P. H., Langer, J., Heavenrich, J., & Nathanson, M. Social learning and Piaget's cognitive theory of moral development. *Journal of Personality and Social Psychology*, 1969, *11*, 261–274.

Coyne, J. C. Depression and the response of others. *Journal of Abnormal Psychology*, 1976, *85*, 186–193.

Craig, K. D. Vicarious reinforcement and non-instrumental punishment in observational learning. *Journal of Personality and Social Psychology*, 1967, *7*, 172–176.

Craig, K. D., Best, H., & Ward, L. M. Social modeling influences on psycho-physical judgments of electrical stimulation. *Journal of Abnormal Psychology*, 1975, *84*, 366–373.

Craig, K. D., & Neidermayer, H. Autonomic correlates of pain thresholds influenced by social modeling. *Journal of Personality and Social Psychology*, 1974, *29*, 246–252.

Cramer, P. A developmental study of errors in memory. *Developmental Psychology*, 1972, *7*, 204–209.

Cramer, P. Evidence for a developmental shift in the basis for memory organization. *Journal of Experimental Child Psychology*, 1973, *16*, 12–22.

Crowley, P. M. Effect of training upon objectivity of moral judgment in grade school children. *Journal of Personality and Social Psychology*, 1968, *8*, 228–232.

Crown, D. P., & Marlowe, D. *The approval motive*. New York: Wiley, 1964.

Danner, F. W., & Taylor, A. M. Integrated pictures and relational imagery training in children's learning. *Journal of Experimental Psychology*, 1973, *16*, 47–54.

Dashiell, J. F. *Fundamentals of general psychology*. (3rd ed.) Cambridge, Massachusetts: Riverside Press, 1949.

Debus, R. L. Effects of brief observation and model behavior on conceptual tempo of impulsive children. *Developmental Psychology*, 1970, *2*, 22–32.

Debus, R. Observation learning of reflective strategies by impulsive children. Presented at the Congrès International de Psychologie, Paris, France, 1976.

Deese, J. *Psycholinguistics*. Boston: Allyn and Bacon, 1971.

Denny, D. R. Modeling and eliciting effects upon conceptual strategies. *Child Development*, 1972, *43*, 105–119. (a)

Denny, D. R. Modeling effects upon conceptual style and cognitive tempo. *Child Development*, 1972, *43*, 105–119. (b)

Denny, D. R. The effects of exemplary and cognitive models and self-rehearsal on children's interrogative strategies. *Journal of Experimental Child Psychology*, 1975, *19*, 476–488.

Denny, D. R., Denny, N. W. & Ziobrowski, M. J. Alterations in the information-processing strategies of young children following observation of adult models. *Developmental Psychology*, 1973, *8*, 202–208.

Denny, N. W., Zeytinoglu, S., & Selzer, S. C. Conservation training in four-year-old children. *Journal of Experimental Child Psychology*, 1977, *24*, 129–146.

Deutsch, M., & Gerard, H. B. A study of normative and informational social influences upon individual judgment. *Journal of Abnormal and Social Psychology*, 1955, *51*, 629–636.

DiVesta, F. J., & Gray, G. S. Listening and note taking. *Journal of Educational Psychology*, 1972, *63*, 8–14.

DiVesta, F. J., & Gray, G. S. Listening and note taking: II. Immediate and delayed recall as functions of variations in thematic continutiy, note taking, and length of listening-review intervals. *Journal of Educational Psychology*, 1973, *64*, 278–287.

Dodd, D. H., Kinsman, R. A., Klipp, R. D., & Bourne, L. E., Jr. Effects of logic pre-training on conceptual rule learning. *Journal of Experimental Psychology*, 1971, *88*, 119–122.

Dorr, D., & Fey, S. Relative power of symbolic adult and peer models in the modification of children's moral choice behavior. *Journal of Personality and Social Psychology*, 1974, *29*, 335–341.

Doyle, A. B. Listening to distraction: A developmental study of selective attention. *Journal of Experimental Child Psychology*, 1973, *15*, 100–115.

Drummond, T. B., Williams, T. M., & Aiken, L. S. Children's use of prototypes in pattern classification. *Child Development*, 1973, *44*, 686–688.

Dubanoski, R. A., & Parton, D. A. The effect of a human model on imitative behavior in children. *Developmental Psychology*, 1971, *4*, 463–468.

Duell, O. K. Effect of type of objective, level of test questions, and the information-processing strategies of young children following observation of adult models. *Developmental Psychology*, 1973, *8*, 202–208.

Duncker, K. On problem solving. *Psychological Monographs*, 1945, *58* (5, Whole No. 270).

Durkin, D. The specificity of children's moral judgments. *Journal of Genetic Psychology*, 1961, *98*, 3–13.

Durling, R., & Schick, C. Concept attainment by pairs and individuals as a function of vocalization. *Journal of Educational Psychology*, 1976, *68*, 83–91.

Durrell, D. E., & Weisberg, P. Imitative play behavior of children: The importance of model distinctiveness and prior imitative training. *Journal of Experimental Child Psychology*, 1973, *16*, 23–31.

Dusek, J. B., & Dietrich, D. M. Informational and motivational components of social reinforcement. *Journal of Experimental Child Psychology*, 1973, *16*, 267–277.

Eimas, P. D. Effects of memory aids on hypothesis behavior and focusing in young children and adults. *Journal of Experimental Child Psychology*, 1970, *10*, 319–336.

Ellis, H. E., Parente, F. J., & Shumate, E. C. Meaningfulness, perceptual grouping, and organization in recognition memory. *Journal of Experimental Psychology*, 1974, *102*, 308–313.

English, H. B., & English, A. C. *A comprehensive dictionary of psychological and psychoanalytical terms*. New York: McKay, 1958.

Entwisle, D. R., & Huggins, W. H. Iconic memory in children. *Child Development*, 1973, *44*, 392–394.

Epstein, L. H., Peterson, G. L., Webster, J., Guanieri, C., & Libby, B. Comparison of stimulus control and reinforcement control effects on imitative behavior. *Journal of Experimental Child Psychology*, 1973, *16*, 98–110.

Ervin, S. M. Imitation and structural changes in children's language. In E. Lenneberg (Ed.), *New directions in the study of language*. Cambridge, Massachusetts: MIT Press, 1964. Pp. 163–189.

Ervin-Tripp, S. M. An overview of theories of grammatical development. In D. I. Slobin (Ed.), *The ontogenesis of grammar.* New York: Academic Press, 1971. Pp. 189–212.

Estes, W. K. The state of the field: General problems and issues of theory and metatheory. In W. K. Estes (Ed.), *Handbook of learning and cognitive processes.* Vol. 1. Hillsdale, New Jersey: Lawrence Erlbaum Associates, 1975. Pp. 1–24.

Evans-Pritchard, E. E. *Witchcraft, magic and oracles among the Azande.* New York: Oxford Univ. Press (Clarendon), 1937.

Farnham-Diggory, S. (Ed.) *Information processing in children.* New York: Academic Press, 1972.

Farnham-Diggory, S., & Gregg, L. W. Color, form, and function as dimensions of natural classification: Developmental changes in eye movements, reaction time and response strategies. *Child Development,* 1975, *46,* 101–114.

Faw, T. T., & Nunnally, J. C. The effects on eye movements of complexity, novelty, and affective tone. *Perception and Psychophysics,* 1967, *2,* 263–267.

Faw, T. T., & Nunnally, J. C. The influence of stimulus complexity, novelty, and affective value on children's visual fixations. *Journal of Experimental Child Psychology,* 1968, *6,* 141–153.

Faw. T. T., & Nunnally, J. C. The influence of affective value on children's patterns of visual selection. *Journal of Experimental Child Psychology,* 1973, *15,* 488–499.

Feist, J. R. Some determinants of resistance to extinction following vicarious reinforcement. Unpublished doctoral dissertation, Univ. of Arizona, 1974.

Feldman, N. S., Klossen, E. C., Parsons, J. E., Rholes, W. S., & Ruble, D. N. Order of information presentation and children's moral judgments. *Child Development,* 1976, *47,* 556–559.

Feldstein, J. H. Effect of uncertainty reduction, material rewards, and variety on children's choice behavior, *Journal of Experimental Child Psychology,* 1973, *15,* 125–136.

Fenichel, O. *The psychoanalytic theory of neurosis.* New York: W. W. Norton, 1945.

Ferguson, R. P., & Bray, N. W. Component processes of an overt rehearsal strategy in young children. *Journal of Experimental Child Psychology,* 1976, *21,* 490–506.

Festinger, L. Informal social communication. *Psychological Review,* 1950, *57,* 271–282.

Feynman, R. *The character of physical law.* Cambridge, Massachusetts: MIT Press, 1965.

Finch, K., Rickard, H. C., & Wilson, W. Personality variables and sexual status in observer performance. *Psychological Reports,* 1970, *26,* 676–678.

Finkel, D. L. A developmental comparison of the processing of two types of visual information. *Journal of Experimental Child Psychology,* 1973, *16,* 250–266.

Finkel, D. L., & Smythe, L. Short-term storage of spatial information. *Developmental Psychology,* 1973, *9,* 424–428.

Fishbein, H. D., Haygood, R. C., & Frieson, D. Relevant and irrelevant saliency in concept learning. *American Journal of Psychology,* 1970, *83,* 544–553.

Fisher, J. L., & Harris, M. B. Effect of note taking and review on recall. *Journal of Educational Psychology,* 1973, *65,* 321–325.

Flanders, J. P. A review of research on imitative behavior. *Psychological Bulletin,* 1968, *69,* 316–337.

Flavell, J. H. *The developmental psychology of Jean Piaget.* Princeton, New Jersey: Von Nostrand-Reinhold, 1963.

Flavell, J. H. Concept development. In P. Mussen (Ed.), *Carmichael's manual of child psychology.* New York: Wiley, 1970. Pp. 983–1059.

Forehand, R., & Yoder, P. Acquisition and transfer of conceptual learning by normals and retardates: The effects of modeling, verbal cues, and reinforcement. *Behavior Research and Therapy,* 1974, *12,* 199–204.

Fouts, R. S., Mellgren, R. L., & Lemmon, W. B. American sign language in the chimpanzee: Chimpanzee-to-chimpanzee communication. Paper presented at the Midwestern Psychological Association convention, Chicago, Illinois, May 1973.

Fowler, H. W., & Fowler, F. G. (Translators) *Works of Lucian of Samasota*. Vol. 2. *The way to write history*. New York: Oxford Univ. Press (Clarendon), 1905.

Frankl, V. E. Group psychotherapeutic experiences in a concentration camp. *Group Psychotherapy*, 1954, *7*, 81–90.

Frankl, V. E. *From death to existentialism*. Boston: Beacon, 1959.

Fraser, C., Bellugi, V., & Brown, R. W. Control of grammar in imitation, comprehension, and production. *Journal of Verbal Learning and Verbal Behavior*, 1963, *2*, 121–135.

Frederiksen, J. D., & Rohwer, W. D. Elaborative prompt effects in children's paired-associate learning: Design and population comparisons. *Journal of Educational Psychology*, 1971, *62*, 1–14.

Frederiksen, N., & Evans, F. R. Effects of models of creative performance on ability to formulate hypotheses. *Journal of Educational Psychology*, 1974, *66*, 67–82.

Freud, A. *The ego and the mechanisms of defense*. New York: International Universities Press, 1946.

Freud, S. The interpretation of dreams (1900). In J. Strachey (Ed.), *The standard edition of the complete psychological works of Sigmund Freud*. Vol. 4. London: Hogarth Press, 1955. (a)

Freud, S. The psychopathology of everyday life (1901). In J. Strachey (Ed.), *The standard edition of the complete psychological works of Sigmund Freud*. Vol. 6. London: Hogarth Press, 1955. (b)

Freud, S. Totem and taboo (1913). In J. Strachey (Ed.), *The standard edition of the complete psychological works of Sigmund Freud*. Vol. 13. London: Hogarth Press, 1955, Pp. 1–162. (c)

Freud, S. Group psychology and the analysis of the ego (1921). In J. Strachey (Ed.), *The standard edition of the complete psychological works of Sigmund Freud*. Vol. 18. London: Hogarth Press, 1955. Pp. 67–143. (d)

Freud, S. A note upon the "mystic writing pad" (1925). In J. Strachey (Ed.), *The standard edition of the complete psychological works of Sigmund Freud*. Vol. 19. London: Hogarth Press, 1955. Pp. 226–232. (e)

Freud, S. Civilization and its discontents (1930. In J. Strachey (Ed.), *The standard edition of the complete psychological works of Sigmund Freud*. Vol. 21. London: Hogarth Press, 1955. Pp. 59–145. (f)

Freud, S. On narcissism: An introduction (1914). In E. Jones (Ed.), *Collected papers of Sigmund Freud*. Vol. 4. New York: Basic Books, 1959. Pp. 30–59. (a)

Freud, S. Mourning and melancholia (1917). In E. Jones (Ed.), *Collected papers of Sigmund Freud*. Vol. 4. New York: Basic Books, 1959. Pp. 152–170. (b)

Freud, S. The economic problem in masochism (1924). In E. Jones (Ed.), *Collected papers of Sigmund Freud*. Vol. 2. New York: Basic Books, 1959. Pp. 255–268. (c)

Friedman, P. Relationship of teacher reinforcement to spontaneous student verbalization within the classroom. *Journal of Educational Psychology*, 1973, *65*, 59–64. (a)

Friedman, P. Student imitation of a teacher's verbal style as a function of natural classroom reinforcement. *Journal of Educational Psychology*, 1973, *64*, 267–273. (b)

Frisch, S. A., & Schumaker, J. B. Training generalized receptive prepositions in retarded children. *Journal of Applied Behavior Analysis*, 1974, *7*, 611–621.

Fugita, S. S. Effects of anxiety and approval on visual interaction. *Journal of Personality and Social Psychology*, 1974, *29*, 586–592.

Fuhrer, M. J., & Baer, P. E. Differential classical conditioning: Verbalization of stimulus contingencies. *Science*, 1965, *150*, 1479–1481.

Furth, H. G. *Piaget and knowledge: Theoretical foundations*. Englewood Cliffs, New Jersey: Prentice-Hall, 1969.

Furth, H. G., & Milgram, N. A. Labeling and grouping effects in the recall of pictures by children. *Child Development*, 1973, *44*, 511–518.

Fygetakis, L., & Gray, B. B. Programmed conditioning of linguistic competence. *Behaviour Research and Therapy*, 1970, *8*, 153–163.

Gagne, R. M. *The conditions of learning*. (2nd ed.). New York: Holt, 1970.

Gaines, R. Matrices and pattern detection by young children. *Developmental Psychology*, 1973, *9*, 143–150.

Galton, F. *Inquiries into human faculty and its development*. New York: Macmillan, 1883.

Garbarino, J. The impact of anticipated reward upon cross-age tutoring. *Journal of Personality and Social Psychology*, 1975, *32*, 421–428.

Garcia, A. B., & Zimmerman, B. J. The effect of examiner ethnicity and language on the performance of bilingual Mexican-American first graders. *Journal of Social Psychology*, 1972, *87*, 3–11.

Garcia, E. The training and generalization of a conversational speech form in nonverbal retardates. *Journal of Applied Behavior Analysis*, 1974, *7*, 137–149.

Garcia, E., Guess, D., & Byrnes, J. Development of syntax in a retarded girl using procedures of imitation, reinforcement and modeling. *Journal of Applied Behavior Analysis*, 1973, *6*, 299–310.

Gavurin, E. I., & Donahue, V. M. Logical sequence and random sequence. *Automated Teaching Bulletin*, 1961, *1*, 3–9.

Geis, M. F., & Hall, D. M. Encoding and incidental memory in children. *Journal of Experimental Child Psychology*, 1976, *22*, 58–66.

Gelfand, D. M. The influence of self-esteem on rate of verbal conditioning and social matching behavior. *Journal of Abnormal and Social Psychology*, 1962, *65*, 259–265.

Gelman, R. Conservation acquisition: A problem of learning to attend to relevant attributes. *Journal of Experimental Child Psychology*, 1969, *7*, 167–187.

Gerst, M. S. Symbolic coding operations in observational learning. *Journal of Personality and Social Psychology*, 1971, *19*, 7–17.

Geshuri, Y. Discriminative observational learning: Effects of observed reward and dependency. *Child Development*, 1975, *46*, 550–554.

Gewirtz, J. L. Mechanisms of social learning: Some roles of stimulation and behavior in early human development. In D. Goslen (Ed.), *The handbook of socialization theory and research*. Chicago: Rand McNally, 1968. Pp. 57–212.

Gewirtz, J. L. Conditional responding as a paradigm for observational, imitative learning and vicarious reinforcement. In H. W. Reese (Ed.), *Advances in child development and behavior*. Vol. 6. New York: Academic Press, 1971. Pp. 273–304. (a)

Gewirtz, J. L. The roles of overt responding and extrinsic reinforcement in "self" and "vicarious-reinforcement" phenomena and in "observational learning" and imitation. In R. Glaser (Ed.), *The nature of reinforcement*. New York: Academic Press, 1971. Pp. 279–309. (b)

Gewirtz, J. L., & Stingle, K. G. Learning of generalized imitation as the basis for identification. *Psychological Review*, 1968, *75*, 374–397.

Gholson, B., & Danzinger, S. Effects of two levels of stimulus complexity upon hypothesis sampling systems among second and sixth grade children. *Journal of Experimental Child Psychology*, 1975, *20*, 105–118.

Gholson, B., & Beilin, H. A developmental model of human learning. In H. W. Reese &

L. P. Lipsett (Eds.), *Advances in child development and behavior,* Vol. 13. New York: Academic Press, in press.

Gholson, B., Levine, M., & Phillips, S. Hypotheses, strategies, and stereotypes in discrimination learning. *Journal of Experimental Child Psychology,* 1972, *13,* 423–446.

Gholson, B., & O'Connor, J. Dimensional control of hypothesis sampling during three-choice discrimination learning. *Child Development,* 1975, *46,* 894–903.

Gholson, B., O'Connor, J., & Stern, I. Hypothesis sampling systems among pre-operational and concrete operational kindergarten children. *Journal of Experimental Child Psychology,* 1976, *21,* 61–76.

Gholson, B., Phillips, S., & Levine, M. Effects of the temporal relationship of feedback and stimulus information upon discrimination learning strategies. *Journal of Experimental Child Psychology,* 1973, *15,* 425–441.

Gholson, B., Theobald, D. E., & Thomas, S. A. Effects of modeling a dimension checking strategy upon the information processing behaviors of pre-operational, transitional, and concrete operational kindergarten children. Unpublished manuscript, Memphis State Univ. 1977.

Goldberg, F. Effects of imagery on learning incidental material in the classroom. *Journal of Educational Psychology,* 1974, *66,* 233–237.

Goldschmid, M., & Bentler, P. M. Dimensions and measurements of conservation. *Child Development,* 1968, *39,* 787–802. (a)

Goldschmid, M., & Bentler, P. M. *Manual: Concept assessment kit, conservation.* San Diego: Educational and Industrial Testing Service, 1968. (b)

Goodnow, J. A test of milieu effects with some of Piaget's tasks. *Psychological Monographs,* 1962, *76*(36, Whole No. 555).

Goodnow, J., & Bethon, G. Piaget's tasks: The effects of schooling and intelligence. *Child Development,* 1966, *37,* 573–582.

Greenfield, P. On culture and conservation, and on culture and equivalence II. In J. S. Bruner, R. R. Olver, & P. M. Greenfield (Eds.), *Studies in cognitive growth.* New York: Wiley, 1966. Pp. 225–256, 270–318.

Greenwald, A. G., & Stuart, M. A. Observational learning: The effects of age, task difficulty and observer's motoric rehearsal. *Journal of Experimental Psychology,* 1968, *76,* 267–272.

Grings, W. W., & Lockhart, R. A. Effects of "anxiety-lessening" instructions and differential set development on the extinction of GSR. *Journal of Experimental Psychology,* 1963, *66,* 292–299.

Gruen, G. J., & Poll, M. Subtraction and the solution of open sentence problems. *Journal of Experimental Child Psychology,* 1973, *16,* 292–302.

Gruenenfelder, T. M., & Borkowski, J. G. Transfer of cumulative-rehearsal strategies in children's short-term memory. *Child Development,* 1975, *46,* 1019–1024.

Grusec, J. E., & Skubiski, S. L. Model nurturance, demand characteristics of the modeling experiment, and altruism. *Journal of Personality and Social Psychology,* 1970, *14,* 352–359.

Guess, D. A functional analysis of receptive language and productive speech: Acquisition of the plural morpheme. *Journal of Applied Behavior Analysis,* 1969, *2,* 55–64.

Guess, D. & Baer, D. M. An analysis of individual differences in generalization between receptive and productive language in retarded children. *Journal of Applied Behavior Analysis,* 1973, *6,* 311–329.

Guess, D., Sailor, W., Rutherford, G., & Baer, D. M. An experimental analysis of linguistic development: The productive use of the plural morpheme. *Journal of Applied Behavior Analysis,* 1968, *1,* 297–306.

Guillaume, P. *Imitation in children*. Chicago: Univ. of Chicago Press, 1971.

Gunzburger, D., Wegner, D., & Anooshian, L. Moral judgment and distributive justice. *Human Development*, 1977, *20*, 160–170.

Guthrie, E. R. *The psychology of learning*. New York: Harper, 1935.

Gutkin, D. C. The effects of systematic story changes in intentionality in children's moral judgments. *Child Development*, 1972, *43*, 187–195.

Haddad, N. F., McCullers, J. C., & Moran, J. D. Satiation and the detrimental effects of material rewards. *Child Development*, 1976, *47*, 547–550.

Hanlon, C. C. The effects of social isolation and characteristics of the model on accent imitation in fourth-grade children. *Journal of Experimental Child Psychology*, 1971, *11*, 322–366.

Hanson, R. W. Temporal factors and retest expectations in an observationally acquired simple concept. Unpublished doctoral dissertation, Univ. of Arizona, 1972.

Harris, M. B. Field studies of modeled aggression. *Journal of Social Psychology*, 1973, *89*, 131–139.

Harris, M. B., & Evans, R. C. Models and creativity. *Psychological Reports*, 1973, *33*, 763–769.

Harris, M. B., & Fisher, J. L. Modeling and flexibility in problem solving. *Psychological Reports*, 1973, *33*, 19–23.

Harris, M. B., & Hassemer, W. G. Some factors affecting the complexity of children's sentences: The effects of modeling, age, sex, and bilingualism. *Journal of Experimental Child Psychology*, 1972, *13*, 447–455.

Harris, M. B., & Siebel, C. E. Effects of sex, occupation, and confidence of model and sex and grade of subject on imitation of language behaviors. *Developmental Psychology*, 1976, *12*, 89–90.

Harris, P. L., & Bassett, E. Reconstruction from the mental image. *Journal of Experimental Child Psychology*, 1976, *21*, 514–523.

Hart, B. M., & Risley, T. R. Establishing use of descriptive adjectives in the spontaneous speech of disadvantaged preschool children. *Journal of Applied Behavior Analysis*, 1968, *1*, 109–120.

Harter, S., & Zigler, E. The assessment of effectance motivation in normal and retarded children. *Developmental Psychology*, 1974, *10*, 169–180.

Hartshorne, H., & May, M. A. *Studies in the nature of character*. Vol. I. *Studies in deceit*. New York: Macmillan, 1928.

Harvey, R. T. Effects of vicarious social punishment and reward, and differential instructions to subjects, in suppressing a rule governed response. Unpublished doctoral dissertation, Univ. of Arizona, 1973.

Hatano, G. A developmental approach to concept formation: A review of neo-Piagetian learning experiments. *Dokkyo University Bulletin of Liberal Arts and Education*, 1971, *5*, 59–76.

Hawkins, H. L., Reicher, G. M., Rogers, M., & Peterson, L. Flexible coding in word recognition. *Journal of Experimental Psychology: Human Perception and Performance*, 1976, *2*, 380–385.

Haygood, R. C. Rule learning and concept formation. Paper presented at the Department of Psychology Colloquium, Univ. of Arizona, Tucson, September 1972.

Haygood, R. C., & Bourne, L. E., Jr. Attribute and rule learning aspects of conceptual behavior. *Psychological Review*, 1965, *72*, 175–195.

Haynes, C. R., & Kulhavy, R. V. Conservation level and category clustering. *Developmental Psychology*, 1976, *12*, 179–184.

Heider, I., & Simmel, M. An experimental study of apparent behavior. *American Journal of Psychology*, 1944, *57*, 243–259.
Helson, H. *Adoptation level theory*. New York: Harper, 1964.
Herbert, E. W., Gelfand, D. M., & Hartman, D. P. Imitation and self-esteem as determinants of self-critical behavior. *Child Development*, 1969, *40*, 421–430.
Hilgard, E. R. *Theories of learning*. (2nd ed.) New York: Appleton, 1956.
Hilgard, E. R., & Bower, G. H. *Theories of learning*. (3rd ed.) New York: Appleton, 1966.
Hiller, J. H. Learning from prose text: Effects of readability level, inserted question difficulty, and individual differences. *Journal of Educational Psychology*, 1974, *66*, 202–211.
Hillix, W. A., & Marx, M. H. Response strengthening by information and effect in human learning. *Journal of Experimental Psychology*, 1960, *60*, 97–102.
Hobhouse, L. T. *Mind in evolution*. New York: Macmillan, 1915.
Holstein, C. B. Irreversible stepwise sequence in the development of moral judgment: A longitudinal study of males and females. *Child Development*, 1976, *47*, 51–61.
Holt, E. B. *Animal drive and the learning process*. New York: Holt, 1931.
Homans, G. *The human group*. New York: Harcourt, 1950.
Hovland, C. I., Janis, I. L., & Kelley, H. H. *Communication and persuasion*. New Haven, Connecticut: Yale Univ. Press, 1953.
Hovland, C. I., & Pritzker, H. A. Extent of opinion change as a function of the amount of change advocated. *Journal of Abnormal and Social Psychology*,*54*, 257–261.
Howie, A. M. Effects of brief exposure to symbolic model behavior on the information-processing strategies of internally and externally oriented children. *Developmental Psychology*, 1975, *11*, 325–333.
Hudson, L. *Frames of mind*. London: Methuen, 1968.
Hull, C. L. Quantitative aspects of the evolution of concepts, an experimental study. *Psychological Monographs*, 1920, *28*(1, Whole No. 123).
Hull, C. L. *Principles of behavior*. New York: Appleton, 1943.
Hull, C. L. *A behavior system*. New Haven, Connecticut: Yale Univ. Press, 1952.
Humphrey, G. Imitation and the conditional reflex. *Pedagogical Seminary*, 1921, *28*, 1–21.
Hunt, D., & Fitzgerald, D. Selective attentional responses and overtraining in a discrimination shift prardigm. *Journal of Experimental Child Psychology*, 1973, *15*, 534–548.
Hursh, D. E., & Sherman, J. A. The effects of parent-presented models and praise on the verbal behavior of their children. *Journal of Experimental Child Psychology*, 1973, *15*, 328–339.
Hyde, P. M. An investigation of Piaget's theories of development of the concept of number. Unpublished doctoral dissertation, Univ. of London, 1959.
Hygge, S. Information about a model's unconditioned stimulus and response in vicarious classical conditioning. *Journal of Personality and Social Psychology*, 1976, *33*, 764–771.
Inhelder, B., & Piaget, J. *The growth of logical thinking from childhood to adolescence*. New York: Basic Books, 1958.
Inhelder, B., & Sinclair, H. Learning cognitive structures. In P. Mussen, J. Langer, & M. Covington (Eds.), *Trends and issues in developmental psychology*. New York: Holt, 1969. Pp. 2–21.
James, S. L., & Miller, J. F. Children's awareness of semantic constraints in sentences. *Child Development*, 1973, *44*, 69–76.
James, W. *The principles of psychology*. New York: Holt, 1890.
Jeffery, R. W. The influence of symbolic and motor rehearsal in observational learning. *Journal of Research in Personality*, 1976, *10*, 116–127.

Jensen, A. R., & Rohwer, W. D., Jr. Syntactical mediation of serial and paired associate learning as a function of age. *Child Development,* 1965, *36,* 601–608.

Jones, A., Bentler, P. M., & Petri, C. The reduction of uncertainty concerning future pain. *Journal of Abnormal Psychology,* 1966, *71,* 87–94.

Kanfer, F. H., Duerfeldt, P. H. Martin, B., & Dorsey, T. E. Effects of model reinforcement, expectation to perform, and task performance on model observation. *Journal of Personality and Social Psychology,* 1971, *20,* 214–217.

Kanfer, F. H., Karoly, P., & Newman, A. Source of feedback observational learning, and attitude change. *Journal of Personality and Social Psychology,* 1974, *29,* 30–38.

Kaplan, R. Effects of grouping and response characteristics of instructional objectives when learning from prose. *Journal of Educational Psychology,* 1976, *68,* 424–430.

Kaufman, A., Baron, A., & Kopp, R. E. Some effects of instructions on human operant behavior. *Psychonomic Monograph Supplements,* 1966, *1,* 243–250.

Kazdin, A. E. Effects of covert modeling, multiple models, and model reinforcement on assertive behavior. *Behavior Therapy,* 1976, *7,* 211–222.

Keasey, C. B. Experimentally induced changes in moral opinions and reasoning. *Journal of Personality and Social Psychology,* 1973, *26,* 30–38.

Keating, D. P., & Caramazza, A. Effects of age and ability on syllogistic reasoning in early adolescence. *Developmental Psychology,* 1975, *11,* 837–842.

Kellas, G., McCauley, C., & McFarland, L. E., Jr. Developmental aspects of storage and retrieval. *Journal of Experimental Child Psychology,* 1975, *19,* 51–62.

Kelley, H. H. The warm-cold variable in first impressions of persons. *Journal of Personality,* 1950, *18,* 431–439.

Kelley, H. H., & Thibaut, J. W. Experimental studies of group problem solving and process. In G. Lindzey (Ed.), *Handbook of social psychology.* Vol. 2. (1st ed.) Redding, Massachusetts: Addison-Wesley, 1954. Pp. 735–785.

Kelley, J. E. Basic psychophysical functions in young children. Unpublished Ph.D dissertation, Univ. of Arizona, Tucson, 1974.

Kelly, M., Scholnick, E. K., Travers, S. H., & Johnson, J. W. Relations among memory, memory appraisal, and memory strategies. *Child Development,* 1976, *47,* 648–659.

Kemler, D. G., Shepp, B. E., & Foote, K. E. The sources of developmental differences in children's incidental processing during discrimination trials. *Journal of Experimental Child Psychology,* 1976, *21,* 226–240.

Kendler, H. H., & Kendler, T. S. Vertical and horizontal processes in problem solving. *Psychological Review,* 1962, *69,* 1–16.

Kendler, T. S., & Kendler, H. H. Reversal and nonreversal shifts in kindergarten children. *Journal of Experimental Psychology,* 1959, *58,* 56–60.

Kendler, T. S., & Kendler, H. H. Experimental analysis of inferential behavior in children. In L. P. Lipsett & C. C. Spiker (Eds.), *Advances in child development and behavior.* Vol. 3. New York: Academic Press, 1967.

Kennedy, B. A., & Miller, D. J. Persistent use of verbal rehearsal as a function of information about its value. *Child Development,* 1976, *47,* 566–569.

Kerst, S., & Levin, J. R. A comparison of experimenter-provided and subject-generated strategies in children's paired-associate learning. *Journal of Educational Psychology,* 1973, *65,* 313–320.

Kessler, K., White, G. M., Rosenthal, T. L., & Phibbs, J. Modeling and overt practice in training a rule-creating rubric. Paper presented at the Rocky Mountain Psychological Association annual convention, Las Vegas, Nevada, May 1973.

Kingsley, R. C., & Hall, V. C. Training conservation through the use of learning sets. *Child Development,* 1967, *38,* 1111–1126.

Kintsch, W. *Learning, memory, and conceptual processes.* New York: Wiley, 1970.

Kirby, M. J. Task factors in observational learning. Unpublished M. A. Thesis, Univ. of Arizona, Tuscon, 1973.

Kirby, M., Rosenthal, T. L., & White, G. M. Task factors in observational learning. Paper presented at the Rocky Mountain Psychological Association annual convention, Las Vegas, Nevada, May 1973.

Klatsky, R. L., Clark, E. V., & Macken, M. Asymmetries in the acquisition of polar adjectives; linguistic or conceptual. *Journal of Experimental Child Psychology*, 1973, *16*, 32–46.

Klein, G. A. Effect of attentional demands on context utilization. *Journal of Educational Psychology*, 1976, *68*, 25–31.

Klein, S. P., Frederiksen, N., & Evans, P. P. Anxiety and learning to formulate hypotheses. *Journal of Educational Psychology*, 1969, *60*, 465–475.

Klima, E. S., & Bellugi, V. Syntactic regularities in the speech of children. In J. Lyons & R. J. Wales (Eds.), *Psycholinguistic papers: The proceedings of the 1966 Edinburgh conference*. Edinburgh Univ. Press, 1966. Pp. 183–208.

Klinger, E. Modeling effects on achievement imagery. *Journal of Personality and Social Psychology*, 1967, *7*, 49–62.

Kluckhohn, C. Navaho witchcraft. *Papers of the Peabody Museum of American Archaeology and Ethnology*, Harvard Univ., 1944, *22*(2).

Kobisigawa, A. The effects of model's problem solving behavior and vicarious reinforcement on children's learning. *Japanese Journal of Psychology*, 1968, *39*, 81–85.

Kobisigawa, A., & Orr, R. R. Free recall and retrieval speed of categorized items by kindergarten children. *Journal of Experimental Child Psychology*, 1973, *15*, 187–192.

Koenigsberg, R. S. An evaluation of visual versus sensorimotor methods for improving orientation discrimination of letter reversals by preschool children. *Child Development*, 1973, *44*, 764–769.

Kohlberg, L. Stage and sequence: The cognitive-developmental approach to socialization. In D. A. Goslin (Ed.), *Handbook of socialization theory and research*. Chicago: Rand McNally, 1968. Pp. 347–480.

Kossuth, G. L. Observational learning of a novel language construction. Unpublished Ph.D. dissertation, Univ. of Arizona, 1972.

Krauss, R. M., & Glucksburg, S. The development of communication: Competence as a function of age. *Child Development*, 1969, *40*, 255–266.

Kraut, A. G. Effects of familiarization on alertness and encoding in children. *Developmental Psychology*, 1976, *12*, 491–496.

Kuhn, D. Inducing development experimentally: Comments on a research paradigm. *Developmental Psychology*, 1974, *10*, 590–600.

Kuhn, D. Relation of two Piagetian stage transitions to I. Q. *Developmental Psychology*, 1976, *12*, 157–161. (a)

Kuhn, D. Short term longitudinal evidence for the sequentiality of Kohlberg's early stages of moral development. *Developmental Psychology*, 1976, *12*, 162–166. (b)

Kunce, J. T., Bruch, M. A., & Thelen, M. H. Vicarious induction of academic achievement behavior in disadvantaged adults. *Journal of Counseling Psychology*, 1974, *21*, 507–510.

Kurtines, W., & Greif, E. The development of moral thought: Review and evaluation of Kohlberg's approval. *Psychological Bulletin*, 1974, *81*, 453–470.

Lahey, B. B. Modification of the frequency of descriptive adjectives in the speech of Head Start children through modeling without reinforcement. *Journal of Applied Behavior Analysis*, 1971, *4*, 19–22.

Lamal, P. A. Imitation learning of information-processing. *Journal of Experimental Child Psychology*, 1971, *12*, 223–227.

Landy, D., Berschied, E., & Walster, E. What is beautiful is good. *Journal of Personality and Social Psychology*, 1972, *24*, 285–290.

Landy, D., & Sigall, H. Beauty is talent: Task evaluation as a function of the performer's physical attractiveness. *Journal of Personality and Social Psychology*, 1974, *29*, 299–304.

Laughlin, P. R., Moss, I. L., & Miller, S. M. Information processing in children as a function of adult model, stimulus display, school grade, and sex. *Journal of Educational Psychology*, 1969, *60*, 188–193.

Lefton, L. A., & Fisher, D. F. Information extraction during visual search: A developmental progression. *Journal of Experimental Child Psychology*, 1976, *22*, 346–361.

Le Furgy, W. G., & Woloshin, G. W. Immediate and long-term effects of experimentally-induced social influence in the modification of adolescents' moral judgments. *Journal of Personality and Social Psychology*, 1969, *12*, 104–110.

Lenneberg, E. H. *Biological foundations of language*. New York: Wiley, 1967.

Leon, M., Oden, G. C., & Anderson, N. H. Functional measurement of social values. *Journal of Personality and Social Psychology*, 1973, *27*, 301–310.

Leonard, L. B. The role of nonlinguistic stimuli and semantic relations in children's acquisition of grammatical utterances. *Journal of Experimental Child Psychology*, 1975, *19*, 346–357.

Lepper, M. R., & Greene, D. Turning play into work: Effects of adult surveillance and extrinsic rewards on children's intrinsic motivation. *Journal of Personality and Social Psychology*, 1975, *31*, 479–486.

Lepper, M. R., Green, D., & Nisbett, R. E. Undermining children's intrinsic interest with extrinsic reward: A test of the over-justification hypothesis. *Journal of Personality and Social Psychology*, 1973, *28*, 129–137.

Lepper, M. R., Sagotsky, G., & Mailer, J. Generalization and persistence of effects of exposure to self-reinforcement models. *Child Development*, 1975, *46*, 618–630.

Levin, J. R., Davidson, R. E., Wolff, P., & Citron, M. A comparison of induced imagery and sentence strategies in children's paired-associate learning. *Journal of Educational Psychology*, 1973, *64*, 306–309.

Levy, L. H. Originality as role-defined behavior. *Journal of Personality and Social Psychology*, 1968, *9*, 72–78.

Levy, M., & Kahn, M. Interpreter bias on the Rorschach test as a function of patients' socioeconomic status. *Journal of Projective Techniques and Personality Assessment*, 1970, *34*, 106–112.

Lewin, K. *A dynamic theory of personality*. New York: McGraw-Hill, 1935.

Lewis, M., & Freedle, R. Mother-infant dyad: The cradle of meaning. In P. Pliner, L. Krames, & T. Alloway (Eds.), *Communication and affect, language and thought*. New York: Academic Press, 1973.

Liberty, C., & Ornstein, P. A. Age differences in organization and recall: The effects of training in categorization. *Journal of Experimental Child Psychology*, 1973, *15*, 169–186.

Liebert, R. M., & Allen, M. K. Effects of rule structure and reward magnitude on the acquisition and adoption of self-reward criteria. *Psychological Reports*, 1967, *21*, 445–452.

Liebert, R. M., & Fernandez, L. E. Vicarious reward and task complexity as determinants of imitative learning. *Psychological Reports*, 1969, *25*, 531–534.

Liebert, R. M., & Fernandez, L. E. Imitation as a function of vicarious and direct reward. *Developmental Psychology*, 1970, *2*, 230–232.

Liebert, R. M., Hanratty, M., & Hill, J. H. Effects of rule structure and training method on the adoption of a self-imposed standard. *Child Development,* 1969, *40,* 93–101. (a)

Liebert, R. M. Odom, R. D., Hill, J. H., & Huff, R. L. The effects of age and rule familiarity on the production of modeled language constructions. *Developmental Psychology,* 1969, *1,* 108–112. (b)

Liebert, R. M., & Swenson, S. A. Abstraction inference, and the process of imitative learning. *Development Psychology,* 1971, *5,* 500–504. (a)

Liebert, R. M., & Swenson, S. A. Association and abstraction as mechanisms of imitative learning. *Developmental Psychology,* 1971, *4,* 289–294. (b)

Lindzey, G. (Ed.) *Handbook of social psychology.* (1st ed.) Reading, Massachusetts: Addison-Wesley, 1954.

Lovaas, O. I. A program for the establishment of speech in psychotic children. In J. K. Wing (Ed.), *Childhood autism.* New York: Macmillan, 1966.

Lovaas, O. I., Berberich, J. P., Perloff, B. F.,& Schaeffer, B. Acquisition of imitative speech by schizophrenic children. *Science,* 1966, *151,* 705–707.

Lovaas, O. I., Freitas, L., Nelson, K., & Whalen, C. The establishment of imitation and its use for the development of complex behavior in schizophrenic children. *Behavior Research and Therapy,* 1967, *5,* 171–181.

Lovell, L., & Dixon, E. M. The growth of the control of grammar in imitation, comprehension, and production. *Journal of Child Psychology and Psychiatry,* 1967, *8,* 31–39.

Luchins, A. S., & Luchins, E. H. New experimental attempts at preventing mechanization in problem solving. *Journal of General Psychology,* 1950, *42,* 279–297.

Lutzker, J. R., & Sherman, J. A. Producing generative sentence usage by imitation and reinforcement procedures. *Journal of Applied Behavior Analysis,* 1974, *7,* 447–460.

Maccoby, M., & Modiano, N. On culture and equivalence. In J. S. Bruner, R. R. Olver, & P. M. Greenfield (Eds.), *Studies in cognitive growth.* New York: Wiley, 1966.

Macri, I. Scope of modeling array in concept attainment. Unpublished M. A. thesis, Univ. of Arizona, Tucson, 1976.

Mahoney, M. J. *Cognition and behavior modification.* Cambridge, Massachusetts: Ballinger, 1974. (a)

Mahoney, M. J. Self-reward and self-monitoring techniques for weight control. *Behavior Therapy,* 1974, *5,* 48–57. (b)

Mahoney, M. J., & Thoresen, C. E. *Self-control: Power to the person.* Monterey, California: Brooks-Cole, 1974.

Maller, J. B. *A controlled association test.* New York: Author, 1936.

Malouf, R. E., & Dodd, D. H. Role of exposure, imitation, and expansion in the acquisition of an artificial grammatical rule. *Developmental Psychology,* 1972, *7,* 195–203.

Mandler, G. Organization and memory. In K. W. Spence & J. T. Spence (Eds.), *The psychology of learning and motivation: Advances in research and theory.* Vol. 1. New York: Academic Press, 1967. Pp. 328–372. (a)

Mandler, G. Verbal learning. In G. Mandler, P. Mussen, N. Kogan, & M. A. Wallach (Eds), *New Directions in psychology III.* New York; Holt, 1967. Pp. 1–50. (b)

Mann, J. Vicarious desensitization of test anxiety through observation of videotaped treatment. *Journal of Counseling Psychology,* 1972, *19,* 1–7.

Mann, R. H., & Baer, D. M. The effects of receptive language training on articulation. *Journal of Applied Behavior Analysis,* 1971, *4,* 291–298.

Maratsos, M. P. Decrease in the understanding of the word "big" in preschool children. *Child Development,* 1973, *44,* 747–752.

Martin, J. A. Generalizing the use of descriptive adjectives through modeling. *Journal of Applied Behavior Analysis*, 1975, *8*, 203–209.

Martin, M., Burkholder, R., Rosenthal, T. L., Tharp, R. G., & Thorne, G. L. Programming behavior change and reintegration into school milieu of extreme adolescent deviates. *Behaviour Research and Therapy*, 1968, *6*, 371–383.

Masters, J. C., & Branch, M. N. Comparison of the relative effectiveness of instructions, modeling, and reinforcement procedures for inducing behavior change. *Journal of Experimental Psychology*, 1969, *80*, 364–368.

Masters, J. C., & Driscoll, S. A. Children's "imitation" as a function of the presence or absence of a model and the description of his instrumental behaviors. *Child Development*, 1971, *42*, 161–170.

Masters, J. C., & Santrock, J. W. Studies in the self-regulation of behavior: Effects of contingent cognitive and affective events. *Developmental Psychology*, 1976, *12*, 334–348.

McConkie, G. W., Rayner, K., & Wilson, S. J. Experimental manipulation of reading strategies. *Journal of Educational Psychology*, 1973, *65*, 1–8.

McCauley, C., & Kellas, G. Induced chunking: Temporal aspects of storage and retrieval. *Journal of Experimental Psychology*, 1974, *102*, 260–265.

McCauley, C., Kellas, G., Dugas, J., & DeVellis, R. F. Effects of serial rehearsal training on memory search. *Journal of Educational Psychology*, 1976, *68*, 474–481.

McDavid, J. W. Effects of ambiguity of environmental cues upon learning to imitate. *Journal of Abnormal and Social Psychology*, 1962, *65*, 381–386.

McDougall, W. *An introduction to social psychology*. (Rev. ed.) Boston: John W. Luce, 1926.

McFarland, C. E., & Kellas, G. Category similarity effects in children's semantic memory retrieval. *Journal of Experimental Child Psychology*, 1975, *20*, 369–376.

McLaughlin, L. J., & Brindley, J. F. Age and observational learning of a multiple-classification test. *Developmental Psychology*, 1973, *9*, 9–15.

McNeill, D. Developmental psycholinguistics. In F. Smith & G. H. Miller (Eds.), *The genesis of language: A psycholinguistic approach*. Cambridge, Massachusetts: MIT Press, 1966. Pp. 15–84.

McNeill, D. *The acquisition of language: The study of developmental psycholinguistics*. New York: Harper, 1970.

McNeill, D. The capacity for the ontogenesis of grammar. In D. Slobin (Ed.), *The ontogenesis of grammar*. New York: Academic Press, 1971, Pp. 17–40.

Meacham, J. A. Patterns of memory abilities in two cultures. *Developmental Psychology*, 1975, *11*, 50–53.

Mead, G. H. Social psychology as counterpart to physiological psychology. *Psychological Bulletin*, 1909, *6*, 401–408.

Meichenbaum, D. Cognitive factors in behavior modification: Modifying what clients say to themselves. In C. M. Franks & G. T. Wilson (Eds.), *Annual review of behavior therapy: Theory and practice*. New York: Brunner-Mazel, 1973. Pp. 416–431.

Mellgren, R. L., Fouts, R. S., & Lemmon, W. B. American Sign Language in the chimpanzee: Semantic and conceptual functions of signs. Paper presented at the Midwestern Psychological Association convention, Chicago, Illinois, May 1973.

Melton, A. W. Learning. In W. S. Monroe (Ed.), *Encyclopedia of educational research*. (Rev. ed.) New York: Macmillan, 1950. Pp. 668–686.

Meltzer, R. H., Martin, J. G., Mills, C. B., Imhoff, D. L., & Zohar, D. Reaction time to temporally-displaced phoneme targets in continuous speech. *Journal of Experimental Psychology: Human Perception and Performance*, 1976, *2*, 277–290.

Menyuk, P. Alternation of rules in children's grammar. *Journal of Verbal Learning and Verbal Behavior*, 1964, *3*, 480–488.

Menyuk, P. *Sentences children use*. Cambridge, Massachusetts: MIT Press, 1969.

Midlarsky, E., Bryan, J. H., & Brickman, P. Aversive approval: Incentive effects of modeling and reinforcement on altruistic behavior. *Child Development*, 1973, *44*, 321–328.

Miller, G. A. The magic number seven, plus or minus two: Some limits on our capacity for processing information. *Psychological Review*, 1956, *63*, 81–97.

Miller, G. A. Some preliminaries to psycholinguistics. *American Psychologist*, 1965, *20*, 15–20.

Miller, G. A., Galanter, E., & Pribram, K. H. *Plans and the structure of behavior*. New York: Holt, 1960.

Miller, N. E. The perception of children: A genetic study employing the critical choice delayed reaction. *Journal of Genetic Psychology*, 1934, *44*, 321–339.

Miller, N. E., & Dollard, J. *Social learning and imitation*. New Haven: Institute of Human Relations, Yale Univ. Press, 1941.

Miller, S. A. Contradiction, surprise, and cognitive change: The effects of disconfirmation of belief on conservers and non-conservers. *Journal of Experimental Child Psychology*, 1973, *15*, 47–62.

Miller, S. A., & Brownell, C. A. Peers, persuasion, and Piaget: Dyadic interaction between conservers and nonconservers. *Child Development*, 1975, *46*, 992–997.

Miller, S. A., Shelton, J., & Flavell, J. H. A test of Luria's hypothesis concerning the development of verbal self-regulation. *Child Development*, 1970, *41*, 651–655.

Mims, R. M., & Gholson, B. Effects of type and amount of feedback upon hypothesis sampling systems among seven- and eight-year-old children. *Journal of Experimental Child Psychology*, 1977, *24*, 358–371.

Mischel, W. *Personality and assessment*. New York: Wiley, 1968.

Mischel, W. Sex-typing and socialization. In P. Mussen (Ed.), *Carmichael's manual of child psychology*. New York: Wiley, 1970. Pp. 3–72.

Mischel, W. Toward a cognitive social learning reconceptualization of personality. *Psychological Review*, 1973, *80*, 252–283.

Mischel, W., Ebbesen, E. B., & Zeiss, A. M. Determinants of selective memory about the self. *Journal of Consulting and Clinical Psychology*, 1976, *44*, 92–103.

Mischel, W., & Grusec, J. Determinants of the rehearsal and transmission of neutral and aversive behaviors. *Journal of Personality and Social Psychology*, 1966, *2*, 197–205.

Mischel, W., & Liebert, R. M. Effects of discrepancies between observed and imposed reward criteria on their acquisition and transmission. *Journal of Personality and Social Psychology*, 1966, *3*, 45–53.

Moerk, E. L. Processes of language teaching and language learning in the interaction of mother-child dyads. *Child Development*, 1976, *47*, 1064–1078.

Moeser, S. D. Memory for meaning and wording in concrete and abstract sentences. *Journal of Verbal Learning and Verbal Behavior*, 1974, *13*, 682–697.

Moore, B., Mischel, W., & Zeiss, A. Comparative effects of the reward stimulus and its cognitive representation in voluntary delay. *Journal of Personality and Social Psychology*, 1976, *34*, 419–424.

Morgan, C. L. *Habit and instinct*. London: E. Arnold, 1896.

Morgan, C. L. *Mind at the crossways*. London: Williams & Norgate, 1929.

Morgan, C. L. *The emergence of novelty*. London: Williams & Norgate, 1933.

Morgulas, S., & Zimmerman, B. J. The role of comprehension in children's observational learning of a syntactic rule. An unpublished manuscript, The Graduate School and Univ. Center of CUNY, New York, 1977.

Morris, L. A. Relational responding to a transposition task as a function of relevant verbalizations and feedback. Unpublished doctoral dissertation, Univ. of Arizona, 1970.

Moss, H. Sex, age, and state as determinants of mother infant interaction. *Merrill-Palmer Quarterly*, 1967, *13*, 19–36.

Mowbray, C. T., & Luria, Z. Effects of labeling on children's visual imagery. *Developmental Psychology*, 1973, *9*, 1–8.

Mowrer, O. H. *Learning theory and symbolic processes.* New York: Wiley, 1960.

Moynahan, E. D. The development of knowledge concerning the effect of categorization upon free recall. *Child Development*, 1973, *44*, 238–246.

Muenzinger, K. F. Vicarious trial and error at a point of choice: I, A general survey of its relation to learning efficiency. *Journal of Genetic Psychology*, 1938, *53*, 75–86.

Murphy, G., Murphy, L. B., & Newcomb, T. M. *Experimental social psychology.* (Rev. ed.) New York: Harper, 1937.

Murray, F. B. Acquisition of conservation through social interaction. *Developmental Psychology*, 1972, *6*, 1–6.

Neihardt, J. C. *Black Elk speaks.* New York: Pocket Books, 1972

Neisser, V. *Cognitive psychology.* New York: Appleton, 1967.

Neisser, V. *Cognition and reality.* San Francisco: Freeman, 1976.

Neisser, V., & Becklen, R. Selective looking: Attending to visually specified events. *Cognitive Psychology*, 1975, *7*, 480–494.

Nelson, D. I., & Brooks, D. H. Retroactive inhibition or rhyme categories in free recall: Inaccessibility or unavailability of information. *Journal of Experimental Psychology*, 1974, *102*, 277–283.

Nelson, K. Structure and strategy in learning to talk. *Monograph of the Society for Research in Child Development*, 1973, *38*(1–2, Serial No. 149).

Nelson, K. Concept, word, and sentence: Intercorrelations in acquisition and development. *Psychological Review*, 1974, *81*, 267–285.

Nelson, K. E., Carskaddon, G., & Bonvillian, J. D. Syntax acquisition: Impact of experimental variation in adult interaction with the child. *Child Development*, 1973, *44*, 497–504.

Nelson, K. E., & Earl, N. Information search by preschool children: Induced use of categories and category hierarchies. *Child Development*, 1973, *44*, 682–685.

Nelson, K. E., & Kosslyn, S. M. Semantic retrieval in children and adults. *Developmental Psychology*, 1975, *11*, 807–813.

Norlin, G. (Translator) *Isocates against the Sophists.* Vol. 2. London: Loeb Classical Library, 1929.

Notterman, J. M., Schoenfeld, W. N. & Bersh, P. J. A comparison of three extinction procedures following heart rate conditioning. *Journal of Abnormal and Social Psychology*, 1952, *87*, 674–677.

Odom, R. D., & Corbin, D. W. Perceptual salience and children's multi-dimensional problem solving. *Child Development*, 1973, *44*, 425–432.

Odóm, R. D., Liebert, R. M., & Fernandez, L. E. Effects of symbolic modeling on the syntactical productions of retardates. *Psychonomic Science*, 1969, *17*, 104–105.

Odom, R. D., Liebert, R. M., & Hill, J. H. The effects of modeling cues, reward, and attention set on the properties of grammatical and ungrammatical syntactic constructions. *Journal of Experimental Child Psychology*, 1968, *6*, 131–140.

O'Reilly, E., & Steger, J. A. Children's use of context in judgment of weight. *Child Development*, 1970, *41*, 1095–1101.

Ornstein, P. A., Naus, M. J., & Liberty, C. Rehearsal and organizational processes in children's memory. *Child Development*, 1975, *46*, 818–830.

Ornstein, P. A., Naus, M. J., & Stone, B. P. Rehearsal training and developmental differences in memory. *Developmental Psychology*, 1977, *13*, 15–24.

Osgood, C. E. *Method and theory in experimental psychology*. New York: Oxford Univ. Press, 1953.

Osler, S. F., & Madden, J. The verbal label: Mediator or classifier? *Journal of Experimental Child Psychology*, 1973, *16*, 303–317.

Osser, H., Wang, M. D., & Zaid, F. The young child's ability to imitate and comprehend speech: A comparison of two subcultural groups. *Child Development*, 1969, *40*, 1063–1075.

Paivio, A. *Imagery and verbal processes*. New York: Holt, 1971.

Palermo, D. S., & Jenkins, J. J. *Word association norms: Grade school through college*. Minneapolis: Univ. of Minnesota Press, 1964.

Paris, S. G., & Carter, A. Y. Semantic and constructive aspects of sentence memory in children. *Developmental Psychology*, 1973, *9*, 109–113.

Parnes, S. J., & Meadow, A. Effects of "brainstorming" on creative problem solving by trained and untrained subjects. *Journal of Educational Psychology*, 1959, *50*, 171–176.

Parton, D. A. Theories of imitation learning. Sociology working paper series 73–8, Univ. of Iowa, Iowa City, 1974.

Parton, D. A., & Geshuri, Y. Learning aggression as a function of presence of human model, response intensity, and the target of the response. *Journal of Experimental Child Psychology*, 1971, *11*, 491–504.

Parton, D. A., & Priefert, M. J. The value of being imitated. *Journal of Experimental Child Psychology*, 1975, *20*, 286–295.

Patterson, C. J., & Mischel, W. Plans to resist distraction. *Developmental Psychology*, 1975, *11*, 369–378.

Patterson, C. J., & Mischel, W. Effects of temptation-inhibiting and task facilitating plans on self-control. *Journal of Personality and Social Psychology*, 1976, *33*, 209–217.

Patterson, K. E., Meltzer, R. H., & Mandler, G. Inter-response times in categorized free recall. *Journal of Verbal Learning and Verbal Behavior*, 1971, *10*, 417–426.

Perlmutter, M., & Meyers, N. A. A developmental study of semantic effects on recognition memory. *Journal of Experimental Child Psychology*, 1976, *22*, 438–453.

Phillips, J. R. Syntax and vocabulary of mothers' speech to young children. *Child Development*, 1973, *44*, 182–185.

Piaget, J. *Judgment and reasoning in the child*. New York: Harcourt, 1928.

Piaget, J. *The moral judgment of the child*. Glencoe, Illinois: Free Press, 1948.

Piaget, J. *The child's conception of number*. New York: Humanities, 1952. (a)

Piaget, J. *The origins of intelligence in children*. New York: International Universities Press, 1952. (b)

Piaget, J. *The language and thought of the child* (3rd ed.). London: Routledge & Kegan-Paul, 1959.

Piaget, J. *Play, dreams and imitation*. New York: W. W. Norton, 1962.

Piaget, J. *Six psychological studies*. New York: Vintage, 1968.

Pick, A. D., & Frankel, C. W. A study of strategies of visual attention. *Developmental Psychology*, 1973, *9*, 348–357.

Plato. *The republic*. New York: Modern Library, 1920.

Pollio, H. R. Associative structure and verbal behavior. In T. R. Dixon & D. L. Horton (Eds.), *Verbal behavior and general behavior theory*. Englewood Cliffs, New Jersey: Prentice-Hall, 1968. Pp. 37–66.

Posnansky, C. J., & Neumann, P. G. The abstraction of visual prototypes by children. *Journal of Experimental Child Psychology*, 1976, *21*, 367–379.

Posner, M. I. Coordination of internal codes. In W. G. Chase (Ed.), *Visual information processing*. New York: Academic Press, 1973.

Premack, D. A functional analysis of language. *Journal of the Experimental Analysis of Behavior*, 1970, *14*, 107–125.

Preminger, A. (Ed.) Imitation. In *Encyclopedia of poetry and poetics*. Princeton: Princeton University Press, 1965.

Prentice, N. M. The influence of live and symbolic modeling on prompting moral judgments of adolescent delinquents. *Journal of Abnormal Psychology*, 1972, *80*, 157–161.

Pressley, G. M. Mental imagery helps eight-year-olds remember what they read. *Journal of Educational Psychology*, 1976, *68*, 355.

Price, J. R., Martuza, V. R., & Grouse, J. H. Construct validity of test items measuring acquisition of information from line graphs. *Journal of Educational Psychology*, 1973, *15*, 63–76.

Price-Williams, D., Gordon, W., & Ramirez. M. Skill and conservation: A study of pottery-making children. *Developmental Psychology*, 1969, *1*, 769.

Rachman, S. J. (Ed.) *Critical essays on psychoanalysis*. New York: Univ. of Oxford Press (Pergamon), 1963.

Rachman, S. J., & Hodgson, R. I. Synchrony and desynchrony in fear and avoidance. *Behaviour Research and Therapy*, 1974, *12*, 311–318.

Rand, C. W. Copying in drawing: The importance of adequate visual analysis versus the ability to utilize drawing rules. *Child Development*, 1973, *44*, 47–53.

Randhawa, B. S. Perceptual information processing of different visual stimuli by eight-year-old children. *Journal of Experimental Child Psychology*, 1973, *16*, 55–62.

Raugh, M. R., & Atkinson, R. C. A mnemonic method for learning a second-language vocabulary. *Journal of Educational Psychology*, 1975, *67*, 1–16.

Reichle, J., Longhurst, T. M., & Stepanich, C. Verbal interaction in mother-child dyads. *Developmental Psychology*, 1976, *12*, 273–277.

Rest, J. The hierarchical nature of moral judgments: A study of patterns of comprehension and preference of moral stages. *Journal of Personality*, 1973, *41*, 86–109.

Rest, J., & Turiel, E., & Kohlberg, L. Level of moral development as a determinant of preference and comprehension of moral judgments made by others. *Journal of Personality*, 1969, *37*, 225–252.

Rice, M. E. The development of responsiveness to vicarious reinforcement. *Developmental Psychology*, 1976, *12*, 540–545.

Richman, S., & Gholson, B. Strategy modeling, age, and information-processing efficiency. *Journal of Experimental Child Psychology*, in press.

Ridberg, E. H., Parke, R. D., & Hetherington, E. M. Modification of impulsive and reflective cognitive style through observation of film-mediated models. *Developmental Psychology*, 1971, *5*, 185–190.

Rigney, J. W., & Lutz, K. A. Effect of graphic analogies in chemistry on learning and attitude. *Journal of Educational Psychology*, 1976, *68*, 305–311.

Risley, T. R., & Reynolds, N. J. Emphasis as a prompt for verbal imitation. *Journal of Applied Behavior Analysis*, 1970, *3*, 185–190.

Robert, M., White, G. M., & Rosenthal, T. L. Format for exposure and complexity of array in observational rule attainment. *Psychological Reports*, 1975, *37*, 999–1007.

Roberts, M. C., Santagrossi, D. A. & Thelen, M. H. The effects of prior task experience in the modeling situation. *Journal of Experimental Child Psychology*, 1976, *21*, 524–531.

Robinson, G. M. Rhythmic organization in speech processing. *Journal of Experimental Psychology: Human Perception and Performance,* 1977, *3,* 83–91.

Rogers, C. J., & Johnson, P. J. Attribute identification in children as a function of stimulus dimensionality. *Journal of Experimental Child Psychology,* 1973, *15,* 216–221.

Rogers, S. P., & Haygood, R. C. Hypothesis behavior in a concept learning task with probabilistic feedback. *Journal of Experimental Psychology,* 1968, *76,* 160–165.

Rohwer, W. D. Decisive research: A means of answering fundamental questions about instruction. *Educational Researcher,* 1972, *1,* 5–11.

Rohwer, W. D., & Matz, R. D. Improving aural comprehension in white and in black children: Pictures versus print. *Journal of Experimental Child Psychology,* 1975, *19,* 23–36.

Rollins, H., & Castle, K. Dimensional preference, pretraining, and attention in children's concept identification. *Child Development,* 1973, *44,* 363–366.

Rosch, E. The nature of mental codes for color categories. *Journal of Experimental Psychology: Human Perception and Performance,* 1975, *1,* 303–322.

Rosch, E., Simpson, C., & Miller, R. S. Structural bases of typicality effects. *Journal of Experimental Psychology: Human Perception and Performance,* 1976, *2,* 491–502.

Rose, S. A., & Blank, M. The potency of context in children's cognition: An illustration through conservation. *Child Development,* 1974, *45,* 499–502.

Rosenbaum, M. E. The effect of verbalization of correct responses by performers and observers on retention. *Child Development,* 1967, *38,* 615–622.

Rosenbaum, M. E., & Arenson, S. J. Einstellung by observation. *Psychological Reports,* 1967, *21,* 345–352.

Rosenbaum, M. E., Chalmers, D. K., & Horne, W. C. Effects of success and failure and the competence of the model on the acquisition and reversal of matching behavior. *Journal of Psychology,* 1962, *54,* 251–258.

Rosenbaum, M. E., & Hewitt, D. J. The effect of electric shock on learning by performers and observers. *Psychonomic Science,* 1966, *5,* 81–82.

Rosenbaum, M. E., & Schultz, L. J. The effects of extraneous response requirements on learning by performers and observers. *Psychonomic Science,* 1967, *8,* 51–52.

Rosenhan, D., Fredrick, F., & Burrows, A. Preaching and practicing: Effects of channel discrepancy on norm internalization. *Child Development,* 1968, *39,* 291–301.

Rosenthal, R. H., White, G. M., & Rosenthal, T. L. Probability matching through direct and vicarious experience. *Psychological Reports,* 1975, *36,* 883–889.

Rosenthal, T. L. Anxiety-proneness and susceptibility to social influence. Unpublished doctoral dissertation, Stanford Univ. 1963.

Rosenthal, T. L. Modeling therapies. In M. Hersen, R. M. Eisler, & P. M. Miller (Eds.), *Progress in behavior modification,* Vol. 2. New York: Academic Press, 1976. Pp. 53–97.

Rosenthal, T. L., Alford, G. S., & Rasp, L. M. Concept attainment, generalization, and retention through observation and verbal coding. *Journal of Experimental Child Psychology,* 1972, *13,* 183–194. (a)

Rosenthal, T. L., & Bandura, A. Psychological modeling: Theory and practice. In S. L. Garfield & A. E. Bergin (Eds.), *Handbook of psychotherapy and behavior change.* (2nd ed.) New York: Wiley, 1978.

Rosenthal, T. L., & Carroll, W. R. Factors in vicarious modification of complex grammatical parameters. *Journal of Educational Psychology,* 1972, *63,* 174–178.

Rosenthal, T. L. Feist, J. R., & Durning, K. Expectation and experimenter-as-model versus experimenter-plus-model design in vicariously induced concept attainment. *Journal of Experimental Education,* 1972, *41,* 82–86. (b)

Rosenthal, T. L., & Hertz, L. Effects of minimal models on ink blot percepts. *Australian Journal of Psychology*, 1972, *24*, 353–361.
Rosenthal, T. L., Hung, J. H., & Kelley, J. E. Therapeutic social influence: Sternly strike while the iron is hot. *Behaviour Research and Therapy*, 1977, *15*, 253–257.
Rosenthal, T. L., Kelley, J. E., & White, G. M. Anchoring and relational judgments by young children and retardates. *Memory and Cognition*, 1974, *2*, 279–282. (a)
Rosenthal, T. L., & Kellogg, J. S. Demonstration versus instructions in concept attainment by mental retardates. *Behavior Research and Therapy*, 1973, *11*, 299–302.
Rosenthal, T. L., Moore, W. B., Dorfman, H., & Nelson, B. Vicarious acquisition of a simple concept with experimenter as model. *Behavior Research and Therapy*, 1971, *9*, 217–227.
Rosenthal, T. L., & Reese S. L. The effects of covert and overt modeling on assertive behavior. *Behavior Research and Therapy*, 1976, *14*, 463–469.
Rosenthal, T. L., Rogers, C., & Durning, K. Sequence of extreme belief incongruent versus neutral information in social perception. *Australian Journal of Psychology*, 1972, *24*, 267–273. (c)
Rosenthal, T. L., Rosenthal, R. H., & Chang, A. F. Vicarious, direct, and imaginal aversion in habit control: Outcomes, heart rates, and subjective perceptions. *Cognitive Therapy and Research*, 1977, *1*, 143–159.
Rosenthal, T. L., & Siegel, B. J. Magic and witchcraft: An interpretation from dissonance theory. *Southwest Journal of Anthropology*, 1959, *15*, 143–167.
Rosenthal, T. L., Underwood, B., & Martin, M. Assessing classroom incentive practices. *Journal of Educational Psychology*, 1969, *60*, 370–376.
Rosenthal, T. L., & White, G. M. Initial probability, rehearsal, and constraint in associative class selection. *Journal of Experimental Child Psychology*, 1972, *13*, 261–274. (a)
Rosenthal, T. L., & White, G. M. On the importance of hair in students' clinical inferences. *Journal of Clinical Psychology*, 1972, *28*, 43–47. (b)
Rosenthal, T. L., White, G. M., & Alford, G. S. Some memory effects with sequential impoverished visual stimuli. *Perceptual and Motor Skills*, 1974, *38*, 1115–1120. (b)
Rosenthal, T. L., & Whitebook, J. S. Incentives versus instructions in transmitting grammatical parameters with experimenter as model. *Behavior Research and Therapy*, 1970, *8*, 187–196.
Rosenthal, T. L., & Zimmerman, B. J. Instructional specificity and outcome expectation in observationally induced question formulation. *Journal of Educational Psychology*, 1972, *63*, 500–504. (a)
Rosenthal, T. L., & Zimmerman, B. J. Modeling by exemplification and instruction in training conservation. *Developmental Psychology*, 1972, *6*, 392–401. (b)
Rosenthal, T. L., & Zimmerman, B. J. Organization, observation, and guided practice in concept attainment and generalization. *Child Development*, 1973, *44*, 606–613.
Rosenthal, T. L., & Zimmerman, B. J. Organization and stability of transfer in vicarious concept attainment. *Child Development*, 1976, *47*, 110–117.
Rosenthal, T. L., Zimmerman, B. J., & Durning, K. Observationally-induced changes in children's interrogative classes. *Journal of Personality and Social Psychology*, 1970, *16*, 681–688.
Ross, E. H. *Social psychology: An outline and sourcebook*. New York: Macmillan, 1908.
Ross, M. The self-perception of intrinsic motivation. In J. H. Harvey, W. J. Ickes, & R. F. Kidd (Eds.), *New directions in attribution research*. Hillsdale, New Jersey: Erlbaum, 1976.
Ross, S. M., & DiVesta, F. J. Oral summary as a review strategy for enhancing recall of textual material. *Journal of Educational Psychology*, 1976, *68*, 689–695.

Rothenburg, B. B., & Orost, J. H. The training of conservation of number in young children. *Child Development,* 1969, *40,* 707–726.

Rothman, G. R. The influence of moral reasoning on behavioral choices. *Child Development,* 1976, *47,* 397–406.

Royer, J. M., & Cable, G. W. Illustrations, analogies, and facilitative transfer in prose learning. *Journal of Educational Psychology,* 1976, *68,* 205–209.

Rubin, K. Egocentrism in childhood: A unitary construct. *Child Development,* 1973, *44,* 102–110.

Russell, J. Nonconservation of area: Do children succeed where adults fail? *Developmental Psychology,* 1976, *12,* 467–468.

Ryan, D., & Kobasigawa, A. Effects of exposure to models on concept identification in kindergarten and second-grade children. *Child Development,* 1971, *42,* 951–955.

Rychlak, J. F. Affective assessment in the recognition of designs and paintings by elementary school children. *Child Development,* 1975, *46,* 62–70.

Rychlak, J. F., Duc Tuan, N., & Schneider, W. E. Formal discipline revisited: Affective assessment and nonspecific transfer. *Journal of Educational Psychology,* 1974, *66,* 152–156.

Rydberg, S., & Arnberg, P. W. Attending and processing broadened within children's concept learning. *Journal of Experimental Child Psychology,* 1976, *22,* 161–177.

Sabo, R. A., & Hagan, J. W. Color cues and rehearsal in short-term memory. *Child Development,* 1973, *44,*77–82.

Sachs, J. D. S. Recognition memory for syntactic and semantic aspects of connected discourse. *Perception and Psychophysics,* 1967, *2,* 437–442.

Safer, M. A. & Leventhal, H. Ear differences in evaluating emotional tones of voice and verbal content. *Journal of Experimental Psychology: Human Perception and Performance,* 1977, *3,* 75–82.

Sailor, W., & Taman, J. Stimulus factors in training of prepositional usage in three autistic children. *Journal of Applied Behavior Analysis,* 1972, *5,* 183–190.

Samuels, S. J., & Tenure, J. E. Attention and reading achievement in first-grade boys and girls. *Journal of Educational Psychology,* 1974, *66,* 29–32.

Sanders, J. R. Retention effects of adjunct questions in written and aural discourse. *Journal of Educational Psychology,* 1973, *65,* 181–186.

Santrock, J. W. Father absence, perceived maternal behavior, and moral development in boys. *Child Development,* 1975, *46,* 753–757.

Santrock, J. W. Affect and facilitative self-control: Influence of ecological setting, cognition, and social agent. *Journal of Educational Psychology,* 1976, *68,* 529–535.

Sarason, I. G. Test anxiety and cognitive modeling. *Journal of Personality and Social Psychology,* 1973, *28,* 58–61.

Sarason, I. G. Test anxiety and the self-disclosing coping model. *Journal of Consulting and Clinical Psychology,* 1975, *43,* 148–153.

Sargent, S. & Williamson, R. C. *Social psychology: An introduction to the study of human relations.* New York: Ronald Press, 1958.

Sax, R. M., & Stollak, G. E. Curiosity and the parent-child relationship. *Child Development,* 1971, *42,* 373–384.

Schachter, S. Deviation, rejection, and communication. *Journal of Abnormal and Social Psychology,* 1951, *46,* 190–207.

Schadler, M. Development of relational learning: Effects of instruction and delay of transfer. *Journal of Experimental Child Psychology,* 1973, *16,* 459–471.

Scheerer, M. Cognition theory. In G. Lindzey (Ed.), *Handbook of social psychology.* Vol. 1. (1st ed.) Reading, Massachusetts: Addison-Wesley, 1954. Pp. 91–142.

Schliefer, M., & Douglas, V. I. Effects of training on the moral judgment of young children. *Journal of Personality and Social Psychology*, 1973, *28*, 62–67.
Schlesinger, I. M. Production of utterances and language acquisition. In D. Slobin (Ed.), *The ontogenesis of grammar.* New York: Academic Press, 1971, Pp. 63–102.
Schoenbaum, R. M. A developmental study of differences in initial coding and recoding of hypothesis information. *Journal of Experimental Child Psychology*, 1973, *16*, 413–423.
Schumaker, J., & Sherman, J. A. Training generative verb usage by imitation and reinforcement procedures. *Journal of Applied Behavior Analysis*, 1970, *3*, 273–287.
Schvaneveldt, R. W., Meyer, D. E., & Becker, C. A. Lexical ambiguity, semantic context, and visual word recognition. *Journal of Experimental Psychology: Human Perception and Performance*, 1976, *2*, 243–256.
Shantz, C. V., & Wilson, K. E. Training communication skills in young children. *Child Development*, 1972, *43*, 693–698.
Shatz, M., & Gelman, R. The development of communication skills modification in the speech of young children as a function of listener. *Monograph of The Society for Research in Child Development*, 1973, *38*(5, Serial No. 152).
Sheingold, K. Developmental differences in intake and storage of visual information. *Journal of Experimental Child Psychology*, 1973, *16*, 1–11.
Sheingold, K., & Shapiro, J. Children's verbal rehearsal in a free-recall task. *Developmental Psychology*, 1976, *12*, 169–170.
Sherif, M. A study of some social factors in perception. *Archives of Psychology*, 1935, *27*, *187*, 1–60.
Sherif, M. *The psychology of social norms.* New York: Harper, 1936.
Sherif, M., & Hovland, C. I. *Social judgment.* New Haven, Connecticut: Yale Univ. Press, 1961.
Sherman, J. A. Imitation and language development. In H. W. Reese (Ed.), *Advances in child development and behavior.* Vol. 6. New York: Academic Press, 1971. Pp. 239–272.
Sherman, J. A., Saunders, R. R., & Brigham, T. A. Transfer of matching and mismatching behavior in preschool children. *Journal of Experimental Child Psychology*, 1970, *9*, 489–498.
Sherrington, C. S. On plastic tonus and proprioceptive reflexes. *Quarterly Journal of Experimental Psychology*, 1909, *2*, 109–156.
Shiffrin, R. M., McKay, D. P., & Shaffer, W. O. Attending to forty-nine spatial positions at once. *Journal of Experimental Psychology: Human Perception and Performance*, 1976, *2*, 14–22.
Shimmerlik, S. M., & Nolan, J. D. Reorganization and the recall of prose. *Journal of Educational Psychology*, 1976, *68*, 779–786.
Siegler, R. S. Defining the locus of developmental differences in children's causal reasoning. *Journal of Experimental Child Psychology*, 1975, *20*, 512–525.
Siegler, R. S., & Atlas, M. Acquisition of formal scientific reasoning by 10- and 13-year-olds: Detecting interactive patterns of data. *Journal of Educational Psychology*, 1976, *68*,360–370.
Siegler, R. S., Liebert, D. E., & Liebert, R. M. Inhelder and Piaget's pendulum problem: Teaching preadolescents to act as scientists. *Developmental Psychology*, 1973, *9*, 97–101.
Siegler, R. S., & Liebert, R. M. Effects of presenting relevant rules and complete feedback on the conservation of liquid quantity task. *Developmental Psychology*, 1972, *7*, 133–138.

Simon, S., Ditrichs, R., & Jamison, N. Vicarious learning of common and uncommon associations in children. *Psychonomic Science,* 1965, *3,* 345–346.

Simpson, C. J., Rosenthal, T. L., Daniel, T. C., & White, G. M. Social influence variations in evaluating managed and unmanaged forest areas. *Journal of Applied Psychology,* 1976, *61,* 759–763.

Skinner, B. F. *Science and human behavior.* New York: Macmillan, 1953.

Skinner, B. F. *Verbal behavior.* New York: Appleton, 1957.

Slobin, D. I. Imitation and grammatical development in children. In N. S. Endler, L. P. Boulter, & H. Osser (Eds.), *Contemporary issues in developmental psychology.* New York: Holt, 1968. Pp. 437–443.

Slobin, D. I., & Welsch, C. A. Elicited imitation as a research tool in developmental psycholinguistics. In C. A. Ferguson & D. I. Slobin (Eds.), *Readings on child language development.* New York: Holt, 1973. Pp. 485–497.

Smedslund, J. The acquisition of conservation of substance and weight in children. II. External reinforcement of conservation of weight and the operations of addition and subtraction. *Scandinavian Journal of Psychology,* 1961, *2,* 71–84. (a)

Smedslund, J. The acquisition of conservation of substance and weight in children. IV. An attempt at extinction of the visual components of the weight concept. *Scandinavian Journal of Psychology,* 1961, *2,* 153–155. (b)

Smith, L. B., Kemler, D. G., & Aronfreed, J. Developmental trends in voluntary selective attention: Differential effects of source distinctness. *Journal of Experimental Child Psychology,* 1975, *20,* 352–362.

Smith, S., & Guthrie, E. R. *General psychology in terms of behavior.* New York: Appleton, 1921.

Snow, C. E. Mothers' speech to children learning language. *Child Development,* 1972, *43,*549–565.

Solomon, R. L. & Turner, L. H. Discriminative classical conditioning in dogs paralyzed by curare can later control discriminative avoidance responses in the normal state. *Psychological Review,* 1962, *69,* 202–219.

Sperling, G. The information available in brief visual presentations. *Psychological Monographs,* 1960, *74*(11, Whole number. 498).

Spiegler, M. D., & Liebert, R. M. Imitation as a function of response commonality, serial order, and vicarious punishment. *Journal of Experimental Child Psychology,* 1973, *15,* 116–124.

Spoehr, K. T., & Smith, E. E. The role of orthographic and phonotaxic rules in perceiving letter patterns. *Journal of Experimental Psychology: Human Perception and Performance,* 1975, *1,*21–34.

Staats, A. W. Verbal Habit-families, concepts, and the operant conditioning of word classes. Psychological Review, 1961, *68,* 190–204.

Staats, A. W. *Learning, language and cognition.* New York: Holt, 1968.

Steinberg, E. R., & Anderson, R. C. Hierarchical semantic organization in six-year-olds. *Journal of Experimental Child Psychology,* 1975, *19,* 544–553.

Stewart, D. M., & Hamilton, M. L. Imitation as a learning strategy in the acquisition of vocabulary. *Journal of Experimental Child Psychology,* 1976, *21,* 380–392.

Stratton, R. P., & Brown, R. Improving creative thinking by training in the production and/or judgment of solutions. *Journal of Educational Psychology,* 1972, *63,* 309–397.

Strauss, S., & Liberman, D. The empirical violation of conservation laws and its relation to structural change. *Journal of Experimental Child Psychology,* 1974, *18,* 464–479.

Stevens-Long, J., & Rasmussen, M. The acquisition of simple and compound sentence structure in an autistic child. *Journal of Applied Behavior Analysis,* 1974, *7,* 473–479.

Suppes, P. The semantics of children's language. *American Psychologist,* 1974, *29,* 103–123.

Swenson, I., & Kulhavy, R. W. Adjunct questions and the comprehension of prose by children. *Journal of Educational Psychology,* 1974, *66,* 212–215.

Tarde, G. *The laws of imitation.* (2nd ed.). New York: Holt, 1903.

Tasch, M. Modeling of prosocial behaviors by preschool subjects of high and low esteem. *Dissertation Abstracts International,* 1971, *32,* 572.

Taub, E., Bacon, R. C., & Berman, A. J. Acquisition of a trace-conditioned avoidance response after deafferentation of the responding limb. *Journal of Comparative and Physiological Psychology,* 1965, *59,* 275–279.

Taub, E., Theodoru, D., Ellman, S. J., Bloom, R. F., & Berman, H. J. Deafferentation in monkeys: Extinction of avoidance responses, discrimination and discrimination reversal. *Psychonomic Science,* 1966, *4,* 323–324.

Tenney, Y. J. The child's conception of organization and recall. *Journal of Experimental Child Psychology,* 1975, *19,* 100–114.

Terman, L. M., & Miles, C. C. *Sex and personality.* New York: McGraw-Hill, 1936.

Thelan, M. A., McGuire, D., Simmonds, D. W., & Akamatsu, T. J. Effect of model reward on the observer's recall of the modeled behavior. *Journal of Personality and Social Psychology,* 1974, *29,* 140–144.

Thoresen, C. E., & Mahoney, M. J. *Behavioral self-control.* New York: Holt, 1974.

Tighe, T. J. Tighe, L. S., & Schechter, J. Memory for instances and categories in children and adults. *Journal of Experimental Child Psychology,* 1975, *20,* 22–37.

Thorndike, E. L. *Animal intelligence: Experimental studies.* New York: Macmillan, 1911.

Thorndike, E. L. *Educational psychology.* Vol. 1. *The original nature of man.* New York: Teachers College, Columbia Univ., 1913.

Thorndike, E. L. *Human nature and the social order.* New York: Macmillan, 1940.

Thorndike, E. L. *Man and his works.* Cambridge, Massachusetts: Harvard Univ. Press, 1943.

Tolman, E. C. *Purposive behavior in animals and man.* New York: Appleton, 1932.

Tolman, E. C. *Drives toward war.* New York: Appleton, 1942.

Tolman, E. C. Cognitive maps in rats and men. *Psychological Review,* 1948, *55,* 189–208.

Tolman, E. C., & Honzik, C. H. Introduction and removal of reward, and the maze performance of rats. *University of California Publications in Psychology,* 1930, *4,* 257–275.

Tracy, J. J. & Cross, H. J. Antecedents of shift in moral judgments. *Journal of Personality and Social Psychology,* 1973, *26,* 238–244.

Tsujimoto, R. N., & Liebert, R. M. Effects of symbolic verbalization by the model on children's observational learning. *Perceptual and Motor Skills,* 1971, *33,* 1079–1082.

Tulving, E. Subjective organization in free recall of unrelated words. *Psychological Review,* 1962, *69,* 344–354.

·Tulving, E. Subjective organization and effects of repetition in multitrial free-recall learning. *Journal of Verbal Learning and Verbal Behavior,* 1966, *5,* 193–197.

Tulving, E. Theoretical issues in free recall. In T. R. Dixon & D. L. Horton (Eds.), *Verbal behavior and general behavior theory.* Englewood Cliffs, New Jersey: Prentice-Hall, 1968, Pp. 2–36.

Tumblin, A., Gholson, B., Rosenthal, T. L., & Kelley, J. E. Vicarious acquisition and problem-solving strategies: Four training conditions. Unpublished manuscript, Memphis State Univ. 1977.

Turiel, E. An experimental test of the sequentiality of development stages in a child's moral judgments. *Journal of Personality and Social Psychology*, 1966, *3*, 611–618.

Tversky, B., & Teiffer, E. Development of strategies for recall and recognition. *Developmental Psychology*, 1976, *12*, 406–410.

Ullmann, L., & Krasner, L. *A psychological approach to abnormal behavior*. (2nd ed.) Englewood Cliffs, New Jersey: Prentice-Hall, 1975.

Ulrich, R., Stachnik, T., & Mabry, J. (Eds.), *Control of human behavior*. Vol. 3. *Behavior modification in education*. Glenview, Illinois: Scott Foresman, 1974.

Uzgiris, I. C. Situational generality of conservation. *Child Development*, 1964, *35*, 831–841.

Valentine, C. W. The psychology of imitation with special reference to early childhood. *British Journal of Psychology*, 1930, *21*, 105–132.

van Hekken, S. M. J. The influence of verbalization on observational learning in a group of non-mediating children. *Human Development*, 1969, *12*, 204–213.

Varley, W. H., Levin, J. R., Severson, R. H., & Wolff, P. Training imagery production in young children through motor involvement. *Journal of Educational Psychology*, 1974, *66*, 262–266.

Vasta, R., & Liebert, R. M. Auditory discrimination of novel prepositional constructions as a function of age and syntactic background. *Developmental Psychology*, 1973, *9*, 79–82.

Von Wright, J. M. Relation between verbal recall and visual recognition of the same stimuli in young children. *Journal of Experimental Child Psychology*, 1973, *15*, 534–548.

Wallach, M. A., & Kogan, N. *Modes of thinking in young children*. New York: Holt, 1965.

Walster, E., Walster, G. W., Piliavin, J., & Schmid, L. "Playing hard to get": Understanding an elusive phenomenon. *Journal of Personality and Social Psychology*, 1973, *26*, 113–121.

Walters, R. H., & Amoroso, D. M. Cognitive and emotional determinants of the occurrence of imitative behavior. *British Journal of Social and Clinical Psychology*, 1967, *6*, 174–185.

Waters, R. H. The influence of tuition upon ideational learning. *Journal of Genetic Psychology*, 1928, *1*, 534–549.

Watson, J. B. *Behavior–an introduction to comparative psychology*. New York: Holt, 1914.

Watson, J. B. *Psychology from the standpoint of a behaviorist*. Philadelphia: Lippincott, 1919.

Watson, J. B. *Behaviorism*. New York: Norton, 1924.

Watson, J. B. *The ways of behaviorism*. New York: Harper, 1928.

Watson, J. B., & McDougall, V. *The battle of behaviorism, an exposition and an exposure*. New York: Norton, 1929.

Watts, M. W. Behavior modeling and self-devaluation with video self-confrontation. *Journal of Educational Psychology*, 1973, *64*, 212–215.

Waugh, N. C., & Norman, D. A. Primary memory. *Psychological Review*, 1965, *72*, 89–104.

Westman, A. S., & Yussef, Z. I. Kindergarten children's use of category membership. *Journal of Experimental Psychology*, 1976, *21*, 507–513.

Wheeler, A. J., & Sulzer, B. Operant training and generalization of a verbal response form in a speech deficient child. *Journal of Applied Behavior Analysis*, 1970, *3*, 139–147.

Wheeler, R. J., & Dusek, J. B. The effects of attentional and cognitive factors on children's incidental learning. *Child Development*, 1973, *44*, 253–258.

Wheeler, R., & Ryan, F. L. Effects of cooperative and competitive classroom environments on attitudes and achievement of elementary school students engaged in social studies inquiry activities. *Journal of Educational Psychology*, 1973, *64*, 402–406.

White, G. M. Contextual determinants of opinion judgments: Field experimental probes of judgmental relativity boundary conditions. *Journal of Personality and Social Psychology*, 1975, *32*, 1047–1054.

White, G. M., & Rosenthal, T. L. Effects of modeling, definitions, rehearsal, and response arbitrariness on associative class selection and retention. Unpublished manuscript, Univ. of Arizona, Tucson, 1973.

White, G. M., & Rosenthal, T. L. Demonstration and lecture in information transmission: A field experiment. *Journal of Experimental Education*, 1974, *43*, 90–96.

White, R. M., & Lindquest, D. Transfer from conceptual rule problems to a truth-table-sorting task. *Developmental Psychology*, 1974, *10*, 155–162.

White, R. T., & Gagne, R. M. Retention of related and unrelated sentences. *Journal of Educational Psychology*, 1976, *68*, 843–852.

Whitehurst, G. J. Generalized labeling on the basis of structural response classes by two young children. *Journal of Experimental Child Psychology*, 1971, *12*, 59–71.

Whitehurst, G. J. Production of novel and grammatical utterances by young children. *Journal of Experimental Child Psychology*, 1972, *13*, 502–515.

Whitehurst, G. J. The development of communication: Changes with age and modeling. *Child Development*, 1976, *47*, 473–482.

Whitehurst, G. J. Comprehension, selective imitation, and the CIP hypothesis. *Journal of Experimental Child Psychology*, 1977, *23*, 23–38.

Whitehurst, G. J., Ironsmith, M., & Goldfein, M. Selective imitation of the passive construction through modeling. *Journal of Experimental Child Psychology*, 1974, *17*, 288–302.

Whitehurst, G. J., & Novak, G. Modeling, imitation training, and the acquisition of sentence phrases. *Journal of Experimental Child Psychology*, 1973, *16*, 332–345.

Whitehurst, G. J., Novak, G., & Zorn, G. A. Delayed speech studies in the home. *Developmental Psychology*, 1972, *7*, 160–177.

Whitehurst, G. J., & Vasta, R. Is language acquired through imitation? *Journal of Psycholinguistic Research*, 1975, *4*, 37–59.

Whiting, B. B. *Paiute sorcery*. New York: Viking Fund Publications in Anthropology, No. 15, 1950.

Whyte, W. F. *Street corner society: The structure of an Italian slum*. Chicago: Univ. of Chicago Press, 1943.

Wickens, D. D., Allen, C. K., & Hill, F. A. Effects of instruction and UCS strength on extinction of the conditioned GSR. *Journal of Experimental Psychology*, 1963, *66*, 235–240.

Williams, M. L., & Willoughby, R. H. Observational learning: The effects of age, task difficulty, and observer's motoric rehearsal. *Journal of Experimental Child Psychology*, 1971, *12*, 146–156.

Winters, J. J., & Brzoska, M. A. Development of the formation of categories by normal and retarded persons. *Developmental Psychology*, 1976, *12*, 125–131.

Wohlwill, J. F. Un essai d'apprentissage dans le domaine de la conservation du nombre. *Etudes d'épistémologie génétique*, 1959, *9*, 125–135.

Wohlwill, J. F., & Lowe, R. C. An experimental analysis of the conservation of number. *Child Development*, 1962, *33*, 153–167.

Wolpe, J. *The practice of behavior therapy*. New York: Oxford Univ. Press (Pergamon), 1969.

Woodson, M. I. C. E. Seven aspects of teaching concepts. *Journal of Educational Psychology*, 1974, *66*, 184–188.

Woodworth, R. S. *Dynamic psychology*. New York: Columbia Univ. Prss, 1918.

Woodworth, R. S. *Psychology*. (Rev. ed.) New York: Holt, 1921.

Woodworth, R. S. *Psychology*. (4th ed.) Nw York: Holt, 1940.

Woodworth, R. S. *Dynamics of behavior*. New York: Holt, 1958.

Yando, R., & Zigler, E. Outer directedness in the problem-solving of normal and retarded children. *Developmental Psychology*, 1971, *4*, 277–288.

Young, K. *Social psychology: An analysis of social behavior*. New York: Crofts, 1930.

Yuille, J. C. Changes in verb meaning and the sentence context effect in PA learning. *Journal of Experimental Child Psychology*, 1973, *15*, 247–253.

Yuille, J. C., & Catchpole, M. J. Associate learning and imagery training in children. *Journal of Experimental Child Psychology*, 1973, *16*, 403–412.

Yuille, J. C., & Paivio, A. Imagery and verbal mediation instructions in paired-associate learning. *Journal of Experimental Psychology*, 1968, *78*, 436–441.

Yussen, S. R. Determinants of visual attention and recall in observational learning by preschoolers and second graders. *Developmental Psychology*, 1974, *10*, 93–100.

Yussen, S. R., & Levy, V. M., Jr. Effects of warm and neutral models on the attention of observational learners. *Journal of Experimental Child Psychology*, 1975, *20*, 66–72.

Ziesat, H. A. Effects of instructions and vicarious reinforcement schedules on extinction resistence and response rate. Unpublished M. A. thesis, Univ. of Arizona, 1974.

Zigler, E., & Yando, R. Outer directedness and the imitative behavior of institutionalized and non-institutionalized younger and older children. *Child Development*, 1972, *43*, 413–425.

Zimbardo, P. G. Involvement and communication discrepancy as determinants of opinion conformity. *Journal of Abnormal and Social Psychology*, 1960, *60*, 86–94.

Zimmerman, B. J. Modification of young children's grouping strategies: The effects of modeling, verbalization, incentives, and praise. *Child Development*, 1974, *45*, 1032–1041.

Zimmerman, B. J. A social learning explanation for age-related changes in children's conceptual behavior. *Contemporary Educational Psychology*, in press.

Zimmerman, B. J., & Bell, J. A. Observer verbalization and abstraction in vicarious rule learning, generalization, and retention. *Developmental Psychology*, 1972, *7*, 227–231.

Zimmerman, B. J., & Brody, G. H. Race and modeling influences on the interpersonal play patterns of boys. *Journal of Educational Psychology*, 1975, *67*, 591–598.

Zimmerman, B. J., & Dialessi, F. Modeling influences on children's creative behavior. *Journal of Educational Psychology*, 1973, *65*, 127–134.

Zimmerman, B. J., & Lanaro, P. Acquiring and retaining conservation of length through modeling and reversibility cues. *Merrill-Palmer Quarterly*, 1974, *20*, 145–161.

Zimmerman, B. J., & Pike, E. O. Effects of modeling and reinforcement on the acquisition and generalization of question asking behavior. *Child Development*, 1972, *43*, 892–907.

Zimmerman, B. J., & Rosenthal, T. L. Concept attainment, transfer, and retention through observation and rule provision. *Journal of Experimental Child Psychology*, 1972, *14*, 139–150. (a)

Zimmerman, B. J., & Rosenthal, T. L. Observation, repetition, and ethnic background in concept attainment and generalization. *Child Development*, 1972, *43*, 605–613. (b)

Zimmerman, B. J., & Rosenthal, T. L. Conceptual generalization and retention by young children: Age, modeling, and feedback effects. *Journal of Genetic Psychology*, 1974, *125*, 233–245. (a)

Zimmerman, B. J. & Rosenthal, T. L. Conserving and retaining equalities and inequalities through observation and correction. *Developmental Psychology*, 1974, *10*, 260–268. (b)

Zimmerman, B. J., & Rosenthal, T. L. Observational learning of rule-governed behavior by children. *Psychological Bulletin*, 1974, *81*, 29–42. (c)

Author Index

Numbers in italics refer to pages on which the complete citations appear.

R

S

T

Subject Index

A
B
C 8
D 9
E 0
F 1
G 2
H 3
I 4
J 5